Total Football

Publisher and Creative Director: Nick Wells
Co-ordination and Design: Chris Herbert
Picture Research: Melinda Révèsz
Commissioning Editor: Polly Willis

Special thanks to: Christine Delaborde,
Jeff Fletcher, Scott Morgan, Sonya Newland,
Sara Robson, Claire Walker

FLAME TREE PUBLISHING

Crabtree Hall, Crabtree Lane
Fulham, London, SW6 6TY
United Kingdom
info@flametreepublishing.com
www.flametreepublishing.com

First published 2005

05 07 09 08 06

1 3 5 7 9 10 8 6 4 2

Flame Tree is part of The Foundry
Creative Media Company Limited

The CIP record for this book is available from
the British Library.

ISBN 1 84451 260 6

Every effort has been made to contact copyright
holders. We apologize in advance for any omissions
and would be pleased to insert the appropriate
acknowledgement in subsequent editions
of this publication.

While every endeavour has been made to ensure the
accuracy of the reproduction of the images in this book,
we would be grateful to receive any comments or
suggestions for inclusion in future reprints.

Printed in China

Authors and contributors

NICK HOLT was born and raised in Bolton. Unlike its
favourite son Nat Lofthouse, he spent much of his
footballing career on the wing. An early penchant for
alcohol and good living produced a wide player in the
John Robertson mould, only without the talent. A natural
abrasiveness made him ill-suited for retail; he is now a
successful buying magnate. He lives in a small village
with wife Emma, rendered less peaceful than it should be
by his four large dogs.

GUY LLOYD was raised and schooled in Slough, and to
his credit managed to survive the experience. He
attended university, but declined their kind offer of a
fifth term. His working career has taken in the wacky
world of record retailing and a number of years in
various roles in publishing. Guy's awesome knowledge
of obscure footballing trivia is of concern to friends and
family alike. At 6 ft 3 in he has the natural physique of
a goalkeeper. If only he'd had the talent.

MARK GONNELLA (Contributor) is a freelance sports
writer with a number of football books to his credit. A
journalist since leaving school, his career has spanned
local and national newspapers and broadcasting. He
also works as a media consultant to a number of
bluechip companies and sporting organisations.
Married with two children, Mark holds an FA coaching
badge, continues to play local league football and is a
lifelong fan of his hometown club Reading.

Picture Credits

All photographs courtesy of Allsport, except: Action Images:
27; Empics: 123, 151, 279, 317, 325, 347, 465, 563,
607, 377; Foundry Arts: 69, 79, 115, 139, 497, 673;
Offside Sports Photography Library: (L'Equipe Archive): 53,
119, 153, 163, 195, 227, 537, 687, 689, 699, 305, 327;
(Mark Leech): 19, 207, 381, 385, 507; (Witters): 25, 85,
143, 383; Orion Books: 225; Popperfoto: 15, 73, 97, 117,
199, 293, 309, 321, 369, 401, 419, 587; Spaarmestad
Fotoarchief/Collection SF: 399 (ANP), 483 (Jan Sterk), 725
(T. van der Reijken), 741 (NFP); Topham: 21, 127, 161,
167, 169, 191, 245, 251, 261, 269, 275, 283, 299, 307,
310 (l), 333, 363, 379, 389, 393, 403, 407, 437, 447,
471, 495, 545, 551 (all), 559, 573, 603, 611, 617, 635,
661, 679, 701, 705, 707; VinMag Archive: 541

Total Football

Nick Holt & Guy Lloyd

Foreword: Sir Bobby Robson

**FLAME TREE
PUBLISHING**

Contents

How To Use This Book

You are encouraged to use this book in a variety of ways, each of which caters for a range of interests, knowledge and uses.

- The book is organized alphabetically by entry.
- The entries relate to all aspects of the game: players, managers, matches, dream teams, national and club sides.
- Also included are entries which focus on everything else about football, from tactics and cheating to fanzines and chanting, stadia and the World Cup to bizarre hairstyles and penalty shoot-outs.
- The A–Z format enables the reader to find well-known names quickly and easily, and to discover less well-known players, teams and topics alongside the familiar ones.
- There is a comprehensive index that allows specific entries to be located.

2. Subtitle gives extra information about the subject of the entry

1. Entry title

3. Information and authors' opinion on the person, team or topic the entry is about

7. Bullet-points give additional information to the main text

4. Photos occasionally have captions if image needs further explanation

6. Stats relating to the entry: players, managers and stadia have vital statistics; teams and matches have line-ups. Entries on individual topics have relevant quotes.

5. Player and manager entries have Legend Ratings

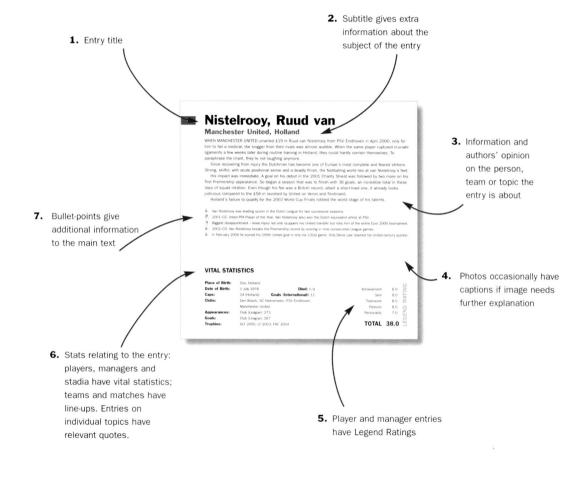

Nistelrooy, Ruud van
Manchester United, Holland

WHEN MANCHESTER UNITED unveiled £19 m Ruud van Nistelrooy from PSV Eindhoven in April 2000, only for him to fail a medical, the snigger from their rivals was almost audible. When the same player ruptured cruciate ligaments a few weeks later during routine training in Holland, they could hardly contain themselves. To paraphrase the chant, they're not laughing anymore.

Since recovering from injury the Dutchman has become one of Europe's most complete and feared strikers. Strong, skilful, with acute positional sense and a deadly finish, the footballing world lies at van Nistelrooy's feet.

His impact was immediate. A goal on his debut in the 2001 Charity Shield was followed by two more on his first Premiership appearance. So began a season that was to finish with 36 goals, an incredible total in these days of squad rotation. Even though his fee was a British record, albeit a short-lived one, it already looks judicious compared to the £58 m lavished by United on Veron and Ferdinand.

Holland's failure to qualify for the 2002 World Cup Finals robbed the world stage of his talents.

- Van Nistelrooy was leading scorer in the Dutch League for two successive seasons.
- 2001-02. Voted PFA Player of the Year. Van Nistelrooy also won the Dutch equivalent whilst at PSV.
- Biggest disappointment – knee injury not only scuppers his United transfer but robs him of the entire Euro 2000 tournament.
- 2002-03. Van Nistelrooy breaks the Premiership record by scoring in nine consecutive League games.
- In February 2004 he scored his 100th United goal in only his 131st game. Only Denis Law reached his United century quicker.

VITAL STATISTICS

Place of Birth:	Oss, Holland				
Date of Birth:	1 July 1976	**Died:** n/a		Achievement	6.0
Caps:	24 (Holland)	**Goals (International):** 11		Skill	9.0
Clubs:	Den Bosch, SC Heerenveen, PSV Eindhoven,			Teamwork	8.0
	Manchester United			Passion	8.0
Appearances:	Club (League): 273			Personality	7.0
Goals:	Club (League): 167				
Trophies:	DLT 2000; LT 2003; FAC 2004			**TOTAL 38.0**	

LEGEND RATING

Foreword

The outstanding success of Euro 2004 in Portugal and the 2002 World Cup Finals in Japan and South Korea demonstrated once again the global popularity of our wonderful game of football.

The remarkable skills of the players – especially the dazzling Brazilians in the World Cup, of course; the amazingly high levels of fitness and stamina, plus the hard-nosed tactical battles fought out by the coaches, made fascinating viewing for all those watching those matches.

Football continues to evolve, and the balance of power may be shifting. It is predicted that an African country will win the World Cup in the near future – and we had better not rule out the possibility of an Asian team from probably becoming World Champions.

Football in the early years of the twenty-first century remains the highest-profile sport on the planet and its future looks very bright indeed. All those lucky enough to earn a living from football – including players, managers and those involved in the media – owe a huge debt to the past giants of the sport.

The players and managers make today's headlines, but it is the supporters of the game of football that form the bedrock of the sport. It is their passion, their enthusiasm and, ultimately, their money that helps keep the game alive.

Thousands of books on football have been published over the years. Some have been notorious and self-seeking, others well-crafted works of literature. And many excellent reference books, containing all kinds of information and statistics, have been produced.

Total Football is a worthy addition to the list. It has been written and compiled *by* genuine football fans *for* genuine football fans. The book is not a just a list of statistics, nor an in-depth history of the game, but one that tries to identify key people, events and themes that have changed or enlivened the game for better or worse.

It pays tribute to the past and present heroes of the game. *Total Football* takes an honest, thoughtful and affectionate view of our marvellous sport and will be a good read for all football fans, young and old.

Sir Bobby Robson

Introduction

Football is unique amongst sports in the degree of passion it arouses in non-combatants. Not for the football fan the pure voyeurism of watching two people belt the living daylights out of each other in a ring, nor the tortuous but cerebral intrigue of a fluctuating test match. Football is about intensity, the thrill of a moment, the excitement of a game revolving around a single piece of action. The fans live every moment, feel every moment, kick every ball.

We've done our share of suffering watching Chelsea under-perform and Bolton get relegated (but not this time, at least for another year!). We've also done our fair share of running around screaming as Chelsea win the FA Cup or Bolton win at Highbury. We've tried to write this book from a fan's perspective, and capture some of the agony and the ecstasy, the hysteria and the humour.

This is not a list of stats; Rothmans and others cover that. Nor is it an in-depth history of the game; that involves too much stuff that no one really cares about – and too much work! This book tries to identify key people and events and themes that have changed or enlivened the game for better or worse. From Hidegkuti to Hairstyles, Nou Camp to Nicknames, we've given a page – no more – to the best and worst of the Beautiful Game. If we think a player was talented but a bit of a lightweight, we've said so; if we think a side was dirty or arrogant, we've said so. We've said so not just because we think we're right, but because football fans want an opinion and an argument.

legend rating

Throughout the book you will note that each player or manager has a legend rating. These are based on the following criteria:

PLAYERS

Achievement: how much the player achieved in football – very little sympathy is accorded players who eschew 'the big move' in this mark.
Skill: pure talent.
Teamwork: ability to turn a game with a moment of skill or leadership.
Passion: overall contribution to a side, heart.
Personality: charisma, personal style.

MANAGERS

Achievement: as above.
Tactical Awareness: ability to read the way a game is going or will go and to act accordingly.
Motivation: gung-ho up-and-at 'em style or man-management – whatever it takes to get the best out of your best.
Transfer Dealing and Team Selection: the ability to distinguish a Cantona from a Marco Boogers.
Personality: as above.

Like the Dream Teams, these are based on opinion, rather than any tangible measurement, and are meant to invite discussion and disagreement. If you think we've rippled Row F rather than the back of the net with our selections, please e-mail us with your abuse (not too ripe!), or your own selections. You could even e-mail us if you agree – but where's the fun in that?

Nick Holt and *Guy Lloyd*
football@flametreepublishing.com

Adams, Tony
Arsenal, England

IN HIS EARLY YEARS Adams was frequently subjected to cries of 'donkey' from the terraces, as he appeared to be a traditional English centre-half – physically dominant but maladroit with the ball at his feet. The fact that he is now treated with universal respect wherever he plays is testimony to the commitment and hard work he has shown in eliminating many of those early deficiencies in his game. The back line of David Seaman, Lee Dixon, Nigel Winterburn and Adams, with first Steve Bould and later Martin Keown, could reasonably lay claim to be the best-ever British club defence.

An outstanding reader of the game, he became a natural leader and an inspirational talisman for both England and Arsenal, both of whom were notably weaker in his absence. Adams' fight against alcohol addiction became a symbol of his strength of character, and his readiness to address personal flaws earned him respect well beyond the football world. His brief stretch in prison gave him a glimpse of life that few of today's pampered professionals would comprehend.

- Arsenal's miserly defence conceded only 18 goals as they waltzed away with the Championship in 1991.
- Adams took over two years to score his first league goal, finally bagging against Liverpool in 1986.
- In Adams's 11 matches as England captain they were only beaten once.
- Adams's honesty and self-awareness has mistakenly led some journalists to use him as a sage and philosopher, when he is clearly neither. He is a decent man who has learned to grow up.
- Adams' long-awaited introduction to management in 2003–04 proved a baptism of fire as he failed to rescue beleaguered Wycombe from relegation, and he resigned in November 2004.

VITAL STATISTICS

Place of Birth:	Romford, England
Date of Birth:	10 October 1966 **Died:** n/a
Caps:	66 (England) **Goals (International):** 5
Clubs:	As Player: Arsenal; As Manager: Wycombe Wanderers
Appearances:	Club (League): 504
Goals:	Club (League): 32
Trophies:	LT 1989, 1991, 1998, 2002; FAC 1993, 1998, 2002; LC 1987, 1993; CWC 1994

LEGEND RATING	
Achievement	8.0
Skill	6.5
Teamwork	8.5
Passion	9.5
Personality	8.0
TOTAL	**40.5**

Ademir Marques de Menezes
Vasco da Gama, Brazil

BRAZIL ENTERED the 1950 World Cup in a state of high expectation. They were the hosts, and the previous year they had won the Copa América with some sensational performances. The stars of the show were their trio of sparkling forwards – Jair Rosa Pinto, Zizinho and Ademir. All slim, nippy and moustachioed, they moved the ball with amazing skill and speed.

Ademir had been playing as an outside left for Vasco da Gama and for his country, but when Brazil moved him inside alongside the other two maestros the results were spectacular. Shimmies, dummies, overhead kicks, half-volleys … all the magic we associate with the 1958 and 1970 Brazil teams was there. Four goals of stunning quality in the final pool match against Sweden was probably Ademir's greatest moment. Only in the last match of the 1950 tournament, when Uruguay detailed their experienced captain, Varela, to mark him, did anyone work out how to cope with his tricks.

☞ No TV footage exists to prove it, but Ademir was said to use a trick of trapping the ball in his heels and hopping over the goalkeeper, still moving at some speed.

👍 The famous English referee Arthur Ellis rated Ademir's overhead kick against Sweden as the best goal he'd ever witnessed.

☞ By the time the 1954 World Cup came around, Ademir, Jair and Zizinho had all gone, and it was 1958 before the next crop of outrageous talent arrived.

☞ So many coaches pulled an extra defender back to counter Ademir that Brazil adopted a 4-2-4 system to help create space for him.

👍 In the 1949 Copa América, Brazil, without Ademir, lost to Paraguay and were forced into a play-off. Our boy put it to rest as Brazil won said play-off 7-0, with Ademir hitting a hat-trick.

VITAL STATISTICS

Place of Birth:	Recife, Brazil
Date of Birth:	8 November 1922 **Died:** 11 May 1996
Caps:	39 (Brazil) **Goals (International):** 32
Clubs:	FC Recife, Vasco da Gama, Fluminense
Trophies:	BLT 1945, 1946, 1947, 1949, 1950, 1952

LEGEND RATING

Achievement	8.0
Skill	9.0
Teamwork	7.0
Passion	8.0
Personality	7.0
TOTAL	**39.0**

Ademir with the Brazilian World Cup squad in 1950 – our man is third from right on the bottom row.

African Nations
The Dream Team

THE AFRICAN NATIONS EMERGED as serious contenders at world level in the 1980s. The continent has since become a recruiting hotbed for the big European clubs. Although the players cannot be blamed for fleeing their homelands, their migration is undermining Africa's efforts to develop its game to its true potential.

This is a great side, full of massive talents. Radebe, so unlucky with injury, was a major force at Leeds as they built a challenging side in the 1990s. Taribo West, green hair notwithstanding, had some great moments at Milan, and Sammi Kuffour has been the corner-stone of Bayern Munich's recent re-emergence as a European force. Oman Biyick scored some spectacular goals for Cameroon alongside the engaging Milla, and Okocha was a joy to watch in the World Cups of 1994 and 1998. Madjer masterminded Algeria's memorable defeat of West Germany in 1982, one of the World Cup's most enjoyable moments. And who could forget George Weah? The Liberian striker was the first African player to make a serious impact on the world stage, and at his peak with AC Milan was deservedly named World Player of the Year. His mantle as the daddy of African football has now passed to Arsenal's Nwankwo Kanu who, as part of a brilliant Ajax team, conquered Europe before his 21st birthday.

- World Cup 1982: Algeria beat West Germany and Chile, and were unlucky not to reach the second phase.
- World Cup 1986: Morocco held England and Poland, beat Portugal and progressed to the second round where they lost due to a late goal from Lothar Matthaus.
- World Cup 1990: Cameroon beat holders Argentina, Romania and Colombia before defensive errors saw them eliminated by England after being 2-1 up.
- World Cups 1994 and 1998: Nigeria played well in the group stages but again failed to cope with experienced European opposition in the knockout rounds.

Manager: Roger Lemerre

3-3-1-3

Thomas Nkono (Cameroon)

Lucas Radebe (S. Africa) Taribo West (Nigeria) Sammi Kuffour (Ghana)

J-J Okocha (Nigeria) Oman Biyick (Cameroon) Mustafa Hadji (Morocco)

Rabah Madjer (Algeria)

Roger Milla (Cameroon) George Weah (Liberia) Nwankwo Kanu (Nigeria)

Subs: Peter Rufai (Nigeria) (G) Mark Fish (S. Africa) (D) Ahmed Ramzy (Egypt) (M) Abedi Pele (Ghana) (M) El Hadji Diouf (Senegal) (F)

Cameroon with the 2002 African Nations Cup.

Ajax
The Dream Team

AJAX HAD NO PEDIGREE before Rinus Michels took over as coach in the 1960s, but since then they have twice developed the best club side in Europe – only to see it broken up by the lure of the lira and, occasionally, the peseta.

The first team was all-Dutch, and contained the cultured defenders Krol and Suurbier, the flying Piet Keizer, the steel of Neeskens and style of Haan in midfield. Oh, and they also had some bloke called Johan Cruyff. That team swept all before them, winning three consecutive European Cups. Only Feyenoord, with Rinus Israel, Wim Van Hanegem and the Swede Owe Kindvall, could compete with them at home while, in Europe, their only serious threat came from the Bayern Munich team of Beckenbauer, Breitner and Müller.

The second side was a much more cosmopolitan affair. By the 1990s, Ajax, like other Dutch sides, were blending home talent with clever imports. Rijkaard and Van Basten had left to team up with Gullit at Milan, but more good youngsters emerged: Reiziger, Davids, Seedorf, Kluivert and the De Boers from Holland, plus Kanu, Litmanen and Finidi George from abroad. Captained by Danny Blind, they won back the European Cup in 1995.

☞ Keizer was an underrated member of the early Ajax side. More direct and aggressive than many of his team-mates, he was often the one to inject some urgency when their play became over-elaborate.

☜ Young Patrick Kluivert was one of the most exciting prospects in European football when he emerged in the mid-1990s. His failure to fulfil that potential must be attributed in part to some unsavoury incidents in his private life.

☞ Guus Hiddink and Louis Van Gaal are accomplished coaches, but Michels is the undisputed father of modern Dutch football – and the only manager to get the best out of the notoriously temperamental Cruyff.

Manager: Rinus Michels

3-4-1-2

Edwin Van Der Sar (90s)

Wim Suurbier (70s) Danny Blind (80s/90s) Rudi Krol (C) (70s)

Piet Keizer (70s) Frank Rijkaard (80s/90s) Johan Neeskens (70s)
Jari Litmanen (90s)

Johan Cruyff (70s)

Marco Van Basten (80s) Dennis Bergkamp (90s)

Subs: Heinz Stuy (G) (70s) Frank De Boer (D) (90s) Arie Haan (M) (70s)
Nwankwo Kanu (F) (90s) Patrick Kluivert (F) (90s)

De Meer, the stadium where Ajax played its dream matches. It was demolished in 1996.

Albert, Florian

Ferencvaros, Hungary

AS THE GREAT HUNGARIAN TEAM of the 1950s was dissolving, the seeds of a new team were being sown. It took a few years, but by the 1966 World Cup Finals some of the young talent was ripening. The jewel among them was Florian Albert, a playmaker with leading club side, Ferencvaros. A gifted centre-forward, he was at the heart of the last Hungarian side to truly compete on the international stage.

In 1962, Albert put paid to English World Cup hopes with a stylish winning goal, and followed it with a hat-trick against Bulgaria. In the 1966 tournament they were drawn in a tough group with Brazil and Portugal. The key game was a 3-1 victory over Brazil and it was a minor classic. Hungary's second, decisive goal involved an eye-blinkingly rapid movement from Albert to Ferenc Bene to Janos Farkas, who crashed in a volley that bulged the net in mouth-watering fashion. In the quarter-finals a strong Soviet side had done their homework; they close-marked Albert and cut off his supply from midfield, a tactic that contributed hugely to their 2-1 victory. The next time the sides met in a Finals tournament was in Mexico 1986. Albert was long gone and the USSR won 6-0.

- Albert and Hungary won the Olympic gold in 1964 and 1968.
- Ujpest Dozsa winger Ferenc Bene, was a great foil for Albert. Quick, and a tidy finisher, he scored all the goals in a 6-0 win over Morocco at the 1964 Olympics.
- Albert's Ferencvaros became the only Hungarian club to win a European trophy when they beat Juventus in the 1965 Fairs Cup Final.
- Albert was named European Footballer of the Year in 1967.
- Ferencvaros returned to the Fairs Cup Final three years later, but lost 1-0 to Leeds over two legs. Bene's Ujpest Dozsa trod the same path the following year, but were beaten by Newcastle.

VITAL STATISTICS

				LEGEND RATING
			Achievement	6.0
			Skill	9.0
Place of Birth:	Hungary		Teamwork	7.0
Date of Birth:	15 September 1941	**Died:** n/a	Passion	9.0
Caps:	75 (Hungary)	**Goals (International):** 27	Personality	7.0
Clubs:	Ferencvaros			
Trophies:	OLT 1963, 1964, 1967, 1968		**TOTAL**	**38.0**

All-Rounders

Sporting Polymaths

LIFE ISN'T FAIR. Most of us would settle for a modicum of talent in any activity; some blessed souls were not only talented enough to play professional football, they excelled at other sports as well.

The doyen was C.B. Fry. The hero of the late-Victorian and Edwardian eras, Fry played football and cricket for England, held the world long-jump record and was offered the throne of Albania for good measure.

Sportsmen who played both football and cricket were relatively commonplace in the days of lower wages and football seasons that didn't extend endlessly into the summer. By the early 1980s, a dwindling breed that included Ted Hemsley, Phil Neale, Jim Cumbes, Arnie Sidebottom and Alan Ramage had disappeared completely.

Pride of place in this era goes to Chris Balderstone, most notably for his efforts on 15 September 1975. After scoring an undefeated fifty for Leicestershire against Derbyshire, a waiting taxi took him to Doncaster, where he turned out in a Fourth Division game for Rovers against Brentford. He returned to Chesterfield the following morning to complete his century.

Follow that Ronaldo!

☞ Sporting brothers Denis & Leslie Compton both played football for Arsenal and England in the pre-and post-war era. They were also county cricketers for Middlesex; Denis is regarded by many as England's finest post-war batsman.

☝ England's World Cup hat-trick hero Geoff Hurst played for the Essex first XI; Gary Lineker also excelled at cricket.

☞ Other athletes have shown good footballing skills in their early years. England cricketer Graham Thorpe was a talented player, as was athlete Duane Ladejo. Viv Richards occasionally turned out for the Leeward Islands.

☞ Alan Hansen, Kenny Dalglish and Michael Owen are all excellent golf players, using their ample leisure time to hone their skills.

'Had he been playing today, there would not have been one unsponsored inch of him.'

Broadcaster and journalist Michael Parkinson pays tribute to Arsenal, Middlesex and England legend Denis Compton

Cricketers who played football: Graham Thorpe and Ian Botham (bottom left, bottom right); and footballers who played cricket: C.B. Fry and Denis Compton (top right and top left).

Anderlecht

The Dream Team

THIS SIDE CONSISTS mainly of Anderlecht's Belgian long-servers throughout the club's history, with a couple of notable exceptions. One of these is the great Dane, Morten Olsen, in the centre of defence. Olsen was a great reader of the game, and was capped more than 100 times by Denmark. He was a mainstay of the Anderlecht side for many years; he is joined at the back by his long-serving and consistent compatriot, Henrik Andersen.

The two Duthcmen, Arie Haan and Rob Rensenbrink both merit inclusion. They were key members of the Anderlecht side that achieved so much in Europe in the 1970s. Haan, a midfield player for Holland, did sterling service as an emergency centre back in many of those games; Rensenbrink scored twice in both Anderlecht's final wins.

Van Binst, Vercauteren, Coeck and Vandenbergh were all part of that triumphant squad. The remaining players represent the stalwarts that have maintained the club at the summit of Belgian football for most of the last 50 years.

- 👍 Anderlecht holds the record of 27 Belgian titles and won the Belgian Cup 8 times.
- 👍 Anderlecht played four European finals in the 1970s, including three in successive years, and two more UEFA Cup finals in the 1980s, winning in 1983 against Benfica.
- ☞ Jef Jurion scored the winner when Sporting Anderlecht became the first team to eliminate Real Madrid, beating the five-time winners 4-3 on aggregate in 1962–63.
- ☞ The Anderlecht stadium named after the club legend Constant Vanden Stock was the first European football ground where companies could invite their patrons in boxes.
- 👍 In 1964 the entire Belgium team for the second half of a game against Holland was made up of Anderlecht players – a unique record.

Manager: Raymond Goethals

4-4-2

Henri Meert

Gilbert van Binst   Georges Heylens
Morten Olsen   Henrik Andersen

Jef Jurion   Paul van Himst   Arie Haan
Frankie Vercauteren

Jan Mulder   Rob Rensenbrink

Subs: Jackie Munaron (G) Lorenzo Verbiest (D) Graeme Rutjes (D)
Ludo Coeck (M) Jef Mermans (F) Erwin Vandenbergh (F)

Archie's Passion

Holland 2 Scotland 3, 1978

GOING INTO THIS MATCH, Scotland's hopes of glory at the 1978 World Cup Finals were already in tatters. With only one point from their first two games they were virtually out of the competition – a fate they could only avoid by beating the mighty Holland by three clear goals. Unbelievably, they came close to pulling it off.

The Scots gave everything. They hit the bar, had a goal disallowed and found themselves a goal down for their troubles, when Rensenbrink converted a penalty. Dalglish volleyed a deserved equaliser just before half-time, and Gemmill scored from the spot after Souness was brought down. Then came the goal that set Scottish hearts beating like the clappers. Gemmill, picking the ball up wide on the right, swerved past two defenders, nutmegged a third and coolly chipped the advancing Jongbloed. As he turned away Gemmill's face was a glorious and unforgettable fusion of elation, determination and passion. A midget player with a giant's heart had scored one of the greatest goals in the history of the game. Sadly for Gemmill, Dalglish and the rest, Scotland could not force a fourth, and had their hopes finally, and emphatically extinguished by Johnny Rep's 30-yard howitzer three minutes later.

☞ No less a judge than the great Dutch coach Rinus Michels had tipped Scotland as dark horses to win the tournament.

☜ Scottish winger Willie Johnston was sent home after the first match for taking a banned substance.

☞ Martin Buchan was chosen as full-back against Peru, where he struggled against Munante, one of the world's fastest wingers.

☜ Ally MacLeod stayed on as manager for one more game before resigning, blaming everyone else for a disastrous tournament.

☜ Complacent and off-key in the first two games, Scotland had been beaten by Peru and drawn with Iran, Ally MacLeod having omitted Graeme Souness for both these games.

SCORERS	**Holland:** Rensenbrink (pen), Rep **Scotland:** Dalglish, Gemmill 2 (1 pen)
EVENT	World Cup group match, Mendoza, 11 June 1978
HOLLAND	(Man: Ernst Happel)
	1. Jongbloed 2. Suurbier 3. Krol 4. Jansen 5. Rijsbergen
	6. Poortvliet 7. van der Kerkhof, R 8. Rep 9. Rensenbrink
	10. Neeskens 11. van der Kerkhof, W
SCOTLAND	(Man: Ally MacLeod)
	1. Rough 2. Kennedy 3. Donachie 4. Rioch 5. Forsyth 6. Buchan
	7. Gemmill 8. Hartford 9. Jordan 10. Souness 11. Dalglish

Ardiles, Osvaldo ('Ossie')
Argentina, Tottenham Hotspur

ARDILES WAS UNKNOWN IN EUROPE before the 1978 World Cup, where he was the fulcrum of the Argentina side that won the tournament, so when he and Ricky Villa were persuaded to come to England immediately after, it was, rightly, regarded as a stunning coup for Spurs. Ardiles returned to the World Cup stage in 1982, but Argentina found it harder work playing in Europe and lost their crown.

With the exception of his 1981 Cup Final performance Villa was only a partial success at Spurs. Ardiles, on the other hand, was a revelation. His push-and-go style was easy to adapt to English football, and he formed a hugely effective partnership with the more flamboyant Glenn Hoddle. A better defence would surely have seen Spurs win more than an FA Cup and UEFA Cup in the early 1980s.

As a manager, Ardiles proved surprisingly inept for such an intelligent player. After a reasonably successful spell at Swindon Town, he suffered disastrous tenures at Newcastle and back at Spurs where, despite bringing in expensive signings such as Jurgen Klinsmann, Gica Popescu and Ilie Dumitrescu, he could not mould the team into an effective unit. In 2003 he settled in Japan as manager of Tokyo Verdy 1969.

☞ His only success as a manager, promotion with Swindon, was annulled due to financial irregularities under the previous incumbent, Lou Macari.

☞ Ardiles and Maradona only briefly overlapped for Argentina, when Ossie was past his energetic best. They would have been some combination in their mutual pomp.

☞ Ardiles' most embarrassing moment was a brief cameo in Spurs' 1981 FA Cup song. The memory of that squeaky little voice trilling out 'Tottingham' still sends shivers down the spine of music lovers everywhere.

☞ Ardiles owned a Yorkshire Terrier called Gazza.

VITAL STATISTICS

Place of Birth:	Cordoba, Argentina	
Date of Birth:	3 August 1952	**Died:** n/a
Caps:	53 (Argentina)	**Goals (International):** 8
Clubs:	Instituto de Cordoba, Huracan, Tottenham Hotspur, Paris	
	Saint Germain, Blackburn Rovers, Queen's Park Rangers	
Appearances:	Club (for Tottenham): 315	
Goals:	Club (for Tottenham): 25	
Trophies:	WorC 1978; FAC 1981; UEFAC 1984	

LEGEND RATING	
Achievement	8.0
Skill	8.0
Teamwork	9.0
Passion	8.0
Personality	7.0
TOTAL	**40.0**

Argentina
The Dream Team

THIS DEFENCE IS FORMIDABLE. In front of arguably the finest South American goalkeeper ever sits a brutal back four. Ruggeri gets in ahead of Sensini and Olguin, while the cultured Ayala would make an interesting contrast with the 6 ft 3 in destroyer Rattin. Marzolini was a world-class attacking full-back and behind him sits one of the great sweepers, the uncompromising Daniel Passarella.

With Ardiles to do the donkey work, Maradona, Di Stefano and the silky pre-war inside forward, Omar Sivori, would be free to run at defences and link up with the lone forward (who needs more than one striker with those three in midfield?). Incredibly, there is no room even on the bench for some serious talent like Ortega, Onega, Veron or Valdano.

Selecting the lone forward was tough; Kempes just gets the nod over Batistuta, as his goals won a World Cup in 1978. No space either for the foppish Caniggia, Artime or Kempes' powerful partner, Luque.

- Guillermo Stabile was Argentina's finest pre-war player, a centre-forward in the team that reached the final of the 1930 World Cup.
- Silvio Marzolini and Roberto Ferreiro were members of the infamous 'Animals'. Ferreiro was a thug, but an effective defender, while Marzolini was a fine player and one of the less obnoxious members of that side.
- Ruggeri was a fine and consistent defender in the 1990s, while Burruchaga, though not the most naturally gifted player, developed into a capable lieutenant for Maradona.
- Both goalkeepers are highly capable – Brazil would look enviously at a bench containing Pumpido.

Manager: Cesar Luis Menotti

1-4-4-1

Ubaldo Fillol (80s)

Daniel Passarella (c) (70s/80s)

Oscar Ruggeri (70s/80s) Antonio Rattin (60s)
Reuben Ayala (90s) Silvio Marzolini (60s)

Ossie Ardiles (70s/80s) Diego Maradona (80s/90s)
Alfredo Di Stefano (50s/60s) Omar Sivori (60s)

Mario Kempes (70s/80s)

Subs: Nery Pumpido (G) (80s) Roberto Ferreiro (D) (30s)
Jorge Burruchaga (M) (80s) Guillermo Stabile (F) (30s) Gabriel Batistuta (F) (90s)

Azteca Stadium

Mexico City

THE NATIONAL STADIUM OF MEXICO, situated 2,240 m above sea level, has a reputation for sapping the strength of even the fittest players with its rarefied atmosphere. With its all-round roof, alarmingly steep stands and six-figure capacity, an Azteca packed to its three-tiered rafters leaves one breathless in more ways than one.

For England fans, the Azteca will always be remembered as the scene of Diego Maradona's infamous 'Hand of God' goal for Argentina against England in the 1986 Finals. Rising to meet Steve Hodge's back pass, the midfielder punched the ball past the stranded Peter Shilton and peeled away in delight. The officials failed to spot the incident and moments later Maradona danced his way past a string of English defenders to score the greatest-ever World Cup goal.

If Maradona was the star performer at the Azteca in 1986, Pele undoubtedly stole the show in 1970, proving that the best performers invariably raise their games on the greatest stages.

The Azteca could provide no greater inspiration. With the relative decline of the Maracana and the reduced capacity of the Bernabeu, there is no finer stadium in the world today.

☞ Although known universally as the Azteca, its name was formally changed in 1997 to the Estadio Guillermo Canedo in memory of the late FIFA vice-president.

☝ The Azteca is the only stadium to host two World Cup Finals, 1970 and 1986. In both tournaments, 19 games were played there, also a Finals record.

☞ The Azteca staged the 1968 Olympic Games football final.

☝ The stadium witnessed the finest ever national team performance, as Brazil outclassed Italy 4-1 to win the 1970 World Cup Final and keep the Jules Rimet trophy.

☞ In 1999, at the end of a tour of Mexico, the Pope addressed 110,000 adoring followers at the Azteca.

VITAL STATISTICS

Location:	Mexico City, Mexico
Local Club:	América (other Mexican clubs use it for important matches)
Date Built:	1966
Current Capacity:	111,000
Max. Capacity:	114,590

Back from the Dead
Comebacks

TEN MINUTES FROM TIME, the ball rolls into touch. The camera catches pitted gaps in the crowd, upturned seats vacated by sections of the crowd who have decided that this one-sided contest is a foregone conclusion. Usually, they're right. Usually...

The greatest comeback? The Valley, 21 December 1957. With an hour played, 10-man Charlton trailed Huddersfield 5-1. Their outside left Johnny Summers suddenly realised a game was taking place and blasted a six-minute hat-trick. With two minutes left Charlton led 6-5 but appeared to have blown it when the Yorkshireman stole an equaliser. Enter Summers, providing John Ryan with a last-gasp winner.

In recent years, Spurs' soft centre has cost them dear. Their capitulation, when 3-0 up, to Manchester United, is worthy of (and gets) its own entry. Whether Mancunian opposition holds a particular terror, we shall never know, but in January 2004 lightning struck again. Spurs hosted City in the FA Cup fourth round. Half-time oranges were sucked secure in the knowledge of a three-goal cushion, whilst City's contribution consisted of a red card for Joey Barton. When Jonathan Macken headed the Sky Blues' winner (and City's fourth goal) in injury time, most Tottenham fans must have begun to wonder whether God was a Gooner. We've all been there.

☞ February 2001. In their fifth-round FA Cup tie Tranmere were 3-0 down at half-time to Premiership Southampton, a Paul Rideout hat-trick and Stuart Barlow's winner earned them a quarter-final dream encounter with Liverpool.

☞ Season 2003-04. Wolves' 4-3 defeat of Leicester was achieved the hard way after the Foxes had led 3-0. Black Country neighbours West Brom provided a carbon copy at Upton Park, this after the Hammers scored three in the first 18 minutes.

☞ Most famous international comeback - the 1966 World Cup Finals. Small-fry South Korea, having already despatched Italy, led 3-0 against fancied Portugal. They reckoned against Eusebio, who roused the Potuguese to a famous 5-3 win.

'Dear Dad, I hope you don't mind but I don't want to be a Spurs fan any more. Love Sam.'

Letter from nine-year-old Sam Curtis to journalist father Adrian, after Tottenham blow a three-goal lead to Manchester City.

Man City battle with Spurs before their injury time winner, January 2004.

Baggio, Roberto
Italy

ONE OF ITALY'S most fêted-strikers of the last 20 years, the more talented Baggio brother played all his club football during the golden years of Serie A. A move outside Italy was never considered, not least because no one outside Serie A could afford the transfer fee. An outstanding schoolboy talent, he made his 1983 debut for Vicenza aged 15 and was snapped up by Fiorentina after only two years. His £8 m transfer in 1990 to Juventus sparked street riots, but it was five years before his goals finally won Serie A for the Turin giants.

A star of the *Azzuri*, his goals saw Italy through to the final of the 1994 World Cup, but the match proved to be his nadir. The memory of Baggio's final penalty sailing harmlessly over the bar to hand Brazil the trophy probably haunts him still, and started a decline that saw his previously unthinkable omission from the Euro 96 squad. A contentious choice for France 98, his chance to lay the World Cup ghost was unsuccessful as Italy again lost on penalties to the eventual winners. Although Baggio formally announced his retirement in December 2003, such was his form in the latter half of the season that a campaign was launched to include him in Italy's Euro 2004 squad. Ultimately, though, he was passed over in favour of the new generation of Italian players – who couldn't even drag the country through to the quarter-finals.

☞ Baggio once refused to take a penalty for Juventus against Fiorentina out of loyalty to his former club – and was promptly substituted by an unsentimental coach.

✍ World and European Footballer of the Year in 1993.

👆 Baggio scored a sensational goal against Czechoslovakia in the 1990 World Cup, sauntering in from the left touchline, drifting past a couple of defenders and scoring in the corner. He produced a carbon copy against Bulgaria in the 1994 semis.

☞ Baggio is a style icon in Italy, his snappy dress-sense and trendy ponytail earning him film-star status with the media.

👆 Scored his 200th Serie A goal in March 2004.

VITAL STATISTICS

Place of Birth:	Caldogno, Italy		Achievement	8.0
Date of Birth:	18 February 1967	**Died:** n/a	Skill	9.0
Caps:	56 (Italy)	**Goals (International):** 27	Teamwork	7.0
Clubs:	Fiorentina, Juventus, AC Milan, Bologna,		Passion	8.0
	Inter Milan, Brescia		Personality	8.0
Appearances:	Club (League): 496			
Goals:	Club (League): 215			
Trophies:	EUFAC 1993; SA 1995, 1996		**TOTAL**	**40.0**

LEGEND RATING

Baggio despairs after missing the final penalty in the 1994 World Cup Final.

Ball, Alan
Everton, Southampton, England

THERE ARE FEW PLAYERS who reach their peak at 21, but as the youngest member of England's World Cup winning side, Alan Ball had the world at his feet. A teenage talent at Blackpool, his six-figure transfer to Everton the same year, the first of that size between English clubs, correctly identified Ball as one of English football's major talents. His Everton years saw Ball in his domestic pomp. With Howard Kendall and Colin Harvey he formed the 'Holy Trinity' that was the Everton midfield and saw them continue the north-west's dominance of the league title. Ball's adherence to the fiery redhead stereotype provided any team with its engine room, but often brought him to the attention of referees and earned him the rare distinction of becoming one of only a handful of players to be sent off while playing for England.

After a lean period at Arsenal, during which his fall-out with Don Revie put paid to his international career, his renaissance at Southampton was typical of other ageing ex-England stars. However, he could not repeat his on-field success in management, where his record thus far reads promotions two, relegations five.

☞ Despite being a World Cup winner, his 1970 league title is Ball's only domestic trophy.

👍 He was the first player to make 100 league appearances for four different clubs (Blackpool, Everton, Arsenal and Southampton).

☞ He scored one of the quickest-ever First Division goals, in 12 seconds for Arsenal v Man Utd.

☞ His £220 k move to Arsenal made Ball England's most expensive player for a second time.

☞ Ball on Revie's England selections: 'Some of the players are donkeys. Give them a lump of sugar and they run all day and play bingo all night.'

VITAL STATISTICS

Place of Birth:	Farnworth, Lancashire, England	
Date of Birth:	12 May 1945	**Died:** n/a
Caps:	72 (England)	**Goals (International):** 8
Clubs:	Blackpool, Everton, Arsenal, Southampton, Bristol Rovers	
Appearances:	Club (League): 743	
Goals:	Club (League): 170	
Trophies:	WorC 1966; LT 1970	

LEGEND RATING	
Achievement	9.0
Skill	7.0
Teamwork	8.0
Passion	9.0
Personality	7.0
TOTAL	**40.0**

Banged Up
Car-Crashers, Counterfeiters and Other Crooks

SADLY, FOOTBALL'S RECORD is as long as your arm. It is not simply that the game is prey to match-fixing, betting scandals and brown envelopes. Some of its participants are just plain criminal.

Top of the crime league is Arsenal. Five players in as many years were banned from driving in the early 1980s, while Tony Adams went one better in 1990, earning a four-month sentence after wrapping his car around a telegraph pole while driving under the influence. Mind you, his efforts were nothing compared to former Gunner Peter Storey. His rap sheet included headbutting a lollipop man, forgery and living off immoral earnings. Small wonder that one of his later trial judges sentenced him with the words 'you already know what prisons are like, Mr Storey'.

The most tragic case is probably that of George Best. The flawed Belfast genius drank and drove once too often but failed to show in court. Eventually tracked to his Chelsea flat, he escaped and later resisted arrest, a small squad of officers being occupied in the process. The magistrate failed to see the funny side and gave him three months. The bigger they are....

- Colombian keeper Rene Higuita is known to English audiences for his spectacular 'scorpion-kick' at Wembley in 1996. Less publicised was his absence from the 1994 World Cup Finals, when he was in jail as a result of kidnapping charges.
- Duncan Ferguson's nickname of 'Duncan Disorderly' came after convictions for violence ended in a three-month jail term. Ferguson had assaulted Raith Rovers' fullback John McStay, a rare example of an on-field incident standing up in court.
- Wrexham's Mickey Thomas was convicted of forgery in 1992. The incriminating evidence included his passing of dodgy banknotes to the club's YTS players.

'For a man who commanded the respect of thousands of people, to find yourself here, believe me, it is heartbreaking.'

Peter Storey's trial judge

1996: Colombian keeper Rene Higuita shows off his scorpion kick at Wembley.

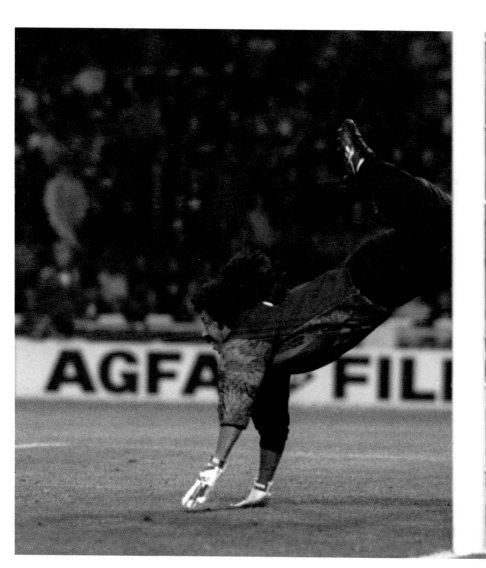

Banks, Gordon

England

ENGLAND'S POST-WAR TRADITION is richer in goalkeepers than in any other position. The pick of a distinguished crop is a man once sacked from Romarsh Welfare in the Yorkshire League after conceding 15 goals in two games. Fortunately for England, Gordon Banks put this disappointment behind him to become his country's automatic choice for nine years, making his debut in Alf Ramsey's second game in charge. It was Ramsey who gave him all his 73 caps, but his worth to England's cause was perhaps most tellingly illustrated by a game he missed. Stricken by a stomach bug the night before the 1970 World Cup quarter-final against West Germany in Mexico, Banks was forced to watch helplessly as his replacement, Peter Bonetti, conceded three goals as England let slip a 2-0 lead. Despite his ability Banks's club career was largely unsuccessful (Leicester and Stoke provided top-division football but little else). Indeed, Leicester practically gave him away to Stoke (£50,000), although they did have an ace up their sleeve in the form of a teenager called Peter Shilton to take over his mantle. The end of his career made headline news for the wrong reasons, the loss of the sight in his right eye following a car crash making his fitness and athleticism irrelevant.

- He lost two FA Cup finals (1961 and 1963) with Leicester in three seasons.
- With Banks between the posts, England lost only nine of 73 games.
- He pulled off what is regarded as the world's greatest-ever save, diving to push a header from Pelé over the bar at the 1970 World Cup Finals in Mexico.
- During his spell with the Fort Lauderdale Strikers in the USA Banks was voted NASL's most valuable keeper. He could only see out of one eye at the time.
- In 1972 he became the first goalkeeper since Bert Trautmann (1956) to win the Footballer of the Year award.

VITAL STATISTICS

Place of Birth:	Sheffield, England	
Date of Birth:	20 December 1937	**Died:** n/a
Caps:	73 (England)	**Goals (International):** 0
Clubs:	Chesterfield, Leicester City, Stoke City,	
	Fort Lauderdale Strikers	
Appearances:	Club (Football League): 510	
Goals:	Club (Football League): 0	
Trophies:	WorC 1966; LC 1964, 1972	

LEGEND RATING	
Achievement	8.0
Skill	10.0
Teamwork	8.0
Passion	9.0
Personality	7.0
TOTAL	**42.0**

Barcelona
The Dream Team

THIS IS PROBABLY not the most talented line-up of Barcelona players, but that would include mainly foreign imports who took the pesetas for a year or two then scarpered for a fat signing-on fee elsewhere. The three overseas stars here stayed long enough to show they wore the red and blue with pride. Koeman was the foundation for the European Cup winning side, Schuster the playmaker through-out the 1980s, and Rivaldo the driving force behind the team in the last five years.

The rest are all Spanish stars, mostly Catalan, and all long-serving players. The defence, in front of the much-capped Zubizarreta, is tough and solid, with sufficient pace and aggression to allow Koeman the freedom to launch attacks with his trademark raking passes. The midfield, too, has strong runners and tacklers supporting the strikingly blond Schuster, and the explosive power of Rivaldo. In attack we have gone for the loyal, ex-coach Rexach, alongside 1950s legend Kubala – both mobile and intelligent. Johan Cruyff will coach this team, which is why he doesn't feature in the starting line-up.

☞ The players left out would make a team in their own right: not featured are Sandor Kocsis, Evaristo, Cesar, Mariano Martin, Ronaldo, Gary Lineker, Hristo Stoichkov, Diego Maradona, Patrick Kluivert, Javier Saviola and, of course, Steve Archibald.

☞ Kubala was Hungarian born. He came to Barca as an outcast and was only able to play after agreeing to adopt Spanish nationality. A goalscoring, inside-forward, many Barca people regard him as the club's best-ever player.

☝ Migueli's 649 appearances for Barcelona remains a club record, with Rexach not far behind.

☞ Pre-war icon Samitier later became president of the club, bringing stars like Kubala, Kocsis and Evaristo to Barcelona.

Manager: Johan Cruyff

4-4-2

Andoni Zubizarretta (C) (80s/90s)

Albert Ferrer (90s) Gustau Biosca (50s) Ronald Koeman (80s/90s) Migueli (70s/80s)

Bernd Schuster (80s) Jose Bakero (90s) Juan Manuel Asensi (70s) Rivaldo (90s)

Carlos Rexach (60s/70s) Ladislao Kubala (50s)

Subs: Antoni Ramallets (G) (40s/50s) Francisco Gallego (D) (60s/70s)
Josep Maria Fuste (M) (60s) Paulino Alcantara (F) (10s/20s) Josep Samitier (F) (20s/30s)

Baresi, Franco
AC Milan, Italy

IN A TEAM OF AC MILAN STARS, none shone brighter than the central defensive wall that was Franco Baresi. A one-club man in an era when most stars shopped around for greater riches, Milan's favourite son was nearly a schoolboy signing for rivals Inter, but big brother Giuseppe was favoured instead. Originally an attacking midfielder, his switch to the back in 1977 began a career for club and country as one of the world's finest and most uncompromising defenders.

His prolonged absence in 1980 with a blood disorder ensured Milan's worst season for years and eventual relegation following a betting scandal, but the ever-loyal Baresi matured still further; four of his six Serie A titles came after he was 30. A third European Cup eluded him – he was suspended for Milan's 1994 triumph – but his biggest disappointment was bowing out of three World Cup tournaments as a loser on penalties, the most gut-wrenching being Italy's defeat to Brazil in the 1994 final. In 1997, the year of his retirement, he was voted Milan's most legendary player. The no. 6 banners that still fly at the San Siro ensure that Baresi's legacy will endure forever.

☞ Baresi's testimonial drew over 50,000 adoring Milanese to the San Siro.

☝ Baresi has never won the World Cup (although named in the victorious 1982 squad, he was not selected).

☝ Baresi played the first game of the World Cup Finals in 1994, was injured and only re-appeared for the final, having had a knee operation in the meantime! He still played a huge game.

☝ In the 1990 World Cup, Baresi marshalled a defence that didn't concede a goal until the sixth game of the tournament.

☝ Baresi scored the first penalty in the shoot-out against Argentina in 1990, but missed in the same circumstances against Brazil in 1994.

VITAL STATISTICS

Place of Birth:	Travagliato, Italy	
Date of Birth:	8 May 1960	**Died:** n/a
Caps:	81 (Italy)	**Goals (International):** 1
Clubs:	AC Milan	
Appearances:	Club (League): 470	
Goals:	Club (League): 12	
Trophies:	SA 1979, 1988, 1992, 1993, 1994, 1996;	
	EC 1989, 1990, 1994; WCC 1989, 1990	

Achievement	9.0
Skill	9.0
Teamwork	8.0
Passion	9.0
Personality	6.0
TOTAL	**41.0**

LEGEND RATING

Basten, Marco van

Ajax, AC Milan, Holland

IF MARCO VAN BASTEN had not been forced out of the game prematurely, who knows what he might have achieved. He was not yet 30 when a suspect ankle gave way in the 1993 European Cup final, a game in which he probably ought not to have played. He was thus denied the opportunity to make amends for the one failure in his career – a miserable performance in an abject Dutch display at the 1990 tournament. Van Basten and Bergkamp would have been interesting.

Better to remember his performances in the 1988 European Championship, when he scored a hat-trick against England, the winner in the semi-final against Germany, and a sensational volley from a nigh-on impossible angle in the final against Russia.

At club level he won the lot. Starting as a 17 year-old with Ajax, he won trophies galore in Holland before a move to AC Milan in 1987. There, with compatriots Gullit and Rijkaard, he was the spearhead of the best club side in Europe, as three Serie A titles and two European Cups testify. His strike rate against the forbidding and cynical defences of the Italian league was remarkable.

Van Basten was a surprise choice to take over as Dutch coach when Dick Advocaat resigned after Euro 2004.

He scored two goals as Milan routed Steaua Bucharest 4-0 in the final of the 1989 European Cup.

He was voted European Footballer of the Year in 1988, 1989 and 1992 and World Player of the Year 1992. He also won the Golden Boot in 1986 – a phenomenal 37 goals in 26 games for Ajax.

In 1991 Van Basten objected to being used as a lone striker for Milan. It is alleged that he gave Milan President Silvio Berlusconi an ultimatum – coach Arrigo Sacchi left to coach Italy that summer.

July 2004 – appointed Dutch national coach, replacing Dick Advocaat.

VITAL STATISTICS

Place of Birth:	Utrecht, Holland	
Date of Birth:	31 October 1964	**Died:** n/a
Caps:	58 (Holland)	**Goals (International):** 24
Clubs:	Ajax, AC Milan	
Appearances:	Club (All Matches): 280	
Goals:	Club (All Matches): 218	
Trophies:	EuroC 1988; EC 1989, 1990; CWC 1987;	
	DLT 1982, 1983, 1985; SA 1988, 1992, 1993	

LEGEND RATING	
Achievement	9.0
Skill	8.5
Teamwork	8.5
Passion	9.0
Personality	7.0
TOTAL	**42.0**

Batistuta, Gabriel Omar
Fiorentina, Argentina

AS A TEENAGER Gabriel Omar Batistuta seemed destined to be a basketball star, but a switch to football at the age of 17 saw a remarkable turnaround. Not the quickest, but hard-working, powerful and sharp, the striker with the rock-star looks made an instant impact. 'Batigol' won the Copa Libertadores (Argentinean championship) at 19, and was top scorer as Argentina won the Copa América for the first time in 32 years in 1991. The inevitable move to Italy followed, but to Fiorentina, the Viola, not one of the Serie A giants. Despite his goals Fiorentina were relegated, but Batigol stayed, and they came back up. In 1999 the Viola pushed hard for the title, but a crucial injury to Batistuta cost them dearly. Finally in 2000 he left for Roma, and promptly inspired them to a Serie A title triumph, a victory his ability and commitment fully merited. After a brief loan-out to Inter Milan in 2003, Batistuta looks set to end his career with Qatar's Al-Arabi.

Batistuta played with distinction in two World Cup tournaments in his time at Fiorentina, proving he lacked no appetite for the big games. The 2002 finals proved to be Batistuta's swansong, as age and creaky legs caught up with him.

- Roma's Serie A title ended an 18-year drought for the club. Batistuta scored over 20 Serie A goals for the fifth time.
- Keegan on Batistuta: 'Batistuta is very good at pulling off defenders.' Whoops.
- Bati scored two hat-tricks in successive World Cups, against Greece in 1994 and Jamaica in 1998 (the one against Jamaica was the only one of the tournament).
- Batistuta is believed to have more websites dedicated to him than any other player – all entirely down to his footballing talent, of course!
- The £22 m Roma paid for Batistuta was the second highest transfer fee at the time.

VITAL STATISTICS

Place of Birth:	Reconquista, Santa Fe, Argentina	
Date of Birth:	2 January 1969	**Died:** n/a
Caps:	78 (Argentina)	**Goals (International):** 57
Clubs:	Newell's Old Boys, River Plate, Boca Juniors,	
	Fiorentina, AS Roma, Inter Milan, Al-Arabi	
Appearances:	Club (All Matches): 428	
Goals:	Club (All Matches): 245	
Trophies:	SA 2001	

LEGEND RATING	
Achievement	7.0
Skill	9.0
Teamwork	7.0
Passion	8.0
Personality	7.0
TOTAL	**38.0**

Battle of Santiago
Italy 0 Chile 2, 1962

'GOOD EVENING. The game you are about to see is the most stupid, appalling, disgusting and disgraceful exhibition in the history of the game.' The words of David Coleman, introducing the BBC's highlights programme, summed up this grim encounter perfectly. There have been many dirty matches, ones that live in the memory more for career-threatening challenges and long-running feuds. If you thought that Arsenal and Manchester United gave no quarter in recent years, their rivalry resembles two kittens toying with a ball of wool compared to this – simply the ugliest game ever played. Chile, having qualified as hosts, realised that in pure footballing terms, they were punching above their weight. So they just punched instead. Sanchez created the mould by breaking Maschio's nose. With South American spittle raining down from all angles, Italy, hardly strangers to cynicism, responded in kind. As the match descended into anarchy, so many separate scores were being settled at any one time that a dozen referees would have developed writer's cramp. The appearance of riot police on the pitch came not a moment too soon. That the mayhem died down long enough for Chile to score twice seems the only mystery. This was a day where the football was entirely incidental.

☞ Chilean sensibilities had been offended before the game, when Italian journalists had questioned in print the appearance and moral fibre of their country's womenfolk.

☞ The Italian team, mindful of the row, feebly offered their hosts compensatory carnations before the game. These were unceremoniously rejected.

✍ Miraculously, only two players were dismissed – both Italian. Ferrini lasted all of 12 minutes. David was sent off after a martial arts kick at Sanchez, he of the nose-breaking left hook.

☞ Beleaguered English referee Ken Aston complained that his preferred linesmen had been superseded by FIFA's own appointments. A timid Mexican and a 'little American from New York' proved too intimidated to offer much assistance.

☞ 'I wasn't reffing a football match. I was acting as an umpire in military manoeuvres.' Aston's disgust was entirely understandable.

SCORERS	Ramirez, Toro
EVENT	World Cup Finals, group match, Estadio Nacional, Santiago, 2 June 1962
CHILE	(Man: Fernando Riera) 1. Escuti 2. Eyzaguirre 3. Sanchez, R 4. Navarro 5. Contreras 6. Rojas 7. Ramirez 8. Toro 9. Landa 10. Fouilloux 11. Sanchez, L
ITALY	(Man: Paolo Mazza) 1. Mattrel 2. David 3. Robotti 4. Salvadore 5. Janich 6. Tumburus 7. Mora 8. Maschio 9. Altafini 10. Ferrini 11. Menichelli

English referee Ken Aston is aided by Chilean military as he sends off Ferrini.

Baxter, Jim
Rangers, Scotland

A MIDFIELD, BALL-PLAYING GENERAL whose medal tally never matched those of a Billy McNeill or an Ally McCoist, but whose skill, personality and lifestyle filled endless column inches on the front and back pages of Scotland's press.

The architect of Rangers' dominance in the early 1960s, Baxter's talent elevated him to the status of team-mate to the likes of Alfredo Di Stefano, Ferenc Puskas and Eusebio in a Wembley appearance for the Rest of the World against England in 1963. Four years later it was the same venue and opponents who provided Baxter with a moment that epitomised his talent and sense of occasion when, during Scotland's famous defeat of the World Champions, he sat on the ball inviting the English players to dispossess him. While the tanner-ball Scottish stereotype suited Baxter, he also lived up to his nation's drinking traditions and a decline following a transfer to Sunderland in 1965 ensured he was never again to win a major trophy. His death at 61 in April 2001 jogged memories of a greater glory and prompted Rangers fans to line the streets in their thousands to mourn his passing.

👍 Baxter's best-ever Rangers performance was probably the 1963 Cup Final replay against Celtic. He was imperious in a 3-0 victory.

👎 Scotland's failure to qualify for the 1966 World Cup Finals was put down largely to the absence of Baxter, who missed crucial qualifiers against Poland and Italy.

👎 Baxter never played in the finals of a major international tournament, so remains largely unknown outside Britain.

👎 After four unsuccessful years away, Baxter returned to Rangers for a last hurrah in 1969, but was not the force of old.

☞ Scotland's 1967 victory at Wembley condemned England to their first defeat since winning the World Cup a year earlier.

VITAL STATISTICS

Place of Birth:	Hill O'Beath, Fife, Scotland	
Date of Birth:	29 September 1939	**Died:** 14 April 2001
Caps:	34 (Scotland)	**Goals (International):** 3
Clubs:	Rangers, Sunderland, Raith Rovers,	
	Nottingham Forest	
Appearances:	Club (for Rangers): 254	
Goals:	Club (for Rangers): 24	
Trophies:	SLT 1961, 1963, 1964; SFAC 1962, 1963, 1964	

LEGEND RATING	
Achievement	6.0
Skill	9.0
Teamwork	7.0
Passion	8.0
Personality	8.0
TOTAL	**38.0**

Bayern Munich
The Dream Team

BAYERN'S TRUE HISTORY started in 1969 when they won their second league title. The first, in 1932, was in a weak league, and the club spent most of the following 30 years in the Second Division.

That all changed when the huge hands of Maier and the genius of Beckenbauer were allied to the finishing of Müller. With the uncompromising Schwarzenbeck at the back, Breitner surging up and down the left, and Hoeness quietly piecing it all together, this was a class act, and they won three consecutive European Cups to prove it.

Bayern have never quite hit those heights again, but they have remained at the top of German football, and have always been a threat in Europe (although it wasn't until 2001 that they won the European Cup again). A good percentage of Germany's best players have started with Bayern, often, like Matthaus and Klinsmann, returning for a second spell after doing the tourist bit in Italy, Spain or England. Bayern's unpopularity with other European clubs is based on their reputation for arrogance; this team would do nothing to alleviate that.

- Markus Babbel, an aggressive and attack-minded defender, was enjoying an excellent spell at Liverpool when he was diagnosed with Guillain Barre syndrome. He missed most of the 2001–02 season because of the illness.
- Samuel Kuffour, the Ghanaian international, has become an integral part of the modern Bayern side; it was a surprise when he was not elected African Footballer of the Year in 2001.
- Apart from Kuffour, Belgian goalkeeper Pfaff is the only other non-German in the side. The successor to Maier, he was one of the earlier successful imports into the Bundesliga.
- Uli Hoeness was an undemonstrative player, but his link play allowed the bigger egos to flourish.

Manager: Franz Beckenbauer

1-4-3-2

Sepp Maier (60s/70s)

Franz Beckenbauer (C) (60s/70s)

Markus Babbel (90s) Georg Schwarzenbeck (70s) Samuel Kuffour (90s)
Paul Breitner (70s)

Uli Hoeness (70s) Lothar Matthaus (80s/90s) Stefan Effenberg (90s)

Gerd Müller (70s) Karl-Heinz Rummenigge (80s)

Subs: Jean-Marie Pfaff (G) (80s) Andreas Brehme (D) (80s) Klaus Augenthaler (D) (80s) Mehmet Scholl (M) (90s) Jurgen Klinsmann (F) (90s)

Referee Colina offers consolation after Bayern's last-gasp defeat in the 1999 Champions League Final.

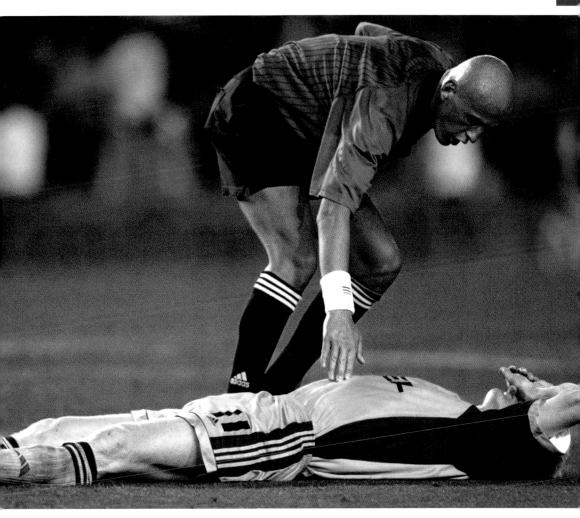

Beckenbauer, Franz
Bayern Munich, Germany

'THE KAISER', as Franz Beckenbauer became known (such were the imperious nature of his displays for club and country), was one of the finest players in the history of the game. An outstanding captain and tactician, it was no surprise that he went on to win everything, including the World Cup as player and manager.

Beginning his international career as a deep-lying midfielder, Beckenbauer revolutionised the notion of the attacking sweeper, bursting out of defence to set up attacks, often even finishing them himself. He had every attribute a footballer requires: control, passing, strength and uncanny vision. Only Ruud Gullit has since shown a comparable range of skills, but he lacked Beckenbauer's iron will. Retiring from international football in 1977, Beckenbauer teamed up with Pelé at New York Cosmos in the North American Soccer League, before returning to claim one last domestic honour with SV Hamburg.

Once retired he was appointed national coach almost immediately, and injected the same discipline and indomitable steel into the German side in the 1980s that it was famed for under his captaincy 10 years earlier. More success followed, and Beckenbauer, as President of Bayern Munich, remains at the forefront of German and European football to this day.

- Many commentators believe Beckenbauer's best performance came in the 3-2 win over England at the 1970 World Cup in Mexico. He inspired the Germans to a 3-2 win after they fell two goals behind.
- Only Mario Zagalo has equalled Beckenbauer's feat of World Cup medals as player and manager; Zagalo was not captain of Brazil.
- Beckenbauer was twice named European Footballer of the Year, in 1972 and 1976.
- He was picked for Germany after only 27 appearances for Bayern.
- Beckenbauer was detailed to man-mark Bobby Charlton in the 1966 World Cup Final, and later admitted he was not ready for the challenge.

VITAL STATISTICS

Place of Birth:	Munich, Germany
Date of Birth:	11 September 1945 **Died:** n/a
Caps:	104 (W. Germany) **Goals (International):** 15
Clubs:	Bayern Munich, Hamburg, New York Cosmos
Appearances:	Club (All Matches): 720
Goals:	Club (All Matches): 94
Trophies:	WorC 1974 (1990); EuroC 1972; BLG 1969, 1973, 1974, 1975, (1994); EC 1974, 1975; CWC 1967

LEGEND RATING	
Achievement	10.0
Skill	9.0
Teamwork	9.0
Passion	9.0
Personality	8.0
TOTAL	**45.0**

Beckenbauer covets the World Cup with the West German team in 1974.

Beckham, David
Manchester United, Real Madrid, England

WHEN DAVID BECKHAM curled a last-minute free kick over the Greek wall to win England a place at the 2002 World Cup finals, it completed a comeback more remarkable than his national side. It also capped one of the most complete performances by any player in an England shirt.

That he has matured beyond adolescent cockiness is more surprising, his looks, style and pop-star wife have made 'Becks' the most hounded footballer since George Best. A much-publicised spat with Alex Ferguson led to Beckham's departure for Real Madrid, where he has sometimes struggled alongside the other galacticos.

Three years previously, he was the nation's hate figure, reviled after his petulant kick and red card against Argentina had cost England their place at France 98. If he had taken the easy option and moved abroad, he may not have become what he is; the single most influential player for his country. His passing and crossing are of the highest order, and his shooting from set pieces is simply Brazilian in its power and accuracy.

- Arrives in English football with an outrageous 50 m goal at Wimbledon.
- France 98. Becomes a national hero by scoring a 25 m free kick against Colombia. Argentina and Diego Simeone were only days away, though.
- 1999. Marries Spice Girl Victoria Beckham. 'Posh and Becks' become Britain's most photographed couple.
- December 2001. Voted BBC Sports Personality of the Year, and runner-up as World Footballer of the Year for a second time.
- October 2004. Claims to have deliberately earned a booking (and subsequent suspension) with a silly tackle in the England v Wales game, as he was injured and would have missed the next game anyway. Apparently this proves he's not stupid. Yes, David.

VITAL STATISTICS

Place of Birth:	Leytonstone, England		
Date of Birth:	2 May 1975	**Died:** n/a	
Caps:	76 (England)	**Goals (International):** 15	
Clubs:	Manchester United, Real Madrid		
Appearances:	Club (All Matches): 453		
Goals:	Club (All Matches): 95		
Trophies:	LT 1996, 1997, 1999, 2000, 2001, 2003;		
	FAC 1996, 1999; EC 1999		

LEGEND RATING	
Achievement	9.0
Skill	8.5
Teamwork	9.0
Passion	8.5
Personality	6.0
TOTAL	**41.0**

Bergkamp, Dennis
Arsenal, Holland

DENNIS BERGKAMP BROKE INTO the Ajax team towards the end of the Gullit, Rijkaard, Van Basten era. Bergkamp gradually made his presence felt, and earned a high-profile move to Inter to replace Jurgen Klinsmann. Not suited to playing as a lone striker, the move did not work out and Inter offloaded him to Arsenal. Initially it seemed as if his spell at Highbury would be equally unfruitful, but the arrival of Arsène Wenger changed all that. Almost immediately Bergkamp was rejuvenated and, in tandem with Nicolas Anelka, inspired the Gunners to a League and Cup double in 1998.

After scoring the two goals at Wembley that effectively eliminated England in the qualifiers, Bergkamp had an outstanding 1994 World Cup in a transitional side. A better side flopped in Euro 96, getting hammered by England, but surprised many by the quality of their play at France 98. Bergkamp showed his divine poise and touch in scoring the goal of the tournament against Argentina. Since then Bergkamp's best has only been seen in glimpses, and he found himself exiled to the fringes of the Arsenal first team until a resurgence of form saw him help the Gunners win another double in 2002 and another title in 2004.

- In August 1997 Bergkamp occupied the top three positions in the *Match Of The Day* goal-of-the-month competition. The winning goal, a cheeky control-and-finish against Leicester, also won the goal-of-the-season award.
- Many Ajax coaches thought Bergkamp wasn't strong enough for pro football, but Johan Cruyff was quick to select him for the first team.
- Bergkamp's fear of flying, which he thought he had conquered, was rekindled by a bomb alert as the Dutch team travelled to the 1994 World Cup in the USA. He has not flown since.
- Bergkamp was named after Denis Law. His parents mistakenly spelt his first name with two 'n's instead of one.

VITAL STATISTICS

Place of Birth:	Amsterdam, Holland
Date of Birth:	18 May 1969 **Died:** n/a
Caps:	79 (Holland) **Goals (International):** 36
Clubs:	Ajax, Inter Milan, Arsenal
Appearances:	Club (League): 528
Goals:	Club (League): 202
Trophies:	LT 1998, 2002, 2004; FAC 1998, 2002, 2003; DLT 1993; EUFAC 1992, 1994

LEGEND RATING	
Achievement	7.0
Skill	9.0
Teamwork	8.0
Passion	7.0
Personality	7.0
TOTAL	**38.0**

Berlusconi's Dream
AC Milan, late 1980s

IN DEBT AND UNSUCCESSFUL, Milan were going nowhere until Silvio Berlusconi's millions (or billions, if we're talking lire!) provided coach Arrigo Sacchi with the funds to strip other European clubs of their prize assets. The ploy had served Milan well in the late 1950s, and was to do so again. The Dutch triumvirate of Gullit, Rijkaard and Van Basten was assembled in front of possibly the greatest club defence of all time; Tassotti and Maldini at full-back and, inside them, the peerless Baresi and Costacurta. In 1989, after a wait of 20 years, they brought home the European Cup, and won it again the following year.

Four years later, this time under Fabio Capello, the European Cup was again brought back to the San Siro, erasing the frustrations of a defeat against Marseille in 1993. The full-backs and the tousle-haired Donadoni were still there, and Marcel Desailly bestrode the midfield. There was a Balkan influence up front, with the Croatian Boban deployed alongside the enigmatic Yugoslav, Savicevic. That was the last great European year for Milan; Savicevic departed and was shortly followed by Desailly, while Baresi was to retire before the decade was out. Their replacements, despite Milan's Champions League victory in 2003, have yet to scale the heights of their predecessors.

- In the 1989 European Cup final the Dutch trio destroyed Steaua Bucharest 4-0, Van Basten and Gullit grabbing a brace each.
- Rijkaard's glory came the following year, as he scored the only goal in the 1-0 win over Benfica.
- In 1994 Savicevic was the tormentor-in-chief. Barcelona were confident of victory going into the game, but they were pulled apart by the Yugoslav genius as Milan again won 4-0.
- Following a corruption enquiry into their owner, Bernard Tapie, Marseille were stripped of their 1993 European Cup title. UEFA decided not to award Milan the trophy by default.
- Franco Baresi missed Barcelona's crushing. It would have been fitting to have one of the club's great servants in their finest hour.

Managers: Arrigo Sacchi and Fabio Capello

Key Players
Paolo Maldini (D) Franco Baresi (D) Alessandro Costacurta (D)
Frank Rijkaard (M) Ruud Gullit (M/F) Marcel Desailly (M)
Roberto Donadoni (M) Daniele Massaro (F)
Marco Van Basten (F) Dejan Savicevic (F)

Trophies
SA 1988, 1992, 1993, 1994 EC 1989, 1990, 1994

Van Basten and Gullit with the European Cup. Nice vest, Ruud!

Bernabeu Stadium
Madrid, Spain

THE CHAMARTIN STADIUM WAS HOME to Real Madrid for their first 23 years. In 1944, ambitious club president Santiago Bernabeu saw work begin on his dream to construct an arena which would propel Real to the top of football's élite. Three years later the boast became reality.

The Bernabeu is a mighty work. It boasts twin towers, similar to those at Wembley, and its steep terraces make it one of the most intimidating football theatres in the world. The Bernabeu played host to the all-conquering Real side of the 1950s, and became a virtual fortress for the home team between 1957–65, as Real played a remarkable 114 matches in succession without defeat. Eight replica European Cups make the trophy room unique, a scale of victory unthinkable without the atmosphere and revenue generated by the Bernabeu.

The stadium was improved still further when Spain hosted the 1982 World Cup Finals. A new roof was added, increasing the crescendo still further. Naturally, the Bernabeu played host to the final itself, Italy beating West Germany 3-1.

- ☞ The first game at the Bernabeu on 14 December 1947 saw Real Madrid beat the Portuguese team Os Belenenses 3-1.
- ☝ A record crowd of 124,000 watched Real beat Fiorentina 2-0 in the 1957 European Cup final.
- ☝ The capacity was drastically reduced in the 1990s following UEFA's insistence on all-seater stadiums.
- ☝ The Bernabeu has hosted three European Cup finals; 1957, 1969 and Nottingham Forest's 1-0 victory over Hamburg SV in 1980.
- ☞ A new stadium has been proposed on a site 5 km away. It has met with stiff opposition from traditionalists, despite the intention to return capacity to 120,000-plus.

VITAL STATISTICS

(Named after long-time Real Madrid president Santiago Bernabeu)

Location:	Madrid, Spain
Local Club:	Real Madrid
Date Built:	1947
Current Capacity:	105,000
Max. Capacity:	125,000

Best Football Team in the World

...Ever

THIS WAS REALLY EASY TO PICK. So few players elevate themselves to the level of these 16 players that the process of elimination is almost automatic. The criteria? Great technical ability, appetite for battle, sustained excellence over a number of years, and an ability to inspire others, either by example or leadership.

None of these players were perfect (although Pelé came close at times) and none are pre-war (football was a cruder game back then and the competition was less fierce), but all satisfy the criteria in abundance. Six of them played in the 1950s, four more started in the 1960s, two in the 1970s, and the last four in the 1980s.

There are nine Europeans and five South Americans (no country has more than two players), and there are no out-and-out full-backs; the restrictive nature of the position makes it unattractive for the very best players. If 4-4-2 were required, Baresi would slot in alongside Moore, and Garrincha or Best would drop to the bench. Only Paolo Maldini is still in active service, and his career is coming to an end. Other current players were considered, but the likes of Luis Figo, Thierry Henry and David Beckham still have plenty to prove before they can be bracketed in this exalted company.

☞ No one got close to either of the goalkeeping slots; the next in line were Shilton, Schmeichel, Zoff and Jennings.

☞ Van Basten is another Dutchman unlucky to miss out, and Eusebio and Bobby Charlton wouldn't have looked out of place.

☞ Daniel Passarella had a case for inclusion, but was less sophisticated than the four defenders picked. Marcel Desailly falls just short of this status.

☞ Gullit is perhaps the most obvious omission from the midfield.

☞ Lothar Matthaus was a great player, but his biggest fan was Lothar Matthaus.

☝ Managing this collection of inflated egos would be impossible, so we thought we might as well appoint ourselves!

Managers: Guy Lloyd and Nick Holt

3-4-1-2

Lev Yashin (USSR)

Franz Beckenbauer (C) (W. Ger) Bobby Moore (Eng) Paolo Maldini (Ita)

Garrincha (Bra) Pelé (Bra)
Michel Platini (Fra) George Best (N. Ire)

Alfredo Di Stefano (Arg)

Johan Cruyff (Hol) Ferenc Puskas (Hun)

Subs: Gordon Banks (G) (Eng) Franco Baresi (D) (Ita) Diego Maradona (M) (Arg)
Juan Schiaffino (F) (Uru) Gerd Muller (F) (W. Ger)

Lev Yashin (USSR)

Franz Beckenbauer (W. Ger) (c)

Bobby Moore (Eng)

Paolo Maldini (Ita)

Garrincha (Bra)

Pelé (Bra)

Michel Platini (Fra)

George Best (N. Ire)

Johan Cruyff (Hol)

Alfredo Di Stefano (Arg)

Ferenc Puskas (Hun)

Best, George

Manchester United, Northern Ireland

'I THINK I'VE FOUND YOU A GENIUS,' claimed the Belfast scout in an excited telephone call to Matt Busby. He wasn't wrong. Signed as a professional on his 17th birthday, George Best thrilled the Old Trafford faithful like no player before or since. Had Best played for a stronger country than Northern Ireland he may now be spoken of with the same reverence as Pelé.

The cocktail of outrageous ball skills and smouldering good looks proved to be an explosive one; Best's transformation from Belfast innocent to international playboy seemed to capture the spirit of the 1960s. He was even dubbed 'El Beatle' by the Portuguese press after a mesmerising display in Benfica's Stadium of Light. The free spirit that was Europe's most feared striker became society's hottest property, an advertiser's dream whose fame and fortune rocketed in a whirl of boutique openings and product endorsement. The inevitable falls from grace were frequent and glaring, and at 28 he was washed-up.

Despite an Indian summer at Fulham with fellow funster Rodney Marsh, and occasional spells in the NASL and elsewhere, the career of George Best has now been restricted to bar-room reminiscences for nearly 30 years.

- Best was originally recommended to Leeds. Unimpressed, the scout left his trial match during the first half.
- 1968. Best's *annus mirabilis*: Joint First Division top-scorer, European Cup winner, English and European Footballer of the Year.
- 1970. Suspended for four weeks for bringing the game into disrepute. On his return, scored six in an 8-2 win at Northampton.
- 1976. Scored after 71 seconds in his debut for Fulham. Also became their first recipient of a red card.
- A liver transplant in 2002 failed to curb Best's drinking bouts and he was convicted of drink driving in January 2004.

VITAL STATISTICS

Place of Birth:	Belfast, Northern Ireland	
Date of Birth:	22 May 1946	**Died:** n/a
Caps:	37 (N. Ireland)	**Goals (International):** 9
Clubs:	Manchester United, Stockport County, Cork Celtic, Los Angeles Aztecs, Fulham, Hibernian, Fort Lauderdale Strikers, San Jose Earthquakes, Golden, Bournemouth	
Appearances:	Club (League for Man Utd): 361	
Goals:	Club (League for Man Utd): 137	
Trophies:	LT 1965, 1967; EC 1968 (all with Man Utd)	

LEGEND RATING	
Achievement	8.0
Skill	10.0
Teamwork	7.0
Passion	8.0
Personality	9.0
TOTAL	**42.0**

Bianconeri
Juventus, early 1980s

AT THE BEGINNING of the 1980s Juventus were a deeply unfulfilled club. Their great rivals from Milan had both won the European Cup in the 1960s and 1970s, but despite a stream of Serie A titles, Juve were perennial failures in their quest for ultimate European glory (they had lost their only final appearance against Ajax in 1973). The defence was rock solid, a formidable barrier that contained experienced keeper Dino Zoff, Scirea at sweeper and the fabled hard-man Gentile in the middle. Coach Trapattoni had tried a number of permutations of overseas stars ahead of them, but it was the combination of Platini and the Polish star Boniek that would prove the key. They came close in 1983, but came up against a stubborn Hamburg in the final. The following year was another dress rehearsal, a victory in the European Cup Winners' Cup over Porto. Sadly, when Juve finally landed their Holy Grail, their victory, against Liverpool in the 1985 final, was tainted with sadness. The deaths of 39 of their fans following the collapse of a wall in the Heysel stadium before kick-off reduced the match to a meaningless and hollow affair. The Cup was lifted, the crowd applauded but there was no joy in the celebrations.

- ☝ Zoff, Gentile, Cabrini, Scirea, Tardelli and Rossi all started the 1982 World Cup Final. Zoff captained the side, Tardelli and Rossi both scored.
- ☞ Juve squeezed past Manchester United in the semi-finals of the 1984 European Cup Winners' Cup, a 2-1 home win seeing them home on aggregate by the odd goal.
- ☞ In 1983, on their way to the European Cup final, they disposed of English opposition, beating Aston Villa home and away.
- ☝ Platini settled the 1985 final with a penalty that shouldn't have been given. The great Frenchman contributed seven goals to Juve's campaign that year.

Manager: Giovanni Trapattoni

Key Players
Dino Zoff (G) Claudio Gentile (D) Antonio Cabrini (D)
Gaetano Scirea (D) Marco Tardelli (M) Zbigniew Boniek (M)
Michel Platini (M/F) Paolo Rossi (F) Roberto Bettega (F)

Trophies
SA 1981, 1982, 1984, 1986 EC 1985 CWC 1984 WCC 1985 ESC 1984

Zbigniew Boniek, 'Il Bello di Notte', celebrates another goal.

Blanchflower, Robert Dennis (Danny)

Tottenham Hotspur, Northern Ireland

DANNY BLANCHFLOWER is best remembered as the playmaker in the 1961 Spurs double-winning side. However, he was by then in the twilight of his career, having emerged in Irish football just after the war.

Not exceptionally quick or powerful, Blanchflower's game was all about passing. Blessed with exceptional vision, his ability to find team-mates with the ball was uncanny. His understanding of the game was deep and intuitive, and he used that knowledge to great effect on the pitch. 'Football is not really about winning ... it's about doing things in style,' he once wrote. Any modern footballer uttering those words would be sold the next day!

After retiring, Blanchflower had a few forays into management. He managed the Northern Ireland national team in a tough spell prior to the golden years of Billy Bingham, and was in charge at Stamford Bridge as Chelsea suffered relegation in 1979. Thereafter he concentrated on his career as a journalist, where his erudite thinking about the game served him better.

☞ He famously refused to take part in the programme *This Is Your Life* when Eamonn Andrews surprised him.

🖑 Danny's younger brother, Jackie, played for Manchester United and was injured in the Munich air crash, never to play again.

👌 Blanchflower was captain of the Northern Ireland team that reached the quarter-finals of the 1958 World Cup.

👌 He was also captain when Northern Ireland beat England at Wembley for the first time in 1957.

✌ He was Player of the Year in 1958 and 1961.

VITAL STATISTICS

Place of Birth:	Belfast, Northern Ireland
Date of Birth:	10 February 1926 **Died:** 9 December 1993
Caps:	56 (N. Ireland) **Goals (International):** 2
Clubs:	Glentoran, Swindon Town, Barnsley, Aston Villa, Tottenham Hotspur
Appearances:	Club (All Matches): 735
Goals:	Club (All Matches): 40
Trophies:	LT 1961; FAC 1961, 1962; CWC 1963

LEGEND RATING	
Achievement	8.0
Skill	9.0
Teamwork	7.0
Passion	8.0
Personality	8.0
TOTAL	**40.0**

Blokhin, Oleg
Dynamo Kiev, USSR

THE SOVIET UNION used to guard its assets with extreme jealousy, so football viewers to the west of the Iron Curtain only tended to see their stars when they came out of their shell in European competition. When Dynamo Kiev beat Ferencvaros in the 1975 European Cup Winners' Cup final they revealed some marvellous talent, not least their flying winger Oleg Blokhin, scorer of their third goal. Fast and with a penchant for cutting inside and heading for goal, Blokhin went on to terrorise the best club defence in Europe the following year, scoring a hat-trick in the 3-0 victory over Bayern Munich in the European Super Cup. Eleven years later Blokhin played in another European Cup Winners' Cup final, this time as the old warhorse in the sublimely talented side coached by Valeri Lobanowski. He contributed a goal to a mesmerising performance in what was a fitting swansong at the top level. In Igor Belanov, another striker who enjoyed attacking from wide positions, Dynamo had a ready-made successor for Blokhin, and they have continued to cover for his absence impressively, nurturing several talented front men including Andrei Shevchenko and Sergei Rebrov.

- Blohkin's cup exploits earned him the European Footballer of the Year award in 1975. His club-mate and compatriot Igor Belanov won the same honour in 1986.
- Kiev almost got to the final of the 1977 European Cup but, after eliminating holders Bayern Munich, they lost 2-1 on aggregate to Borussia Monchengladbach in the semi-final.
- Blokhin became the first Soviet player to win 100 caps. Let's hope no one catches his final target of 101, because if they do it means the tanks have rolled again.
- At the end of his career Blokhin was allowed to leave the Soviet Union and earn a pension in Austrian football. He later became manager of Olympiakos in Greece, and is now breathing new life into the Ukrainian national team in preparation for World Cup 2006.

VITAL STATISTICS

Place of Birth:	Kiev, Russia		
Date of Birth:	5 November 1952	**Died:** n/a	
Caps:	101 (USSR)	**Goals (International):** 39	
Clubs:	Dynamo Kiev, Vorwarts Styer		
Appearances:	Club (All Matches): 432		
Goals:	Club (All Matches): 211		
Trophies:	LT 1971, 1974, 1975, 1980, 1981, 1985, 1986;		
	CWC 1975, 1986		

Achievement	8.0
Skill	8.0
Teamwork	8.0
Passion	7.0
Personality	6.0
TOTAL	**37.0**

LEGEND RATING

Blonde Bombshells
A Scandinavian Select

SWEDEN AND DENMARK DOMINATE this strong selection, as befits the two countries with the greatest pedigree at international level. Eriksson is the most successful coach from any of those nations, so gets the manager's job.

Sweden have been a competitive side since the war, reaching the final of the 1958 World Cup on home soil with a team including the adaptable Liedholm, the energetic Gren and the great goalscorer Gunnar Nordahl, and managed by Englishman George Raynor. They usually qualify for the finals and rarely disgrace themselves. Denamrk's remarkable win at Euro 92 put them on the footballing map, and the skills of the Laudrup brothers have kept them there. Their best side was prior to that win, in 1986 under German Sepp Piontek, with the great Morten Olsen holding court at sweeper.

Norway flirted with major tournaments in the 1990s but Egil Olsen's dour tactics always stifled the better players. Bratseth, a world-class defender, represents them here. Finland are an improving side, with the brilliant Jari Litmanen an inspiration for future generations. Iceland, too, are no longer cannon fodder; in qualification for Euro 2000 they gave a superb account of themselves in a group containing France, Russia and Ukraine.

👍 Sweden have had several top-class international strikers. In the 1970s Ralf Edstrom was a towering player, Thomas Brolin was their playmaker, and their recent duo of Kennet Andersson and Henrik Larsson paired two-high calibre finishers.

👍 Denmark, too, have had notable strikers. Preben Elkjaer and Fleming Povlsen, were both excellent players; Elkjaer was a fine foil for Micahel Laudrup, with his phenomenal stamina and work-rate.

☞ Iceland, and its future, are represented by Chelsea's Eidur Gudjohnsen, whose father also plays for the country.

☞ With the precocious Mikael Forsell in their ranks, Finland gave England two tough matches in the 2002 World Cup qualifiers.

Manager: Sven-Goran Eriksson (Swe)

1-3-3-1-2

Peter Schmeichel (Den) (90s)

Morten Olsen (C) (Den) (80s)

Nils Liedholm (Swe) (50s) Bjorn Nordqvist (Swe) (60s/70s)
Rune Bratseth (Nor) (80s/90s)

Gunnar Gren (Swe) (50s) Jan Molby (Den) (80s)
Jari Litmanen (Fin) (90s) Michael Laudrup (Den) (90s)

Henrik Larsson (Swe) (90s/00s) Gunnar Nordahl (Swe) (50s/60s)

Subs: Tomas Ravelli (Swe) (G) (80s/90s) Patrik Andersson (Swe) (D) (90s)
Kurt Hamrin (Swe) (M/F) Eidur Gudjohnsen (Ice) (F) (00s)
Allan Simonsen (Den) (F) (70s/80s)

Bloomer, Steve
Derby County, England

WITH HIS SLIGHT BUILD and sallow appearance, Steve Bloomer was an unlikely athlete. A dressing-room nickname of 'paleface' hardly suggested a man brimming with rude health but, during a remarkable career of 21 seasons, he became English football's first great goalscoring hero, and its undoubted star during the pre-First World War era.

His 352 league goals (a record that only Dixie Dean has beaten) were achieved courtesy of rare, two-footed skills that made him one of the game's most entertaining dribblers. His influence was exemplified by the 1903 FA Cup. Bloomer's goals had guided Derby to the final but, for the big day itself, he was absent with injury. Without him Derby succumbed 6-0 to Bury in what remains the heaviest final defeat of all time.

Two years later he made up one half of British football's then-biggest transfer, as Middlesbrough swooped for Bloomer and Sunderland's Alf Common in the first-ever four-figure deal. The gamble paid off. Boro, seemingly destined for relegation, hauled themselves clear in the final weeks of the season. For Bloomer, carrying inferior team-mates became the story of his career.

- He was England's seventh-highest scorer with 28 goals, despite winning only 23 caps.
- Bloomer never won a trophy, twice finishing on the losing side in the FA Cup final.
- 1914. Coaching in Berlin, Bloomer's career was only ended when he was interned at the onset of the First World War.
- Bloomer had a typically direct approach to the game: 'The purpose of play is the scoring of goals.'
- He was the leading league scorer five times in eight seasons.

VITAL STATISTICS

Place of Birth:	Cradley Heath, England
Date of Birth:	20 January 1874 **Died:** 16 April 1938
Caps:	23 (England) **Goals (International):** 28
Clubs:	Derby County, Middlesbrough
Appearances:	Club (League): 598
Goals:	Club (League): 352
Trophies:	None

LEGEND RATING	
Achievement	5.0
Skill	8.0
Teamwork	8.0
Passion	9.0
Personality	6.0
TOTAL	**36.0**

Bloomer (front row, seated second from left) poses with the England team.

Blue Heaven
The Chelsea Dream Team

THE 1955 TEAM may have won Chelsea's only title, but its sum was always greater than its individual parts. Hence captain and inspiration Roy Bentley is its only representative in this Dream Team, the remaining players being provided by teams of the 1970s and the late 1990s.

The agile Bonetti was a better goalkeeper than England fans will ever credit. The rest of the defence is dominated by the recent sides, with the exception of full-backs, where Shellito and McCreadie shade the more reliable Ferrer and sometimes unpredictable Le Saux. With Gullit and the fabulous Marcel Desailly at the back, there's no shortage of ability on the ball. Dennis Wise adds a bit of attitude to the midfield alongside the gifted yet underachieving Hudson. Gus Poyet provides all-day running and a good goal quota. The puck-like skills of Gianfranco Zola are used in their best position, just behind the front two (the only downside to this being that ball artists Nevin and Cooke have to settle for a place on the bench).

In attack Osgood, a truly complete centre-forward who should have played more internationals for England, is a fine spearhead alongside the industrious Bentley. Hughie Gallagher, perhaps better known as a Newcastle player, makes a potent substitute.

☞ Gullit is included in defence, despite being better known as an attacking midfielder.

☜ No place for Jimmy Greaves. Despite 124 goals in 157 games, his name is synonymous with Spurs.

☞ Bonetti is one of Chelsea's shorter keepers, dwarfed by 'Fatty' Foulke and Ed de Goey.

☞ Osgood and Le Saux both had two spells at the club. Osgood is included for his first, Le Saux his second.

☞ None of the current squad's expensive recruits merits inclusion just yet – England internationals John Terry and Frank Lampard seem the most likely.

Manager: Glenn Hoddle

4-3-1-2

Peter Bonetti (60s/70s)

Ken Shellito (60s) Marcel Desailly (90s)
Ruud Gullit (90s) Eddie McCreadie (70s)

Dennis Wise (90s) Alan Hudson (70s) Gus Poyet (90s)

Gianfranco Zola (90s)

Roy Bentley (50s) Peter Osgood (60s/70s)

Subs: Carlo Cudicini (G) (80s) Graeme Le Saux (D) (90s) Pat Nevin (W) (80s) Charlie Cooke (W) (60s/70s) Hughie Gallagher (F) (30s)

Ron Harris (left) and Peter Osgood (right) brandish the FA Cup after Chelsea's victory in 1970.

De Boer, Frank

Ajax, Barcelona, Holland

FROM THE MOMENT he first pulled on the orange jersey at the age of 20, Frank de Boer exuded an air of permanence. Fourteen years and 112 appearances later, he retired from international football as Holland's most-capped player and his country's most consistent defender.

What would the Dutch have given for him in 1974? All the soul-searching after the World Cup Final defeat to Germany could have been avoided if Holland's central defence had been marshalled by a player with the same unflappable authority. A fine distributor and unruffled when bringing the ball out of defence, he often seemed to be a chip off the Beckenbauer block. His career blossomed at Ajax, highlighting in the dazzling 1995 Champions League victory. Domestic league winner's medals became the norm but it became clear that a greater challenge was needed. Like many of the Ajax team, he eventually followed coach Louis van Gaal to Barcelona but his career suddenly turned sour. He struggled to command a place and faced a season's ban after failing a dope test in 2001. By 2003, he had become surplus to requirements and his club career never recovered. Later spells at Galatasaray and a four-month stint at Glasgow Rangers never threatened to scale previous heights.

☞ His international appearances with identical twin brother Ronald continued a Dutch sibling tradition. The brothers Witschge, van de Kerkhof and Koeman also played together.

👍 Best international moment: v Argentina in a 1998 World Cup quarter-final. Frank struck a pinpoint 60-metre pass to Bergkamp, who scored arguably Holland's best-ever goal and an 89-minute winner.

👎 Worst international moment: v Italy in a Euro 2000 semi-final. Frank missed two penalties; one in normal time and one in the shoot-out, as Holland crashed out.

VITAL STATISTICS

Place of Birth:	Hoorn, Holland	
Date of Birth:	15 May 1970	**Died:** n/a
Caps:	112 (Holland)	**Goals (International):** 13
Clubs:	Ajax, Barcelona, Galatasaray, Glasgow Rangers,	
	Al-Rayyan	
Appearances:	Club (League for Ajax and Barcelona): 352	
Goals:	Club (League for Ajax and Barcelona): 33	
Trophies:	DLT 1990, 1994–96, 1998; UEFAC 1992;	
	EC 1995; WCC1995; ESC 1996; PLA 1999	

LEGEND RATING	
Achievement	0.0
Skill	0.0
Teamwork	0.0
Passion	0.0
Personality	0.0
TOTAL	**0.0**

Boniek, Zbigniew
Juventus, Poland

AFTER EMERGING as a potential star with his local team, Zbigniew Boniek was picked up by Widzew Lodz, one of the top Polish sides. As his international reputation grew, so did the interest in him from scouts operating on behalf of the top clubs in Spain and Italy. He joined Juventus in 1982, forming an awesome midfield with Michel Platini and Marco Tardelli in one of the great European club sides.

Boniek was the perfect compliment to elegant playmaker Platini. Quick, skilful and industrious, he pulled defenders all over the pitch creating space and goals for both the Frenchman and striker Paolo Rossi.

At international level he appeared in three World Cups for Poland. On his first appearance, in 1978, he was still a raw novice, but by 1982 a strong Polish side was erected around his talents, and who knows what might have happened had he not been suspended for the semi-final against Italy? His last World Cup Finals appearance at Mexico 86 is probably best forgotten. Slow and ineffective playing as a sweeper, he was humiliated as a waning Polish team crashed 4-0 to Brazil in the second round.

- He was christened *Bello di Notte* ('Beauty of the Night') by Juventus president Gianni Agnelli for his stunning performances in night matches.
- He now works as a commentator on Polish TV.
- Boniek scored a great hat-trick in a second phase match against Belgium in the 1982 World Cup.
- He scored the winner in the 1984 European Cup Winners' Cup final against Porto.
- The £1.1 m Juventus paid for Boniek was a record for a Polish player.

VITAL STATISTICS

Place of Birth:	Bydgoszcz, Poland	
Date of Birth:	3 March 1956	**Died:** n/a
Caps:	80 (Poland)	**Goals (International):** 24
Clubs:	Zawisza Bydgoszcz, Widzew Lodz, Juventus, Roma	
Trophies:	EC 1985; CWC 1984; SA 1984	

LEGEND RATING	
Achievement	8.0
Skill	8.0
Teamwork	7.0
Passion	9.0
Personality	7.0
TOTAL	**39.0**

Boot Room, The

Liverpool, 1972–90

IT SEEMS A LITTLE HARSH to lump this lot together and count them as one team, but to separate them would be to undervalue their core strength, namely the great continuity that ran through the club for nearly 30 years. Liverpool's legendary ability to hand over from one manager to the next, and to replace one great player with another was the platform on which their success was built.

Shankly stood down for Paisley and, briefly, Fagan. Lawrenson slotted in effortlessly for Thompson, Keegan became Dalglish – every few years the face of the team would morph like Dr Who and a new line-up would emerge, just as powerful as the last. The circuit seemed to have been broken with the installation of Dalglish as the team's first player-manager, but the mercurial Scot understood the Liverpool ethos, and brought more success, including the club's first League and Cup double in 1986. Liverpool won games on reputation alone – lesser teams quailed at the prospect of playing them, and Anfield became a fortress. They lost only nine home league games in the 1970s, compared with 33 in the less successful 1990s.

- Phil Neal, the right-back, amassed eight championship medals, a record held jointly with Hansen. Add 50 caps and you have a remarkable tally for a player of modest abilities.
- Ray Kennedy, a double winner with Arsenal in 1971, missed the chance to become the first player to achieve that feat with a second club when Liverpool were beaten by Manchester United in the 1977 FA Cup final.
- Ronnie Whelan was an underrated player – athletic and strong, he could run all day and was a wonderful foil for the less mobile talents of Souness and Jan Molby.
- Liverpool never replaced the solidity of Ray Clemence in goal; current keeper Jerzy Dudek looked for a while to be a promising substitute, but has recently fallen from favour.

Managers: Bill Shankly, Bob Paisley, Joe Fagan, Kenny Dalglish

Key Players

Ray Clemence (G) Emlyn Hughes (D) Phil Thompson (D)
Phil Neal (D) Alan Hansen (D) Mark Lawrenson (D)
Graeme Souness (M) Jimmy Case (M) Ray Kennedy (M)
Ronnie Whelan (M) John Barnes (W) Kevin Keegan (F)
Kenny Dalglish (F) Peter Beardsley (F) Ian Rush (F)

Trophies

LT 1973, 1976, 1977, 1979, 1980, 1982, 1983, 1984, 1986, 1988, 1990;
FAC 1986; LC 1981–84; UEFAC 1973, 1976; EC 1977, 1978, 1981, 1984

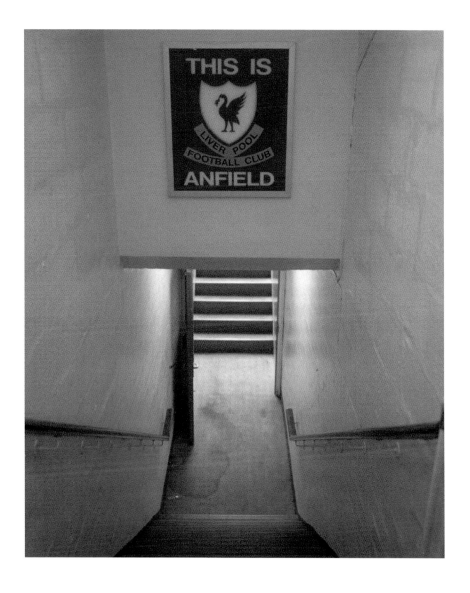

Bosman, Jean-Marc
FC Liege

IN 1988, an unremarkable Belgian midfielder entered into a dispute with his club over what appeared to be nothing more than a contractual technicality. Seven years later, the outcome of this legal spat was to change football forever. Jean-Marc Bosman was signed by RFC Liege on a two-year contract in 1988. On its expiry, a prospective new deal would have reduced his wages by 60 per cent. A potential solution was offered in the form of French club Dunkerque, but their transfer valuation of Bosman was less than half the £250,000 that Liege were demanding. He remained stuck in Belgium. Undeterred, Bosman started a legal process that inched its way to the European Court of Justice. His argument was that by retaining his registration, and demanding a transfer fee even after his contract had expired, Liege were in breach of European Union law, which was supposed to safeguard the free movement of workers between member states. In December 1995, the court agreed and ruled in Bosman's favour. The ruling has made players more powerful than ever before, with many of them, like England stars Steve McManaman and Sol Campbell, choosing to see out their contracts in order to negotiate lucrative moves away from clubs where they had been nurtured, developed and idolised.

☞ The same ruling also quashed a UEFA regulation limiting the number of foreign players that could appear in European competition for a single club.

👌 The beneficiaries? Top players, as clubs began to offer improved wages to attract out-of-contract stars.

👎 The losers? Small clubs, who had relied on the transfer income from their rising talent. Bigger teams could now wait for their contracts to expire and pick them up for nothing.

VITAL STATISTICS

Place of Birth:	Belgium	Achievement	4.0
Date of Birth:	30 October 1964	**Died:** n/a	Skill	6.0
Caps:	0	**Goals (International):** 0	Teamwork	7.0
Clubs:	FC Liege	Passion	8.0
Appearances:	Club (League): 73	Personality	9.0
Goals:	Club (League): 3	
Trophies:	None	**TOTAL 34.0**

LEGEND RATING

Brady, Liam
Arsenal, Juventus, Republic of Ireland

LIAM BRADY'S SKILL on the ball was a joy to behold – great touch, excellent dribbling skills and a sublime left foot. Little wonder then, that Arsenal fans quickly took him to their hearts. 'Chippy', as he became known, inspired the Gunners to their dramatic 3-2 FA Cup final win over Manchester United in 1979, creating the winning goal for Alan Sunderland in the dying moments.

A year later he was instrumental in Arsenal's run to the final of the European Cup Winners' Cup but, on the night, it was Brady's missed penalty in the shoot-out that handed the Cup to Valencia.

Possibly operating on the philosophy of 'if you can't beat 'em join 'em', Brady later moved to the continent where he became a huge success, winning two Serie A titles with Juventus, where he played alongside greats like Roberto Bettega in what many Juve fans still regard as their finest-ever team. Oddly though, Brady never played in a championship-winning side for Arsenal. In England Brady is perhaps best remembered for a goal he scored during a 5-0 thrashing of Spurs, an outrageous left-footed shot that curled into the top corner of the net.

👍 Brady was voted PFA Player Of The Year in 1979.

👍 He scored the penalty that sealed Juve's second successive title in 1982.

☞ Both Brady's brothers played professional football in Ireland.

👎 Brady had an unhappy two years as manager of Celtic, citing internal politics as his reason for leaving.

☞ He won surprisingly little in England, just his 1979 FA Cup medal.

VITAL STATISTICS

Place of Birth:	Dublin, Ireland	
Date of Birth:	13 February 1956	**Died:** n/a
Caps:	72 (R. Ireland)	**Goals (International):** 9
Clubs:	Arsenal, Juventus, Inter Milan, Ascoli, West Ham	
Appearances:	Club (for Arsenal): 306	
Goals:	Club (for Arsenal): 59	
Trophies:	FAC 1979; SA 1981, 1982	

Achievement	6.0
Skill	9.0
Teamwork	7.0
Passion	8.0
Personality	7.0
TOTAL	**37.0**

LEGEND RATING

Breitner, Paul
Bayern Munich, West Germany

GERMANY HAVE RARELY been short of a decent left-back. Andreas Brehme was justifiably acclaimed as the best player in the world in his position during the 1980s and early 1990s, but Paul Breitner had a range of skills that eclipsed even those of the former Inter star. Quick, strong and with a keen eye for the goal, Breitner was the complete full-back, a player so comfortable on the ball that in the latter stages of his career he developed into an equally impressive midfield player.

Breitner was picked for West Germany at 20 in 1971, and was a key member of the team that won the 1972 European Championship and the 1974 World Cup. After a dispute with the management he was absent from the international scene for a number of years, but returned to play in the 1982 World Cup as a midfield general, some say at the behest of Karl-Heinz Rummenigge. Breitner's club career saw him win a plethora of league titles with Bayern Munich and Real Madrid, and he also appeared in the first of Bayern's three consecutive European Cup wins in the mid-1970s.

☞ Breitner scored in two World Cup Finals, a penalty in 1974, and West Germany's consolation in the 1982 final.

👍 Before the 1974 final, Breitner had already scored twice in the tournament against Chile and Yugoslavia.

☞ Breitner was known for his left-wing political views; not a common trait in a professional footballer!

☞ Breitner was known as 'Der Afro' on account of his disco-frizz hairdo.

VITAL STATISTICS

Place of Birth:	Freilassung, Germany
Date of Birth:	5 September 1951 **Died:** n/a
Caps:	48 (W. Germany) **Goals (International):** 10
Clubs:	Bayern Munich, Real Madrid, Eintracht Braunschweig
Appearances:	Club (for Bayern Munich): 255
Goals:	Club (for Bayern Munich): 83
Trophies:	WorC 1974; EuroC 1972; EC 1974; PLA 1975, 1976; BLG 1972, 1973, 1974, 1980, 1981

LEGEND RATING	
Achievement	10.0
Skill	8.0
Teamwork	8.0
Passion	7.0
Personality	8.0
TOTAL	**41.0**

Bremner, Billy

Leeds United, Scotland

THE FIRST GREAT LEEDS SIDE may have been created by Don Revie, but Billy Bremner was its midfield heartbeat. An assessment of him could just as easily describe the team itself – tough-tackling, measured in the pass and with a combative spirit that was by turns inspirational and illegal.

Bremner was indispensable even in a team packed with pedigree, a fact emphasised by a glance at the Elland Road record books. Incredibly, Bremner led Leeds to six of the seven major trophy successes in their entire history (the championship win of 1992 being the only triumph in which he did not participate).

Often in trouble with referees, the sight of Bremner throwing his shirt to the ground after becoming, with Kevin Keegan, the first British player to be dismissed at Wembley, led to parliamentary calls for him to be permanently suspended.

It was similar at an international level. In 1974 he captained a Scotland squad that emerged from the World Cup Finals as the only unbeaten team, but was shortly banned for life following incidents in a Danish nightclub after a game. His departure from Elland Road to Hull City in 1976 signalled the break-up of the great Leeds team, a schism which took the Yorkshire club 16 years to recover from.

☞ Bremner made his Leeds debut aged 17, as a winger.

⚫ 1965. Scored Leeds' first-ever goal at Wembley but they lose 2-1 to Liverpool in the FA Cup final.

⚫ 1970. Scored in British football's most epic club game, but Leeds went down to Celtic in a European Cup semi-final.

☝ 1985. Became Leeds' manager by popular demand. Failed to revive an average Second Division team and was sacked in 1988.

☝ 1997. His sudden death from a heart attack shocked and saddened the football world.

VITAL STATISTICS

Place of Birth:	Stirling, Scotland
Date of Birth:	9 December 1942 **Died:** 7 December 1997
Caps:	54 (Scotland) **Goals (International):** 3
Clubs:	Leeds United, Hull City, Doncaster Rovers
Appearances:	Club (League for Leeds Utd): 586
Goals:	Club (League for Leeds Utd): 90
Trophies:	LT 1969, 1974; FAC 1972; LC 1968; UEFAC 1968, 1971

LEGEND RATING	
Achievement	8.0
Skill	7.0
Teamwork	9.0
Passion	9.0
Personality	6.0
TOTAL	**39.0**

Wembley 1968: Bremner lifts Leeds' first major trophy, the League Cup.

Brilliant Orange
The Holland Dream Team

PERHAPS NOT SURPRISINGLY, all these players are from the modern era. Holland were no great shakes until around 1960, when Rinus Michels began to bring through a generation of players at Ajax that would change the face of football for ever. His method of play became known as 'Total Football' and it spawned a team of creative, flexible players capable of performing wherever they happened to find themselves on the field.

All the defenders in this team are comfortable on the ball (although Koeman had a tendency to dwell on it), and all the midfield players could defend when necessary. Gullit and Rijkaard give the midfield strength and Rep, who is picked ahead of Van Hanegem, provides width. Their only genuine winger, Marc Overmars, has failed too often on the big occasion to warrant selection.

The forward line is wonderful. The movement of Cruyff and Bergkamp would have defences marking shadows, and the pure goalscoring genius of Van Basten means a decent percentage of the chances would be put away without fuss. In a Dream Team World Cup they would produce performances to drool over, probably surpassing even Brazil at their best. But they would inevitably lose in the final and all blame each other.

- The side lacks a quality goalkeeper like Sepp Maier, Gordon Banks or Dino Zoff.
- Only four of the XVI are still playing, Holland not being the force they were: no De Boer, Kluivert, Cocu or Davids.
- Bergkamp's inclusion is, of course, dependent on the fixtures being held in western Europe. Van Nistelrooy will fill in for away fixtures that require air travel.
- Van Nistelrooy gets in without any great international pedigree simply because we couldn't leave him out after his breathtaking displays for Man United. If Holland screw up in the next World Cup qualifiers he may become one of the greatest players never to make the Finals.

Manager: Rinus Michels

3-4-3

Hans Van Breukelen (80s)

Wim Suurbier (70s) Ronald Koeman (C) (80s/90s) Rudi Krol (70s)

Frank Rijkaard (80s) Ruud Gullit (80s)
Johann Neeskens (70s) Wim van Hanegem (70s)

Johann Cruyff (70s) Marco Van Basten (80s) Dennis Bergkamp (90s)

Subs: Edwin Van Der Saar (G) (90s) Frank De Boer (D) (90s)
Arie Haan (M) (70s) Johnny Rep (M) (70s) Ruud Van Nistelrooy (F) (00s)

Bring on Brazil
Italy 4 West Germany 3, 1970

LET'S GIVE DUE CREDIT to Karl-Heinz Schnellinger. This semi-final was drifting towards a sterile 1-0 Italian victory when he emerged in the last minute to smash a volleyed equaliser, thus setting up the greatest extra-time ever. Germany then appeared to have completed their smash-and-grab raid when Müller took advantage of an underhit back pass but, uncharacteristically, the German defence went to sleep, and two goals in six minutes saw the first period of extra-time finish with Italy 3-2 ahead.

The plot had yet more twists. An apparently harmless header from Müller was left by substitute Rivera – who had anticipated a goal kick – and the ball crept inside the post. But within a minute, the villain had turned hero, calmly placing the ball past a floundering Sepp Maier for the game's fifth goal in a breathless 22 minutes. In the light of what had gone before, a goalless last nine minutes was unexpected. By the final whistle, players and spectators were completely drained.

- England should have been playing in this match, but had blown a 2-0 lead against Germany in the quarter-finals.
- Goals may have flowed in this game, but Burgnich's effort was rare: in his 66 internationals, this was his second and last.
- The high altitude of Mexico produced enervating conditions. Extra-time was always likely to lead to a higher incidence of errors and goals.
- This is not a game Franz Beckenbauer will remember fondly. Germany's sweeper finished with four in the debit column and a heavily strapped arm.
- For Italy, victory proved bittersweet. Brazil were waiting to pick them off in the final.

SCORERS **Italy:** Boninsegna, Burgnich, Riva, Rivera
W. Germany: Schnellinger, Müller (2)
EVENT World Cup semi-final, Azteca stadium, Mexico City, 17 June 1970

ITALY (Man: Feruccio Valcareggio)
1. Albertosi 2. Burgnich 3. Facchetti 4. Bertini 5. Rosato 6. Cera
7. Domenghini 8. Mazzola 9. Boninsegna 10. Di Sisti 11. Riva
W. GERMANY (Man: Helmut Schoen)
1. Maier 2. Vogts 3. Patzke 4. Beckenbauer 5. Schnellinger 6. Schulz
7. Grabowski 8. Seeler 9. Müller 10. Overath 11. Lohr

Rivera wraps himself around a post as Müller levels the scores at 3-3.

Brothers' Farewell
Brazil 3 Denmark 2, 1998

BOTH TEAMS CAME into the match on good form. Brazil had thrashed Chile 4-1 in the second round of the tournament, and their most celebrated player, Ronaldo, had been in sparkling form. More surprisingly, Denmark, inspired by the gifted Laudrup brothers, had beaten the highly fancied Nigerians by the same score.

The brothers were awesome against Brazil, too. Brian Laudrup set up a simple goal after two minutes for Jorgensen, while Michael gave the Brazilian defence a torrid time all night, even when the favourites were enjoying the bulk of possession. Brazil's armoury was still formidable, though, and they quickly restored parity, Bebeto breaking away from his marker to score past Schmeichel. Then, before the first half came to a close, they took the lead through Rivaldo. In the second half a mistake by Roberto Carlos let in Brian Laudrup, and the Dane inflicted full punishment. Denmark then poured forward in search of a winning goal, but suddenly Dunga released Rivaldo, who finished with a trademark piledriver. Rieper was thrust into the attack and hit the bar as the Danes applied late pressure, but Brazil clung on. Both Laudrups retired from international football after this game, bringing a golden era of Danish football to an end.

☞ Michael Laudrup threw his boots into the crowd at the end of the match – a clear statement of his intent. His younger brother followed him into retirement a few days later.

☝ Brazil's semi-final was another pulsating game, as Holland hung on, forcing a penalty shoot-out, but couldn't hold their nerve.

☞ The Danes, and the Dutch in the next round, exposed a weakness in the Brazilian defence that the French exploited in the final.

☝ After a disastrous Euro 2000, Denmark, coached by their former captain Morten Olsen, regrouped well and reached the second round of World Cup 2002. They went one better at Euro 2004, making it through to the quarter-finals.

SCORERS	**Brazil:** Bebeto 11 Rivaldo 27, 60
	Denmark: Jorgensen 2 Brian Laudrup 50
EVENT	World Cup quarter-final, Nantes, 3 July 1998
BRAZIL	(Man: Mario Zagallo)
	1. Taffarel 2. Cafu 3. Roberto. Carlos 4. Junior. Baiano 5. Aldair
	6. Cesar Sampaio 7. Leonardo 8. Dunga 9. Ronaldo 10. Bebeto 11. Rivaldo
DENMARK	(Man: Bo Johansson)
	1. Schmeichel 2. Helveg 3. Heintze 4. Colding 5. Rieper 6. Hogh 7. Jorgensen
	8. Nielsen 9. Laudrup, B 10. Laudrup, M 11. Moller

Busby Babes
Manchester United, 1955–58

ANY MENTION OF THE Manchester United team that dominated English football in the late 1950s inevitably evokes images of the terrible Munich air crash. The death of eight of football's brightest young talents was a tragedy that touched the lives of football fans all over the world. But just as tragic is that the players who perished are now largely remembered as passengers on an ill-fated aircraft rather than for what they were: extraordinary and remarkable footballers who might easily have gone on to dominate Europe for a decade.

At the heart of the team was Duncan Edwards. Looking at photographs now, it seems impossible to believe that such an imposing presence was only 21 when he died. Mark Jones was a similarly towering figure at centre-half, while in goal Harry Gregg combined agility with rare courage (many press pictures of the time show him diving boldly at the feet of oncoming strikers).

Like all great United teams though, their strength lay in attack. Tommy Taylor was a fearless centre-forward in the best English tradition, and Dennis Viollet and Bobby Charlton both chipped in with more than their fair share of goals. This team was together for less than two seasons. Yet even in this short time they established themselves as a formidable and widely feared European force.

☞ Under Busby, United had already won the league in 1952, but that ageing side was dismantled to make way for the Babes.

✎ United won the league in 1956 and 1957. They should have won the double in 1957, but lost to Aston Villa in the final.

✎ United were the first British entrants to the European Cup in 1956–57, defying the wishes of the myopic Football League. They reached the semi-finals in their first two competitions.

✎ The last league match played by the Busby Babes, five days before Munich, was one of their most memorable games. Arsenal 4 United 5 brought the curtain down in typical style.

✎ Of the Munich survivors, Bill Foulkes and Bobby Charlton were eventual European Cup winners in 1968.

Manager: Matt Busby

Key Players
Harry Gregg (G) Duncan Edwards (D)
Tommy Taylor (F) Bobby Charlton (M/F) Bill Foulkes (D)
Dennis Viollet (M) Roger Byrne (D)

Trophies
LT 1956, 1957

The last line-up of the Busby Babes, 5 February 1958, Belgrade. From left to right: Edwards, Colman, Jones, Morgans,

Busby, Matt
Manchester United

IN 1945 MATT BUSBY became manager of Manchester United, a club whose 67 years had yielded just two league titles and a solitary FA Cup. The trophy cabinet had been bare for 34 years, Old Trafford was a bomb site and United were lodging at Maine Road. On his retirement in 1969, Matt Busby had added five Championships, two FA Cups and United had become England's first winners of the European Cup.

Although a remarkable haul, it would surely have been more but for the tragic Munich air crash in 1958 that robbed English football of one of its greatest-ever teams. It was indicative of his tenacity and strength of will that Busby not only cheated death himself in the disaster but that, within seven years, he had made United champions again, rebuilding his team around George Best, Denis Law and Bobby Charlton. The end of his tenure saw them relegated within five years.

A journey to Old Trafford today finishes with a walk down Sir Matt Busby Way to his statue. One senses a modest, hard-working Scotsman from humble, working-class origins would have been uneasy with such acclaim. However, for a club with legends to spare, it is fitting that the tribute is for him alone.

☞ No mean player himself, Busby played for United's deadliest rivals Manchester City and Liverpool!

☞ He was born within a few miles of two other managerial legends, Jock Stein and Alex Ferguson.

🖑 He was awarded a CBE in 1958 and knighted 10 years later.

☞ On winning the European Cup: 'When Bobby took the cup it cleansed me. It eased the pain of going into Europe. It was my justification.'

☞ He defied the Football League to enter United as England's first European Cup contestants in 1956. The rift took 26 years to heal, before Busby was elected Football League vice-president in 1982.

VITAL STATISTICS

Place of Birth:	Bellshill, Glasgow, Scotland	
Date of Birth:	26 May 1909	**Died:** 20 January 1994
Caps:	1 (Scotland)	**Goals (International):** 0
Clubs:	As Player: Manchester City, Liverpool;	
	As Manager: Manchester United	
Trophies:	FAC 1948, 1963; LT 1952, 1956, 1957, 1965, 1967; EC 1968	

LEGEND RATING	
Achievement	10
Tactical Awareness	9
Motivation	10
Team Selection/Transfers	9
Personality	8
TOTAL	**46**

Campbell, Sol
Tottenham, Arsenal, England

SOL CAMPBELL was destined for big things at an early age. A schoolboy prodigy, he was one of the early vindications of the FA School of Excellence before signing professional forms with Spurs in 1992.

He immediately started attracting the sort of praise normally reserved for continental central defenders. Not only could he take the knocks and command in the air, he possessed the first touch, distribution and prescience that brought comparisons with Bobby Moore.

Despite becoming a permanent fixture for England, it became clear that major domestic honours would elude Campbell at White Hart Lane. In the summer of 2001, as a free agent, he became the most talked-about transfer in years when he thought the unthinkable, broke Spurs' hearts and became a Gunner.

The inevitable yet depressing hate campaign followed, Campbell's dignified response was typical of a player who has always let his feet do the talking. The answer was the Double in his first season.

Despite the fierce competition for England's centre-back places (even allowing for Rio Ferdinand's absence from Euro 2004 following a ban for failing to attend a drugs test), Campbell looks set to remain the senior partner to Woodgate, Terry, et al for some time.

👍 December 1992 – scores on his first-team debut against Chelsea.

👍 Only 23 yellow cards in over 400 games are testament to Campbell's pace and clean tackling.

☞ At the 1998 World Cup Finals, Campbell has an 81st-minute 'winner' against Argentina disallowed for Shearer's earlier foul. Sadly the rest is history.

👍 Campbell's first international goal is England's opener at the 2002 World Cup Finals, as he powers home a header against Sweden.

👍 2002 – Campbell is named in FIFA's Team of the World Cup Finals, surprisingly edging out the superior Ferdinand.

VITAL STATISTICS

Place of Birth:	London, England	
Date of Birth:	18 September 1974	**Died:** n/a
Caps:	64 (England)	**Goals (International):** 1
Clubs:	Tottenham Hotspur, Arsenal	
Appearances:	Club (All Matches): 457	
Goals:	Club (All Matches): 23	
Trophies:	LT 2002, 2004; FAC 2002; LC 1999	

Achievement	7.0
Skill	9.0
Teamwork	7.0
Passion	8.0
Personality	7.0
TOTAL	**38.0**

LEGEND RATING

'What's up with you?', Sol Campbell asks of Brazil's Rivaldo during England's clash with Brazil on 21 June 2002.

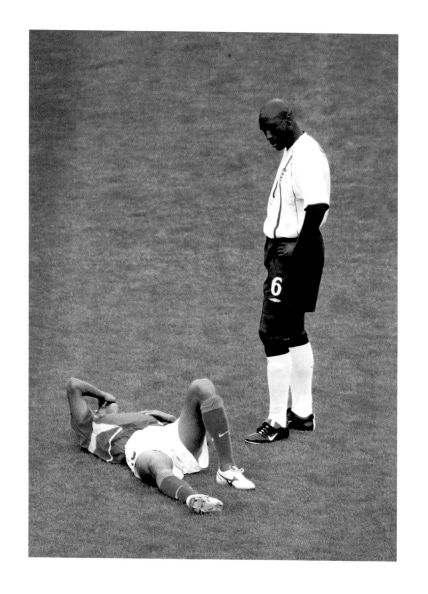

Cantona, Eric
Manchester United, France

WHETHER FOR HIS FOOTBALLING exploits or temperamental outbursts, few players have provoked headlines or incited debate like Eric Cantona. Not one to suffer fools gladly, he was too hot to handle for five French clubs.

An instant hit at Leeds, his arrival provided the Yorkshire club with the impetus to clinch the League title in 1992 but, while the fans idolised him, rumours of his clashes with manager Howard Wilkinson were rife. His shock £1.2 m transfer to Manchester United indicated Leeds' desire to be rid of him, but it turned out to be the most injudicious transfer sale of all time, as Cantona went on to inspire United to a period of domination unrivalled since Liverpool's run of success in the 1970s and 1980s.

It is a sad fact that Cantona will be remembered for one moment of madness when, at Crystal Palace in 1995, making his way off the pitch following yet another red card, Cantona launched a two-footed kung fu kick at a spectator who had racially abused him. A less gifted player may have been sacked, but Cantona survived and returned to lead United to more championship success. He retired at 31, and his recent incarnations as an actor and sports promoter have enhanced his reputation as the modern renaissance footballer.

- 1988. Banned from the French national side after describing manager Henri Michel as a 'sack of sh*t'.
- PFA Player of the Year, 1994 and 1996. Footballer of the Year 1996.
- 1994. Arrested and handcuffed by security guards after a row with officials at USA 94. Cantona was just there to watch.
- He had five league titles in six English seasons 1992–97, missing out only in 1995.
- He was voted Manchester United's most valuable player ever in 1999.

VITAL STATISTICS

Place of Birth:	Paris, France
Date of Birth:	24 May 1966 **Died:** n/a
Caps:	45 (France) **Goals (International):** 19
Clubs:	Martigues, Auxerre, Marseille, Bordeaux, Montpellier, Leeds United, Manchester United
Appearances:	Club (for Man Utd): 142
Goals:	Club (for Man Utd): 64
Trophies:	LT 1992, 1993, 1994, 1996, 1997; FAC 1994, 1996

LEGEND RATING	
Achievement	8.0
Skill	9.0
Teamwork	7.0
Passion	9.0
Personality	9.0
TOTAL	**42.0**

Capped and Cast-Off
An Ill-Treated England Team

THERE WILL ALWAYS be players who feel hard done by when international caps are handed out. But there can be good reasons why a player does not receive the international acclaim he feels he deserves. Sometimes players fail to reproduce their club form at international level (Steve McManaman), lack the touch to compete against the world's best (Les Ferdinand and Ian Wright), or simply don't fit into the framework of a team (Matt Le Tissier).

Most of this team do not fit into any of these categories. These players were omitted because their faces, for some reason, just didn't fit. In some cases a player was kept out of the side by another player who most people (except the manager) could see was inferior: Phil Neal kept out Dave Clement, and Kenny Sansom won 86 caps to Derek Statham's three. The woeful Peter Barnes was somehow selected ahead of Gordon Hill, and Alan Hudson had to sit on the sidelines while the likes of Colin Viljoen and Dave Thomas pulled on England jerseys. Clough and Shackleton were omitted for different reasons. Notoriously vocal and headstrong, both were rejected by an establishment that didn't like to be challenged.

☞ Why Shilton? Because Ray Clemence and Chris Woods won 85 caps between them while Shilton was still playing. Clemence was a great keeper, but Shilton was better. Woods was not in the same league.

☝ Mortimer was the fetcher and carrier in the Aston Villa side that won the First Division title in 1981. He was an excellent team player and deserved England honours.

☝ Clough and Shackleton's exclusion was echoed in the 1970s, when Revie's suspicion of flair players saw talents like Hudson, Bowles and Worthington miss out on international recognition.

☞ How did Sammy Lee win 14 caps and Jimmy Case none? Lee was a good player, but certainly no better than Case.

Manager: Terry Venables

4-4-2

Shilton (125)

Dave Clement (5) Colin Todd (27)
Kevin Beattie (9) Derek Statham (3)

Alan Devonshire (8) Dennis Mortimer (0)
Alan Hudson (2) Jimmy Case (0)

Brian Clough (2) Len Shackleton (5)

Kevin Beattie, a nine-times capped player.

Capped and Clueless
All-Time Worst England Team

EVEN AT THEIR PEAK this lot would have struggled to win a pub league. Anyone with at least one functioning eye could see this, except, it seems, the England managers who selected them. You want detail? Okay, here we go.

Beasant was error-prone and nervy.... Bardsley was nondescript.... Foster and Blockley were cumbersome and slow.... Ruddock was overweight and over-rated.... Phelan looked a decent player at Norwich but became a laughing stock at Old Trafford ... while Geoff Thomas was a plodding journeyman elevated to the role of international playmaker (he and his Palace team-mate Andy Gray were selected on the basis of getting to the Cup final). And who on earth was Nick Pickering?

Peter Ward? Hands up if you were there on the day he played the stormer that earned him selection for the national side. Michael Ricketts was picked on the back of a scoring streak at Bolton that ended when he earned his cap and decided he was an international.

This XI are by no means the only players who should never have been picked for England, but they remain the most startling examples.

☞ We've restricted ourselves to players from our own era. It's unfair to deride a player you've never seen.

☞ Both Ward and Pickering made their appearances in tour friendlies against Australia. Only Thomas of this team was a contender for a place in a first-choice England team.

☞ Foster compounded his lack of ability by wearing that absurd headband. It added nothing to his game and looked ridiculous.

☞ Ruddock had a nice left foot, but was too slow to cope with top-class forwards, and lacked the wit to make up for it with anticipation and experience.

☞ Kevin Keegan, for all his tactical shortcomings, seemed to know the best players when he saw them.

Manager: Don Revie

4-4-2

Dave Beasant (2) (90)

David Bardsley (2) (93)   Steve Foster (3) (82)
Jeff Blockley (1) (73)   Neil Ruddock (1) (95)

Michael Phelan (1) (90)   Geoff Thomas (9) (91, 92)
Andy Gray (1) (92)   Nick Pickering (1) (83)

Peter Ward (1) (80)   Michael Ricketts (1) (2002)

Catenaccio Kings
Inter Milan, 1960s

INTERNAZIONALE, or Inter Milan as they tend to be known in Britain, is a huge club which has never made the impact expected of them in European football. Except in the 1960s, that is. In the decade of flower power and the Beatles Inter, managed by Argentinian Helenio Herrera, were top dogs. Herrera was a fiery character and a flamboyant coach who had previously enjoyed spells with Barcelona and, briefly, the Spanish national team. At Inter he developed the formidable *catenaccio* system, the first formal tactical system to use a sweeper behind a back four. Wrongly interpreted by British observers as an entirely negative formation, it allowed the full-backs license to attack, and dispensed with the need for two wingers. Two successive European Cup wins in 1964 and 1965 were the fruits of Herrera's work, but defeat against Celtic in the 1967 final was the beginning of a decline in the club's fortunes. An ageing team reached the final in 1972 but were no match for Ajax, particularly Johan Cruyff who destroyed them almost single-handedly.

☞ Facchetti was one of the first beneficiaries of *Catenaccio*; tall for a full-back, quick and energetic, he was an early 'wing-back'. Facchetti was outstanding in Italy's 1970 World Cup campaign.

✎ Mazzola was a one-club man, and his rivalry with Milan's Gianni Rivera is legendary. He enjoys a status at Inter similar to that accorded Bobby Charlton at Manchester United.

✐ Inter haven't reached a European Cup Final since 1972, although they won three UEFA Cup trophies in the 1990s.

☞ Herrera's most significant signing was Luis Suarez from his old club, Barcelona. Suarez's combination with Mazzola gave Inter the ability to play keep-ball to a degree not previously seen in European club football.

Manager: Helenio Herrera

Key Players
Sarti (G) Tarcisio Burgnich (D) Giacinto Facchetti (D)
Guarneri (D) Jair (W) Sandro Mazzola (M)
Luis Suarez (M/F) Angelo Domenghini (M)

Trophies
SA 1963, 1965, 1966, 1971 EC 1964, 1965

Ceulemans, Jan
Lierse SK, Club Brugge, Belgium

BELGIAN FOOTBALL'S FINEST MOMENT? A 4-3 win over a highly rated USSR side in the last 16 of the 1986 World Cup. The mainstays of that excellent team were goalkeeper Pfaff, the tough, bearded full-back Gerets, the young Enzo Scifo, and the inspirational captain, Jan Ceulemans.

Ceulemans was a tall player, 6 ft 3 in (190 cm), but still comfortable with the ball at his feet. His considerable stamina allowed him to play his part in defence and then burst forward with aggressive runs, in a manner echoed in recent years by Steven Gerrard. He had come to prominence as a young workhorse in the Belgium team that reached the final of the 1980 European Championships.

In the next round after the USSR match, Ceulemans was again the key figure, winning the game against Spain with a spectacular diving header. Eventual winners, Argentina, proved a bridge too far in the semi-final, but Belgium and their talismanic captain had earned their ticker-tape welcome in Brussels.

At home, after leaving his home town team, Lierse, Ceulemans would stay with Club Brugge for the remainder of his career, eschewing a move to Milan in 1981, persuaded by his mother, some claim. While he was in his prime, the power of Brugge and Anderlechtois in Belgian competition had been broken.

- In the 1986 semi-final Maradona broke Belgian hearts by scoring a solo goal to eclipse even the wonder-goal he had scored against England in the previous round.
- Ceulemans played in three World Cup Finals tournaments, scoring three goals in 15 games.
- Ceulemans' 96 caps remains a record for Belgium. Twenty-three goals was a decent strike rate in those games.
- The coach of the Belgium team in both 1980 and 1986 was the great Guy Thys, who died in 2003, aged 80.
- Ceulemans is now coach of Belgian club side, Westerlo.

VITAL STATISTICS

Place of Birth:	Lierse, Belgium		Achievement	6.0	
Date of Birth:	28 February 1957	**Died:** n/a	Skill	7.0	
Caps:	96 (Belgium)	**Goals (International):** 23	Teamwork	8.0	
Clubs:	Lierse SK, Club Brugge		Passion	9.0	
Appearances:	Club (League): 518		Personality	6.0	
Goals:	Club (League): 229				
Trophies:	BLT 1980, 1988, 1990		**TOTAL**	**36.0**	

LEGEND RATING

Champions League
The Ultimate Test

THERE WAS A TIME when the European Cup was simple. If you won your domestic title, you qualified for a 32-team knockout competition, where each tie was a home and away two-legged affair. Then in 1992/93 the Champions League was born. As with most schemes approved by UEFA's bigwigs, it was a dog's dinner. In 1999, however, it became a canine banquet. The previous format of teams playing in a league system to qualify for the quarter-finals was complicated further by an expansion to 32 teams, with two group stages meaning 12 games now had to be played before the knockout stage of the last eight. Teams reaching the final had to play a total of 17 matches.

Of course, true competition had little to do with it. Rich European clubs, frustrated by their domestic authorities' refusal to sanction a breakaway super league, simply dangled the sponsors cash in front of UEFA and created one anyway. The current revenue of £416 m is difficult to ignore. UEFA takes £112 m while the rest goes to the participating clubs. From 2003–04 UEFA, nervous of the reduced interest and potential advertising revenue caused by two group stages, wisely replaced the second of these with a knockout competition featuring the 16 teams left from the first group phase. This has failed to eliminate completely the feeling that TV rights remain overpriced.

☞ Most extraordinary result of the 2003–04 competition: Monaco 8 Deportivo la Coruna 3. Both teams reached the quarter-finals.

👎 Biggest villain from 2003–04: Sinisa Mihajlovic. The Lazio defender was banned for eight matches after kicking and spitting at Chelsea's Adrian Mutu. He was charged after TV evidence was produced, the offence having been missed by the referee.

👍 Fortunately, some attractive football is still played. The best final was in 1994, when Milan cuffed Barcelona 4–0, probably the finest European club display since Real Madrid won 7-3 in 1960.

'If we want to make more money we have to change the concept.'

UEFA's Gerhard Aigner explains the reasons for the further expansion of the Champions League in 1998

Andrei Shevchenko ensures AC Milan come out on top in the 2003 Champions League final at Old Trafford

Chanting
Ee-aye-addio and All That

IN THE 1870s it would have appeared rather vulgar. One can't imagine the Old Carthusians goalkeeper standing resolute with flat cap and Victorian moustache to a backdrop of 'Who ate all the pies?' from the massed top hats of the Royal Engineers. Some contemporary chanting can claim a distinguished pedigree. 'The Pompey Chimes' were ringing out at Fratton Park for the title winning teams of over 50 years ago, while 'I'm Forever Blowing Bubbles' has been handed down through the generations at Upton Park (although opposition fans now tend to shout their own alternative over the cockney chorus).

Over the past 30 years, club choirs have broadened their repertoires considerably from the quaint 'Ee-aye-addio'. The greater televising of matches means that copyrights can be quickly violated – a player can be vocally ridiculed at Old Trafford one week and hear the identical chant at Stamford Bridge the next. One fact remains a certainty, though. Any player guilty of the merest physical deformity, tabloid headline or on-field mishap can be sure it will be pointed out. For anyone playing in front of more than two men and a dog, 'you can run but you can't hide' is the biggest truism of all.

☞ To opposition fans scarce in number: 'Is that all you take away?', 'You must have come in a taxi,' or 'We'll see you both outside'.

☞ 'He's fat, he's round' also prefaced a memorable chant about Jan Molby, namely: 'He's fat, he's round, his car is in the pound.'

☞ To expensive opposition striker, preferably one who's just missed an open goal: 'What a waste of money', 'Hallo, hallo [insert previous club here] reject' (repeat to fade).

✍ Silliest chant: 'Boing! Boing! Baggies! Baggies!', accompanied by a vigorous pogo from West Bromwich Albion fans.

✍ References in this section to Elton John, Leslie Ash or Trevor Morley would be libelous. But you know what we're getting at, right?

'He's fat, he's round, he's never in the
ground, Captain Bob.'

**Oxford fans to absent chairman
Robert Maxwell**

Gallic chic noticeably absent as French fans raise the roof.

Chapman, Herbert

Arsenal, Huddersfield

MANY GREAT MANAGERS have built one great team at one club, but Herbert Chapman is among the élite who have done it twice. An unconventional manager, he surrounded himself with intelligent players who fed him ideas and tactics. He responded to a change in the offside law by introducing a 3-4-3 formation with a defensive centre-half, and he was the first manager to encourage his wingers, notably Cliff Bastin, to cut inside the full-back and go for goal.

His first great side was the Huddersfield Town team of the 1920s, built around the intelligent playmaker Clem Stephenson. He left Huddersfield for the challenge of managing Arsenal and turned them into the dominant side of the next decade. The Arsenal side featured many of the great players of that generation, often providing five, six or even seven players to the England team of that era. Under his stewardship Arsenal went on to win the title four times in five years, but tragically Chapman died of pneumonia in 1934, aged 55, and didn't enjoy the full fruits of his work. He was the game's first managerial genius.

☞ Chapman was a great innovator, and was an early advocate of floodlights, artificial pitches and numbered shirts.

☞ He was instrumental in the renaming of Gillespie Road tube station as 'Arsenal'.

☞ He was one of the first managers to offer a fee to lure big-name players away from other clubs. His purchase of David Jack from Bolton was the first £10,000 transfer.

☞ Most of the Arsenal team only heard of Chapman's death as they turned up to play a match. The pallbearers at the funeral were Cliff Bastin, Eddie Hapgood, Joe Hume, David Jack, Alex James and Jack Lambert.

VITAL STATISTICS

Place of Birth:	Kiverton Park, England
Date of Birth:	19 January 1878 **Died:** 6 January 1934
Caps:	0 **Goals (International):** 0
Clubs:	As Player: Kiverton Park, Ashton North End, Stalybridge Rovers, Rochdale, Grimbsy Town, Sheppey United, Worksop, Northampton Town, Sheffield United, Notts County, Tottenham Hotspur; As Manager: Northampton Town, Leeds City, Huddersfield Town, Arsenal
Trophies:	LT 1924, 1925, 1926, 1931, 1933; FAC 1922, 1930

LEGEND RATING	
Achievement	10
Tactical Awareness	9
Motivation	9
Team Selection/Transfers	9
Personality	9
TOTAL	**46**

Chapman's Champions
Arsenal, 1930s

WHEN HERBERT CHAPMAN took over as Arsenal manager in 1925 the team was a mid-table side who had won nothing. By the time war broke out they had won their first trophy, the FA Cup in 1930, and followed it with four league championships and another FA Cup in between. In 1932, one of their fallow years, they were runners-up in both competitions. Sadly Chapman was to die soon after, his life taken by a bout of pneumonia in 1934.

In the infamous England international against Italy that became known as 'The Battle of Highbury' Arsenal provided no less than seven players to the England team (Moss, Hapgood, Copping, Bastin, Drake, Bowden and Male). Arsenal skipper Eddie Hapgood captained his country that day, and his successor in the role was the other Arsenal full-back, George Male.

The team's innovative tactics and willingness to spend money to bring in new, better players ensured they stayed at or near the top for the whole decade. Indeed, such was their residual strength that an ageing team continued to compete at the top of the table in the immediate post-war years. The only blot on their record in the decade was the cup defeat by Third Division Walsall in 1933 – arguably the most seismic upset in FA Cup history.

☞ Male was a half-back converted to full-back by Chapman. Within a year he was in the England team. He remained with the club in various capacities until his retirement in 1975.

✍ Lambert was a crunching, old-fashioned, centre-forward with a good goal scoring record. There were eyebrows raised when he was replaced with Drake, but the latter proved even more deadly.

✍ Frank Moss was injured in a crucial league game against Everton in March, 1935. With no substitutes allowed he went out to the wing as a passenger leaving Hapgood to take over in goal. Arsenal won 2-0. Moss scored.

✍ In the 'Battle of Highbury', Wilf Copping inspired his team to a 3-2 victory over the World Cup winners.

Manager: Herbert Chapman

Key Players

Frank Moss (England, goalkeeper) Eddie Hapgood (England, full-back)
Alex James (Scotland, playmaker) Cliff Bastin (England, winger)
Joe Hulme (England, winger) David Jack (England, inside-forward)
Jack Lambert (Scotland, centre-forward) Ted Drake (England, Lambert's replacement) Wilf Copping (England, half-back, hard man)
Leslie Compton (England, half-back) George Male (England, full-back)

Trophies
LT 1931, 1933, 1934, 1935, 1938 FAC 1930, 1936

Arsenal players line up to pay their respects at the great man's funeral.

Charles, John

Leeds United, Juventus, Wales

WHETHER OPERATING AT centre-half or centre-forward John Charles was the most complete footballer Wales has ever produced. Although a hero at Leeds and Cardiff, he became the first British player to settle successfully on the Continent, succeeding for five years in Italy where Jimmy Greaves and Denis Law were later to fail. So adored was he in Turin that Juventus fans dubbed him the 'Gentle Giant' due to his power and sportsmanship.

As an international, he was the key to Wales's most successful era, a period that culminated in their appearance in the 1958 World Cup quarter-final in Sweden. Sadly, Charles was absent through injury that day and the Welsh went down narrowly 1-0 to the eventual winners Brazil.

Lured back to Leeds by Don Revie, he failed to settle and returned to his adopted Italy with AS Roma before ending his career at Cardiff, adding thousands to the Ninian Park attendances. In a land where sporting heroes have traditionally played with an oval ball, Charles increased the stature of football in the Valleys like no player before or since. His death in February 2004 was mourned equally in Britain and Italy. It signalled the passing of a true sporting gentleman.

- ☞ 1957. Charles moves from Leeds to Juventus for £70,000, more than double the British transfer record.
- ☝ He never won a trophy in Britain, but has three Italian titles and two cups to his name.
- ☞ The first rich British footballer, Charles' wages in Italy were £60 per week, more than four times the maximum permitted in Britain. A signing-on fee of £10,000 added to his fortune.
- ☞ He played with brother, Mel, in the same Welsh team as the Allchurch brothers, Len and Ivor. Two sets of brothers have never appeared together in any other international team.
- ☝ 1973. Years after retirement, Charles lined up for Europe, scoring a hat-trick against Great Britain in a friendly international.

VITAL STATISTICS

Place of Birth:	Swansea, Wales
Date of Birth:	27 December 1931 **Died:** 21 February 2004
Caps:	38 (Wales) **Goals (International):** 15
Clubs:	Leeds United, Juventus, Roma, Cardiff City, Hereford United
Appearances:	Club (League for Juventus): 150
Goals:	Club (League for Juventus): 93
Trophies:	SA 1958, 1960, 1961

LEGEND RATING	
Achievement	7.0
Skill	9.0
Teamwork	8.0
Passion	9.0
Personality	7.0
TOTAL	**40.0**

Charlton, Bobby
Manchester United, England

HAVING SURVIVED THE Munich air crash, Bobby Charlton seized his chance to become one of England's most successful and admired players. He never commanded the huge transfer fees paid for Denis Law, nor could he boast the natural flair and ability of George Best, but in terms of achievement Charlton was by far the most successful of United's most famous forward line. His application was total. As a young player he would often train wearing just a slipper on his right foot – a ploy designed to make him practice shooting with his left until it could generate the same venomous power as his right.

For England, he became a national hero after helping them win the 1966 World Cup, but it was his substitution in the 1970 quarter-final against Germany that fans remember almost as vividly; brought off by Alf Ramsey with the score at 2-1 to England, Charlton's absence upset the balance of the team and they eventually capitulated 3-2. Charlton bowed out in 1973 – on the same day as his brother, Jack – when over 60,000 fans packed Old Trafford for his testimonial. Knighted in 1994, he remains a director at Old Trafford and ambassador for both United and the Football Association.

- His league appearances (606) and goals (199) remain United club records.
- Best England goal? A 30-yard rasper versus Mexico in the 1966 World Cup Finals.
- 106 caps was an England record only Bobby Moore and Peter Shilton have overtaken, his 49 goals remain unequalled.
- 1966. English and European Footballer of the Year. He also received a special PFA merit award in 1974.
- He was one of only two Munich air crash survivors to play in the European Cup winning side 10 years later. Bill Foulkes was the other.

VITAL STATISTICS

Place of Birth:	Ashington, Northumberland, England
Date of Birth:	11 October 1937 **Died:** n/a
Caps:	106 (England) **Goals (International):** 49
Clubs:	Manchester United, Preston North End
Appearances:	Club (All Matches): 798
Goals:	Club (All Matches): 257
Trophies:	WorC 1966; EC 1968; LT 1957, 1965, 1967; FAC 1963

LEGEND RATING	
Achievement	10.0
Skill	8.0
Teamwork	9.0
Passion	8.0
Personality	7.0
TOTAL	**42.0**

Charlton, Jack
Leeds, England, Republic of Ireland

AN ENGLAND WORLD-CUP WINNER he may have been, and the defensive rock of Don Revie's Leeds he undoubtedly was, but Jack Charlton's most celebrated achievements came more recently across the Irish sea. Foreign managers taking control of other countries' national teams no longer raises eyebrows, but Charlton's appointment to the Republic of Ireland post was a revolutionary step. Using the no-frills approach that had served him well in English club management, Charlton rebuilt the Irish team. Eschewing continental niceties for a long-ball style that was effective rather than pretty, and recruiting players through long-lost Irish family connections, he affected a dramatic turnaround in their international fortunes. The Republic qualified for the European Championships and the World Cup in 1988 and 1990 respectively. The World Cup in Italy was his finest hour, especially the penalty shoot-out victory over Romania that set up a quarter-final with Italy, bringing the nation to a standstill. The Republic's 1-0 defeat to the Italians cemented his status as Ireland's second most popular icon after the Pope. USA 94 saw revenge against Italy, but Ireland's lack of imagination cost them. Imagination wasn't a word associated with him as a player either, but he stood tall against some of the best the game could throw at him.

- Success arrived late for Charlton the player; not picked for England until nearly 30, he was a World Cup winner and Footballer of the Year (1967) in the two seasons that followed.
- 1965. Policeman intervened during a Fairs Cup tie to stop Charlton exacting revenge on a Valencia player. Charlton and two Spaniards were dismissed.
- 1973/74. His first season in management saw Middlesbrough win Division Two by 15 points.
- Charlton was criticised as Irish manager for seeking out players with distant Irish heritage, but the practice is now common.
- He is the only member of England's 1966 World Cup winning side who made a success of management.

VITAL STATISTICS

		MANAGER		PLAYER	
Place of Birth:	Ashington, Northumberland, England				
Date of Birth:	8 May 1935 **Died:** n/a	Achievement	6	Achievement	9
Caps:	35 (England)	Tactical Awareness	8	Skill	6
Goals (International): 6		Motivation	9	Teamwork	7
Clubs:	As Player: Leeds United; As Manager:	Team Selection/Transfers	7	Passion	8
	Middlesbrough, Sheffield Wednesday,	Personality	8	Personality	7
	Republic of Ireland national side				
Trophies:	As Player: WorC 1966; LT 1969;	**TOTAL**	**38**	**TOTAL**	**37**
	FAC 1972; LC 1968; None as manager				

LEGEND RATING

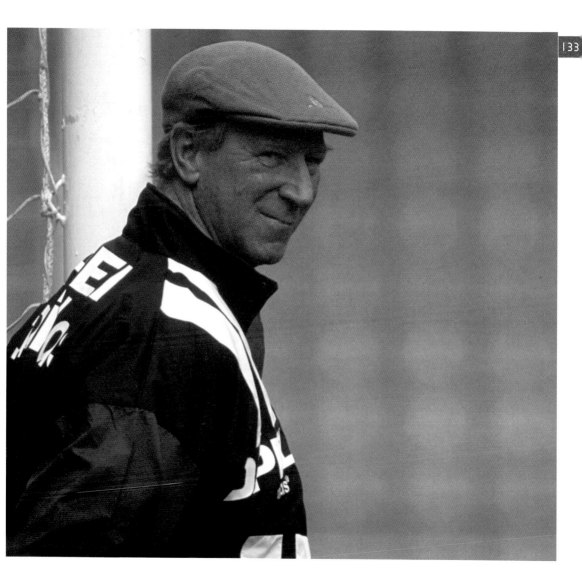

Cheating
The Unacceptable Face

THE ORIGINAL CHEAT was also the biggest. One can only imagine what was going through William Webb Ellis's mind as he picked up the ball and sprinted for the goal-line. The referee's action was even more inexplicable. Instead of an automatic red, Ellis was slapped on the back and credited with inventing a new game. If only he'd gone to Our Lady of the Sacred Heart, rugby might never have got off the ground. In football, modern discussion is centred on the dive. While some xenophobic opinion incorrectly identifies diving as an exclusively foreign pastime, it is true that Jurgen Klinsmann raised the art to a new level. Still, at least he had the self-deprecating charm to diffuse the criticism that came his way, famously making an ironic plunge turfwards after scoring on his Spurs debut at Hillsborough. The Daddy of all cheats, though, is Maradona, who saved the 1986 World Cup quarter-final against England for his party piece. Although Diego lied, the camera didn't, and the image of his hand palming the ball past Peter Shilton still raises the ire of all England fans.

☞ Frank Skinner gag during Euro 92: 'I brushed past the television and Klinsmann fell over.'

☜ Drugs have played their part. Jaap Stam is one of the latest to fall foul of the authorities for use of banned substances.

☜ Referees are not untouchables. The Greek referee was widely believed to have cheated Leeds out of the 1973 European Cup Winners' Cup final. Even his countrymen in the Salonika crowd booed him at the final whistle.

☞ The complaint of players collapsing to the ground clutching non-existent head wounds provokes strong reactions. Leicester boss Dave Bassett accused Spurs' Mauricio Taricco of cheating after a league match in 2002; a bit rich from Robbie Savage's boss.

'It was scored partly by the hand of God and partly by the head of Maradona.'

Diego puts a personal spin on THAT goal, 1986

The 'Hand of God' strikes. Maradona's hand reaches the ball marginally before Peter Shilton.

Chilavert, Jose Luis

Paraguay

THEY SAY GOALKEEPERS are a different breed, and there is no denying the position has boasted its fair share of larger-than-life characters. There's Yashin, Schmeichel and Higuita for starters. But even these men are bashful wallflowers compared to Jose Luis Chilavert. Paraguay's most famous player came from humble farming stock, but lost his humility at an early age. 'I'm the best goalkeeper in the world,' was a typical self-assessment. After quickly outgrowing Paraguayan domestic football he came to prominence in Argentina – and not just for his prowess between the sticks. 'El Chila' also insisted on taking free-kicks. Most keepers in opposition territory are generally regarded as little more than novelty acts, but Chilavert proved to be highly accomplished and deadly accurate; his 19 goals in the last five seasons probably make him the highest-scoring custodian in history. Chilavert's disciplinary record can be politely described as 'colourful'; the targets of his ire have included the president of the Paraguayan Olympic committee and a ballboy whom he berated for not doing his job with sufficient alacrity. Japan and Korea was a tournament too far: Chilavert was a parody of himself.

👍 Chilavert's goalscoring exploits began in the last minute of an international against Colombia in 1989. With all his colleagues reluctant to take a penalty, Chilavert rushed up-field to smash the winner past Rene Higuita.

👍 Chilavert is the only goalkeeper ever to win the South American Footballer of the Year award (1997).

👎 His showmanship has brought volatile reactions from Argentine crowds. He was once narrowly missed by a knife, while a more accurately thrown firecracker left him with concussion.

☞ He has stated his intention to run for the Paraguayan presidency on his retirement. Judging by the standard of his predecessors and his adored status in his native land, he is probably a good bet.

VITAL STATISTICS

Place of Birth:	Luque, Paraguay
Date of Birth:	27 July 1965 **Died:** n/a
Caps:	74 (Paraguay) **Goals (International):** 8
Clubs:	Cerro Porteno, Real Zaragoza, San Lorenzo, Velez Sarsfield, RC Strasbourg, Penarol
Appearances:	Club (All Matches): 521
Goals:	Club (All Matches): 24
Trophies:	None

LEGEND RATING	
Achievement	6.0
Skill	9.0
Teamwork	7.0
Passion	9.0
Personality	9.0
TOTAL	**40.0**

Christmas Trees and Catenaccio

Tactics

IN THE EARLY PART of the last century, tactics did not invite the degree of discussion they do today. Teams played with two defenders, a centre-half, two half-backs – who were expected to do most of the running – two inside forwards to create and score, two wingers to supply, and a centre-forward. But in the 1930s, innovative managers like Arsenal's Herbert Chapman and Italy's Vittorio Pozzo tweaked this system. In their teams the centre-half became a defender, and the inside forwards started to drop a little deeper. Wingers, too, were encouraged to add to their repertoire and tuck slightly further infield.

Throughout the 1950s Austria and Hungary introduced new attacking ideas and styles, and their intricate passing and use of a deep-lying centre-forward initially confused many of their more conventionally structured opponents. Brazil's World Cup success started when they adopted a back four, with attacking full-backs and two forwards feeding off two wingers. The Italian club sides in the 1960s introduced the notion of the sweeper behind two centre-halves, and Franz Beckenbauer advanced that role. The Dutch threw away the book entirely in the 1970s, laying the foundations for the fluid, modern football we see today.

☞ 'Contrary to what some people might think I do not want to see the ball booted aimlessly up-field – but the truly great players hurt the opposition with one devastating pass.' Graham Taylor, defending the tactics of a team containing Geoff Thomas.

☞ The advent of substitutes and large squads has allowed managers more flexibility with tactics. 'I don't drop players, I make changes.' Bill Shankly.

☞ Once the players are out there it's beyond the manager's control: 'I went down to pass on some technical information to the team like the fact the game had started.' Ron Atkinson forsakes his seat in the stand as things don't go to plan.

'I do want to play the long ball, and I do want to play the short ball. I think long and short balls are what football is all about.'

Bobby Robson

Clockwise from top left: old-style 2-3-5, 4-4-2, 90s-style Christmas tree, sweeper system with overlapping full-backs.

Clough, Brian

Middlesbrough, Derby County, Nottingham Forest, England

REMEMBERED BY MODERN SUPPORTERS as one of the great managers of his era, Clough was also a fine player. A phenomenal scoring record at Middlesbrough and then Sunderland was down to a sharp turn of speed and clinical finishing. Clough's playing career was cut short by a serious knee injury suffered on Boxing Day 1962, after which he concentrated on management, initially at Hartlepool, where he was joined by Peter Taylor, an old team-mate from his Middlesbrough days. The pair moved to Derby where Clough won his first league title in 1972. In October 1973, Clough resigned from Derby and joined Brighton. In July 1974, Clough was appointed by Leeds for his infamous 44 days. Elland Road just wasn't big enough for all those egos.

It was at Forest that Clough really hit the heights. Reunited with Taylor, he built a successful, well-organised side that continually managed to punch above its weight, winning two European Cups in 1979 and 1980. Clough finally left Forest towards the end of the 1992/93 season, with the club relegated, in disarray, and amid accusations of excessive drinking. It was a sad end to a glorious and charismatic career. His death in September 2004 inspired almost unprecedented respect.

- After resigning due to ill health, Peter Taylor returned to management at Derby, and promptly poached John Robertson, one of Forest's key players. He and Clough never spoke again before Taylor's death.
- Players at Derby threatened to strike when Clough left in 1973.
- Two caps was a risible return for such a fine striker.
- Forest were unbeaten for a record 42 league matches between November 1977 and December 1978.
- Forest only once finished outside the top 10 in the First Division during Clough's 18 years, prior to the relegation season.
- Was passed over for the England manager's job in the mid-70s. The FA knew they could never have handled him.

VITAL STATISTICS

			MANAGER		PLAYER	
Place of Birth:	Middlesbrough, England					
Date of Birth:	21 March 1935 **Died:** 20 September 2004		Achievement	9	Achievement	6
Caps:	2 (England) **Goals (International):** 0		Tactical Awareness	9	Skill	9
Clubs:	As Player: Middlesbrough, Sunderland;		Motivation	9	Teamwork	7
	As Manager: Hartlepool United,		Team Selection/Transfers	8	Passion	8
	Derby County, Brighton & Hove Albion,		Personality	10	Personality	7
	Leeds United, Nottingham Forest					
Trophies:	LT 1972, 1975, 1978; EC 1979, 1980; LC 1978, 1979, 1989, 1990		**TOTAL**	**45**	**TOTAL**	**37**

LEGEND RATING

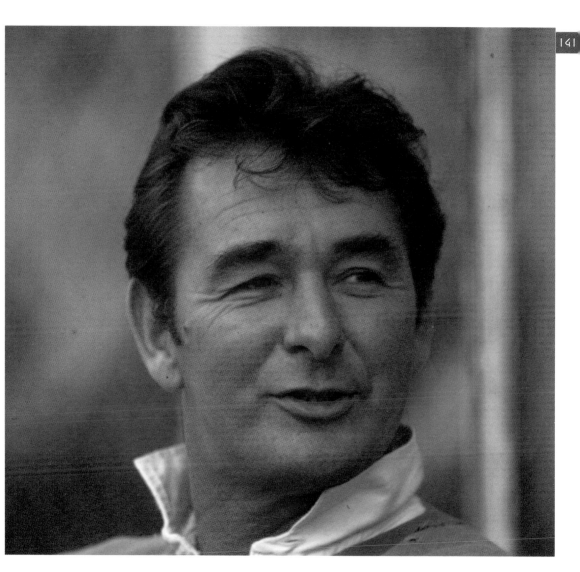

Club Bruges
The Dream Team

DESPITE HAVING PLAYED second fiddle to Anderlecht for much of their history, Bruges remain the only Belgian team to reach a European Cup final, losing 1-0 to Liverpool at Wembley in 1978. In the current economic climate, the achievement of Ernst Happel's squad will not be matched.

The core of this Dream Team comes from that squad; the prankster goalie, Jensen, Bastijns, the captain and 'Mac The Knife' Leekens, an uncompromising centre half, were all part of a miserly defence. The languid Australian defender, Paul Okon, would later make his reputation in Belgium before throwing it away in Italy and England, and the modern left back Borkelmans completes the defensive line-up. The hardworking Cools and the Dane, Le Fevre, join the 1980s superstars, Jan Ceulemans and Franky van der Elst in midfield – a midfield rich in goalscoring potential. Ceulemans' emergence coincided with a revival in Bruges' fortunes after a few lean years. Marc Degryse – another who found life tough in England – was the spearhead of that 1980s side.

The team is completed by the giant Raoul Lambert, a formidable goalscorer who started two decades of service to Bruges in the 1960s. Lambert's 300 goals for the club would have been exceeded had he not been so prone to injury, but he was fine finisher with a deft touch for such a huge man.

👆 Birger Jensen played the match of his life in the Wembley final, frustrating mighty Liverpool until the 69th minute.

☞ Georges Leekens: as a player he was already an inspirator, later the most successful coach of his team-mates. He was manager of Bruges for two years and took the Belgian national team to the 1998 World Cup.

☞ Jan Ceulemans: 'Strong Jan' was offered a move to AC Milan after Euro 1980, but preferred to stay in Belgium. He was tranquillity incarnate, never a word in the wrong place at the wrong time.

☞ Raoul Lambert was the only one who was born and bred in Bruges. For years he was national coach Raymond Goethals' favourite spearhead. He was the pet of the Bruges crowd.

Manager: Ernst Happel
4-4-2

Birger Jensen (70s/80s)

Fons Bastijns (c) (70s) Georges Leekens (70s) Paul Okon (90s)
Vital Borkelmans (90s)

Julien Cools (70s) Franky van der Elst (80s/90s) Jan Ceulemans (80s)
Ulrik Le Fèvre (70s)

Marc Degryse (80s) Raoul Lambert (70s/80s)

Subs: Dany Verlinden (G) (90s/00s) Erwin Vandendaele (D) (60s/70s) Johny Thio (M) (60s/70s) Pierre Carteus (M) (60s/70s) Gert Verheyen (F) (90s/00s) Fernand Goyvaerts (F) (50s/60s)

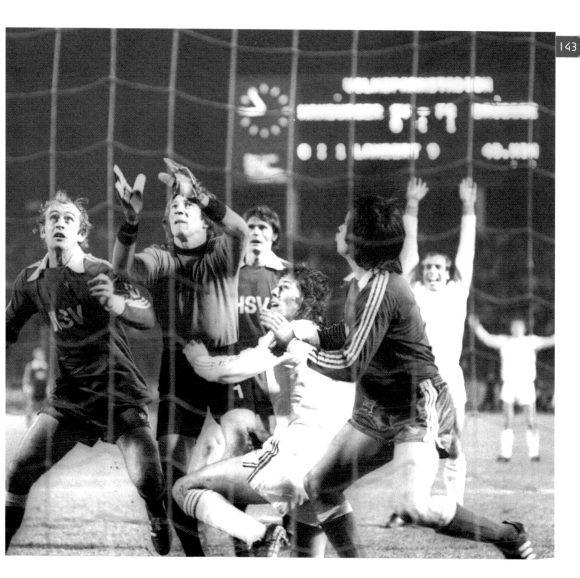

Commentators
Nice Work, If You Can Get It

LOVE THEM OR LOATHE THEM, commentators are an integral part of the modern football-watcher's perception of the game. Initially, especially in Kenneth Wolstenholme's early broadcasts, commentary was simply a scientific narrative of the match, but as the art developed they became more intrusive, sharing opinions and statistical nuggets of information with their audience. John Motson became the master of the trivial aside, relishing every opportunity to embellish his reports with whimsical extras. ITV joined the fray, and Brian Moore's voice soon became as familiar as that of Motty and David Coleman.

New technology led to increased coverage, and an increase in the studio body count. Suddenly, presenters like Desmond Lynam were joined by teams of 'expert' summarisers, usually retired, or uninvolved current players. The two-commentator broadcast became ever-more popular, with a pundit sitting alongside a match commentator, sharing views and an occasional bit of banter.

All in all, football commentary and punditry has made a disappointing contribution to the game; intelligent and articulate people are shackled by fear of upsetting one faction or the other, or even a sponsor, and the result is too often bland and innocuous.

☞ The first radio broadcast was on 2 January 1927. The game? Arsenal versus Sheffield United.

☞ The first TV broadcast was in 1936, and was followed a year later by the first live TV broadcast (1938 FA Cup final, Preston versus Huddersfield). The BBC tested their 'live' technology with a test broadcast of Arsenal versus Arsenal Reserves.

☞ *Match of the Day* began in 1964, with Kenneth Wolstenholme as commentator.

☞ Why ex-footballers or managers? Why not people trained professionally to talk, not play? That way we could avoid the cliché and banality offered by Messrs Brooking, Charlton, Pleat, Keegan, Francis and Atkinson.

'Poland nil, England nil, though England are now looking better value for their nil.'

Barry Davies, 1989

John Motson, poised to deliver another statistic.

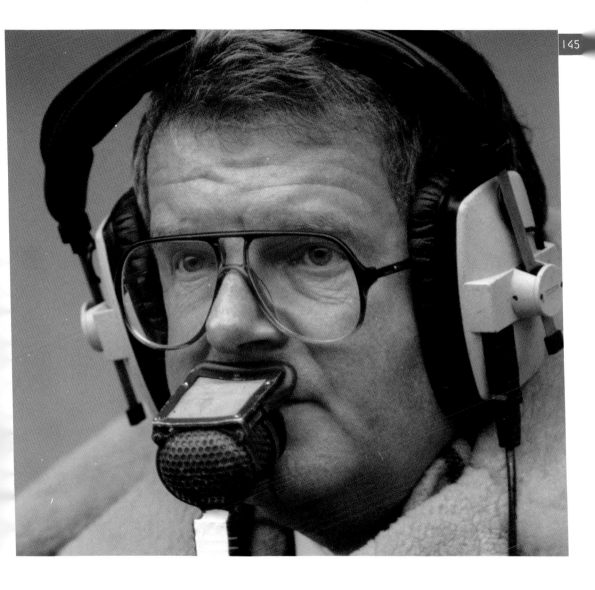

Crawford's Cracker
Colchester United 3 Leeds United 2, 1971

'THE MOST FANTASTIC RESULT you'll ever see!' For once, this was a headline that avoided hyperbole. Although not non-leaguers, Fourth Division Colchester's feat was, in relative terms, more notable than any previous Cup giant-killing. This was Leeds. Don Revie's Leeds. The best team in the country, a line-up replete with seasoned internationals and a reputation for hard-man cynicism that made them the least likely of pushovers.

Colchester had one international up their sleeve. True, Ray Crawford's two England caps had been won nine years earlier and at 34 his star was hardly in the ascendant. But all this counted for nothing as Crawford's double swept Colchester to an incredible 3-0 lead just after half-time. Normal service was partly resumed as Hunter and Giles set up a frantic finish that saw Leeds keeper, Gary Sprake, reduced to a role as a distant onlooker. But his counterpart in the Colchester goal, Graham Smith, proved equal to the bombardment and the Essex club held out to produce a result that provoked open-mouthed astonishment across the country. Revie's Leeds had their share of big-match disappointments, but none was as humiliating as this.

- Colchester hero Ray Crawford has a league championship medal, won with Ipswich in 1962.
- Manager Dick Graham had promised a free fortnight's holiday for his players and their wives if they won. He paid up.
- A triumph for experience; six Colchester players were over 30.
- Colchester lost 5-0 at Everton in the sixth round.

SCORERS	**Colchester:** Crawford 2, Simmons
	Leeds: Hunter, Giles
EVENT	FA Cup Fifth Round, Layer Road, Colchester, 13 February 1971
COLCHESTER	(Man: Dick Graham)
	1. Smith G. 2. Hall 3. Cram 4. Gilchrist 5. Garvey 6. Kurila 7. Lewis 8. Simmons 9. Mahon 10. Crawford 11. Gibbs
LEEDS	(Man: Don Revie)
	1. Sprake 2. Reaney 3. Cooper 4. Bates 5 . Charlton 6 . Hunter 7. Lorimer 8. Clarke 9. Jones 10. Giles 11. Madeley

Ray Crawford (left foreground) turns away after scoring one of his giant-killing goals

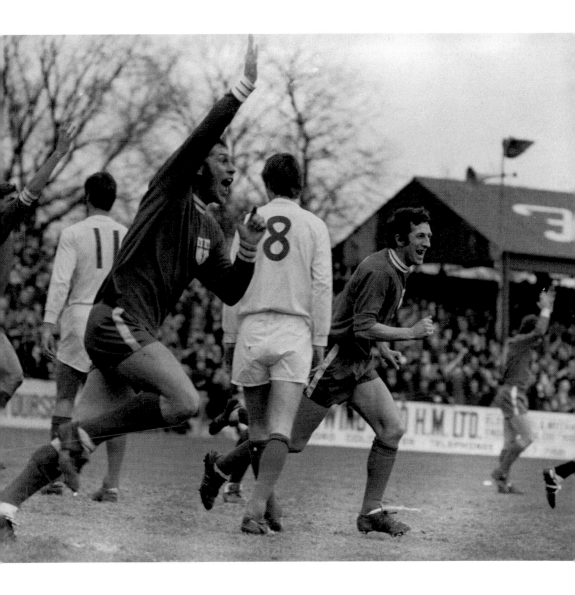

Cruyff, Johan
Ajax, Amsterdam, Barcelona, Holland

JOHAN CRUYFF'S MOTHER worked as a cleaner at Ajax's ground in Amsterdam, and the club were persuaded to give the youngster trials. One suspects they didn't regret it. He was fortunate to develop under the legendary Ajax coach Rinus Michels, but not as fortunate as Ajax were to have such an extraordinary talent born on their doorstep. Cruyff had the lot: pace and strength allied to nigh-perfect ball control, and a punishing finish with either foot. But, as is often the case with men of genius, Cruyff had a flawed side to his personality. An irritable and greedy nature saw him often at odds with authority and meant he was lost far too early to international football.

As a manager he was quixotic and opinionated too, and brought great success to Barcelona, landing them the coveted European Cup, but his tenure at the Nou Camp was plagued by clashes with key players, notably Hristo Stoichkov and the Brazilian striker, Romario. Despite his arrogance and irritability, Cruyff will be remembered as a breathtaking footballer to rank with the best in the world. Living in his native Holland, he has retired from management after developing a heart problem due to his penchant for chain-smoking.

👍 Cruyff destroyed Inter in the 1972 European Cup final, scoring both goals in Ajax's 2-0 win.

☞ Legendary sports writer David Miller dubbed Cruyff 'Pythagoras in boots', such was the geometric precision of his passing.

☞ After a bust-up with Ajax at the end of his playing career, Cruyff responded by joining their arch-rivals Feyenoord as player-coach, promptly winning the double for the old enemy.

✍ He is one of only three players to have won the European Player of the Year award three times, in 1971, 1973 and 1974 (the others were Michel Platini and Marco van Basten).

VITAL STATISTICS

		MANAGER		PLAYER	
Place of Birth:	Amsterdam, Holland				
Date of Birth:	25 April 1947 **Died:** n/a				
Caps:	48 (Holland) **Goals (International):** 33				
Clubs:	Ajax, Barcelona, Los Angeles Aztecs,	Achievement	9	Achievement	9
	Washington Diplomats, Levants, Feyenoord	Tactical Awareness	8	Skill	10
Appearances:	Club (All Matches): 704	Motivation	6	Teamwork	10
Goals:	Club (All Matches): 392	Team Selection/Transfers	9	Passion	9
Trophies:	OLT 1966–68, 1970, 1972–73, 1982–84,	Personality	7	Personality	7
	(1986, 1987); PLA 1974, (1991–94);				
	EC 1971–72, (1992); CWC 1987, 1989	**TOTAL**	**39**	**TOTAL**	**45**

LEGEND RATING

Cubillas, Teofilo
Peru

'NENE' CUBILLAS IS Peru's most famous player, his two World Cup Finals' appearances, eight years apart, guaranteeing his status as national hero and international star. As an unknown 20-year-old in 1970, his attacking skills and combination with the experienced Hector Chumpitaz helped Peru reach the quarter-finals in Mexico and placed him in the international shop window. Curiously, it took three years before he left local club side Alianza for FC Basel, but an impressive spell in the Swiss league saw him transferred to FC Porto the following year. He was never to settle in Europe, however, and returned for a second spell with Alianza.

Back on home soil, Cubillas enhanced his reputation further by helping Peru fend off the twin giants of Brazil and Argentina to take the South American Championship in 1975, and three years later he was to score twice as Peru shocked Scotland in the 1978 World Cup Finals in Argentina. His performance that day was typical. Always one to raise his game on the big occasion, his two World Cup Finals' appearances brought him 10 goals, making him one of the highest scorers in the tournament's history.

☞ Cubillas finished his career in the NASL with Fort Lauderdale, where he enjoyed a striking partnership with George Best.

👍 He was South American Footballer of the Year, 1972.

👍 Cubillas inspired the Peru side that burst the Ally MacLeod bubble in the 1978 World Cup Finals, scoring twice in seven minutes in a 3-1 victory.

👍 Unlike Scotland, Cubillas was more than a match for Iran in that tournament, and helped himself to a hat-trick.

👎 Cubillas' World Cup career came to a sadly undignified end in 1978. With Argentina requiring a heavy victory to progress, Peru capitulated 6-0 in abject fashion amidst whispers of bribery.

VITAL STATISTICS

Place of Birth:	Puente Piedra, near Lima, Peru
Date of Birth:	8 March 1949 **Died:** n/a
Caps:	117 (Peru) **Goals (International):** 47
Clubs:	Alianza, Basel, FC Porto, Fort Lauderdale Strikers
Goals:	Club (for Alianza de Lima): 295

LEGEND RATING	
Achievement	5.0
Skill	9.0
Teamwork	7.0
Passion	8.0
Personality	7.0
TOTAL	**36.0**

Cup Winners' Cup Winners. Twice
Anderlecht In The 70s

RSC ANDERLECHTOIS, as they were still known in the seventies, had dominated post-war Belgian football, but had never made much of a stir in European competition.

That changed in 1976, when a favourable draw (including Wrexham) saw them through to the CWC Final against West Ham at the Heysel stadium. The game was a ding-dong do, and Anderlecht ran out 4-2 winners with two goals apiece for the livewire Van Der Elst and the skilful Dutchman, Rensenbrink. With another Dutch international, Arie Haan, pulling the strings, and a tight defence, the Belgian club had announced themselves as a force.

Sterner opposition were overcome the following year as Anderlechtois reached the final again, but the mighty SV Hamburg proved a bridge too far, and won with two late goals. Revenge was sweet the following year as the Belgians drew the holders in an early round. A superb Rensenbrink goal saw the Germans beaten 2-1 at home, but Anderlechtois still had to endure a fraught return, clinging on for a 1-1 draw and aggregate win.

The addition of young Frank Vercauteren added a new dimension to the team and they cruised through the rest of the tournament. Porto and FC Twente were brushed aside and FK Austria Wien were routed 4-0 in the final at the Parc des Princes, Paris.

👍 Anderlecht added the European Super-Cup in 1976 and 1978. Yeah, we know. So what?

☞ The club only changed its name to RSC Anderlecht in 1984.

👍 The 1978 final saw Rensenbrink add another brace to the two he scored against West Ham. Full-back Gilbert Van Binst also scored twice.

☞ Anderlecht added UEFA Cup success in 1983, beating Benfica 2-1 on aggregate. They reached the final again the following season but were edged out on penalties by Tottenham.

👍 Anderlecht's success heralded a bit of a Golden Age for the Belgians; the National side would reach the final of Euro 1980 and the semi-finals of the 1986 World Cup.

> **Managers: Hand Croon (76), Raymond Goethals (77, 78)**
>
> **Key Players**
> Gilbert Van Binst (D) Jean Thissen (D) Ludo Coeck (M) Arie Haan (M)
> Francky Van Der Elst (F) Rob Rensenbrink (F)

Czech Out the Dutch
Czech Republic 3 Holland 2, 2004

THIS WAS A SNORTER. Not only the best match of Euro 2004 by a distance, but one of the best in the game's history. Two gifted sides, both with a preference for attacking football, going at it hammer and tongs.

A close game didn't look on the cards after 20 minutes with Holland two-up. Two goals from crosses by the dangerous Arjen Robben left the Czechs with a mountain to climb. Instead the mountain pulled back a goal, after a disastrous misplaced pass from Cocu let in Baros to set up a tap-in for Koller. The game swung to and fro, with great shooting from distance by both teams, none better than a daisy-cutter from Davids that hit the post.

The second half was all Czech Republic. Robben was inexplicably withdrawn, and replaced with Bosvelt, the intention being to stifle the increasingly influential Pavel Nedved. Instead Nedved continuing to run riot, at one point surging past the despairing Bosvelt and leaving the crossbar shaking with a 30-yard thunderbolt. The Dutch wing-backs were all over the place – Heitinga was dismissed for a second caution, and Van Bronckhorst gave the ball away for Poborsky to fire in the shot leading to Vladimir Smicer's winner.

The Dutch were distraught. The Czechs were through.

☞ Both sides came off the back of hesitant openers. The Czechs had to come from behind to beat Latvia, while Holland scraped a draw with a late rally against Germany.

☞ A further mystery of Advocaat's substitutions was the fact that Van Hooijdonk, whose introduction had turned the game against Germany, remained on the bench.

☞ Compare Bruckner's removal of his right back, given a torrid time by Robben, after 25 minutes. The replacement was Smicer, an attacking midfield player.

☞ Nedved fully justified his nomination as European player of the year in 2003, and his injury in the match against Greece may have cost his team a place in the final they probably deserved.

SCORERS	**Czech Rep:** Koller, Baros, Smicer
	Holland: Bouma, Van Nistelrooy
EVENT	Euro 2004 group match, 19 June 2004
CZECH REP	(Man: Karel Bruckner)
	1. Cech 2. Grygera (Smicer) 3. Jiranek 4. Ujfalusi 5. Jankulowski
	6. Poborsky 7. Galasek (Heinz) 8. Nedved 9. Rosicky 10. Baros
	11. Koller (Rozehnal)
HOLLAND	(Man: Dick Advocaat)
	1. Van Der Saar 2. Stam 3. Cocu 4. Bouma 5. Hettinga 6. Seedorf
	(Van Der Vart) 7. Davids 8. Van Bronckhorst 9. Van Der Meyde (Reiziger)
	10. Van Nistelrooy 11. Robben (Bosvelt)

Dalglish, Kenny
Celtic, Liverpool, Scotland

KENNY DALGLISH EMERGED as a major force with Celtic in the early 1970s, in a side that dominated Scottish domestic football. It did not take him long to establish himself in the Scottish national team or to convince Liverpool to part with a massive £440,000 to take him to Anfield as a successor for the departing Kevin Keegan. Dalglish repaid their faith in him immediately forming a deadly combination with Ian Rush. It is hard to envisage a harder player to mark – subtle, strong and two-footed, he could turn defenders any which way he wanted.

When Liverpool needed a manager to keep up the boot-room succession, they surprised many by turning to Dalglish as player-manager in 1985. Again their faith was repaid. Dalglish became the first (and remains the only) player-manager to win the League and Cup double.

Dalglish later retired as Liverpool manager, blaming cumulative stress partially brought on by the Hillsborough disaster. A year later, though, he returned to football as manager of Blackburn Rovers, whom he led to the Premiership title in 1995. More recently spells at Newcastle and Celtic, where he took up a role as technical director, both ended in acrimony and failure. But who's to say he won't be back?

- Dalglish scored Liverpool's only goal in the 1978 European Cup final against Bruges.
- He is the only player to score 100 goals for English and Scottish clubs.
- Dalglish is a superb golfer, and could have been good enough to play professionally.
- He was one of only three managers to win the English First Division with two different clubs.
- He was PFA and Football Writers' Player of the Year, 1983.

VITAL STATISTICS

Place of Birth:	Glasgow, Scotland					
Date of Birth:	4 March 1951		**Died:** n/a			
Caps:	102 (Scotland)	**Goals (International):** 30				
Clubs:	Celtic, Liverpool			MANAGER	PLAYER	
Appearances:	Club (League): 559		Achievement	9	Achievement	9
Goals:	Club (League): 230		Tactical Awareness	8	Skill	8
Trophies:	SLT 1972, 1973, 1974, 1977; SFAC	Motivation	8	Teamwork	9	
	1972, 1974, 1975, 1977; EC 1978,	Team Selection/Transfers	7	Passion	9	
	1981, 1984; LT 1979, 1980, 1982-4,	Personality	6	Personality	7	
	(1986), (1988), (1990); LC 1981,					
	1982, 1983, 1984; FAC (1986), (1989)	**TOTAL**	**38**	**TOTAL**	**42**	

LEGEND RATING

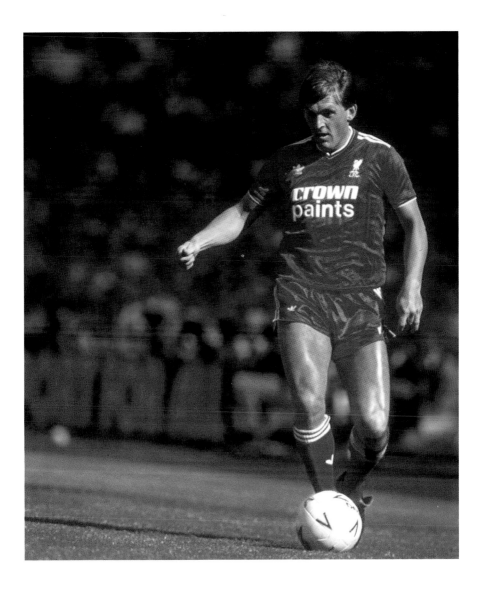

Danny's Boys
Tottenham Hotspur, 1961

BY 1961 the general consensus among the football fraternity was that the League and Cup double was impossible. Aston Villa and Preston's achievements were distant memories that belonged to another century, while Cullis's Wolves and the Busby Babes had both faltered in recent years when the prize seemed within their grasp. The genesis of the team that finally cracked it was 10 years earlier, when Arthur Rowe's side won the title with a style its critics labelled 'push and run'. By the time Bill Nicholson took over in 1958, he realised that this style could be honed to greater effect. Rather than players remaining in static positions, Nicholson figured that if they worked harder, passed the ball earlier and found space to receive it quickly, they would out-manoeuvre most opponents. It was a prototype of 'Total Football'.

The blend was irresistible, particularly in midfield where the silky passing of Blanchflower dovetailed perfectly with the powerhouse tackling of Mackay and the industry of John White. Maurice Norman was the rock at centre-half, while the free-scoring talents of Smith, Allen and Greaves ran riot through immobile defences. Their prime was the double season of 1961. They made it look easy.

- Spurs won the League by eight points in 1961, setting records galore. They won their first 11 games, won 16 away matches and equalled Arsenal's 1931 points total of 66.
- Jimmy Greaves arrived six months after the double was won, and he was instrumental in maintaining Spurs' success. He helped Spurs retain the FA Cup the following year.
- Nicholson knew early he was on to a good thing. His first game in charge finished Spurs 10 Everton 4.
- Spurs were the first British team to win a European trophy, collecting the European Cup Winners' Cup in 1963.
- Although Arthur Rowe's 1951 team was largely home grown, Nicholson's side was built with players from the transfer market.

Manager: Bill Nicholson

Key Players
Maurice Norman (D) Danny Blanchflower (M) Dave Mackay (M)
John White (F) Cliff Jones (W) Bobby Smith (F) Jimmy Greaves (F)

Trophies
LT 1961 FAC 1961

Das Wunderteam
Austria, 1930–50

EITHER SIDE OF THE WAR Austria had teams that were briefly rated as the world's best. In the early 1930s Jewish banker Hugo Meisl built 'Das Wunderteam,' the finest Austrian side in history. They beat Scotland 5-0, Germany 6-0, Switzerland 8-1 and Hungary 8-2. In 1932 they lost 4-3 to England at Stamford Bridge in a fabulous game that gave English fans their first glimpse of the Austrians' elaborate passing movements. They went into the 1934 World Cup as the favourites, where they eliminated France and Hungary (after an ill-tempered clash), before meeting with hosts Italy on a muddy pitch in Milan. Sindelar, their pale but athletic playmaker, was mauled by Luis Monti, and the Austrians were narrowly beaten 1-0. Another formidable side was built after the war but, as in 1934, the team was marginally past its best by the time the Finals came around in 1954. With Ocwirk pulling the strings, they hammered the Czechs thanks to a brilliant hat-trick from Probst, recovered from 3-0 down to beat Switzerland 7-5, but were then inexplicably trounced 6-1 by West Germany. The team had shot its bolt, and Austria's days as a major force were over.

☞ Matthias Sindelar looked more like a schoolteacher than a footballer, playing with a studiousness befitting his appearance. He was a Jew and didn't survive the German invasion.

☞ Many others in the Austrian team were annexed to the German squad for the 1938 World Cup, only a month after the Nazi invasion. 'Bimbo' Binder was one of them – he played 20 times for Austria and nine times for 'Greater Germany'.

☞ Ernst Ocwirk was one of the finest attacking centre-halves in the game, but by 1954 Austria's tactics were out of date, and the powerful German inside-forwards swamped their defence.

☞ Hanappi and Happel were great defenders, and the versatile Hanappi often played at half-back and at inside-forward.

Managers: Hugo Meisl (pre-war)
Walter Mausch (post-war)

Pre-War
Rudi Hiden (G) Pepi Smistik (M) Josef Bican (F)
Matthias Sindelar (F) Franz Binder (F)

Post-War:
Gerhard Hanappi (F/B) Ernst Happel (F/B)
Ernst Ocwirk (M) Robert and Alfred Korner (W)
Erich Probst (F)

Matthias Sindelar the illfated Austrian playmaker

Davids, Edgar
Ajax, Milan, Juventus, Inter, Holland

EDGAR DAVIDS DOESN'T LIKE penalty shoot-outs. Having played in the Dutch side that exited the 1998 World Cup and Euro 2000 on penalties, he then suffered the same fate with Juve in the sterile 2003 Champions League final against Milan.

Unlike some others, at least Davids had the consolation of one winner's medal; he was one of many exciting new talents in the young Ajax side that won the 1995 European Cup. His performances at Ajax earned him a high-profile and lucrative move to Milan, but he never settled there, and Juve snapped him up in December 1997. Davids' blood and thunder non-stop style provided the heartbeat for a Juventus side that won three Serie A titles in his six years at the club. It earned the distinctively dreadlocked midfielder a series of bookings and red cards along the way.

No stranger to appearing before the authorities, Davids has endured a ban for a positive drug test, and left the Dutch squad before Euro 96 after a fierce row with coach Guus Hiddink. 2004 saw Davids out of favour at Juventus, and a loan with Barcelona was followed by a move to Inter in the summer.

☞ Davids' trademark goggles are to protect his eyes from glare after he was diagnosed with glaucoma.

☞ Davids' abrasive style has earned him the nickname Pitbull – he has been described in Britain as a "dreadlocked Roy Keane"!

🖑 The row with Hiddink blew up when Davids accused the coach of racism after he was left on the bench for the opening two games.

🖑 The defeat in the Champions League Final in 2003 was a third disappointment for Davids; he had lost with Ajax in 1996 and Juve in 1998 as well.

🖑 Davids strenuously denied the positive test (for nandrolone), but served his ban nevertheless.

VITAL STATISTICS

Place of Birth:	Paramaribo, Surinam	
Date of Birth:	13 March 1973	**Died:** n/a
Caps:	73 (Holland)	**Goals (International):** 6
Clubs:	Ajax, AC Milan, Juventus, Barcelona, Inter Milan	
Appearances:	Club (All Matches): 352	
Goals:	Club (All Matches): 29	
Trophies:	EC 1995; UEFAC 1992; DLT 1994, 1995, 1996; SA 1998, 2002, 2003; WCC 1995	

LEGEND RATING	
Achievement	7.0
Skill	7.0
Teamwork	8.0
Passion	9.0
Personality	7.0
TOTAL	**38.0**

Dean, William 'Dixie'
Everton, England

FOOTBALL'S MOST PROLIFIC pre-war goal machine was the original English centre-forward. Lawton, Lofthouse and Milburn may have carried on the tradition, but none of them scored goals like Dixie Dean. His British record of 379 is one that will stand forever. True, today's superior marking and packed defences would have prevented this avalanche, while Dean's bustling strength would have incurred the displeasure of modern referees, but none of this should overshadow the man's talent – at times he seemed to challenge Arsenal's dominance of the league title almost single-handedly, shooting Everton to a brace of league titles and an FA Cup in six seasons.

Dean was born, raised and remained in the north-west all his life, retiring in modest circumstances before a disgracefully overdue testimonial in 1964 drew 40,000 to Goodison Park. Fittingly Dean even took his last breath at his beloved Everton's ground, passing away at Goodison after watching a Merseyside derby in 1980.

- 1928/29 season. Scored 60 goals in 39 games for Everton in the First Division, a record that still stands.
- Lived most of his life with a steel plate in his head, after fracturing his skull in a motorcycle crash as a youth.
- 1936. Overhauled Steve Bloomer's record of 352 league goals.
- Dean scored twice on his debut for England and hit hat-tricks in his second and fifth matches.
- He preferred his real name William to his life-long nickname Dixie.

VITAL STATISTICS

Place of Birth:	Birkenhead, England
Date of Birth:	27 January 1907 **Died:** 1 March 1980
Caps:	16 (England) **Goals (International):** 18
Clubs:	Tranmere, Everton, Notts County
Appearances:	Club (League): 438
Goals:	Club (League): 379
Trophies:	LT 1928, 1932; FAC 1933

LEGEND RATING	
Achievement	8.0
Skill	8.0
Teamwork	10.0
Passion	9.0
Personality	6.0
TOTAL	**41.0**

Der Kaiser und Der Bomber
West Germany, 1970s

SO CONSISTENT have been their performances over the last 50 years, it seems almost ill-mannered to single out a particular German team for special praise. But, for their comprehensive domination of the early 1970s, the team of Beckenbauer, Breitner and Müller, stands out, even ahead of their all-conquering successors in the 1990s. After losing in an exciting semi-final against Italy in the 1970 World Cup, the Germans regrouped and emerged even stronger for the 1972 Euros. Inspired by Gunther Netzer, the brilliant, if unpredictable, midfielder, they won the tournament with ease, including an exemplary victory at Wembley to effectively eliminate England. Their 1974 World Cup winning side was typical West Germany. In defence they boasted an enviable array of talent including Bertie Vogts, a blond terrier of a full-back, the attacking marauder Paul Breitner, the redoubtable Karl-Heinz Schnellinger and, of course, Beckenbauer. Ahead of them stood a midfield of rare athleticism and energy, Grabowski's wing play providing an outlet for Wolfgang Overath's silky left foot, and ammunition for the urgent running of new star Rainer Bonhof. At the tip of their arrow was Gerd Müller, a striker with the priceless knack of producing a goal, even when the rest of his colleagues were struggling. This was no Dream Team. It was real.

☞ West Germany, and later Germany, have been blessed with a succession of world-class forwards. Seeler was succeeded by Müller, and Rummenigge, Voller and Klinsmann followed.

👆 Jurgen Grabowski was a frustrating talent, brilliant one minute, mediocre the next. His successor, Pierre Littbarski, though a potential match-winner, rarely rose to the big occasion.

☞ Uli Hoeness was the link player in the team, an unfussy player he rarely gave the ball away.

👆 West Germany won the 1974 World Cup the hard way, against a Dutch team regarded as one of the greats. The Germans hardly touched the ball for the first 20 minutes, but showed typical resilience to come back from a goal down to win 2-1.

Manager: Helmut Schoen

Key Players
Sepp Maier (G) Franz Beckenbauer (D/SW) Berti Vogts (D)
Paul Breitner (D) Wolfgang Overath (M) Uli Hoeness (M)
Rainer Bonhof (M) Gunter Netzer (M) Gerd Müller (F)

Trophies
EuroC 1972, 1980 WorC 1974

West Germany line-up before the 1974 WC Finals. See if you can spot Paul Breitner's afro.

Desailly, Marcel

AC Milan, Chelsea, France

THE FRENCH HAVE OFTEN mined foreign territories in search of new talent, with West Africa proving to be one of their richest seams. Among the gems to have been uncovered in their excavations is a tall, loose-limbed Ghanian by the name of Marcel Desailly. In France Desailly began his career with Nantes, later moving on to Bernard Tapie's Olympique Marseille where he became a mainstay of their French championship-winning teams of the early 1990s.

An imperious midfield general, his languid and nonchalant style has often brought accusations of arrogance, but he has proved to be a loyal and dependable professional, well-liked and respected by colleagues wherever he's played. After Marseille's surprise win in the 1993 European Cup final, the vanquished Milan immediately signed him, and it was perhaps no coincidence that the trophy followed him to the San Siro the following season. By now Desailly was at the heart of the defence, from where he helped guide France to their triumphs at France 98 and Euro 2000. On his arrival at Chelsea in 1998, many thought him another fading foreign star in search of a final payday, but that was a criminal underestimation of both man and player. Only since 2003 has Desailly started to look mortal. Euro 2004 was a sad and unworthy end to his international career.

- After financial scandal rocked Marseille and forced Tapie's hand, Desailly's transfer brought income that was desperately needed.
- On his return to the San Siro with Chelsea, Desailly received a warmer reception than some members of the Milan team.
- His goals are rare, but his canter through the Barcelona defence before applying the coup de grâce in the 1994 European Cup final is an obvious highlight.
- Playing with Angloma and Boli in a Marseille defence known as the 'black guard', Desailly won over the crowd in France's most racist city.
- His five different major honours make Desailly's trophy cabinet one of the most complete, and varied, in Europe.

VITAL STATISTICS

Place of Birth:	Accra, Ghana		
Date of Birth:	7 September 1968	**Died:** n/a	
Caps:	116 (France)	**Goals (International):** 3	
Clubs:	Nantes, Marseille, AC Milan, Chelsea		
Appearances:	Club (League): 508		
Goals:	Club (League): 17		
Trophies:	WorC 1998; EuroC 2000; EC 1993, 1994; SA 1994, 1996; FAC 2000		

LEGEND RATING	
Achievement	10.0
Skill	9.0
Teamwork	8.0
Passion	7.0
Personality	7.0
TOTAL	**41.0**

Deschamps, Didier
Nantes, Marseilles, Juventus, Chelsea, Valencia, France

MOST NEUTRAL OBSERVERS, fans and pundits never remember Didier Deschamps as a remarkable footballer. Talk to his contemporaries and you get a clearer picture. Any great midfield needs a 'sitter', a player prepared to do the boring stuff for the flair players, to hold back when the surges of Gallic passion carry the rest forward on a cavalry charge. The great midfield that France boasted in the late 1990s had Deschamps; undemonstrative, unspectacular, but vital. Bad players do not win 103 caps in a strong team. Bad players do not keep Patrick Vieira out of the side, even a Vieira yet to reach his awesome peak.

So forget the uninspired figure seen in the Premiership at Chelsea, and remember the busy, neat general who led his country to back-to-back wins in the World Cup and the European Championship. Or consider the fact that Juventus, having won diddly-squat for a decade, won every trophy going in the five years Deschamps was there.

Deschamps' record suggests a highly intelligent player; a notion reinforced by the immediate impact he has made as coach on an ailing Monaco side. Unable to buy players, Deschamps took a raggle-taggle bunch to a Champions League final, beating Real Madrid and Chelsea along the way.

☞ Deschamps played for Marseilles in the 1-0 Champions League win over Milan; they were stripped of the title after the corruption of Bernard Tapie was exposed the following year.

👍 Three more Champions League finals came at Juventus, including a winner's medal in 1996.

☞ A record of 4 goals in 103 internationals shows one of Deschamps' main failings – without pace or a fierce shot, he was very ordinary in the last quarter of the pitch.

☞ At Monaco, Deschamps has shown his astuteness and put together a fearsome front two by combining the little-known Croatian, Dado Prso and on-loan Fernando Morientes from Real Madrid.

VITAL STATISTICS

Place of Birth:	Bayonne, France
Date of Birth:	15 October 1968 **Died:** n/a
Caps:	103 (France) **Goals (International):** 4
Clubs:	As Player: Nantes, Marseille, Bordeaux, Marseille, Juventus, Chelsea, Valencia; As Manager: Monaco
Appearances:	Club (League): 407
Goals:	Club (League): 16
Trophies:	FLT 1989–93; SA 1995, 1997, 1998; FAC 2000; EC 1993, 1996; EuroC 2000; WorC 1998

LEGEND RATING

Achievement	10.0
Skill	6.0
Teamwork	9.0
Passion	8.0
Personality	7.0
TOTAL	**40.0**

Deutschland Unter Alles
The Decline of Germany

WE KNEW THAT THIS wasn't the Germany of Beckenbauer, Netzer or Rummenigge. Even this second-string squad, though, had thrown off the indignity of a 5-1 home humiliation against England to reach a World Cup final less than 12 months later. 'Don't write them off' had become an insurance policy for any pre-tournament assessment of Germany's failings.

This appeared an even-more sensible caveat after the first game, in which the Germans proved more than a match for the talented individualism of Holland. They led until the 81st minute and had reduced the Dutch to using substitute Van Hooijdonk as an aerial battering ram. Van Nilstelrooy's brilliant volley, after he eluded Worns for the first time, cost Germany the victory they deserved.

Grounds for optimism were removed after their second game. The goalless draw with Latvia, the tournament's only genuine minnows, was as insipid a German performance as any in living memory.

The Czechs, guaranteed to top the group after two wins, fielded a reserve team, giving hope to the bealeaguered Rudi Voller. On twenty minutes, Ballack's strike appeared to restore the natural order. By the end, a free-kick special from Heinz and a winner from the rejuvenated Baros meant that Germany were reduced to relying on Latvia.

- Despite topping their qualifying group, Germany's pre-tournament form was woeful. It included a 5-1 stuffing by Romania, a team who failed to reach the finals.
- Ballack, and the youngsters, Schweinsteiger and Lahm, should be the only players exempt from criticism. The former retained his class and industry, despite being surrounded by makeweights.
- None of the five players selected as strikers could muster a goal. Midfielders Ballack and Frings fired the only bullets.
- 'Wunderbar!' Not a German headline, but a cheeky effort from the Dutch paper *Algemeen Dagblad*, greeting the Czech defeat of the alt enemy with undisguised glee.

'Rudi, we were the idiots of Europe.'

German tabloid *Bild* delivers its damning verdict on German coach Rudi Voller.

Coach Rudi Voller can't bear to watch as Germany crash out of Euro 2004.

Di Canio, Paolo
Celtic, Sheffield Wednesday, West Ham United

LIKE FELLOW MAVERICK Eric Cantona, Paolo di Canio's talents have been more appreciated in Britain than in his home country. Volatility and indiscipline have led successive Italian managers to ignore him, and have resulted in a lengthy exile from his homeland following precocious beginnings at Milan. The case against was most vividly illustrated in 1998 when, reacting to being issued with a red card playing for Sheffield Wednesday against Arsenal, he pushed referee Paul Durkin to the ground. The shove inflicted only bruised pride, but left another manager resigned to parting with a wayward talent.

With passion and skill complementing his sublime touch and striker's instinct, Di Canio has been a folk hero at every club from the San Siro to Celtic Park, always resurrecting a career that has appeared irretrievably damaged. His hunger and commitment to the team are often obscured by his moments of indiscretion, but those that have watched him regularly will vouch for his skill and influence. Alex Ferguson's efforts to sign him for Manchester United in 2002 are an indication that, even at 34, he still had much to offer on football's biggest stages. Following the Hammers' relegation, Di Canio remained in the Premiership limelight at Charlton.

- Di Canio even takes penalties in style; his trademark chips continue to embarrass keepers.
- 2000. Outrageous volley v Wimbledon wins BBC's goal of the season.
- 2001. Won Fair Play award after catching the ball to allow Everton's fallen keeper to receive treatment when he might have pulled the ball down and scored.
- He has never won a trophy in Britain.
- West Ham fans chanted his name to the tune of an aria from Verdi's 'Rigoletto'.

VITAL STATISTICS

Place of Birth:	Rome, Italy			
Date of Birth:	9 July 1968	**Died:** n/a		
Caps:	0 (Italy)	**Goals (International):** 0	Achievement	4.0
Clubs:	Terrana, Lazio, Juventus, Napoli, AC Milan,		Skill	9.0
	Celtic, Sheffield Wednesday, West Ham,		Teamwork	8.0
	Charlton		Passion	10.0
Appearances:	Club (League): 358		Personality	9.0
Goals:	Club (League): 94			
Trophies:	UEFAC 1993		**TOTAL**	**40.0**

LEGEND RATING

Di Stefano, Alfredo
Real Madrid, Argentina, Colombia, Spain

ONE OF THE GREATEST-EVER strikers, Alfredo Di Stefano's name was initially made in South American football where, after leading a players' strike and starring in a breakaway league, he stood out as much for his militancy as his ability on the ball. Europe beckoned and it was as the captain and inspiration of the mighty Real Madrid team of the 1950s for which he is now best remembered.

His partnership with the brilliant Hungarian Ferenc Puskas was one of the great attacking combinations in the game's history and reached its high point in the last of Madrid's five consecutive European Cups from 1956–60. In a 7-3 demolition of Eintracht Frankfurt Di Stefano scored a hat-trick, while Puskas weighed in with the other four! With the 'White Arrow' spearheading their attack, Real carried all before them in La Liga for nigh on a decade. After leaving Real in 1964, ending an 11-year love affair at the Bernabeu, he played one final season in Spain with Espanol but, at 38, he was unable to sustain the brilliance for which he was famed, sparkling only in flashes. Coaching spells in Spain and Argentina brought him a La Liga title with Valencia in 1971, but it is as a player of rare and inspirational skill that he left his most enduring imprint on the sport.

☞ He is the only player to have played for three countries: Argentina, Colombia and Spain.

✍ He was European Player of the Year 1957 and 1959.

☝ Di Stefano's 49 European club goals remains a record, although Raul looks set to take it from him.

☞ Real beat Man United 5-3 on aggregate in a classic two-leg semi-final in the 1957 European Cup. But for the Munich disaster the two teams would have surely battled each other for Europe's top award for many years.

☞ Di Stefano joins George Best as the only members of our World XI never to grace a World Cup Finals tournament.

VITAL STATISTICS

Place of Birth:	Barracas, Argentina
Date of Birth:	4 July 1926 **Died:** n/a
Caps:	7 (Argentina); 2 (Columbia); 31 (Spain)
Goals (International):	7 (Argentina); 0 (Columbia); 23 (Spain)
Clubs:	Los Cardales, River Plate, Huracan, Millonarios, Real Madrid, Espanyol
Appearances:	Club (All Matches for Real Madrid): 510
Goals:	Club (All Matches for Real Madrid): 418
Trophies:	EC 1956–60; PLA 1954, 1955, 1957–59, 1961, 1963, 1964, (1971)

LEGEND RATING	
Achievement	8.0
Skill	10.0
Teamwork	9.0
Passion	9.0
Personality	8.0
TOTAL	**44.0**

Dirtiest Cup Final Ever
Chelsea 2 Leeds United 1, 1970

THIS INFAMOUS MATCH was a bloodbath. Chelsea were the fancydan southerners, flashy and inconsistent with a reputation for boozy late nights, while Leeds were the no-nonsense, cynical professionals whose pre-match evenings were spent playing dominoes. Both teams viewed each other with contempt. At Wembley, Eddie Gray had tormented Chelsea's right-back David Webb, and the tactic of switching Webb with Ron Harris for the replay had the desired effect within minutes. Gray became a limping passenger for the rest of the game. 'Chopper' had set the tone.

In a tit-for-tat response that would have brought approval from hardliners in the Middle East, Bonetti was taken out moments later, subsequently giving a commendable display on one leg. From then on, a pulsating and skilful Cup final was routinely punctuated by outbreaks of violence. Hutchinson and Charlton traded blows, while McCreadie's two-footed lunge at Bremner's neck introduced kung fu to a British audience several years before Bruce Lee. Yet for all the 'southern softies' jibes, it was Chelsea who prevailed. A goal down at half-time, they hit back through a diving header from Osgood and scrambled a winner courtesy of Webb's right ear.

☞ When Chelsea finally went ahead in extra-time, it was the first time they had led in the tie. They had pegged Leeds back at Wembley with two equalisers.

☞ Osgood's goal meant he had scored in every round.

☞ This was the first FA Cup final settled outside Wembley since it became the venue in 1923.

☞ Referee Jennings must have forgotten his pencil. Despite the violence not one player was cautioned.

☞ David Harvey was the only change from the teams who contested the first match. Gary Sprake was left out after a trademark howler had gifted Chelsea their first equaliser.

SCORERS **Chelsea:** Osgood, Webb
Leeds: Jones

EVENT FA Cup Final Replay, Old Trafford, 29 April, 1970

CHELSEA (Man: Dave Sexton)
1. Bonetti 2. Harris, R 3. McCreadie 4. Hollins 5. Dempsey 6. Webb
7. Baldwin 8. Cooke 9. Osgood 10. Hutchinson 11. Houseman

LEEDS (Man: Don Revie)
1. Harvey 2. Madeley 3. Cooper 4. Bremner 5. Charlton 6. Hunter
7. Lorimer 8. Clarke 9. Jones 10. Giles 11. Gray, E.

Disasters
Footballing Tragedies

FOOTBALL ATTRACTS MORE SPECTATORS than any other sport in the world. The downside to this is that when things go wrong they go wrong in a big way. Recent advances in stadium safety seem to have eradicated most of the problems, but it took a scandalously long time for the authorities to take action. In 1946, a wall collapsed under pressure from spectators eager to watch Bolton's FA Cup quarter-final against Stoke. Thirty-three people were crushed to death. After this the luck of the authorities held until 1971, when 66 people died at Ibrox. Rangers fans were filing down a staircase, believing their team to have been beaten in the New Year derby. A last-minute equaliser caused thousands to turn back and the crush barriers failed to take their weight.

Ibrox's legacy was the Safety of Sports Grounds Act, which, although a development, failed to address the problem of old wooden structures and fire risk. In 1985, this oversight resulted in the deaths of 56 fans from a fire started by one cigarette, dropped on to rubbish under a stand at Valley Park. Though most British grounds are safer now, the mixture of weak stadium, bad policing, hooliganism and panic can result in tragedy anywhere in the world. It is inevitable that, one day, this page will require updating.

- 1982. In a chilling echo of Ibrox, 340 people died at a European Cup match in Moscow after a late goal. Russian officials claimed the death toll was 61 in an attempt to disguise poor policing.
- Locked gates and an exiting human tide have proved a fatal combination. 74 people were crushed at an Argentine game in 1968; 71 died for the same reason in Katmandu 20 years later.
- In 1964 police fired shots as a crowd 'control' exercise in Lima. Over 300 people died in the resulting panic.
- African crowd control has not kept pace with modern improvements. Three unnecessary uses of tear-gas have produced separate disasters in the last few years.
- 26 people died at Ibrox in 1902 after a stand collapsed.

'Football is not a matter of life and death – it's much more important than that.'

In the context of Heysel and Hillsborough, Bill Shankly's words have a hollow ring

Don't Expect it to Happen Again
Liverpool 4 Newcastle United 3, 1996

IN 10 YEARS of the Premier League, there had never been a game quite like it. With the season approaching its climax, both teams were straining for the Champions League, while Newcastle were also slugging it out with Man United for the title.

Under the circumstances a cagey, low-scoring affair would have been understandable. Instead, both teams came at each other from the off, and after an extraordinary opening 15 minutes Newcastle were 2-1 to the good, having overturned Robbie Fowler's second-minute strike. A sense of normality returned for the following 30 minutes but half-time only served to recharge the batteries. Fowler slid in an equaliser 10 minutes after the restart, only for Asprilla to restore Newcastle's lead within another two. A spectator for 68 minutes, Stan Collymore woke up sufficiently to turn in McAteer's cross to level the scores again. A draw seemed the fair result, but Ian Rush had other ideas. His appearance as an 82nd-minute substitute spurred Liverpool for one last effort and two minutes into injury time Anfield's greatest goalscorer turned provider, combining with John Barnes to set up an unmarked Collymore for the winner. Fairytale stuff.

☞ 'If they score three, we'll score four.' Keegan's words earlier in the season characterised Newcastle's approach and so nearly proved prophetic.

✑ For Newcastle it was another away defeat in a stuttering run that cost them the title. They had been 12 points ahead at the turn of the year.

✑ Best moment of the match? Asprilla nutmegging Ruddock before scoring Newcastle's third.

☞ Radio Five Live's captain smugness, Alan Green, before the corresponding fixture the following season: 'Welcome to a packed Anfield. And do yourselves a favour folks: don't expect 4-3. That happens once every 10 years.' You've guessed it....

SCORERS	**Liverpool:** Fowler (2), Collymore (2)
	Newcastle: Ferdinand, Ginola, Asprilla
EVENT	FA Premiership, Anfield, 3 April 1996
LIVERPOOL	(Man: Roy Evans)
	1. James 2. Wright 3. Scales 4. Ruddock 5. McAteer 6. Redknapp
	7. Barnes 8. McManaman 9. Jones 10. Fowler 11. Collymore
NEWCASTLE	(Man: Kevin Keegan)
	1. Srnicek 2. Watson 3. Howey 4. Albert 5. Beresford 6. Beardsley
	7. Lee 8. Batty 9. Ginola 10. Ferdinand 11. Asprilla

Michael Owen leaves Newcastle's Steve Watson floundering

Double, The

Impossible!

THE SIGHT OF an open-topped bus inching its way through an adoring throng is a familiar end-of-season ritual, but the spectacle of beaming players displaying both the League Championship and the FA Cup is relatively rare. Only seven clubs have achieved the double in over 100 seasons of competition (ten times in all). It seemed so easy when Preston won it in the league's first season, so when Aston Villa completed the same feat eight years later it barely raised an eyebrow. But for the next 64 years the double acquired the status of a holy grail as numerous teams stumbled near the summit. Chapman's Huddersfield and Arsenal, and the Busby Babes, all went close without igniting the proverbial cigar.

It was the push-and-run of Nicholson's Spurs that ended the drought, a feat repeated to general surprise by their North London neighbours a decade later. The fact that the double has been won relatively frequently in recent years is a symbol of the recent polarisation of power in the game. Indeed, following Man United's capture of the League, FA Cup and European Cup treble in 1999, the status of the domestic double has probably been undermined for good.

- 1889/2004. Preston North End/Arsenal remained unbeaten all season.
- 1897. Aston Villa's toughest obstacle was an FA Cup quarter-final epic with Preston lasting three games.
- 1994, 1996, 1999. Man United raise the stakes with a 'double-double,' followed by their *annus mirabilis* three years later.
- 1971. Arsenal climbed Everest the hard way, overhauling Leeds in the final game and coming from behind in the FA Cup Final.
- 1986. Liverpool's cake was iced by beating Everton in the first all-Merseyside Cup final.
- Arsenal followed Manchester United with further Doubles in 1998 and 2002.

'We were the last Manchester club to finish as Champions … and we'll be the next.'

Peter Swales, Manchester City chairman in 1992

Kenny Dalglish with the spoils in 1986.

Drake, Ted
Arsenal, England

WHEN HERBERT CHAPMAN decided he needed a replacement for his centre-forward Jack Lambert, he had only one target in mind: Ted Drake, the barnstorming Southampton striker. And so, for the princely sum of £6,500, Drake moved to Arsenal, becoming the latest piece in Chapman's ever-shifting jigsaw. The attacking line-up in the 1934/35 season read thus: Bastin, Jack, Drake, James and Hulme. Like Lambert, Drake was strong and fearless, often playing through injuries that would have ruled out lesser men. In 1935 Arsenal beat Aston Villa 7-1, a game in which Drake had nine attempts at goal. One was saved, one hit the bar and he scored with the other seven.

The vagaries of international selection in those days meant he played only five times for England; it is testimony to his striking instincts that he still managed to notch six goals. After the war Drake tried his hand at management, and enjoyed a nine-year spell at Chelsea, during which he led the club to its only league title, in 1955. A tall, handsome, athletic man, but without excessive vanity, Drake would have been a marketing manager's dream had he played today.

- Scored the only goal in the 1936 FA Cup Final.
- In 1963 Drake became a member of the first ever pools panel, convened in the 'big freeze' of that winter.
- Drake's tackle on Italy's Luisito Monti sparked off the 'Battle of Highbury,' a bruising encounter between Italy and England in 1934. England won 3-2, Drake scored.
- He scored 42 league goals in his first season at Arsenal, including four in a match on four occasions.
- His seven goals against Aston Villa (see main text) were made even more remarkable by the fact that Drake played with a heavily-strapped knee.

VITAL STATISTICS

Place of Birth:	Southampton, England		Achievement	7.0
Date of Birth:	16 August 1912	**Died:** 30 May 1995	Skill	8.0
Caps:	5 (England)	**Goals (International):** 6	Teamwork	7.0
Clubs:	Southampton, Arsenal		Passion	9.0
Appearances:	Club (All Matches for Arsenal): 184		Personality	6.0
Goals:	Club (All Matches for Arsenal): 139			
Trophies:	LT 1935, 1938, (1955); FAC 1936		**TOTAL**	**37.0**

LEGEND RATING

Dream Dragons
The Wales Dream Team

HARDLY SCINTILLATING IS IT? Welsh football has had its moments, but they have tended to come when a team made up mainly of ordinary players has elevated itself by dint of endeavour and passion. The squad of 16 below contains no more than half a dozen world class players, and neither Giggs nor Rush produced their best for Wales. This team is not reflective of the players with the most caps, otherwise the midfield might comprise Peter Nicholas, Brian Flynn, Barry Horne and Mickey Thomas, if he's out of jail.

At least the keeper is world class, and Kevin Ratcliffe was a hugely under-rated defender. John Charles would start at the back, but could also bolster the attack. Two decent wingers, Meredith from the early part of the last century, and the whippet-like Cliff Jones from Spurs double-winning side, might create some problems, and leave Giggs to try and cause damage wherever. Hughes would give anyone a hard game, even if he wasn't a prolific scorer, and Rush, in this company, might do what he never really did for Wales.

- Fred Keenor was captain of the Welsh team which won the Home Internationals in the 1920s, and also captained the Cardiff City side which won the 1927 FA Cup. He would be a solid ball-winner.
- Mike Smith oversaw a Welsh team that achieved more than its collective parts suggested it was capable of – which was more than many of his better known successors managed.
- We went for a 3-4-3 to avoid picking Joey Jones.
- John Charles' brother, Mel, was also up for selection, as were a few other Jonesies apart from Cliff. As were Mark Aizlewood, Glynn Hodges, Clayton Blackmore, Kenny Jackett and Eric Young. We didn't pick them either. Not because they had brothers but because they weren't very good.
- Mark Hughes' promising tenure as Welsh manager came to an end in Autumn, 2004. His successor, John Toshack, faces a tough task, as Speed retired after the England game, and Giggs will surely follow suit soon.

Manager: Mike Smith (80s)

3-4-1-2

Neville Southall (80s/90s)

Kevin Ratcliffe (80s) Mike England (70s) John Charles (60s)

Billy Meredith (00s/10s) Fred Keenor (20s)
Gary Speed (90s/2000s) Cliff Jones (C) (50s/60s)

Ryan Giggs (90s)

Mark Hughes (80s/90s) Ian Rush (80s)

Subs: Jack Kelsey (G) (50s) Len Allchurch (D) (50s)
Ivor Allchurch (50s) Trevor Ford (F) (40s/50s) Ted Vizard (W) (20s)

Dreaming in Red
Liverpool's All-Time XI

IT WAS SURPRISING, when we started to examine the Liverpool players of the last 35 years as individuals, how few of them stood out as genuine world class performers. The likes of Tommy Smith, Brian Hall, Phil Neal, Sammy Lee and Jimmy Case were crucial parts of the Anfield jigsaw, but taken out of that context were relatively unremarkable players.

But an endless cycle of international players in recent years was not allowed to blur the fact that it was the more prosaic home-grown talents – the likes of full-backs Lawler and Hughes that brought Liverpool their vast array of trophies over two decades. Those two, with Lawrenson (narrowly over Ron Yeats) and Hansen – probably the best ever pairing in English club football – and the redoubtable Clemence in goal make up a formidable back five.

The midfield choices ignored the claims of St John, McDermott and Molby, but allies work-rate to skill, the selection of Liddell, acknowledges the other great Liverpool teams in the early part of the last century.

Keegan and Dalglish could interchange, and Rush would surely relish service of the quality this team could provide. If he didn't, there's always Roger Hunt or Michael Owen to replace him!

☞ The Kop, originally standing on a mound of ashes and cinders, was named after the Spion Kop, a hill successfully defended by the Boers in the Boer War.

☞ Club anthem 'You'll Never Walk Alone' came from a hit by Merseybeat singer Gerry Marsden. The phrase is now carved into the wrought-iron gates at the ground.

☝ No Heighway, Toshack, Aldridge, Beardsley, Barnes, Fowler. Simply no room at the inn.

☝ Only Owen from the current crop – though in three or four years Hyppia and Kewell may push for consideration.

☞ "Mind you, I've been here during the bad times too – one year we came second." Bob Paisley

---

Manager: Bill Shankly (60s/70s)

4-4-2

Ray Clemence (70s/80s)

Chris Lawler (60s/70s) Mark Lawrenson (80s)
Alan Hansen (70s/80s) Emlyn Hughes (C) (70s)

Kevin Keegan (70s) Graeme Souness (80s)
Steven Gerrard (00s) Billy Liddell (40s)

Kenny Dalglish (70s/80s) Ian Rush (80s)

Subs: Elisha Scott (G) (20s) Ron Yeats (D) (60s) Roger Hunt (F) (60s)
Ian Callaghan (M) (60s/70s) Michael Owen (F) (90s/00s)

Duff, Damien

Blackburn Rovers, Chelsea, Republic of Ireland

AMIDST ALL THE KERFUFFLE of Roy Keane's exit from the 2002 World Cup Finals, many journalists passed the opinion that Ireland had lost their only world class player. They were wrong. For a year or two, the stocky Blackburn Rovers winger, Damien Duff, had been tormenting Premiership right backs, providing a stream of crosses for his forwards, and notching a few goals himself.

Able to go either way, with great balance and a sporty extra gear, Duff was the envy of many of the Premiership big-boys, always on the lookout for a lock to pick stubborn defences. His performances, post-Keane, in the 2002 World Cup, did nothing to damage that reputation. After exciting in the group matches, especially in the vital draw with Germany, he was simply outstanding in the defeat by Spain on penalties. That form carried on into Blackburn's excellent 2002–03 season in the Premiership, a season that made an approach from one of the Champions League clubs inevitable.

In an injury-hit first season at Chelsea, Duff's talent was more evident in how much the team missed him than for his dangerous contributions when he was fit. Without him, Blackburn, too, looked a shadow of the team they were the previous season. The best should be yet to come.

☞ On his U-21 Ireland debut, the team were housed in a basic hotel in poverty-stricken Moldova. Duff responded by sleeping for 12 hours while the others complained.

☞ Chelsea had to pay £17 m for Duff's services, then a club record; this figure triggered a break clause in his contract at Blackburn.

☞ In the 2002 World Cup, Mick McCarthy used Duff as a support striker rather than a winger. A debate still goes on as to where he is most effective.

☞ Summer 2004. Duff publicised his displeasure at Chelsea's signing of Dutch winger and first-team threat Arjen Robben. Both players, when fit, have been included in the starting line-up.

VITAL STATISTICS

Place of Birth:	Ballyboden, Ireland	
Date of Birth:	2 March 1979	**Died:** n/a
Caps:	48 (R. Ireland)	**Goals (International):** 6
Clubs:	Blackburn Rovers, Chelsea	
Appearances:	Club (League): 200	
Goals:	Club (League): 40	
Trophies:	None	

Achievement	5.0
Skill	9.0
Teamwork	7.0
Passion	7.0
Personality	7.0
TOTAL	**35.0**

LEGEND RATING

Dutch Oven Too Hot For Hoops
Feyenoord 2 Celtic 1, 1970

FOR FEYENOORD, this was particularly sweet. Ajax had dominated the Dutch league in the late sixties and were seasoned campaigners in the competition. In the previous year, the ultimate prize was within their grasp, as they won through to the final, only to freeze in Milan's dazzling headlights. So it was left to the Rotterdam side to become Holland's first European Cup winners.

The final threatened to become and end-to-end classic. Feyenoord were attacking liberos, while Celtic's up-and-at-'em 4-2-4 was typical of the style that had won them the competition three years before. Gemmell stunned Feyenoord on the half-hour withe a 25 m piledriver, only for 'Iron' Rinus Israel to head an equaliser within three minutes from a set piece. Surprisingly, the game died in the second half. Celtic burnt themselves out and their sparse central midfield was repeatedly overrun. Feyenoord should have killed the game off in normal time but finally did so in the 116th minute courtesy of a lapse from the unlikeliest of sources, Billy McNeill.

Misjudging an upfield punt, the Celtic captain tried desperately to handle the ball away, flailing and failing in the process. Waiting was the Swedish centre-forward Kindvall, whose precise finish ensured Rotterdam revelry.

☞ Celtic had beaten Leeds in the semi-final, the only occasion that two British teams have reached the last four.

☞ Gemmell, a full-back, is the only British player to score in separate European Cup Finals.

👆 Feyenoord's progress to the Final included a 16-0 aggregate win (12-0 and 4-0) over Reykjavic. Both games were played in Rotterdam, as Icelandic facilities weren't up to the task.

👆 Feyenoord also eliminated the holders Milan, a victory made all the sweeter as the Italians had defeated Ajax in the previous season's final.

👆 Jansen and Van Hanegem were later to grace an even bigger stage, in the 1974 World Cup Final against West Germany.

SCORERS   **Feyenoord:** Israel, Kindvall
                Celtic: Gemmell

EVENT   European Cup Final, San Siro Stadium, Milan, 6 May 1970

FEYENOORD (Man: Ernst Happel)
                1. Pieters Graafland 2. Romeijn (Haak) 3. Israel 4. Laseroms 5. Jansen
                6. Van Duivenbode 7. Hasil 8. Van Hanegem 9. Wery 10. Kindvall 11. Moulijn

CELTIC   (Man: Jock Stein)
                1. Williams 2. Hay 3. Gemmell 4. Murdoch 5. McNeill 6. Brogan
                7. Johnstone 8. Wallace 9. Hughes 10. Auld (Connelly) 11. Lennox

Dutch Revival
Ajax, mid 1990s

VAN GAAL TOOK OVER as head coach at Ajax in 1991 and, following the departures of Rijkaard, Van Basten, Bergkamp, Winter and Jonk, was immediately charged with the onerous task of finding suitable replacements. Three years later, with the returning Rijkaard in their team, they won the Dutch title and went on to reclaim their status as Europe's premier club side. Van Gaal was successfully able to blend emerging Dutch stars with well-chosen imports; Jari Litmanen, the imaginative Finnish playmaker, and two young Nigerians, Finidi George and the freakishly large-footed Nwankwo Kanu. They finally announced themselves in the 1995 Champions League, beating AC Milan twice in the group stages and romping through to a tough semi-final against Bayern Munich. After a 0-0 draw in Munich, a similarly close second leg was expected. But, inspired by Litmanen, Ajax tore into Bayern, winning 5-2. A hard-fought match against AC Milan brought a third win against the Italians, and the return of the trophy Ajax had dominated in the early 1970s. Another fine campaign the following year ended in disappointment as they lost to Juventus on penalties in the final.

☞ During the 1995/96 European campaign, Van Gaal almost took his players off the pitch in Budapest in protest at the racial abuse being hurled at Ajax's black players. They settled for a 4-0 win.

☞ Van Gaal had a spell at Barcelona after Ajax; when Frank Rijkaard resigned as Dutch coach after Euro 2000, Van Gaal took over.

☞ Ronald and Frank De Boer both moved to Barcelona from Ajax – the twins have since split up, Ronald moving on to Rangers.

☞ Since their European Cup win the team has broken up again; all its best players have been sold (Van Der Saar, Overmars, Kanu, George and Litmanen all played in the Premiership).

✎ Ajax look to be on the rise again, claiming a domestic league and cup double in 2002.

Manager: Louis Van Gaal

Key Players
Edwin Van Der Saar (G) Frank De Boer (D) Danny Blind (D)
Frank Rijkaard (D) Edgar Davids (M) Marc Overmars (W)
Jari Litmanen (F) Patrick Kluivert (F) Finidi George (F)
Ronald De Boer (W) Kanu (F)

Trophies
OLT 1994, 1995, 1996 EC 1995 UEFAC 1992
ESC 1995 WCC 1995

Eastern Promise
An Eastern Europe Select

THIS IS A WORLD CLASS line-up, in spades. Every one of the 16 players performed well at the highest level, but only rarely have the respective nations performed collectively well. Czechoslovakia and the USSR both won European Championships, and Croatia and Poland have reached World Cup semi-finals, but no Eastern European side has ever seriously threatened to win a World Cup.

The defence is sound; the under-rated Belodedici was one of the finest defenders of the last decade, and Zmuda marshalled the highly effective Polish team of the 1970s. Behind them is probably the world's greatest ever goalkeeper. Masopust was a craftsman, and the architect of a Czechoslovakia team that reached the 1962 World Cup final. Boniek was all power and precision, a free-scoring midfielder, with bite and stamina. Hagi was an enigma; at times appearing overweight and lethargic, he possessed one of the games' most gifted left feet – with him and Stoichkov in the team, best not to concede free-kicks!

Up front the rapier quick Lato, one of the most prolific goalscorers in World Cup Finals' history, partners Shevchenko, who has never appeared in the Finals. Nonetheless the Ukrainian's performances for AC Milan mark him as one of the most penetrative target-men in modern football.

- The USSR side of the late 1980's, largely comprising players from an outrageously talented Dinamo Kiev side, was probably the best East European side to take the field – they were beaten 4-3 by Belgium in a rousing match. Demianenko was the captain of that side.
- No Hungarians included – they have their own space for their glory years elsewhere, and have had no players to threaten this squad since Florian Albert in the sixties.
- Viktor Onopko can play anywhere in the back four; in his prolific later years he has featured mainly as a sweeper.
- Savicevic would be a wild card substitute – which one would come on? Infuriating layabout or match-winning genius?
- Sinisa Mihailovic was not considered. We don't pick racists.

Manager: Boris Milutinovic

4-3-3

Lev Yashin (SU) (50s/60s)

V. Onopko (SU) (90s) W. Zmuda (Pol) (70s) M. Belodedici (Rom) (90s)

A. Demianenko (SU) (80s)

Zbigniew Boniek (Pol) (80s) Josef Masopust (Cze) (60s) Gheorghe Hagi (Rom) (90s)

Grzegorz Lato (Pol) (70s) Andrei Shevchenko (Ukr) (90s/00s) Hristo Stoichkov (Bul) (90s)

Subs: Ranat Dasaev (USSR) (80s) Vladislav Bigicevic (Ygv) (70s) Alexei Mihailichenko (Rus) (90s) Pavel Nedved (Cze) (90s/00s) Dejan Savicevic (Ygv) (90s)

Poland's winning goal against Brazil in the 1974 World Cup.

Edwards, Duncan
Manchester United, England

FROM THE MOMENT Duncan Edwards died in Munich, losing a desperate battle for life two weeks after seven team-mates had perished on the runway, his status as a footballing immortal was assured. Only 21 years of age when he died from his injuries, his achievements at the heart of the famous Busby Babes team were the pipe dreams of most players 15 years his senior. Wistful debates have continued for over 40 years as to what he might have achieved, but Sir Duncan Edwards with a World Cup winner's medal and a century of England caps is a realistic, some might say even conservative, projection.

Edwards was earmarked for stardom at an early age, excelling for England's under-14s and creating a queue for his signature that saw the wily Matt Busby at its head. He was equally at home at centre-half or half-back but his physique, strength and authority (unprecedented in a teenager) meant he could operate pretty much wherever Busby wanted him to. All deaths at Munich were individual tragedies of equal measure, but Edwards' loss was the biggest for English football.

- 1953. Edwards made his professional debut for Manchester United aged only 16 years 185 days.
- 1955. Became England's youngest debutant of the century at 18 years 183 days. Scotland are trounced 7-2.
- He played for England at five different levels.
- He won two league titles before his 21st birthday.
- Had he lived, Edwards would now be a pensioner, having reached 65 in October 2001.

VITAL STATISTICS

Place of Birth:	Dudley, England	
Date of Birth:	1 October 1936	**Died:** 21 February 1958
Caps:	18 (England)	**Goals (International):** 5
Clubs:	Manchester United	
Appearances:	Club (League): 175	
Goals:	Club (League): 21	
Trophies:	LT 1956, 1957	

LEGEND RATING

Achievement	7.0
Skill	8.0
Teamwork	9.0
Passion	9.0
Personality	7.0
TOTAL	**40.0**

Eleven Lions in their Shirts
The England Dream Team

WE WERE TEMPTED BY 3-5-2 due to lack of great full-backs, but that would not be England, so 4-4-2 it is. Unfortunately, this means we had to omit one of three great centre-halves, the much-capped Billy Wright. Leaving out Moore was unthinkable, and the monolithic Duncan Edwards adds much-needed strength and attacking power. Eddie Hapgood switches to the right – he was the best of the pre-war, old-fashioned full-backs. Roger Byrne, who like Edwards had his life tragically cut short by the Munich air crash, gets in on the left ahead of Terry Cooper and Stuart Pearce. Finney wins our version of the ever-raging debate and gets in ahead of Sir Stanley for his greater all-round contribution and for his goal-scoring.

Beckham gives defences a different problem on the other side, and adds his set-piece flair. Meanwhile, Robson's tackling and stamina allow Charlton to push behind the front two. We opted for the big man/quick man combination up front, with Lineker shading Greaves and Jackie Milburn in the quick-man stakes. Dean was a towering presence, creating as well as scoring goals with his aerial power. But then, to be fair, so would Drake, Lawton, Lofthouse or Tommy Taylor. Decisions, decisions....

☞ We would like to point out that we mean Billy Wright, as opposed to Mark Wright or, indeed, Ian Wright playing out of position.

☞ The assumption that all players are operating at the peak of their career means only one of Bryan Robson's legs is currently broken.

👍 Dean would need to be briefed on law-changes as smacking the keeper into the net is simply not done any more, chaps!

☞ Alf Ramsey would only be given the job if he signed a contract agreeing to play wingers.

👍 Lineker would take the penalties, as Le Tissier didn't make the 16, and Beckham would be spoilt for choice over who to pick out from free-kicks.

Manager: Alf Ramsey

4-4-2

Gordon Banks (60s)

Eddie Hapgood (30s)   Duncan Edwards (50s)
Bobby Moore (C) (60s)   Roger Byrne (50s)

David Beckham (90s)   Bobby Charlton (60s)
Bryan Robson (80s)   Tom Finney (50s)

Gary Lineker (80s/90s)   Dixie Dean (20s/30s)

Subs: Peter Shilton (G) (70s/80s) Billy Wright (D) (50s) Alan Shearer (F) (90s) Stanley Matthews (W) (40s/50s) Jimmy Greaves (F) (60s)

Emerald Eleven
The Republic of Ireland Dream Team

MANY PUNDITS have criticised Jack Charlton's Irish team for being negative and unimaginative, and point out that their achievements in the World Cup were, despite the hype, relatively modest. Fair enough, but they would do well to remember that until Charlton took over and started picking players with Irish grannies, the Republic had been swimming with the minnows. Suddenly a team emerged. Celtic goalkeeper Packy Bonner, Lawrenson, O'Leary, Brady and Stapleton were the core of the first side while Manchester United's long-serving full-back Dennis Irwin, Staunton, McGrath, Keane and Quinn took them into another decade and, some would say, on to another level. In our team Johnny Carey is the sole representative of the old guard.

This side would do what Irish sides do best – scrap for everything and hope that their limited forwards (Stapleton was hard-working and intelligent, but not world class) made the most of the chances. Bonner became a top goalkeeper, and O'Leary and Lawrenson would be a genuine barrier, especially with McGrath in front of them. The midfield is superb, three world-class players with complimentary styles, and there are few better wingers in the game now than Duff.

- The biggest challenge would be keeping Keane and Giles on the pitch – two great players, neither afraid of putting the boot in.
- Charlton could bring out the best in players of limited ability, Mick McCarthy and Tony Cascarino being good examples.
- The back-up midfield is top-quality, too. Sheedy was a talented player who achieved less than he should have and Heighway held down a place in a fantastic Liverpool team.
- The redoubtable Mick McCarthy would be employed as a coach – against expectations he has maintained the Republic's record of qualifying for tournaments from tough groups.
- No place for John Aldridge – prolific at club level, consistently off target for his country.

Managers: Jack Charlton with Mick McCarthy

4-1-4-1

Packy Bonner (80s/90s)

Johnny Carey (50s) Mark Lawrenson (80s) David O'Leary (80s) Dennis Irwin (90s)

Paul McGrath (C) (80s/90s)

Damian Duff (00s) Johnny Giles (60s/70s) Roy Keane (90s) Liam Brady (70s/80s)

Frank Stapleton (70s)

Subs: Jim McDonagh (G) (70s) Steve Staunton (D) (90s)
Kevin Sheedy (M) (80s) Steve Heighway (M) (70s) Niall Quinn (F) (90s)

England's Dreaming
England, 2006?

THERE ARE MANY different opinions as to why England has unearthed a rich seam of young footballing talent at the start of the twenty-first century. The FA will probably take the praise; but the main reason is certainly not the new academy system (it will be another decade before the fruits of that tree ripen).

Perhaps the proliferation of the much-criticised foreign legion has forced the young English players to work that much harder to cement their place and prove themselves? When you have to fight for your club place with a seasoned international, it does tend to concentrate the mind.

With one or two exceptions, the current generation of England players are much of an age. The manager's challenge will be to incorporate changes as seamlessly as possible, and not spend too long trying players who are palpably short of the requisite attitude or ability.

With proper encouragement for these young players – the removal of David Platt as U-21 manager was a good move – there is some optimism for believing that England can win one of the major international trophies during this decade. With Wayne Rooney in the side, who knows what could happen…

☞ Other possibles: Robert Green (Norwich, b. 1980), Nicky Hunt (Bolton, b. 1983), Wes Brown (Man Utd, b. 1979), Jonathan Woodgate (Real Madrid, b. 1980), Wayne Bridge (Chelsea, b. 1983), Darren Ambrose (Newcastle, b. 1984); Frank Lampard (Chelsea, b. 1979), James Milner (Leeds, b. 1986), Jermaine Pennant (Leeds Utd, b. 1983), Dean Ashton (Crewe, b. 1983), Ian Westlake (Ipswich, b. 1983), Alan Smith (Man Utd, b. 1979). Ledley King (Tottenham, b. 1980)

☞ Some omissions: Michael Owen (will his body survive until 2006?), Scott Parker & Joe Cole (Chelsea reserves…), Jermaine Jenas & Kieron Dyer (grow up), Darius Vassell (will be in Div. 1 by 2006), Zat Knight (other centre-halves who will be better than him).

Manager: Sven-Goran Eriksson
(if our media hasn't driven him away)

4-4-2 (clubs as of Dec 2004)

Chris Kirkland (Liverpool, b. 1981)

Glen Johnson (Chelsea, b. 1984)   Rio Ferdinand (Man Utd, b. 1978)
John Terry (Chelsea, b. 1980)   Ashley Cole (Arsenal, b. 1980)

David Bentley (Arsenal, b. 1984)   David Beckham (Real Madrid, b. 1975)
Steven Gerrard (Liverpool, b. 1980)   Lee Holmes (Derby, b. 1987)

Wayne Rooney (Man Utd, b. 1985)   Jermaine Defoe (Tottenham, b. 1984)

Eriksson, Sven-Goran
IFK Gothenburg, Benfica, Lazio, England

UNASSUMING, softly spoken and seemingly dispassionate, Sven-Goran Eriksson has many qualities you would not expect to find in a football manager. He also possesses plenty of common sense, which appears to have stood him in good stead.

An unremarkable playing career was ended early by a knee injury; he then commenced a coaching career that has taken in a number of the biggest clubs in Europe and seen him collect an impressive list of national titles plus a smattering of European trophies.

Then the bombshell: for the first time in history, England appoint a foreigner as manager of the national team! Despite opposition from the sceptics – not all of them motivated by moronic nationalism – Eriksson quickly settled into his new role. Recognising the talent available to him Eriksson set about organising his players and, with improved tactics and discipline, virtually the same squad that lost at home to Germany in a World Cup qualifier under Kevin Keegan tore the Germans apart in the reverse fixture in Munich, winning 5-1 and sending a minor tremor through European football.

- A five-year spell at Sampdoria was something of a mid-career hiccup for Eriksson, as he failed to galvanise the unfashionable side.
- Eriksson seems to have blunted the venom of the English tabloids by appearing to be unaware of their supposed influence and power. He simply pretends they aren't there.
- He cleverly installed Beckham as regular England captain and saw the player rise to spectacular new heights.
- Eriksson's appointment appears to have coincided with a decline in the influence of Howard Wilkinson on the England scene. Attaboy Sven!

VITAL STATISTICS

Place of Birth:	Torsby, Sweden
Date of Birth:	5 February 1948 **Died:** n/a
Caps:	0 **Goals (International):** 0
Clubs:	As Player: KB Karlskoga; As Manager: Degerfors IF, IFK Göteburg, Benfica, AS Roma, Fiorentina AC, Sampdoria, Lazio, England national side
Trophies:	SA 2000; SLT 1981; PLT 1983, 1984, 1991; UEFAC 1982; CWC 1999; ESC 1999

LEGEND RATING	
Achievement	8
Tactical Awareness	9
Motivation	8
Team Selection/Transfers	8
Personality	7
TOTAL	**40**

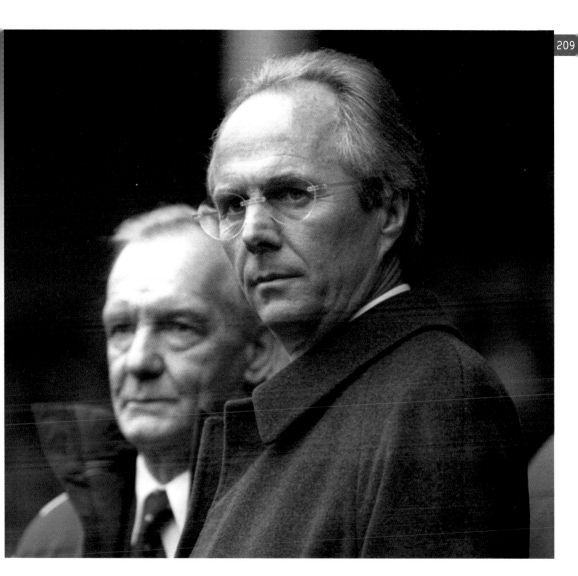

Eusébio
Benfica, Portugal

MOZAMBIQUE-BORN EUSÉBIO da Silva Ferreira was the first great African player and remains the continent's most famous footballing ambassador. His ability to run past players at pace, and hit fierce shots at speed, helped him maintain a goalscoring record so impressive that comparisons with Pelé are not inappropriate.

At Benfica, where he played most of his career, his goals tally was an unrivalled 316 from 294 games, and he appeared in four European Cup finals for the Lisbon club (sadly, wining only one).

English audiences warmed to Eusébio, having adopted him during the 1966 World Cup where, after North Korea had taken a 3-0 lead in the quarter-final, he hauled his side back into the game, scoring four as Portugal ran out 5-3 winners. The semi-final against England, where his duel with Nobby Stiles was the tournament's highlight, saw him in the role of gallant loser. His tears at the end of that Wembley clash were repeated at the same stadium two years later when Benfica lost out to Matt Busby's Man United in the European Cup final, a match in which the 'Black Panther' had a chance to give his team the lead in the dying moments but shot straight at United's Alex Stepney. Despite his disappointment Eusébio turned to shake hands with Stepney and applaud the save.

- After a spell in the NASL, Eusébio retired after a serious knee injury, aged only 32.
- He was European Footballer of the Year in 1965.
- Benfica cheekily snatched the young Eusébio from rivals Sporting Lisbon; he had begun his career with Sporting's nursery club.
- He was top scorer in Europe twice (1968 and 1973), and also at the 1966 World Cup, with nine.
- A statue at Benfica's Estadio da Luz is a fitting tribute to a club and a nation's greatest footballer.

VITAL STATISTICS

Place of Birth:	Lourenco-Marques (now Maputo), Mozambique
Date of Birth:	25 January 1942 **Died:** n/a
Caps:	64 (Portugal) **Goals (International):** 41
Clubs:	Sporting Club of Lourenco-Marques, Benfica, Monterrey, Boston Minutemen, Toronto, Metros-Croatia, Las Vegas Quicksilver
Appearances:	Club (League for Benfica): 294
Goals:	Club (League for Benfica): 316
Trophies:	PLT 1961, 1963, 1964, 1965, 1967, 1968, 1969, 1971, 1972, 1973, 1974; EC 1962

Achievement	8.0
Skill	10.0
Teamwork	8.0
Passion	9.0
Personality	7.0
TOTAL	**42.0**

LEGEND RATING

FA Cup
The Blue Riband

ON 16 OCTOBER 1871, 13 teams entered a knockout competition dreamt up by FA secretary Charles Alcock. It thrives today with the same name, the Football Association Challenge Cup.

Little did Alcock know what he had started. The first final was played in front of 2,000 spectators at the Kennington Oval. As the competition grew in stature, so did the venues, until the twin towers of the newly built Wembley became the permanent home for finalists in 1923. Even then, the Cup's popularity was underestimated; the first final was not all-ticket and over 200,000 turned up, leaving a white horse called Billy to shepherd spectators off the pitch.

The Graf Zeppelin's visit in 1930 … Bert Trautmann massaging his broken neck in 1956 … Jim Montgomery's miraculous save for Sunderland in 1973 … the final has produced memories that have endured through generations, passed on from father to son. Once it was the dream of every minnow to reach the final. That has long passed but the Cup's value to the lesser lights should not be underestimated; one tie against a top division club can bring more revenue than they would usually amass in an entire season. Other competitions come and go, but the oldest and best will always be known, quite simply, as The Cup. And long may it continue.

☞ Ten venues have staged the FA Cup final. In 1920 the final was scheduled for Stamford Bridge. Chelsea were knocked out in the semi by Aston Villa, saving the FA from the potentially embarrassing situation of having to rewrite their rule book (the final is supposed to be played on a neutral ground).

☝ The best final? It has got to be 1953 when, inspired by Stanley Matthews, Blackpool recovered from 3-1 down to win in the last minute.

☞ There have been four trophies. The first cost £20 to make but was stolen in 1895. The present design was created for the 1911 final by Italian silversmiths in Bradford, Messrs Fattorini and Sons. Appropriately, Bradford were its first winners.

'The Crazy Gang have beaten the Culture Club.'

John Motson describing Wimbledon's surprise victory over Liverpool in the 1988 final

Fashion Victims, Part 1
Hair

THE CATEGORY WINNERS IN THE 'SILLIEST HAIR IN FOOTBALL' AWARDS ARE AS FOLLOWS:

CATEGORY	GOLD	SILVER	BRONZE
Mullet	Brian Kilcline	Kevin Keegan	Chris Waddle
Comb-Over	Ralph Coates	Sir Bobby Charlton	Uwe Seeler
Perm	Tommy Caton	Bob Latchford	Terry McDermott
Dreadlocks	Jason Lee	Henrik Larsson	Tony Daley
Ponytail	Roberto Baggio	David Seaman	Darren Peacock
Beard	Trevor Hockey (aka Chewbacca)	Abel Xavier	Alexei Lalas
Dyed	Taribo West	Ian Wright	Romania, 2000
Outrageous	Abel Xavier	Carlos Valderrama	Alexei Lalas
Girlie	Charlie George	Barry Venison	Mario Kempes
AND THE WINNER IS:	**Abel Xavier**	**Jason Lee**	**Alexei Lalas**

☞ Xavier scores in two categories: outrageous hair and silly beard. He could easily have featured in dyed. Overall, a worthy winner.

☞ Jason Lee appeared confused and hurt when his coiffured 'pineapple' was met with derision from the terraces. His manager saw fit to defend him against a barrage of abuse from comedy duo Baddiel & Skinner, but that hair was indefensible.

☞ The 1970s was a shocking decade for haircuts in football. Starting with Charlie George looking like a big girl's blouse, the decade moved into bubble perms, ending with the mullet.

☞ The influence of style icons like Gullit and Batistuta has spawned a generation of wannabees. White men in dreads and sweaty Englishmen attempting windswept Latin locks. Yeeuch!

KEY

Mullet: grievous 1970s rear overhang.
Comb-over: bald and in denial.
Perm: deliberate attempt to look like a show dog.
Dreadlocks: cool on Ruud, but pineapples were never in.
Ponytail: old and in denial.
Beard: aerodynamically unsound, visually absurd.
Dyed: last resort of the immature.
Outrageous: says it all.
Girlie: 'La la la, superstar, he looks like a woman and he wears a bra.'

Fashion Victims, Part 2
Silly Strips

IT WAS EASIER in the old days. Back then it was safe to rally your team with cries of 'Come on you blues/reds/whites.' Now it's not so simple. 'Come on you azures with the sienna trim, epaulettes and unfeasibly large logo,' just doesn't have the same ring to it does it? In the last 25 years, football kits have gone from simple, functional designs to the sort of garish tat normally peddled by the likes of Zandra Rhodes. The decline started in the late 1970s when manufacturers' logos joined club badges as a staple decoration on your standard jersey; these grew from discreet chest emblems to covering entire sleeves. Once clubs realised that fans would line up like sheep to part with £50 ever other year for a shirt with a minutely modified collar, filthy lucre instantly kicked tradition into touch. Nowadays, a successful performance in the club shop is more important than a Cup run. Manchester United have become the world's richest club by selling not just strips, but lampshades, duvet covers and credit cards. Traditionalists and parents may moan, but the biggest culprits are not the clubs but the fans. There is no law that states we have to buy a replica shirt, no one puts a gun to our heads. Guns to heads? Now there's an idea. Anyone know the way to Umbro's design department?

- Worst away-kit offenders? Chelsea. Jade green was offensive enough, while the 'tangerine and graphite' efforts in the mid-1990s were enough to trigger epilepsy.
- Manchester United famously changed their kit at half-time following a disastrous 45 minutes at the Dell. Alex Ferguson claimed their new grey strip made the players difficult to see.
- The pioneers of the silly strip were Coventry, who as early as the 1970s appeared in a chocolate-brown away kit.
- Shiny kits in the 1980s were a big mistake. The sight of Jan Molby and Paul Stewart squeezing their ample torsos into them rendered pre-match pies even more indigestible.

'For those of you watching in black and white, Spurs are the team in yellow.'

John Motson describes Tottenham's away strip

Fat Lady Forgets to Show
Spain 4 Yugoslavia 3, 2000

SPAIN DO NOT HAVE an impressive record at major finals, and at Euro 2000 they looked destined for yet another ignominious first-round exit. In their final group match they needed to beat Yugoslavia to ensure qualification for the second round, while their opponents required only a draw. After half an hour of frantic activity the first goal of the match finally arrived, Savo Milosevic bulleting a header past Canizares. But Yugoslavia could not hold their lead. Before half-time Raul, who had uncharacteristically spurned several chances of his own, set up Alfonso to equalise. Yugoslav substitute Govedarica restored their lead shortly after half-time, but again their lead was short-lived, Munitis levelling for Spain just two minutes later. It was breathless stuff. Spain pounded the Yugoslavs, but left themselves open to the counter-attack, and were punished by Komljenovic with just 15 minutes left. So to the finale. Deep into injury time Abelardo was baulked in the box, and Mendieta kept his head with the penalty to draw Spain level at 3-3. Amazingly, there was still time for more. With the Yugoslavia fans whistling desperately for the ref to blow for full-time Alfonso, left unmarked by 10-man Yugoslavia (Jokanovic was sent off), waltzed through to score the winner. Cue chaos. A potential non-event had turned into drama of the highest order.

- The drama didn't end with the final whistle; the Yugoslavs dejection turned to joy as they discovered Slovenia had held Norway, and they too were through to the quarter-finals.
- This was Yugoslavia's second extraordinary game. In their opener against Slovenia they came from 3-0 down to draw 3-3 – with 10 men!
- To Aston Villa supporters' disbelief, Savo Milosevic was Yugoslavia's tournament star, scoring five goals in four matches.
- Jokanovic's sending off against Spain made it three in three for Yugoslavia. In the previous encounter against Norway, Kezman was sent off a minute after coming on as a substitute. Mihailovic saw red in their opening match against Slovenia.

SCORERS   **Spain:** Alfonso (2), Munitis, Mendieta (pen)
             Yugoslavia: Milosevic, Govedarica, Kremljenovic
EVENT   Euro 2000 group stage, Bruges, 21 June 2000

SPAIN   (Man: Jose Antonio Camacho)
             1. Canizares 2. Salgado 3. Abelardo 4. Helguera 5. Sergi 6. Mendieta
             7. Paco 8. Fran 9. Guardiola 10. Alfonso 11. Raul
YUGOSLAVIA (Man: Vujadin Boskov)
             1. Kralj 2. Djorovic 3. Jokanovic 4. Djukic 5. Jugovic 6. Mijatovic
             7. Milosevic 8. Stojkovic 9. Mihailovic 10. Komljenovic 11. Drulovic

Fergie's Generation
Manchester United, 1990s

ROTATION HAS BEEN a key-word at Manchester United in the last decade. Not just Alex Ferguson's much publicised policy of resting players, but also his impeccable judgement in deciding when to bring players into Old Trafford and, just as crucially, when to let them go. Ferguson has recognised that to continue to compete in every tournament, every season, the team must evolve and improve.

Jaap Stam was a cornerstone of the team that won the Treble in 1999, but a loss of form saw him moved on without the blink of an eye. Andrei Kanchelskis and Andy Cole were also offloaded while still first-team players. The genius of Cantona was irreplaceable, but after a fallow season, Teddy Sheringham began to exert a similar, talismanic influence. Others like Bruce, Hughes, McClair and Irwin were allowed to grow old with dignity at the club, and leave with full honours.

Most of the recent changes have taken place in the defence and forward line. The midfield of Beckham, Scholes, Keane and Giggs, with Butt in support remained the same for a few seasons, and was the heart of United's success. Beckham's departure and Keane's decline leave Ferguson with a problem that may signal a decline of sorts.

☞ Critics talk of luck in the European Cup final, but it's never over till it's over. And United were missing both Keane and Scholes....

👍 Andy Cole's improvement as a footballer under Ferguson and his coaches was remarkable, expunging memories of a disgruntled Cantona scowling as his partner conducted an oral examination of the latest gift horse.

👎 Others have taken a year or two to blossom at United, and the press are often too quick to question Ferguson's judgement. There have been very few dodgy signings at Manchester United in recent years.

👍 Many doubted the wisdom of retaining Roy Keane ahead of Paul Ince. Not now.

☞ The talent in the squad eventually covered Cantona's departure, but Schmeichel has never been replaced. Barthez has merely substituted presence with tomfoolery.

Manager: Alex Ferguson

Key Players
Peter Schmeichel (G) Gary Neville (D) Jaap Stam (D)
David Beckham (M) Paul Scholes (M) Roy Keane (M)
Ryan Giggs (W) Eric Cantona (F) Andy Cole (F)
Teddy Sheringham (F)

Trophies
LT 1993, 1994, 1996, 1997, 1999 FAC 1990, 1994, 1996, 1999
LC 1992 CWC 1991 EC 1999

Ferguson, Alex
Aberdeen, Manchester United, Scotland

RUTHLESS AS A PLAYER and driven as a manager, Alex Ferguson's record is one that only Bob Paisley can match. His background from the school of hard knocks in Govan served him well, requiring a commitment and self-discipline that he has always demanded, and received, from his players. Strange that such a professional started his footballing life with archetypal amateurs Queen's Park, but it was as Aberdeen manager that he really made his mark. For six years the Old Firm dominance was interrupted as three titles and a European trophy arrived at Pittodrie. Manchester United, desperate to escape Liverpool's shadow, broke the bank, and Aberdonian hearts, to get their man. Although his 18-year tenure is the Premiership's longest, the first trophy did not arrive for four years amid mutterings that the Midas touch had vanished.

In 1993 he landed United's first title for 26 years and their subsequent run of success ought to have made his depature unthinkable. Arsenal's recent rise and the near-legal spat in 2003–04 with United's major shareholder, J.P. McManus, over the stud rights of the racehorse Rock of Gibraltar threatened an acromonious departure. An uneasy truce was declared when Ferguson signed a rolling one-year contract. If he goes, it will be on his terms.

- A tearaway player, Ferguson was sent off seven times in the days when once was a rarity.
- 1978. St. Mirren sacked Ferguson for the only time in his career after 'unpardonable swearing at a lady on club premises'. The hair-drying technique was honed later.
- 1989. United fans called for Ferguson's head after a 5-1 defeat to local rivals City.
- 1999. Knighted following United's unique treble of League, FA Cup and European Cup.
- 2001. Won his seventh English league title to beat Bob Paisley's record.

VITAL STATISTICS

Place of Birth:	Glasgow, Scotland
Date of Birth:	31 December 1941 **Died:** n/a
Caps:	0 **Goals (International):** 0
Clubs:	As Player: Queens Park, St Johnstone, Dunfermline, Rangers, Falkirk, Ayr United; As Manager: East Stirling, St Mirren, Aberdeen, Scotland national side (as caretaker manager), Manchester United
Trophies:	SLT 1980, 1984–85; SFAC 1982–84, 1986; CWC 1983, 1991; FAC 1990, 1994, 1996, 2004; LC 1992; LT 1993, 1994, 1996, 1997, 1999–01, 2003; EC 1999

LEGEND RATING	
Achievement	10
Tactical Awareness	9
Motivation	10
Team Selection/Transfers	9
Personality	8
TOTAL	**46**

Fever Pitch
Football Writing

THERE HAVE ALWAYS BEEN good football books. Hunter Davies' *The Glory Game* (1972) and Eamon Dunphy's *Only A Game* (1976), are examples of superb tomes published pre-Nick Hornby. Yet these books were released almost apologetically by publishers, as if they could never truly bring themselves to believe that football supporters actually had the ability to read. Hornby changed all that. *Fever Pitch* (1992) redefined football publishing. People with no interest in the game read and – often to their great surprise – even enjoyed it, impressed by Hornby's passion and insight. This was no journalist recounting his views from the press box, no retired player explaining why a fat has-been wasn't picked for the Cup final. This was a true fan, a terrace sweat, living out the triumph and the torture of the national game. Inevitably, the accelerating bandwagon was leapt upon enthusiastically, with publishers falling over themselves to print the memoirs of every two-bob sports journalist they could get their hands on. Wanabe Hornby's were rife, and the world was inundated with entries for soccer's 'Pseuds' corner'.

☞ *The Glory Game* is Hunter Davies' account of a year behind the scenes at Tottenham. An early insight into professional football, it remains an absorbing read.

☞ Recent footballing biographies have been written with greater care and consideration in the light of Hornby's achievement. Alex Ferguson's autobiography, by Hugh McIlvanney, and Tony Adams' searching *Addicted*, were bestsellers.

☞ Lesser players produce fascinating insights too. Gary Nelson's *Left Foot Forward*, and Steve Claridge's *Tales From The Boot Camp* are fine examples of this sub-genre.

☞ Splenetic and acerbic, *Only A Game* is a journeyman footballer's exploration of the whys and wherefores of the game.

'A feminist colleague of mine literally refused to believe that I watched Arsenal, a disbelief that apparently had its roots in the fact that we once had a conversation about a feminist novel.'

Nick Hornby

FEVER
P*I*TCH

Nick Hornby

'Funny, wise and true'
RODDY DOYLE

Feyenoord
The Dream Team

FEYENOORD HAS THE BEST stadium ('de Kuip') and the most fanatical supporters in Holland. The club has the image of a hard-working team reflecting the working nature of Rotterdam, a major port city. The image is a cliché; Feyenoord has had its fair share of technically gifted players. The Feyenoord Dream Team is made up principally of die-hard Dutch players; together they won 470 national caps, many league titles and three European Cups. Eddy Pieters Graafland is the gentleman of the side. His stylish and efficient performance between the posts mirrored his invariably elegant coiffure. The defenders are a tough bunch grouped around the peerless Rinus Israel – centre-half and playmaker. The midfield is the strongest part of this Dream Team. Wim Jansen personalized the club motto, 'No words, just action'. Puck van Heel was for decades the record cap-winner for the Dutch national team. And above them all is Willem van Hanegem: simply sublime. The only overseas player is Swede Ove Kindvall: his winning goal in the European Cup final against Celtic sealed the club's finest moment.

☞ The winning goal of Ove Kindvall in the Europe Cup final against Celtic in 1970 was the reason for the novel 'The Dreamgoal', written by Peter Hopstaken.

☞ In the 1960s the top Dutch players were semi-professional. Pieters Graafland owned a sportshop, Rinus Israel a newsagents and Coen Moulijn a fashion boutique.

☞ Substitutes include Johan Cruyff and Ronald Koeman. Key players naturally (Cruyff is chosen as the best European Football player of the 20th century) but both played for Feyenoord in the final stage of their careers.

👍 Ernst Happel, a hero as a player for Austria in the 1950s, was the absolute boss, never yielding to star players or arrogant board members. A tactical genius, he invariably chose the right moment to tinker.

☞ Coen Moulijn is the most popular Feyenoord player of all time. He played 519 matches in the red, white and black.

Manager: Ernst Happel

4-3-3

Eddy Pieters Graafland (50s/60s)

Bennie Wijnstekers (70s/80s) Wim Rijsbergen (70s) Rinus Israel (C) (60s/70s)
Cor Veldhoen (60s)

Wim Jansen (60s/70s) Puck van Heel (20s/30s) Willem van Hanegem (60s – 80s)

Ruud Gullit (80s) Ove Kindval (60s/70s) Coen Moulijn (50s – 70s)

Subs: Ed de Goey (G) (90s) Ronald Koeman (D) (90s) Paul Bosvelt (M) (90s/00s)
Johan Cruyff (F) (80) Pierre van Hooijdonk (F) (00s)

FIFA
Bureaucrats and Balloons

IF THE MANDARINS of the British game had won the argument, football would still be played only in its own backyard and the Home Internationals would be the World Cup. Hats off to the French for attempting to broaden its appeal. The Federation Internationale de Football Association was formed in Paris on 21 May 1904. The original signatories were seven European nations, but within 10 years Africa and South America were also represented.

Its third president, Jules Rimet, took the concept of togetherness even further, laying the foundations for the first World Cup in 1930. On his retirement in 1954, FIFA boasted 85 members.

The advent of television coverage, especially of the World Cup Finals, helped spread the gospel even further and by the 1960s even insular Britain had acknowledged FIFA's influence, providing Stanley Rous in 1961 as its sixth president. As World Cup tournaments grew, so did FIFA's income. The startling increase in the value of television rights has seen it rise from a small association into a major corporation. From its beginnings with a backroom staff of 12, FIFA now employs over 120 in its role as the game's international powerbroker.

☞ FIFA has more members than the United Nations.

☞ The four UK nations, peeved at FIFA's growing influence, withdrew after the First World War. They returned only in 1946.

☞ Most African countries have joined FIFA more recently, but South Africa were its first non-European members, in 1909. They joined before any of the four British nations.

☞ FIFA operates as a private institution. It receives no government grants or subsidies.

☜ Increased power and money have brought the inevitable whiff of sleaze. President Joao Havelange's retirement in 1998 was tainted by allegations of corruption.

'People are always kicking, old or young. Even an unborn child is kicking.'

Sepp Blatter, FIFA secretary-general, wobbles a few chins in 1990

Figo Stands Tall
Portugal 2 Holland 1

INSPIRATION FINALLY ARRIVED for Luis Figo. England's customary failure in a penalty shoot-out had reprieved a man who had departed the quarter-final sullen and substituted. This was a tournament dominated by big-name underachievement, mention of which had hitherto merited the Portuguese captain's inclusion.

Figo's was by turns a performance of high-octane wing-play and midfield dominance. His was the corner from which a scandalously unmarked Ronaldo headed Portugal in front after 26 minutes. Figo could have sealed the game minutes before half-time, had a curling drive, following an outrageous piece of footwork, not struck the opposite post with Van der Sar a nervous spectator.

A fluctuating match saw Portugal's winner arrive from nowhere. Ronaldo outwitted the Dutch defence with a flat delivery to Maniche, loitering 25 yards from goal. Advancing towards the left edge of the area, his swerving missile of a shot sped into the far top corner.

Portugal earned their victory by staying positive, refusing to abandon their game plan and not retreating to their own penalty area. A place in their first major final had been hard-fought and well won.

☞ This was Figo's 109th and penultimate senior cap. He had already announced his international retirement.

✍ Figo's highlight: a 60-yard run in the 18th minute that set up a chance for Ronaldo. It was but one of four, dazzling bursts that terrorised the Dutch in the first half.

☝ Turning point no. 1: two minutes after Ronaldo's opening goal, an unmarked Overmars volleys over from eight yards.

☞ Turning point no. 2: a marginal but correct offside flag cancels out Van Nistelrooy's precise, 16-yard finish. Typically, Overmars is booked for dissent.

☞ Lasting moment: the sight of Van Nistelrooy congratulating and exchanging shirts with Ronaldo, his Manchester United team-mate.

SCORERS	**Portugal:** Ronaldo, Maniche
	Holland: Andrade (og)
EVENT	Euro 2004, first semi-final, 30 June 2004
PORTUGAL	(Man: Luiz Felipe Scolari)
	1. Ricardo 2. Miguel 3. Andrade 4. Carvalho 5. Nuno Valente 6. Maniche (Couto)
	7. Costinha 8. Figo 9. Deco 10. Ronaldo (Petit) 11. Pauleta (Nuno Gomes)
HOLLAND	(Man: Dick Advocaat)
	1. Van Der Sar 2. Reiziger 3. Stam 4. Bouma (Van Der Vaart) 5. Van Bronckhorst
	6. Cocu 7. Seedorf 8. Davids 9. Overmars (Makaay) 10. Van Nistelrooy
	11. Robben (Van Hooijdonk)

Figo, Luis
Barcelona, Real Madrid, Portugal

IN AN ERA when many top European footballers are fêted, paid king's ransoms and live life in a constant spotlight, some remain out in front of the chasing group. Luis Figo is one such player; no one stands taller in world football today. For all football's changes, it is comforting to find that Figo's origins and rise strike a familiar chord. Plucked from street football in a working-class district of Lisbon, he joined local club Sporting at 11, graduating from schoolboy to captain of the first team.

Figo is the complete midfielder, with a strong tackle, deft touch and deadly shot, and yet he failed to realise his full potential until being converted to a right winger by Johan Cruyff. Unlike some of Cruyff's tactical experiments it proved to be a masterstroke, though in truth such an embodiment of 'Total Football' could probably play anywhere. Figo's world-record move to Real Madrid later saw him teamed with his only contemporary peer, Zinedine Zidane – a midfield partnership to excite everyone except possibly Catalans and Real's bank manager. At international level, he is the key reason for Portugal's rise from also-rans to serious world contenders (and back again at the 2002 World Cup).

- He made his first-team debut for Sporting Lisbon at the age of 16.
- 1995/96. Banned from playing in Italy for two years after signing holding contracts with both Parma and Juventus. Serie A's loss was Barcelona's gain.
- Euro 2000. Figo was the Player of the Tournament but Portugal lost in the semi-finals.
- He was European Footballer of the Year 2000 and World Footballer of the Year 2001.
- 2000. Sold by Barcelona to deadliest rivals Real Madrid for £40 m, a then world record. Barcelona's profit was £38.6 m!
- February 2004. 'Football for me does not finish at Real Madrid.' He's obviously not planning full retirement just yet…

VITAL STATISTICS

Place of Birth:	Lisbon, Portugal
Date of Birth:	4 November 1972 **Died:** n/a
Caps:	107 (Portugal) **Goals (International):** 31
Clubs:	Sporting Lisbon, Barcelona, Real Madrid
Appearances:	Club (Spanish League): 392
Goals:	Club (Spanish League): 85
Trophies:	PLA 1998, 1999, 2001; CWC 1997; EC 2002

Achievement	7.0
Skill	9.0
Teamwork	9.0
Passion	9.0
Personality	6.0
TOTAL	**40.0**

LEGEND RATING

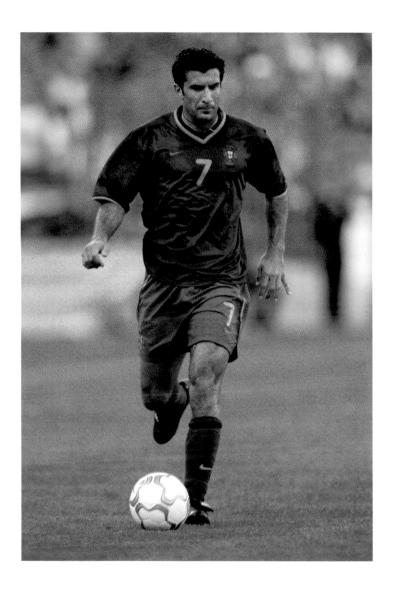

Finney, Tom
Preston North End, England

'TOM FINNEY WOULD HAVE been great in any team, in any match and in any age … even if he had been wearing an overcoat.' So said Bill Shankly. Speculation as to how the great players of the 1940s and 1950s would have fared in the modern game is a favourite subject of bar-room, but it would take a brave man to dispute Shankly's assessment of his former Preston team-mate. There is no doubt that Finney's dribbling ability was the equal of his contemporary, Stanley Matthews, and many have argued that his reading of the game, and his shooting, were far superior. Whether he was better than Matthews will always be a matter of opinion.

After the war, Finney became the star of a great England side. His performances in a 10-0 demolition of Portugal and 4-0 thrashing of reigning World Champions Italy, were highlights of his early career. He continued playing for England until the age of 36, and his 30 goals for his country remained a record for many years. The maximum wage ruling meant Finney never earned the financial rewards his talents probably merited. It also tied him to Preston, which meant his medal collection was nothing to write home about either.

- Aged 40, Finney made a belated appearance in Europe. At the invitation of George Eastham he played for Irish club Distillery against Benfica in 1963. Distillery emerged with a heroic 3-3 draw.
- He was named Football Writers' Player of the Year in 1954 and 1957, the first player to win the award twice.
- Finney received an OBE in 1961 and a belated knighthood in 1999.
- Like Stanley Matthews, he was never booked in his career.
- Finney blew his one chance to win the FA Cup, having an uncharacteristically poor game in the 1954 final. North End lost 3-2.

VITAL STATISTICS

Place of Birth:	Preston, England		
Date of Birth:	5 April 1922	**Died:** n/a	
Caps:	76 (England)	**Goals (International):** 30	
Clubs:	Preston North End		
Appearances:	Club (League): 433		
Goals:	Club (League): 187		
Trophies:	None		

Achievement	6.0
Skill	10.0
Teamwork	9.0
Passion	8.0
Personality	7.0
TOTAL	**40.0**

LEGEND RATING

Fists and Fury, Part 1
Racing Club 1 Celtic 0, 1968

THE BATTLES OF BERNE AND SANTIAGO may give it a run for its money, but all things considered this was probably the dirtiest game ever. It was an ill-advised match to begin with. The champions of Europe and South America had already battled it out (often literally) to a 2-2 stalemate over two legs, so setting up a final, decisive fixture was inviting trouble. After the Argentines had conducted a cynical campaign of thuggery in the first two matches, particularly against their tormentor Jimmy Johnstone, there were several outstanding scores to be settled. A neutral referee was appointed to officiate, probably in the hope that this would ease tensions. It didn't.

While the Argentines must shoulder most of the responsibility for setting the tone, it's fair to say that Celtic were no shrinking violets. Once Jock Stein's team snapped, the game developed into a free-for-all punctuated by occasional moments of football. Rulli's sending off in the 37th minute inspired a brawl bringing two more dismissals and the intervention of local riot police. Johnstone was the fourth player to go. Pushed beyond endurance, a flailing elbow saw him depart to the disappointment of the locals. The referee's humiliation was complete in the final minute, when Bertie Auld ignored his dismissal and completed the game. Oh, the score? Racing won 1-0.

- Those five red cards: Rulli, Basile, Lennox, Johnstone, Auld.
- Celtic keeper Ronnie Simpson was felled by a bottle in the pre-match warm up before the second leg in Buenos Aires. He was led from the field bleeding and replaced by John Fallon.
- Under modern rules, a third game would never have taken place. Although they lost the second game 2-1, Celtic would have taken the trophy on away goals.
- Having qualified as Argentine champions, Racing Club failed to win another title for 35 years, finally triumphing in 2001. Celtic's record in the same period was 16 league wins.
- Celtic won the first game 1-0 at Hampden Park in front of 103,000 with a Billy McNeill goal.

SCORERS	**Racing Club:** Cardenas
EVENT	World Club Championship Final play-off.
	Estadio Centenario, Montevideo, Uruguay, 5 November 1967
RACING	(Man: Juan José Pizzuti)
	1. Cejas 2. Perfumo 3. Chabay 4. Martin 5. Rulli 6 Basile 7. Cardoso
	8. Maschio 9. Cardenas 10. Rodriguez 11. Raffo
CELTIC	(Man: Jock Stein)
	1. Fallon 2. Craig 3. Gemmell 4. Murdoch 5. McNeill 6. Clark 7. Johnstone
	8. Lennox 9. Wallace 10. Auld 11. Hughes

Fists and Fury, Part 2
Italy 1 Argentina 1, 1990

FOR HOSTS buoyed by fervent and total support, this was a bitter pill to swallow. Italy's progress had been a procession, a series of national celebrations in the wake of seemingly inexorable progress. Their awakening could not have been ruder.

Argentina didn't quite tie their victims to railway tracks while twirling their moustaches, but they played the part of tournament villains to the full. Cynical, defensive and dirty, they set out to spoil Italy from the outset. In fairness, dampening a fanatical home crowd is a legitimate tactic, but it looked to have backfired when the irrepressible Schillachi shot the home team into a 17th minute lead. Even then, Argentina's tactics remained far from cavalier. They were saved by the honed striking instincts of Caniggia, who converted their one genuine opening mid-way through the second-half.

The goal was a cue for Argentina to retreat back into their shell, and the loss of Ricardo Giusti, sent off in extra-time, only hardened their defensive attitude. The penalty shoot-out came as a merciful relief. Both teams began the shoot-out in composed mood, with the first six attempts all finding their target. But the weight of expectation proved too much for the Italians, notably Donadoni and Serena who both cracked under the strain. A nation shared their grief.

☞ Penalty shoot-out: Italy; Baresi, Baggio, De Agostini, Donadoni (missed). Serena (missed). Argentina; Serrizuela, Burruchaga, Olarticoechea, Maradona.

🖑 At the ground where he had been such a favourite for Napoli Maradona's winning penalty was not well received. After the match Italians stoned his house.

🖑 Argentina were officially the dirtiest team of the tournament. They conceded 152 fouls, an average of one every four minutes. Four of their players missed the final through suspension.

🖑 To the host nation's relief, Argentina were beaten 1-0 by Germany in the final. Two boorish and unattractive teams served up the World Cup's worst-ever final.

SCORERS	**Italy:** Schillachi
	Argentina: Caniggia
EVENT	World Cup semi-final, Napoli, 3 July 1990
ITALY	(Man: Azeglio Vicini)
	1. Zenga 2. Baresi 3. Bergomi 4. De Agostini 5. Ferri 6. Maldini
	7. Donadoni 8. De Napoli 9. Giannini 10. Vialli 11. Schillachi
ARGENTINA	(Man: Carlos Bilardo)
	1. Goycoechea 2. Ruggeri 3. Simon 4. Olarticoechea 5. Serrizuela 6. Giusti
	7. Burruchaga 8. Basualdo 9. Calderon 10. Caniggia 11. Maradona

Five Times Champions!
Real Madrid 7 Eintracht Frankfurt 3, 1960

IT WAS A TREAT for the fans in Glasgow and is widely touted as the finest-ever display by a club side. Frankfurt, physical and formidable, arrived to challenge the mighty Real. Gone for Real were the smooth skills of Kopa and Rial, but they still had the two giants Puskas and Di Stefano who, even if the rest of the team were misfiring, could usually be relied upon to produce something special. At 1-0 down after 20 minutes the Spanish team began to find their rhythm, and soon it was clear that both Madrid's great players were on top form – which was just as well because Santamaria and his defence were being made to look ponderous by the quick German forwards.

By half-time Di Stefano had scored twice and Puskas once. Puskas completed a hat-trick before the hour to make it 5-1, and then two more goals for each side in a breathless four-minute spell completed a fine night's entertainment. It was to be the last of Real Madrid's run of five consecutive European Cup trophies. What a way to end an era.

☞ Some claim Frankfurt were poor opposition, but Rangers probably wouldn't agree; in the semi-finals they went down to them 12-4 on aggregate.

☞ It was to be 14 years before another German team reached the final, Bayern Munich winning the first of their three consecutive victories in 1974.

☞ The Germans were also criticised for their tactics, but surely the only way to beat Real was to attack their vulnerable defence; it was hugely optimistic to hope for a clean sheet against that forward line.

✍ While they never attained this level again, Real reached three further finals in the 1960s, winning in 1966.

SCORERS	**Real Madrid:** Di Stefano 3, Puskas 4
	Eintracht Frankfurt: Kress, Stein 2
EVENT	European Cup Final, Hampden Park, Glasgow, 18 May 1960, a crowd of 134,000!
REAL	(Man: Miguel Munoz)
	1. Dominguez 2. Marquitos 3. Pachin 4. Vidal 5. Santamaria 6. Zarraga 7. Canario 8. Del Sol 9. Di Stefano 10. Puskas 11. Gento
FRANKFURT	(Man: Paul Osswald)
	1. Loy 2. Lutz 3. Hofer 4. Weilbacher 5. Eigenbrodt 6. Stinka 7. Kress 8. Lindner 9. Stein 10. Pfaff 11. Meier

Flair and Failure
The Demise of the Gifted in the 1970s

THE 1970s, an otherwise dour period for English football, was enlivened by a handful of rebellious and talented individuals. They never seemed to feature much in the England set-up – perhaps that was why England were so poor – because Ramsey and Revie were mistrustful of their maverick talents.

Frank Worthington (eight caps), the strutting Elvis dress-a-like, won most of his caps under Joe Mercer. The conceited but gifted Alan Hudson (two caps) played two matches under Revie (both wins) and was discarded. Stan Bowles (five caps), a god at Loftus Road, was barely an apostle for England, much like his predecessor Rodney Marsh (eight caps). The most capped of the 1970s entertainers was Tony Currie (17 caps), but his international career was spread over seven years. All these players, gifted as they were, invited criticism over their attitude. Hudson's career declined early, and Marsh always promised more than he delivered. By contrast, Bowles and Worthington, for all their flamboyance and apparent nonchalance, were fit and diligent players, with Worthington playing league football into his late 30s.

- Bowles scored 11 goals in QPR's UEFA Cup campaign in 1976/77, playing brilliantly throughout the tournament. Three years later he walked out on Brian Clough and Nottingham Forest, and became a forgotten man.
- Hudson's first cap was against World Cup holders West Germany in 1975. He orchestrated a 2-0 win, showing awesome confidence for a debutant. A 5-0 win over Cyprus followed, and then oblivion.
- Asked which opponent he most feared, Worthington's answer was: 'My wife.' His autobiography was entitled *One Hump Or Two*. Frank was an entertaining footballer with a host of clubs, and remains an idol at Huddersfield, Leicester and Bolton.

'I never seem to miss England quite enough. I might only be operating at about 30 per cent of my potential as a manager, but the lifestyle makes up for the rest.'

Rodney Marsh, comfortably ensconced at Tampa Bay Rowdies, reveals why he was such a perennial underachiever

Flower of Scotland
The Scotland Dream Team

THE KEEN-SIGHTED AMONG YOU will probably notice that we have not selected a goalkeeper. We make no apologies for this, reasoning that this team would have more chance of preventing goals with Alan Hansen as a sweeper cum rush-goalie than if we had selected any of the other clowns that have worn the Scottish number one jersey down the years. It also allows us to atone for the errors of various Scots managers and actually pick Hansen, who makes up a revolutionary back four with McLeish, Miller and Young. Apologies to John Greig, Martin Buchan, Richard Gough and Tom Boyd, who don't even make the 16.

The presence of the biting Bremner in midfield adds to the defensive cover, Baxter supplies enigmatic vision and Alex James combines ceaseless industry with neat footwork. On the wing Jimmy Johnstone provides flair out wide, so no place for Archie Gemmill who sits on the bench, ahead of other contenders Strachan and Souness.

The forward line picked itself. Skill, strength, imagination, pace and finishing – and that's just Kenny Dalglish! Craig Brown got a sympathy vote as manager, as he deserves the chance to work with some decent players. And because none of the truly great Scottish players have managed Scotland, at least not effectively.

✋ George Young, the Rangers defender, won over 50 caps immediately after the war, and was the mainstay of Rangers' famous 'Iron Curtain' defence.

✍ Unlucky omissions? Talented wingers like Lennox, Cooke, Morgan and Robertson. Alex Jackson (a 1920s striker), Ally McCoist and also Danny McGrain, a fine attacking full-back.

✍ Deserving omissions? Paul McStay and Maurice Malpas – 77 and 55 caps respectively but neither fulfilled his potential.

☞ No current players make this team. Never before have Scotland had such a dearth of talent.

Manager: Craig Brown

1-3-4-3

Alan Hansen (SW) (70s/80s) George Young (50s)
Alex McLeish (80s) Willie Miller (80s)

Jimmy Johnstone (60s/70s) Billy Bremner (C) (60s/70s)
Jim Baxter (60s) Alex James (20s/30s)

Kenny Dalglish (70s/80s) Hughie Gallagher (20s/30s)
Denis Law (60s/70s)

Subs: Dave Mackay (D/M) (60s/70s) Billy McNeill (D) (60s)
Archie Gemmill (M) (70s/80s) Billy Liddell (F) (00s) Andy Gray (F) (80s)

Fontaine, Just
Reims, France

JUST FONTAINE, France's first genuinely great player, was actually a Moroccan who only moved to France in 1953 to start a career with Nice. His incisive forward play and goalscoring later saw him attract the attention of Reims, where he went on to win the League and Cup double in 1958.

It was his World Cup exploits the same year that shot him to international fame, though. His 13 goals in the Finals in Sweden set a record that still stands today. Fontaine scored six times in the group matches, including a hat-trick against Paraguay, and followed this with two more goals in the quarter-final win over Northern Ireland.

In the semis France met Brazil and, in truth, were overwhelmed in a 5-2 defeat. Fontaine scored only once in that match but, in the third-place play-off against defending champions Germany, he picked up the pace again, scoring four times as France ran out 6-3 winners. Despite France's semi-final defeat, Fontaine's place in World Cup history was assured. Tragically, the 1958 Finals proved to be his zenith as a player – a twice-broken leg forced him into premature retirement in 1962. In total Fontaine hit 30 goals in 21 appearances for France, the best ratio in the post-war era so far.

- Fontaine scored a hat-trick on his international debut in a 7-0 demolition of Luxembourg.
- He became the first president of the French Football Union.
- Fontaine only made his starting line-up in the first match against Paraguay because regular centre-forward Rene Bliard was injured.
- Thirty goals in 21 internationals is the highest post-war ratio of any striker, apart from the odd one or two-cap wonder.
- Fontaine scored 10 goals in Reims 1958–59 European Cup campaign, albeit against some poor sides.

VITAL STATISTICS

Place of Birth:	Marrakesh, Morocco	
Date of Birth:	18 August 1933	**Died:** n/a
Caps:	21 (France)	**Goals (International):** 30
	(record 13 goals in 1958 Finals)	
Clubs:	AC Marrakesh, USM Casablanca, Nice, Reims	
Appearances:	Club (All Matches): 213	
Goals:	Club (All Matches): 200	
Trophies:	FLT 1956, 1958, 1960, 1962	

LEGEND RATING	
Achievement	6.0
Skill	8.0
Teamwork	7.0
Passion	8.0
Personality	6.0
TOTAL	**35.0**

Football's Coming Home
England 4 Holland 1, 1996

ENGLAND'S LAST GAME in the opening phase of Euro 96 promised to be a tight affair, as the two best teams in the group met with Terry Venables' men needing only a draw to progress to the quarter-finals. The first half was tight, with Alan Shearer's penalty the only difference between the teams, but the second period left fans open-mouthed as, in a glorious 11 minutes, England tore one of Europe's finest sides to shreds. The newly discovered combination of Sheringham and Shearer ran riot.

Holland's night was summed up by Van der Sar's fumble from Anderton's shot that allowed Sheringham to score England's fourth, although, in truth, the Dutch keeper didn't know what had hit him. With Gascoigne at his impish best, McManaman raiding down the flanks and Anderton finding space galore, England were irresistible, for once performing with the uninhibited style that has characterised so many of their successful club sides. If the Gazza-inspired victory over Scotland in the previous game had revived the hosts' expectations, this result raised them to euphoric levels.

☞ At 4-0, England had inadvertently thrown Scotland a lifeline. Only Patrick Kluivert's late consolation for Holland prevented the Scots pipping the Dutch to a quarter-final place.

👍 This game formed part of Shearer's finest spell for England; he finished as top scorer in the tournament.

👍 As if this wasn't exciting enough, both England's quarter-final against Spain and semi-final versus Germany went to penalties.

👍 This result was sweet revenge for England, who had been eliminated by the Dutch during qualifying for the 1994 World Cup.

👎 Euro 96 was to end for England in familiar fashion, losing to Germany on penalties.

SCORERS	**England:** Shearer 2 (1 pen), Sheringham 2 **Holland:** Kluivert
EVENT	Group Stage, European Championship Finals, Wembley, 18 June 1996
ENGLAND	(Man: Terry Venables) 1. Seaman 2. Neville, G 3. Pearce 4. Ince (Platt) 5. Adams 6. Southgate 7. Gascoigne 8. Shearer (Barmby) 9. Sheringham (Fowler) 10. Anderton 11. McManaman
HOLLAND	(Man: Guus Hiddink) 1. Van der Sar 2. Reiziger 3. Blind 4. Seedorf 5. De Boer (Kluivert) 6. Bergkamp 7. Hoekstra (Cocu 72) 8. Winter 9. Witschge (De Kock) 10. Bogarde 11. Cruyff

Forza Azzurri
The Italian Dream Team

MANAGER POZZO was one of the first genuine tacticians – a simple ploy of having his wingers switch positions every so often completely bamboozled the Czechs in the 1934 World Cup Final.

Deploying the classic Italian sweeper formation, this would be an imposing defence (only an all-time German defence would be its equal). Get past the uncompromising attentions of Claudio Gentile and the timing of Scirea and Maldini, and you've still got to go through Baresi and Zoff. Maldini plays in his less-preferred position in the centre to accommodate Facchetti, the rampaging attacking back of the late 1960s.

If that weren't protection enough, the great playmaker from the 1930s Luis Monto sits in front of them – he made Gentile look like a pussy cat. Tardelli adds huge endeavour and Mazzola craft and subtlety.

Meazza is another from the great sides of the 1930s; he gets in alongside the great Luigi Riva ahead of substitutes Baggio and Piola, (a 1930s contemporary), leaving no room for Bettega, Boninsegna or Totti.

☞ Baggio's inclusion in the starting line-up was jeopardised by his liking for fashion fripperies – theres more to cool than a pigtail, Roberto.

👌 In Baresi, Maldini and Scirea, Italy have had three of the most accomplished defenders of the modern era – you hardly ever saw them on the floor – Frank Leboeuf take note.

👆 Paolo Rossi was unavailable, perhaps he was down at the bookies?!

☞ The Italian public have great expectations of their team – if this lot failed they would get more than tomatoes chucked at them!

☞ Bizarrely the most skilful modern players have been ignored by Italian managers in the 90s. Zola has scandalously few caps and Di Canio has none. Others, like Del Piero and Lentini, have flattered to deceive.

Manager: Vittorio Pozzo

1-4-3-2

Dino Zoff (70s)

Franco Baresi (C) (80s/90s)

Claudio Gentile (80s) Gaetano Scirea (80s)
Paolo Maldini (80s/90s) Giacinto Facchetti (60s)

Marco Tardelli (80s) Luis Monti (30s) Sandro Mazzola (60s)

Guiseppe Meazza (30s) Gigi Riva (60s)

Subs: Fabio Cudicini (G) (60s) Alessandro Costacurta (D) (90s)
Gianni Rivera (M) (60s) Roberto Baggio (F) (90s) Paolo Rossi (F) (80s)

Francescoli, Enzo
River Plate, Uruguay

SOUTH AMERICAN FOOTBALLERS tend to be categorised into two stereotypes. One is the cynical hatchet-man defender, inscrutably taking out an opponent off the ball, and the other is the prima donna forward, locks streaming as he swallow dives in the box several metres from the nearest defender. But you can cast aside these impure thoughts when considering Enzo Francescoli Uriarte. The Gary Lineker of Uruguay is universally respected as one of the most gifted and honest forwards of the past 20 years. Idolised in Buenos Aires, his two spells at River Plate saw him sign off in 1987 with the most emotional farewell for a foreign player ever seen in Argentina. The intervening years brought him a French title at Marseille and four seasons leading the line for less fashionable Cagliari and Torino in Serie A. His 40 per cent strike rate is remarkable considering he spent most of his career playing in some of the most sterile, defensive leagues in the world. Since retiring in 1987 'The Prince' has enhanced his nice-guy reputation yet further by becoming Uruguay's ambassador for the world children's charity, UNICEF.

- Francescoli was playing for nursery club Real Cadys Junior at the age of six, and signed junior forms with Uruguayan team Wanderers at 14.
- Three times Argentine Player of the Year, Francescoli won the South American award in 1985.
- He has disappointed in World Cup Finals. Eight appearances in 1986 and 1990 brought only one goal.
- Francescoli was hugely respected at Olympique Marseille, winning the award for best foreign player in France in 1987.
- Francescoli was Zidane's hero as a child, the Frenchman named one of his sons Enzo in his honour. When Juventus played River Plate in a 1996 friendly, Zidane swapped shirts with his hero.

VITAL STATISTICS

Place of Birth:	Montevideo, Uruguay			
Date of Birth:	12 November 1961	**Died:** n/a	Achievement	7.0
Caps:	122 (Uruguay)	**Goals (International):** 20	Skill	8.0
Clubs:	Wanderers, River Plate, Matra Racing,		Teamwork	8.0
	Marseille, Cagliari, Torino		Passion	8.0
Appearances:	Club (River Plate): 197		Personality	7.0
Goals:	Club (River Plate): 115			
Trophies:	FLT 1990		**TOTAL**	**38.0**

LEGEND RATING

Gallic Flair, Part 1
France, 1984

MUCH LIKE THE ALL-CONQUERING French team of recent years, the great French team of the 1980s thrived despite the absence of a quality striker. Their talents, again like the recent French team, were concentrated in midfield. Fernandez, a supreme fetcher and carrier, was a forerunner of Didier Deschamps, while Giresse and Tigana offered the power and athleticism currently provided by the likes of Vieria and Petit. Then there was was Platini, probably the most complete European footballer since Johan Cruyff. Zidane might be a world-class player, but Platini's gifts were not of this planet. He was a footballing god. And in the 1984 European Championships he played like one, scoring eight goals as France won the competition on home soil. If St Etienne's Dominique Rocheteau, their one half-decent forward, had managed to stay fit they might easily have added a World Cup crown to their sideboard. But, in 1982 and 1986, their challenge foundered at the semi-final stage. France's elimination in the 1982 World Cup was particularly painful. Defeat by Germany on penalties was bad, but to see the German goalkeeper, Schumacher, escape unpunished for a foul on Battiston added injury to insult. It was Germany again in 1986, but this time a half-fit Platini failed to exert his influence. It was a last hurrah at the top level for this squad.

☞ Like Henry in 1998, Jean Pierre Papin was too raw to influence the 1986 World Cup campaign. Papin in his prime would have made this a formidable side indeed.

☝ The opening game of Euro 84 was full of incident. Denmark's Allan Simonsen was left screaming for over a minute by the referee after he broke his leg, while Amoros was sent off for an atrocious head-butt.

☝ France failed to qualify for Euro 88; automatic qualification for the holders didn't apply, and they were eliminated by a strong Soviet team in the groups.

Managers: Michel Hidalgo and Henri Michel

Key Players
Joel Bats (G) Manuel Amoros (D) Patrick Battiston (D)
Max Bossis (D) Jean Tigana (M) Alain Giresse (M)
Luis Fernandez (M) Michel Platini (genius)
Dominique Rocheteau (F)

Trophies
EuroC 1984

Gallic Flair, Part 2
France, 2000

FRANCE WERE NOT HIGHLY fancied to win the 1998 World Cup, even on home soil. True, they had a solid-looking defence and an excellent midfield made up of wonderfully complimentary talents; Deschamps and Petit doing the donkey work with Djorkaeff and Zidane waving the wands. The reason no one fancied them was because their forwards were nondescript. The critics, not for the first time, were wrong. France won, although it has to be said Brazil did them a favour by not bothering to turn up for the final. France were indebted to Lilian Thuram for their 2-1 win over Croatia in the 1998 World Cup semi-final. Thuram had never scored for France before, but got two great goals to see his country through to the final.

Two years later at Euro 2000 the back four of Thuram, Desailly, Blanc and Lizarazu was still intact, the midfield had the added steel of Vieira, and Thierry Henry had blossomed into a convincing striker (not the lightweight winger he was at France 98). This time they were the favourites and justified it. Italy made a go of it in the final, but when David Trezeguet hit the golden-goal winner in extra-time it was no more than the French deserved.

- Barthez; Desailly; Blanc; Lebouef; Silvestre; Malbranque; Vieira; Petit; Pires; Henry; Saha. All Premiership players – we have been treated to the best in the world over the last few years.
- Full-back Lizarazu was a key member of the powerful Bayern Munich, playing in the 1999 and 2001 European Cup finals.
- The 1998 strikers must rate as the worst to win the World Cup. Dugarry and Guivarc'h were barely international standard, while Henry still thought he was a winger and Trezeguet was raw.
- Many were sceptical when Wenger recruited Pires to replace Marc Overmars. He took some time to settle, but he has proved himself a better all-round player than the conceited Dutchman.

Managers: Aime Jacquet (WC 1998) and Roger Lemerre (EC 2000)

Key Players
Fabien Barthez (G)   Lilian Thuram (D)   Bixente Lizarazu (D)
Marcel Desailly (D)   Laurent Blanc (D)   Zinedine Zidane (M)
Didier Deschamps (M)   Youri Djorkaeff (M)   Emmanuel Petit (M)
Patrick Vieira (M)   Thierry Henry (F)   Robert Pires (W)

Trophies
WorC 1998   EuroC 2000

Game of Two Halves
Tottenham Hotspur 3 Manchester United 5, 2001

IT IS OFTEN SAID that football is a game of two halves, and on a bright London afternoon in September 2001, Tottenham and Man Utd endorsed the accuracy of this cliché in a match that will be talked about until young men are old. Spurs, keen to capitalise on United's uncertain start to the season, began brightly and took a 2-0 lead with goals from Dean Richards and Les Ferdinand. United were a shambles in defence and it was no surprise when, two minutes before half-time, Spurs claimed a third goal through Christian Ziege.

The heat from Alex Ferguson's team talk must have curdled the milk in the half-time tea. His practical response was to switch Irwin with Silvestre for more pace on the left flank, with Solskjaer providing a third attacker at Butt's expense. The effect was dramatic. Once Cole's header had reduced the deficit in the first minute after the break, Spurs played as if hypnotised. Blanc scored from a corner, and then Van Nistelrooy's head restored parity. United sensed Tottenham's anxiety and went for the kill. Solskjaer and Scholes combined sweetly for Veron to put them ahead 4-3 then, with four minutes remaining, Beckham hammered an emphatic swerving shot past a shell-shocked Sullivan to complete the greatest turnaround in Premier League history.

- For £8 m new signing Dean Richards, it was a bitter-sweet debut. His move from Southampton produced a goal after eight minutes. If only it was a game of one half.
- For Teddy Sheringham, the game was a particular embarrassment. He had moved back to Spurs from United in the close season and was team captain for the day.
- One Spurs fan watched the second half with horror. He had bet £10,000 on a home win at half-time. The odds were 1-16.
- Hoddle was forthright: 'It looks like a Jekyl and Hyde performance from both sides.' Unfortunately it was his players who swallowed the wrong potion at half-time.

SCORERS   **Tottenham:** Richards, Ferdinand, Ziege
                   Manchester United: Cole, Blanc, Van Nistelrooy, Veron, Beckham

EVENT   FA Premier League, White Hart Lane, 29 September 2001

TOTTENHAM (Man: Glenn Hoddle)
               1. Sullivan 2. Richards 3. King 4. Perry 5. Taricco 6. Ziege 7. Freund
               8. Anderton 9. Poyet 10. Ferdinand 11. Sheringham

MAN. UTD. (Man: Alex Ferguson)
               1. Barthez 2. G Neville 3. Irwin (Silvestre) 4. Johnsen 5. Blanc 6. Beckham
               7. Butt (Solskjaer) 8. Veron 9. Cole 10. Van Nistelrooy 11. Scholes

Garra

Uruguay, 1930–54

'OTHER COUNTRIES HAVE THEIR HISTORY, Uruguay has its football.' It's not known who first said this, or even if they said it at all, but it's a quote Uruguayans often use to explain the importance of the national football team to the inhabitants of their tiny nation.

Modern football enthusiasts have a tendency to overlook the abilities of players from earlier generations. For that reason it is often forgotten that for 30 years Uruguay were the undisputed daddies of world football. During their period of supremacy their 'garra' (a word used to signify determination, collective belief and strength of purpose) carried them over some significant hurdles.

In 1930 they came from behind to beat Argentina in the first World Cup Final (four of the selected players are from the 1930 team: Nasazzi, Jose Andrade, Scarone and Cea). Twenty years later in the Maracana they defeated Brazil 2-1 in the decisive match of the competition. In 1954 they came up against the Mighty Magyars in the semi-finals and, even with a weakened team, pushed the Hungarians all the way, eventually going down 4-2 in a fantastic match. Since those days Uruguay have had good players rather than good teams, and their 'garra' has too often mutated from grit and determination into spite and violence.

- Ghiggia was a brilliant winger, blessed with pace, skill and clinical finishing ability. He overshadowed the great Schiaffino in the 1950 tournament, scoring the winner in the final.
- Ghiggia's successor, Abbadie, was a more than decent replacement. Another quick, goal-scoring winger he, along with Varela and Miguez, missed the semi-final against Hungary.
- Centre-forward Miguez played in 1950 and 1954, scoring eight goals in the Finals. Though a top-class finisher, he was eclipsed by the genius of Schiaffino and Ghiggia.
- Victor Andrade (of the 1950s team) was the nephew of Jose Andrade. Jose was one of the first successful black players, some years before Leonidas made his impact for Brazil.

Managers: Alberto Suppici (1930s)
and Juan Lopez (1950s)

Key Players
Roque Maspoli (G) Jose Nasazzi (D) Jose Santamaria (D)
Obdulio Varela (D) Jose Andrade (M) Victor Andrade (M)
Alcide Ghiggia (W) Julio Cesar Abbadie (W) Juan Schiaffino (F)
Pedro Cea (F) Hector Scarone (F) Omar Miguez (F)

Garrincha
Brazil

MANUEL DOS SANTOS FRANCISCO, otherwise known as Garrincha, was like a character from a fairytale. Born into poverty, and with a disability that meant his legs were bowed in opposite directions, he somehow managed to become one of the most feared attackers in the history of the game. Great balance and superb close control made him a deadly dribbler, and he was the first of the great Brazilian players to perfect the 'banana' shot.

He was 24 before he forced his way into the national side, but his exploits in three World Cups, particularly the successful 1958 and 1962 campaigns, earned him his place in Brazilian folklore. Perhaps his greatest moment was in 1962 when, after Pelé had bowed out of the tournament with injury, he took on the responsibility of leading the Brazilian attack. Garrincha destroyed England in the quarter-finals, then did the same to the violent hosts Chile in the semis and, despite his sending-off late in that game, he was allowed to appear in the final where he collected his second winner's medal. Unlike most modern Brazilian players, Garrincha played his domestic football in his home country, notably with Botafogo, whose rivalry with Pelé's Santos was a feature of the era.

☞ Garrincha means 'Little Bird,' although not many defenders caught this pigeon!

👎 Garrincha wasn't a stranger to scandal. He had well-publicised pay rows with Botafogo, got in trouble with the tax authorities, and left his wife and eight children for a singer.

☞ When Brazil fell to Hungary in the 1966 World Cup it was Garrincha's first defeat in the yellow shirt in 60 games. No team ever defeated Brazil when Garrincha and Pelé were both in the side.

👎 A fondness for the good life led to Garrincha's untimely death, aged only 49.

👍 Garrincha announced himself emphatically, scoring a hat-trick on his debut for Botafogo in 1953.

VITAL STATISTICS

Place of Birth:	Pau Grande, Brazil
Date of Birth:	28 October 1933 **Died:** 20 January 1983
Caps:	50 (Brazil) **Goals (International):** 13
Clubs:	Botafogo, Santos, Corinthians, Flamengo, Bangu, Portuguesa Santista, Olaria, AJ Barranquilla, Red Star Paris
Appearances:	Club (Botafogo): 581
Goals:	Club (Botafogo): 232
Trophies:	BLT 1964, 1965; WorC 1958, 1962

LEGEND RATING	
Achievement	9.0
Skill	10.0
Teamwork	8.0
Passion	8.0
Personality	9.0
TOTAL	**44.0**

Gascoigne, Paul

England, Tottenham Hotspur, Lazio, Rangers

IT IS A SAD FACT that the most talented footballer of his generation has also been the most self-destructive. 'He wears a No 10 jersey. I thought it was his position but it turns out to be his IQ,' said George Best in 1992 – and Georgie knew a drunken waster when he saw one. Gascoigne's excesses ranged from endearingly playful to crass and unpalatable, but his football, when fit, was sublime.

Blessed with superb control, Gascoigne also had a deceptive change of pace, a terrific shot, and great vision. He could turn a game in an instant, against opponents of the highest quality. The stunning free-kick he crashed past David Seaman in the 1991 FA Cup semi-final and the cheeky goal against Scotland in Euro 96 stand out as two of his finest moments.

Despite his poor fitness and dodgy temperament, clubs queued up to sign him. Newcastle, Spurs, Lazio and Rangers all saw glimpses of Gascoigne at his most inspired. Later, at Middlesbrough and Everton, the physio saw a lot more of Gazza than the fans.

- 1990. Sports Personality Of The Year after fine performances in the World Cup, including well-documented tears after earning the booking which would have kept him out of the final.
- The reckless tackle that saw him carried off with a broken leg in the 1991 Cup final delayed his move to Italy by a year and cost Spurs about £2 m in transfer fees.
- Once asked if he had a message for Norway prior to a World Cup qualifier, Gazza replied, 'F*** off!'
- Gazza's best mate and drinking buddy, Jimmy 'Five-Bellies' Gardner became a short-lived, cult micro-celebrity.
- Gascoigne's recent attempts to resurrect his career abroad and in England have made an unedifying spectacle.

VITAL STATISTICS

		LEGEND RATING
Place of Birth:	Gateshead, England	
Date of Birth:	27 May 1967 **Died:** n/a	Achievement 7.0
Caps:	57 (England) **Goals (International):** 10	Skill 9.0
Clubs:	Newcastle United, Tottenham, Lazio, Rangers,	Teamwork 8.0
	Middlesbrough, Everton, Burnley, Boston United	Passion 9.0
Appearances:	Club (All Matches): 413	Personality 7.5
Goals:	Club (All Matches): 108	
Trophies:	FAC 1991; SLT 1996, 1997; SFAC 1996	**TOTAL 40.5**

Gazza's Tears
England 1 West Germany 1, 1990

IT COULD HAVE ALL been so different. Their best World Cup showing since 1966 had seen England edge past an unlucky Belgium with a last-gasp winner in the second round then, thanks largely to Gary Lineker's prowess from the penalty spot, narrowly defeat African challengers Cameroon in the quarter-finals. But in the semi-final they met their nemesis, the Germans.

Germany began as favourites but were more than equalled by England in a tense encounter. The match is probably most famous for Gascoigne's tears, the young midfielder breaking down after receiving a booking that, had England won, would have kept him out of the final. On the hour, Germany got lucky when Brehme's free-kick, seemingly innocuous, took an extravagant deflection off Paul Parker and looped agonisingly over Shilton into the net. It looked to be enough, but with 10 minutes left Lineker eluded his marker to place a low shot across Illgner for the equaliser.

Both teams hit the woodwork in extra-time but could not break the deadlock, so a penalty shoot-out ensued. The tension was unbearable. After six successful kicks, England faltered, Stuart Pearce firing into Illgner's legs. Waddle fired his kick high into the blackness of the Turin night. Their pride was intact, but England were out.

☞ Penalty shoot-out: England: Lineker, Beardsley, Platt, Pearce (missed), Waddle (missed). Germany: Brehme, Matthaus, Riedle, Thon.

☞ 'Football is a game played by 22 players. And then Germany win'. Lineker's quote reflected the Indian sign Germany appeared to hold over England.

☞ Gascoigne was reportedly so upset that he accidentally climbed aboard the German team coach after the game.

☞ The day before, the first semi-final had produced an identical result. Italy lost 4-3 on penalties to Argentina after a 1-1 draw.

☞ Lightning was to strike for a second time six years later. England lost a second semi-final on penalties to Germany in Euro 96.

SCORERS	**England:** Lineker
	Germany: Brehme
EVENT	World Cup semi-final, Turin, 4 July 1990
ENGLAND	(Man: Bobby Robson)
	1. Shilton 2. Parker 3. Walker 4. Butcher 5. Wright 6. Pearce 7. Gascoigne
	8. Platt 9. Lineker 10. Beardsley 11. Waddle
GERMANY	(Man: Franz Beckenbauer)
	1. Illgner 2. Brehme 3. Kohler 4. Augenthaler 5. Buchwald 6. Berthold
	7. Hassler 8. Thon 9. Matthaus 10. Klinsmann 11. Voller

Genius, Part 1
Brazil, 1958

MOST MODERN SUPPORTERS remember the 1970 team as the apotheosis of Brazilian football, but older supporters often claim that this was Brazil's second incarnation of greatness. Their first was in 1958. The World Cup Finals of that year were held in Sweden, and began with no clear favourites. Brazil had stuttered through qualification, and were thought of as a talented but disorganised side. That perception was quickly changed, though. In a flurry of attacking football, Brazil blew away the opposition, winning both the semi-final and final 5-2. The Brazilians played a new 4-4-2/4-2-4 system with two hard-working wingers supporting two forwards. They chopped and changed the side throughout the tournament, and yet the end result was always the same: dazzling, winning football. The revelation of the tournament was Pelé, a 17-year-old whose talent and maturity astonished in equal measure. The strolling Didi was also a huge influence, waltzing his way through 90 minutes scarcely drawing a breath.

By the 1962 Finals Brazil were a settled and confident side who started the competition as clear favourites – and, despite an early injury to Pelé, they justified the bookmakers' faith in them, crushing the Czechs 3-1 in the final.

☞ Garrincha was a big influence in the latter stages of the 1958 tournament – a deputation of players, led by Nilton Santos demanded his inclusion. He saved his finest displays for 1962, when he was brought in as cover following an injury to Pelé.

☞ Both Nilton and Djalma Santos played in the 1958 and 1962 Finals. For the 1958 final Djalma was drafted in to combat the Swedish wingers Skoglund and Hamrin, forcing the unlucky de Sordi to miss out.

✍ Gylmar was probably the best keeper the Brazilians have ever had.

☞ The 1958 quarter-final against Wales was Mazzola's last game for Brazil. Reverting to his birth name, Jose Altafini, he represented his adopted country, Italy, in the 1962 Finals.

Manager: Vicente Feola

Key Players
Gylmar (G) Nilton Santos (D) Djalma Santos (D)
Didi (M) Zagallo (W) Garrincha (M) Pelé (F)
Mazzola – aka Jose Altafini (F) Vava (F)

Genius, Part 2
Brazil, 1970

THEY WERE PROBABLY the best football team ever. The fact that their goalkeeper would have struggled to make it as a park footballer, and that the rest of their defence was unconvincing at best, is irrelevant. When they got the ball they kept it. The movement and industry of the midfield and forwards was phenomenal, and those frail backs suddenly looked a whole lot better coming out to support the attacks.

1966 had been a hiccup, with Brazil eliminated in the group stage for the only time after the Portuguese cynically hacked Pelé out of the tournament. Now the great man was looking for a last hurrah on the big stage. Playing deeper than in the Finals of 1958 and 1962, he was the fulcrum of Brazil's play alongside the strolling Gerson, and the bustling, moustachioed Rivelino. The ball was played at speed with uncanny precision; man-marking was impossible as the flicks and tricks took out defenders with ease, and when the final ball was delivered, there was always Jairzinho or the selfless Tostao to receive. Four years later only Jairzinho and Rivelino remained, albeit with a better defence. Their football was disappointingly cautious, and they were easily brushed aside by the Dutch.

☞ Considering many of the Brazilians were heavy smokers, their fitness was impressive. Ignore the rose-tinted memories of them walking the ball around; these guys were like fluttering ribbons off the ball.

👍 Brazil's last goal in the final was not their only great goal of the tournament. Against Uruguay in the semi-final they scored three peaches: a one-two and finish from Clodoaldo; a tasty end to a passing move from Jairzinho; and a net-buster from Rivelino.

👎 Brazil's goalkeeping problems have never really gone away. Felix was awful, Waldir Peres an embarrassment in the great 1982 team, and Taffarel, the keeper throughout the 1990s, was only a marginal improvement.

Manager: Mario Zagallo

Key Players
Carlos Alberto (D) Gerson (M) Rivelino (M) Pelé (M/F)
Jairzinho (F)

Trophies
WorC 1970 (Won World Cup for third time and kept Jules Rimet Trophy)

Gentile, Claudio
Juventus, Italy

IF YOU WERE TO SELECT an all-time World XI from just two nations, Brazil could supply the forwards and most of the midfield, but the defence would have to be all Italian. And Claudio Gentile would have to be in it. Like all the best Italian defenders, he was comfortable at full-back, centre-half or sweeper. Gentile's reading of the game was such that he always seemed to appear in the right place at the most opportune moment; desperate lunges and last-ditch tackles just weren't his style. Intimidation, on the other hand, most definitely was.

In domestic football, like Roberto Bettega, Gentile was Juventus through and through, winning six Serie A titles in his 11 seasons with the Turin giants. For Italy, his career highlight was an obvious one: the 1982 World Cup. Although Rossi's goals grabbed the headlines in the later stages, it was their back line, marshalled by Zoff and Gentile, that prevented an early flight home. (Italy's dismal group performances saw them scrape through with three draws, including an embarrassing 1-1 with Cameroon.) Sparkling victories over Argentina, Brazil and West Germany ensured they scaled Everest the hard way. Gentile played in every game.

- A World Cup winner in 1982, Gentile also played in the 1978 Finals, appearing in all six games as Italy finished fourth.
- Goals were a responsibility Gentile was content to leave with others. He failed to score in his last six seasons in Serie A.
- Best game? The 1982 World Cup clash with Argentina. Gentile's shadowing of Maradona verged on GBH, but a niggled Diego was subdued.
- Gentile's 13 games in World Cup Finals brought only two defeats.
- He was appointed coach of the Italian U-21s in December 2000, and led them to Olympic bronze in 2004.

VITAL STATISTICS

Place of Birth:	Libya, Tripoli
Date of Birth:	27 September 1953　　**Died:** n/a
Caps:	71 (Italy)　　**Goals (International):** 1
Clubs:	Arona, Varesse, Juventus, Fiorentina
Appearances:	Club (League): 473
Goals:	Club (League): 14
Trophies:	SA 1975, 1977, 1978, 1981, 1982, 1984, 1986; UEFAC 1977; CWC 1984; WorC 1982

Achievement	9.0
Skill	8.0
Teamwork	9.0
Passion	8.0
Personality	6.0
TOTAL	**40.0**

LEGEND RATING

Gento, Francisco
Real Madrid, Spain

THERE HAVE ALWAYS BEEN quick players. Take Jackie Milburn, Jimmy Greaves and Ryan Giggs – all really quick and, it should be said, very good. Then there are the really, really quick players, like Tony Daley and Franz Carr who, to be honest, weren't very good at all. But occasionally a player comes along who is both really, really quick and very good. One such was Francisco Gento, the flying Spanish winger.

Blessed with frightening pace generated by his immense thighs (Jimmy Greaves considered him the fastest player he had ever seen), Gento also had great control, and could finish when called upon. Sadly, he was never seen at his best in the World Cup, but the European Cup was another matter. Gento was an integral component of the Real Madrid team that dominated the early years of the competition. Everyone remembers Di Stefano and Puskas, but it was Gento's pace that provided the team with that extra edge, especially when fed by the talented inside-left Rial. Even after five consecutive trophies, Gento wasn't done with the competition, returning for two more losing finals before winning for a sixth time in 1966. It was another 32 years before Real won the trophy again.

☞ Gento was always under pressure to maintain his form; Spain had another excellent left-winger in Atletico Madrid's Enrique Collar.

🏅 Gento's six European Cup wins are still a record.

👍 Gento scored the winner in the 1958 European Cup final against Milan, in an unscheduled period of extra-time. This followed a goal in the previous year's final against Fiorentina.

👍 Twelve Spanish league titles wasn't a bad haul, either. Nor were his 800 appearances.

☞ Gento's Real career lasted 18 years (1953–71). Di Stefano, who joined the club in the same year, left seven years before him.

VITAL STATISTICS

Place of Birth: Guarnizo, Spain

Date of Birth: 22 October 1933   **Died:** n/a

Caps: 43 (Spain)   **Goals (International):** 5

Clubs: Nuevo Montana, Astillero, Rayo Cantabria, Real Santander, Real Madrid

Appearances: Club (Real Madrid): 605

Goals: Club (Real Madrid): 181

Trophies: EC 1956, 1957, 1958, 1959, 1960, 1966; PLA 1954, 1955, 1957, 1958, 1961, 1962, 1963, 1964, 1965, 1967, 1968, 1969

LEGEND RATING	
Achievement	8.0
Skill	9.0
Teamwork	7.0
Passion	8.0
Personality	7.0
TOTAL	**39.0**

Gers Decade
Rangers, 1990s

BEFORE 1986/87 being a Rangers fan meant living in the past. The title was a distant memory and Aberdeen were threatening to make the Old Firm irrelevant. Enter Graeme Souness. Although his combative style won him few friends outside Ibrox, particularly in the early days as player-manager, he deserves credit for ignoring the club's sectarian bigotry and picking players purely on ability. The effect was dramatic, as the Gers romped to nine straight Scottish titles.

They were not without their critics. Souness's policy of buying in players from outside Scotland led to Rangers being labelled an 'anglo' or foreign club. While it was true that imports were high, two of their best players were Scottish; Richard Gough formed a formidable partnership with Terry Butcher in central defence, while up front Ally McCoist wrote himself into the Scottish goalscoring record books.

The imported players were their prime inspiration. Paul Gascoigne, bought from Lazio, became a terrace hero but, despite his flickering genius, he was overshadowed by the brilliance of Brian Laudrup. Against the lesser lights in the SPL the Danish midfielder hardly broke sweat, and was their consistent performer in disappointing forays into the European Cup. After being Scotland's third club, Rangers reigned supreme. It took Celtic a decade to win back their crown.

- Rangers won nine successive Scottish championships (1989–97), equalling the record of Jock Stein's Celtic.
- Rangers' only poor record was their disciplinary one. Souness set the tone when he was sent off in his first match in charge.
- Despite being perennial entrants to the European Cup and later the Champions League, Rangers always struggled. One of their notable successes was a defeat of Leeds United in 1993.
- Before 1986/87 Rangers had gone nine years without a championship victory. And their record in the FA Cup wasn't much better, winning it only once in the 1980s.
- Other notable English signings included Chris Woods, Trevor Steven and Ray Wilkins. Oh, and Terry Hurlock. Whoops.

Manager: Graeme Souness

Key Players
Richard Gough (D) Terry Butcher (D) Graeme Souness (M) Ian Durrant (M)
Brian Laudrup (M) Paul Gascoigne (M) Ally McCoist (F)

Trophies
SLT 1990, 1991, 1992, 1993, 1994, 1995, 1996, 1997, 1999,
2000 SFAC 1992, 1993, 1996, 1999, 2000

Giant Killers
Davids and their Goliaths

CRAWFORD'S QUOTE SAYS IT ALL. For small clubs, struggling on meagre attendances with only the occasional local derby to lift the gloom, a major Cup scalp is talked about for years. Down the ages, the recipe for a giant-killing has remained the same. Combine a mudheap of a pitch, a freezing winter's afternoon and a ramshackle stadium jammed to the corner flags, and add complacent opposition who would rather be playing golf. Then sit back and watch the temperature rise. Yeovil Town and their famous sloping pitch created one of the biggest upsets, removing Sunderland in 1949. But the Mackems are just one of Yeovil's 17 league scalps – a record for a team outside the top four divisions. Scoring a goal in a Cup upset is a guaranteed ticket to enduring celebrity, even if it's the only achievement of note in your entire career. Ronnie Radford and Ricky George are still D-list celebrities more than 30 years after their strikes for Hereford knocked out Newcastle. Roy Essandoh answered an Internet advertisement to sign for Wycombe, scored the only goal to knock out Leicester in the 2001 quarter-final and promptly vanished. For technical ability, a clash between the world's best wins hands down. But for sheer excitement, nothing tops a Cup giant-killing.

- ☞ In the days before automatic promotion, many clubs achieved league status on the back of their giant-killing exploits. Peterborough, Hereford and Wimbledon all won promotion to the professional ranks this way.
- ☞ Most giant killers win at home. Altrincham were the last non-leaguers to win at a top-flight ground, upsetting Birmingham 2-1 in 1986.
- ☜ FA Cup giant killers rarely progress to the later stages but the League Cup has produced two Third Division winners – QPR and Swindon.
- ☞ International shocks are rarer still. The USA's win over England in the 1950 World Cup was a shock of seismic proportions.

'This was the match of a lifetime and a day I will never forget.'

Colchester hero Ray Crawford after their epic FA Cup win over Leeds in 1971

Giggs, Ryan
Manchester United, Wales

THE PARALLEL GROWTH of Ryan Giggs and Manchester United since 1991 is no coincidence. The best left winger in British football burst on to the scene as a 17-year-old, scoring the only goal in a Manchester derby. Although success appeared to come easy, it is to his credit that the tabloid mud accurately thrown at his peers has never stuck. Nurtured and protected by Alex Ferguson he has developed into an indispensable player; only Roy Keane or David Beckham can claim a similar influence.

Like George Best, with whom he has often been compared, Giggs seems destined never to play at a major international tournament. Wales again failed to qualify for the 2002 World Cup Finals and missed out on a trip to Portugal for Euro 2004, despite winning their first four games. There is a growing suspicion that Giggs is now more concerned with channelling his efforts into club football – indeed, his propensity for crying off with minor injuries before international fixtures has already prompted many fans to accuse of him of lacking commitment to his country. Despite his loyalty to United over many seasons, indifferent form in 2002–03 provoked disquiet amongst some fans and rumours persisted of a move to Italy. However, a wrangle over only being offered a one-year renewal at Man United in November 2004 suggests he'd like to stay.

☞ He made his professional and full international debut at 17.

☞ He played for England schoolboys but adopted his mother's Welsh homeland. What would England now give for Giggs to fill a left-sided gap?

👆 He had won seven League titles before his 28th birthday.

👆 1999. His best goal ever, a dribble from the half-way line, destroyed England's meanest club defence and won United the FA Cup semi-final against Arsenal.

✋ 2001. A great disciplinary record is blemished when Giggs was sent off for the first time in his career, as Welsh captain.

VITAL STATISTICS

Place of Birth:	Cardiff, Wales	
Date of Birth:	29 November 1973	**Died:** n/a
Caps:	49 (Wales)	**Goals (International):** 8
Clubs:	Manchester United	
Appearances:	Club (All Matches): 611	
Goals:	Club (All Matches): 127	
Trophies:	LC 1992; LT 1993, 1994, 1996, 1997, 1999, 2000, 2001, 2003; FAC 1994, 1996, 1999, 2004; EC 1999	

LEGEND RATING	
Achievement	9.0
Skill	10.0
Teamwork	8.0
Passion	8.0
Personality	7.0
TOTAL	**42.0**

Glory Game
The Tottenham Hotspur Dream Team

IT REALLY WOULDN'T BE SPURS if they didn't have mesmerising attacking players and a mundane defence would it? Starting at the back they do have an all-time great in Jennings, but full-backs Stephen Carr (promising) and 'Nice One' Cyril Knowles (functional) would surely find George Best and Ryan Giggs a bit of a handful.

The choice of Sol Campbell might rankle, but loyalists Gary Mabbutt and Steve Perryman were just not that good. Dave Mackay wasn't really an orthodox centre-half but, on the basis of his spell at Derby, where he briefly occupied the position, he wins selection thus freeing up space in midfield where Spurs have traditionally enjoyed an embarrassment of riches. Who to leave out? After much soul-searching it was Mullery and Gascoigne who had to settle for the bench, leaving Ardiles, Hoddle, Blanchflower and winger Jones to strut their stuff.

The choice of forwards was mouth-watering, with Bobby Smith, Alan Gilzean, Martin Chivers, Steve Archibald and Herr Klinsmann not even making the bench. Sheringham got the nod ahead of Lineker on the grounds of longevity, and our hunch that he would be a better foil for Jimmy Greaves.

☞ Cyril Knowles and Joe Kinnear were Spurs' full-backs for most of the 1970s.

✍ No one from the 1901 Cup winning side makes the team – Spurs were a non-league club at the time! This victory started the 'year ends in one' tradition. Trophies followed in 1921, 1951, 1961, 1971, 1981 and 1991. In 2001 Alan Sugar relinquished control of the club, which was a triumph of sorts.

☝ Stephen Carr missed most of the 2000/01 season with injury.

☞ Tottenham's first meeting with (Royal) Arsenal was abandoned 15 minutes from the end 'owing to darkness'.

✍ Steve Perryman made the most appearances for Tottenham, but was never more than a competent honest pro.

Manager: Bill Nicholson

4-4-2

Pat Jennings (60s/70s)

Stephen Carr (90s) Sol Campbell (90s)
Dave Mackay (C) (60s) Cyril Knowles (60s)

Danny Blanchflower (50s/60s) Ossie Ardiles (80s)
Glenn Hoddle (80s) Cliff Jones (60s)

Jimmy Greaves (60s) Teddy Sheringham (90s)

Subs: Ted Ditchburn (G) (40s/50s) Alan Mullery (M) (60s)
John White (M) (60s) Paul Gascoigne (M) (90s) Gary Lineker (F) (90s)

Glory Glory Man United

Manchester United, late 1960s

AS THE DARK MEMORIES of the Munich air crash receded, a revitalised Manchester United swung into the 1960s with a rebuilt team and new stars. Crash survivors Bill Foulkes and Bobby Charlton were retained, with Foulkes forming a redoubtable defensive barrier alongside David Sadler, while Charlton formed an effective midfield partnership with arch-stroller, Paddy Crerand. Up front Denis 'The Law-man' Law was racking up the goals, and George Best was in his pomp.

Marking Best was like trying to catch soap in the bath. Twice in the European Cup he destroyed Benfica; first in the 1966 quarter-final, and then again two years later in the final at Wembley. But the big prize represented the beginning of the end for this United side. The team was ageing and Busby, memories of the air crash still fresh in his mind, had been looking to bury ghosts rather than build for the next decade. The following year they suffered the indignity of losing the First Division title to rivals Man City, presaging a few years of mediocrity before their tumble into Division Two in 1974. Busby had retired by then so didn't preside over the club's decline. Arguments rage over which is the best United side ever: the original Busby Babes, the 1968 European champions, or Ferguson's 1999 Treble winners? A debate that will continue long after we have kicked our last ball.

👍 Foulkes and Sadler got United to Wembley for their encounter with destiny, scoring a goal apiece in the second half in Madrid to see off Real.

☞ Some believe that had Busby replaced his ageing stars and relied on Best, he might have maintained the success and saved the errant maverick's soul.

☞ Law on Crerand: 'I used to say he was a great asset to television, because they didn't need slow-motion when he was on the ball.'

☞ Law was leading scorer in both United's title-winning seasons in the 1960s but, playing for Man City in 1974, he scored the goal that sent United into Division Two.

Manager: Matt Busby

Key Players:
Alex Stepney (G) Bill Foulkes (D) Tony Dunne (D)
Paddy Crerand (M) Bobby Charlton (M/F)
Denis Law (F) George Best (genius)

Trophies
LT 1967 EC 1968 (First English side to win European Cup)

Goal!!!

Beauty and Ballet

EVERY SEASON there are special goals; curled free kicks, overhead kicks, almighty 30-yarders, ribbons of passing finished with a tap-in. But every now and then one stands out from the crowd – a goal tinged with genius. Le Tissier, Beckham, Bergkamp – all seem incapable of scoring boring goals, probably because they are the sort of players who have innate confidence in their ability to do outrageous things.

But, occasionally, players with more parochial gifts produce crackers too. Blackpool's Micky Walsh was a nondescript Division Two player who earned his place in history with a blistering strike, while Justin Fashanu secured himself a £1 m move to Nottingham Forest on the basis of a stunning turn and volley for Norwich against Liverpool in the 1980s. Perhaps the most memorable of all was the 'donkey kick' goal scored by Coventry's Ernie Hunt against Everton in the 1970s; Hunt cracked a dipping volley over the wall and into the net after his team-mate, Willie Carr, had flicked the ball up to him with his heels. Great concept, even better execution.

- ✎ The best goal involving Beckham was scored by Paul Scholes; an edge-of-the-box volley direct from a pinpoint Beckham corner.
- ✎ Dennis Bergkamp once filled the top three positions in the *MOTD* Goal of the Month competition. A special effort against Leicester eventually won goal of the season, but a sand wedge against Bayern Leverkusen in 2002 wasn't far behind.
- ✎ Trevor Sinclair is known for spectacular acrobatics; an overhead kick playing for QPR flew into the net from all of 25 yards. He's done it consistently enough since to prove it was no fluke.
- ☞ Personal favourite? Frank Worthington teeing the ball up, flicking it over his head between two defenders and volleying it in for Bolton against Ipswich in 1978.

'I went up to him afterwards, shook his hand and called him a b*****d.'

Neil Sullivan, then Wimbledon goalkeeper, after David Beckham beat him from the half-way line

Gray, Andy

Wolverhampton Wanderers, Aston Villa, Everton, Scotland

MEMORIES OF ANDY GRAY as a player conjure up images of a fearless battering ram throwing himself into the fray, diving in with his head amongst flailing feet. It was no wonder Gray was so often injured; few men have played the game with such scant regard for their own safety. Gray was not just a big bloke who put himself around, though. He was a prodigious header of the ball and, while not dazzling with the ball at his feet, his touch was still the equal of most of his contemporaries.

All his clubs enjoyed successful periods with him as their spearhead in attack, but it was his spell at Everton that brought him the rewards he deserved. Toffees boss Howard Kendall took a gamble purchasing Gray (at the time many regarded him to be past his best, and with dodgy knees to boot) but his partnership with his young countryman and acolyte, Graeme Sharp, provided the goals that brought the title back to Goodison. The purchase of Gary Lineker two years later saw Gray exit to Aston Villa, and retirement soon followed. Through the last decade Gray has worked as a pundit for Sky television, where his enthusiasm and entertaining use of high-tech graphics have done much to help the Rupert Murdoch-funded operation overcome initial antagonism towards their franchise.

- Gray and Sharp scored the goals that won the 1984 FA Cup Final.
- He scored the winner for Wolves in the 1980 League Cup final.
- Voted PFA Player of the Year and Young Player of the Year, 1977.
- Wolves paid Villa a then British record fee of £1,469,000 for Gray in 1979.
- Gray was a surprising omission from Ally MacLeod's 1978 World Cup squad. Oh, how they missed him.

VITAL STATISTICS

Place of Birth:	Glasgow, Scotland		
Date of Birth:	30 November 1955	**Died:** n/a	
Caps:	20 (Scotland)	**Goals (International):** 6	
Clubs:	Dundee United, Aston Villa, Wolves, Everton,		
	West Bromwich Albion, Rangers, Cheltenham Town		
Appearances:	Club (All Matches): 593		
Goals:	Club (All Matches): 202		
Trophies:	LC 1980; FAC 1984; LT 1985; CWC 1985; SLT 1989		

Achievement	6.0
Skill	6.0
Teamwork	8.0
Passion	10.0
Personality	8.0
TOTAL	**38.0**

LEGEND RATING

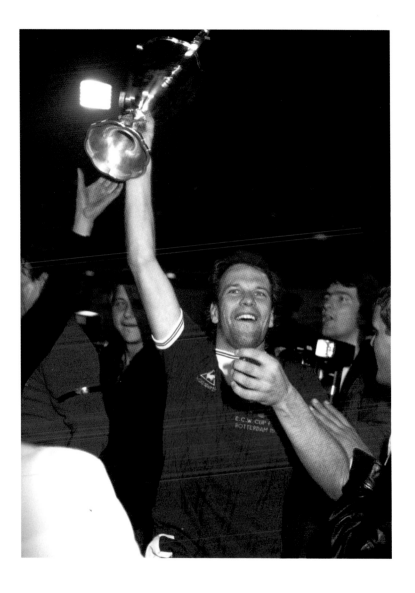

Great Gunners
The Arsenal Dream Team

FOR ALL ARSENAL'S modern flair and expensive foreign talent, the bedrock of this team is steeped in history. Herbert Chapman's team was Arsenal's first great one, sweeping all before them in the 1930s. It's from this side that we have selected both full-backs, Eddie Hapgood and George Male (Dixon and Winterburn have racked up the appearances they don't possess the same pedigree).

In central defence, the newer guard holds sway. Both O'Leary and Adams possess the talent and leadership, and have the happy knack of rising to the big occasion. The midfield combination is both a League of Nations and a Rock of Ages. Pires gives width and penetration and pace; Vieira and Alex James provide a fascinating blend and Cliff Bastin would provide provide goal-scoring support for the two strikers. Not that the front two would be liable to dry up. Drake's direct approach and Henry's subtle skills would always boost the goal difference – the pair provide a dream combination of aerial power and blinding pace.

☞ Hardest man to leave out? Liam Brady. He with the sweetest left foot Highbury's ever seen would play a part in any squad rotation.

☞ The sight of Pat Jennings in goal will continue to stick in the throat of any Spurs fan. Blame Keith Burkinshaw for selling him.

✍ Herbert Chapman is the least contentious choice of manager. His Arsenal team won three successive titles, and he set new standards in tactics, professionalism and commercial awareness.

✍ No places for either record club goalscorer Ian Wright or record England cap winner Kenny Sansom.

☞ 2004. Another season or two at the current extraordinary levels of performance may force the inclusion of others from the exceptional squad.

Manager: Herbert Chapman
4-4-2

Pat Jennings (70s/80s)

George Male (30s) Tony Adams (80s/90s) David O'Leary (70s/80s)
Eddie Hapgood (C) (30s)

Robert Pires (00s) Patrick Vieira (90s) Alex James (30s)
Cliff Bastin (30s)

Ted Drake (30s) Thierry Henry (90s/00s)

Subs: Bob Wilson (G) (60s/70s) Sol Campbell (D) (00s)
Liam Brady (M) (70s) Joe Mercer (M) (40s/50s) Dennis Bergkamp (F) (90s)

Greatest Game Ever?
Hungary 4 Uruguay 2 (aet), 1954

THE REIGNING CHAMPIONS against the favourites. Hungary had scored 21 goals in their first three matches, Uruguay a mere 13 (including four against a disappointing England), but both sides were missing key players, notably Puskas for Hungary and Varela for Uruguay. Yet still one sensed the game would provide thrills and spills aplenty.

Hungary dominated early on, taking a 2-0 lead early in the second half through Czibor and Hidegkuti, the second a wonderful diving header to finish a typically clinical move. In the last quarter of normal time Uruguay, driven on by the dribbling skills of their great forward Juan Schiaffino, again showed the gutsy spirit that had brought them the trophy four years previously, and equalised with two goals from Hohberg, making his first appearance of the tournament. So to extra time, and with Schiaffino carrying a knock the Hungarians regained the upper hand. Pinpoint crosses from first Budai and then Bozsik found Sandor Kocsis, and the man they called 'Golden Head' duly put them away. Hungary were through to the final – and surely couldn't lose to a side they had beaten 8-3 in the group stage.

☞ Only three of the Uruguayan team had played in the 1950 final – Maspoli, Andrade and Schiaffino.

👍 Happily, concerns that the game would descend into a brawl like Hungary's quarter-final against Brazil proved ill-founded.

👍 Just as at the Olympics two years earlier, Kocsis scored in every round except the final.

☞ The Uruguayan number two is the same Santamaria who played at the heart of the great Real Madrid side later that decade.

👎 Hungary, of course, did lose the final, 3-2 to West Germany.

SCORERS	**Hungary:** Czibor, Hidegkuti, Kocsis (2)
	Uruguay: Hohberg (2)
EVENT	World Cup semi-final, Lausanne, 1954
HUNGARY	(Man: Gustav Sebes)
	1. Grosics 2. Buzansky 3. Lantos 4. Bozsik 5. Lorant 6. Zakarias 7. Budai
	8. Kocsis 9. Palotas 10. Hidegkuti 11. Czibor
URUGUAY	(Man: Juan Lopez)
	1. Maspoli 2 Santamaria 3. Martinez 4. Andrade 5. Carballo 6. Cruz
	7. Souto 8. Ambrois 9. Schiaffino 10. Hohberg 11. Borges

Greaves, Jimmy
Tottenham Hotspur, England

ONE OF THE GREAT GOAL SCORERS, Greaves scored at a similar rate to strikers of the 1930s in the more defensive 1960s and 1970s. Although small for a forward, at only 5 ft 8 in and 10 stones wet through, he was fast and had quicksilver feet.

The sight of Greaves dancing around defenders and smacking in yet another hat-trick was one of the treats of the time. Like many natural-born goal scorers he could be selfish, when he received possession he rarely had more than one thought on his mind, and if his team were under pressure he had a tendency to go missing. Greaves maintained his scoring record in internationals, but never really fired in World Cup Finals (only one goal in seven appearances). His greatest disappointment was missing the 1966 World Cup Final; he started the tournament but got injured and was unable to win back his place from Geoff Hurst.

Greaves started drinking heavily at the end of his career, but recovered well and later formed a successful TV double-act with Ian St John on ITV's *The Saint & Greavsie Show*. Greaves made an entertainingly informal pundit (St John was wooden and unfunny).

- Greaves scored on his debut for every club (including a hat-trick on his Spurs debut), and for England.
- He still holds the Spurs record for league goals in a season, 37 in 1963.
- He became the first player to score 100 goals before he was 21.
- Bill Nicholson, unwilling to saddle Greaves with the label of the first £100,000 player, paid Milan £99,999 for his services.
- Greaves once bemoaned, in his role as a pundit, the absence in the modern game of 'the old hey-diddle-diddle-down-the-middle and stick it in the net'.

VITAL STATISTICS

Place of Birth:	London, England		
Date of Birth:	20 February 1940	**Died:** n/a	
Caps:	57 (England)	**Goals (International):** 44	
Clubs:	Chelsea, AC Milan, Tottenham, West Ham		
Appearances:	Club (All Matches): 528		
Goals:	Club (All Matches): 366		
Trophies:	FAC 1962, 1967; CWC 1963		

Achievement	6.0
Skill	10.0
Teamwork	6.0
Passion	8.0
Personality	8.0
TOTAL	**38.0**

LEGEND RATING

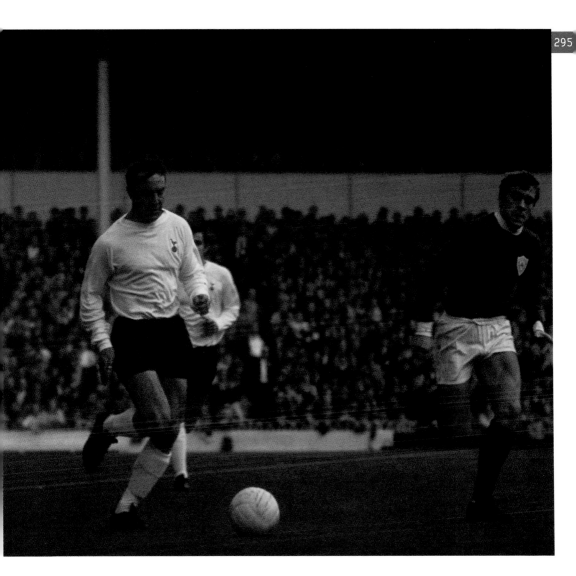

Greece is the Word!
Euro 2004. 100-1. And Few Takers

UNLIKE THE WEAKER teams in the other groups, Greece had a game plan. They didn't turn up simply hoping not to embarrass themselves, they set their stall out to be as competitive as possible in each of their games.

Against Portugal in the opener they went out hard, hoping to capitalise on the hosts' nervousness. The ploy worked a treat as a 2-0 lead ensured three points, and enough credit to mean only one point from the next two games still saw them qualify. A ora, Espana.

France, then. No worries. Actually, there weren't that many, as Greece outplayed France in the first half and then resisted their pressure in the second, scoring an excellent goal on the break to take them into the semis. Au revoir, les bleus.

The Czech Republic had played with panache and courage on their way to the semis, winning all their games. In patches they dominated possession and put the Greeks on the back foot. But Greece survived each Czech purple patch and came again, clinching the game with a header from the outstanding Dellas in the last minute of the first half of extra time. A silver goal.

Three days later. Oh-oh, those summer nights...

👍 The outstanding centre back Traianos Dellas once had a couple of unsuccessful seasons at Sheffield United. Must say something about The Blades' strength in depth. Or not.

☞ Perhaps Greece shouldn't have gone into the tournament as such underdogs. After all, they qualified top of their group ahead of Spain, beating them 1-0 in Madrid.

☞ For all the talent on show from the top Premiership clubs, the only one who ended with a winner's medal was Bolton's Stelios Giannakopoulos.

☞ Like England, Greece defended deep against France to negate Henry's pace. Unlike England they still pressed the ball in midfield and refused to concede space to the opposition's playmakers.

👎 Perhaps Greece only enjoy starting as underdogs. Their World Cup 2006 qualifying campaign began with a defeat by Albania. Already, qualification looks a distant prospect.

'I made certain decisions. These decisions have been followed by the players. I only advise the players and we have great results.'

Coach of the tournament Otto Rehhagel proves that it's a simple game.

Greig, John
Rangers, Scotland

ONE OF AN ELITE BAND to have won the league with the same club as both player and manager, no individual contributed more to the success of the post-war Rangers team than John Greig. An inspiration at centre-half after moving from right-half early in his career, he became, in 1964, only the second Scot to captain a treble-winning side, but Celtic's later dominance frustrated his title ambitions for a further 11 years. His consolation was becoming the only Rangers captain to lift a European trophy, the Cup Winners' Cup in 1972.

Greig's move, during a whirlwind three weeks, from captain to the manager's desk in 1978 seemed a natural one, but in five seasons he failed to bring the title to Ibrox. It was an indication of his reputation among the fans that he kept his job for so long; an outsider with a similar record would have been dismissed without hesitation. Greig's commitment, strength and leadership, plus his telepathic understanding with playmaker Jim Baxter, served Scotland well too, never more so than in the famous 3-2 defeat of England at Wembley in 1967.

☞ His 44th and final cap against Denmark in 1976 came five years after his previous Scottish appearance.

👍 He was twice Scottish player of the year and received an MBE in 1997.

👍 He played a record 496 league games for Rangers, and scored a remarkable 120 goals from defence and right-half.

☞ Greig endeared himself to the community by tirelessly leading his team to funerals and services after the Ibrox disaster in 1971.

👍 In 1999 Greig was voted 'Greatest Ever Ranger' in a fans' poll. Greig actually supported Hearts as a boy.

VITAL STATISTICS

Place of Birth:	Edinburgh, Scotland
Date of Birth:	11 September 1942 **Died:** n/a
Caps:	44 (Scotland) **Goals (International):** 3
Clubs:	Rangers
Appearances:	Club (All Matches): 755
Goals:	Club (All Matches): 120
Trophies:	SLT 1963, 1964, 1975, 1976, (1978);
	SFAC 1963, 1964, 1966, 1973, 1976, (1978),
	(1979), (1981); CWC 1972

LEGEND RATING	
Achievement	7.0
Skill	7.0
Teamwork	8.0
Passion	9.0
Personality	6.0
TOTAL	**37.0**

Gullit, Ruud
Feyenoord, PSV, AC Milan, Holland

ONE OF THE GREAT PLAYERS of the modern generation, Ruud Gullit had the lot – heading, shooting, passing, and tackling all came so easily to him that he was like four players rolled into one. After starting his career as a sweeper at Feyenoord, Gullit moved on to PSV where he was quickly converted to striker, a position he also later occupied at AC Milan alongside his Dutch colleague Marco van Basten.

For his country though, Gullit turned out mostly in midfield and it was from here that he skippered the Dutch to their European Championship victory in 1988. Glenn Hoddle brought him to Chelsea in 1994, and after one season he succeeded the former Spurs midfielder as player-manager. Although he introduced some exciting overseas players to the Premiership and brought Cup success, the league championship evaded him and, after Ken Bates accused him of being a greedy playboy, he was eventually sacked in 1998. A dire spell as manager of Newcastle, where Gullit failed to adjust to the Geordie culture, left an impression that here was a man not prepared for compromise – it was his way or, er, his way. Sadly, his way didn't work.

☞ The £5.5 m Milan paid PSV for Gullit was a world record at the time.

👍 Gullit was the first overseas coach in England to win a domestic trophy (the FA Cup with Chelsea in 1997).

☞ The distinctive dreadlocks worn as a player won admirers of both sexes, and were copied by many of his younger contemporaries.

✌ He was voted European Player of the Year in 1987.

👍 He scored in Holland's win over Russia in the 1988 European Championship final, and repeated the feat for Milan in their 4-0 win over Steaua Bucharest in the European Cup final a year later.

VITAL STATISTICS

Place of Birth:	Amsterdam, Holland	
Date of Birth:	1 September 1962	**Died:** n/a
Caps:	66 (Holland)	**Goals (International):** 17
Clubs:	Haarlem, Feyenoord, PSV Eindhoven, AC Milan, Sampdoria, Chelsea	
Appearances:	Club (League): 465	
Goals:	Club (League): 175	
Trophies:	EuroC 1998; DLT 1984, 1986, 1987; SA 1988, 1992, 1993; EC 1989, 1990; FAC (1997)	

LEGEND RATING	
Achievement	9.0
Skill	9.0
Teamwork	9.0
Passion	7.0
Personality	9.0
TOTAL	**43.0**

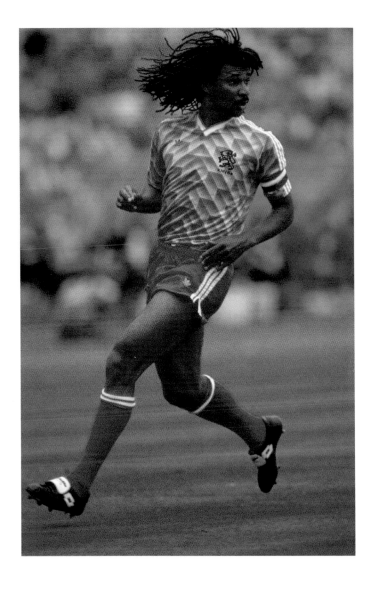

Hagi, Gheorghe
Romania

MADDENINGLY VOLATILE but sublimely talented, the list of great Romanian footballers can be headed by only one man. Gheorghe Hagi remained untamed by a succession of club and international managers, continuing in his mid-30s to explode the myth that one mellows with age.

Short and stocky, he was as much at home leading the attack as he was leaving full-backs for dead on the wing. Such was his hunger for the ball he would often drop back into his own half to start moves that he would sometimes finish himself, making him virtually impossible to man-mark.

The star of the Romania team in five European and World Cup Finals tournaments, his 17-year international career came to a peak in USA 94. Improbably, Romania reached the quarter-finals, a run that included a memorable defeat of Argentina that was inspired by the man they used to call the 'Maradona of the Carpathians'. Only penalties denied Hagi's team a place in the last four. Fittingly, his last major club side was Galatasaray, where his passion and volatility was more than matched by the Turkish supporters. Whether being booked for dissent or turning a game with a moment of brilliance, you ignored him at your peril.

👍 He is the most-capped Romanian and his country's top goalscorer with 35.

👍 He came equal 12th in the most-capped world list; he shares his tally of 125 with Peter Shilton.

👍 Best goal? His 30-m scorcher against Colombia in the 1994 World Cup Finals.

👎 He was sent off for an outrageous dive against Italy in the quarter-finals of Euro 2000.

👍 He has been voted Romanian Player of the Year six times.

VITAL STATISTICS

Place of Birth:	Constanta, Romania
Date of Birth:	5 February 1965 **Died:** n/a
Caps:	125 (Romania) **Goals (International):** 35
Clubs:	Farul Constanta, Sportul Studentesc, Steaua Bucharest, Real Madrid, Brescia, Barcelona, Galatasaray
Appearances:	Club (All Matches): 550
Goals:	Club (All Matches): 269
Trophies:	RLT 1987–90; TLT 1997–2000; UEFAC 2000

LEGEND RATING	
Achievement	6.0
Skill	10.0
Teamwork	8.0
Passion	10.0
Personality	7.0
TOTAL	**41.0**

Hanegem, Wim van
Feyenoord, Utrecht, Holland

BANDY-LEGGED AND SHORT-SIGHTED, Wim van Hanegem was not an obvious footballing specimen. Neither was Nobby Stiles, nor Berti Vogts. But they'd be one of the first on the team-sheet. Ask any manager who makes any team tick and adds the indispensable ingredients of blood, sweat and tears and they will name a player such as van Hanegem.

In the 1960s and 1970s, the simultaneous rise of Wim and Holland was no coincidence. While Cruyff strutted and Krol and Neeskens roamed free, van Hanegem patrolled his left-midfield furrow, providing the apparently shapeless Holland with cohesion and balance. His finest moments, like many of his peers, came during the 1974 World Cup Finals. He shared in the pain of final defeat to West Germany and at 30, it appeared to be his last chance. It was a tribute to his tenacity and fitness that he made the squad for Argentina four years later. As usual, internal Dutch politics was to intervene. Days before the tournament started, van Hanegem walked out in a dispute over the distribution of players' bonuses. A team man and egalitarian to the end, he took issue with some senior players' attitude in keeping lucrative sponsorship cash for themselves instead of dividing it equally. Although his international career continued for another 15 months, this was effectively the end.

☞ Nicknamed 'De Kromme' ('the Crooked') due to his bandy legs.

✎ Worst footballing moment: being red-carded for dissent by the ever-wilful Clive Thomas in the 1976 European Championship semi-final v Czechoslovakia. His initial refusal to leave the pitch nearly led to an abandoned match.

☞ In 1975 van Hanegem was offered a lucrative chance to leave Feyenoord for Olympique Marseille. Legend has it that he gave his dog the casting vote after the issue split the family down the middle. The dog stayed silent and van Hanegem stayed…apparently.

VITAL STATISTICS

Place of Birth:	Breskens, Holland	
Date of Birth:	20 February 1944	**Died:** n/a
Caps:	52 (Holland)	**Goals (International):** 6
Clubs:	Velox, Xerxes, Feyenoord, AZ Alkmaar, Utrecht	
Appearances:	Club (League): 518	
Goals:	Club (League): 128	
Trophies:	DLT 1969, 1971, 1974; EC 1970; WCC 1970; UEFAC 1974	

Achievement	7.0
Skill	7.0
Teamwork	9.0
Passion	8.0
Personality	8.0
TOTAL	**39.0**

LEGEND RATING

Hansen, Alan
Liverpool, Scotland

ONE OF THE MOST elegant defenders in the game's history. Hansen played over 600 matches for Liverpool without appearing to break sweat, a trait that prompted colleague Phil Neal, at the end of every game, to ask, jokingly: 'Did Hansen get dirty today?' His reading of the game was so good that he never appeared stretched but, when required, his tackling and heading were sound, and his distribution was more reminiscent of a foreign sweeper than a British stopper. Bought for £100,000 from Partick Thistle, Hansen was eased into the Liverpool side as a replacement for Emlyn Hughes. His partnerships over 13 seasons at Anfield, with Phil Thompson, Mark Lawrenson and Gary Gillespie coincided with the most successful period in the club's history.

Why successive Scottish managers chose to award Hansen only 26 caps between them remains a mystery. He would have walked into most other national teams, and Scotland were hardly blessed with high-calibre defenders. Eschewing the managerial career many predicted for him upon retirement, Hansen became a TV pundit where his scathing dismissals of Jimmy Hill's opinions on the BBC enlivened many a dull match. Ironically, as a pundit he has achieved more fame and recognition than he ever enjoyed as a player.

☞ Like his pal, Kenny Dalglish, Hansen is a top-class golfer and also played volleyball, basketball and squash to a high standard.

👍 Hansen wasn't a frequent goal scorer, but he did hit the winner against West Ham in the 1981 League Cup final replay.

☞ He memorably uttered the famous line: 'You'll never win anything with kids.' The kids in question, Man United's young side of the mid-1990s, proceeded to waltz away with the Premiership title.

☞ The Aberdeen pairing of McLeish and Miller kept Hansen out of the Scotland side – a modern coach would have played five at the back with Hansen as an attacking sweeper.

👍 Hansen won eight league titles, a record he shares with Liverpool colleague Phil Neal.

VITAL STATISTICS

Place of Birth:	Clackmannanshire, Scotland
Date of Birth:	13 June 1955 **Died:** n/a
Caps:	26 (Scotland) **Goals (International):** 0
Clubs:	Partick Thistle, Liverpool
Appearances:	Club (Liverpool): 623
Goals:	Club (Liverpool): 13
Trophies:	LT 1979, 1980, 1982, 1983, 1984, 1986, 1988, 1990; FAC 1986, 1989; LC 1981, 1983, 1984; EC 1978, 1981, 1984

LEGEND RATING	
Achievement	9.0
Skill	9.0
Teamwork	8.0
Passion	8.0
Personality	6.0
TOTAL	**40.0**

Happel, Ernst
Rapid Vienna, Feyenoord, Hamburg, Austria, Holland

ERNST HAPPEL WAS ONE of the cornerstones of the tip-top Austrian side of the early 1950s. In a methodical passing team, organised by the midfield maestro Ernst Ocwirk he and Gerhard Hanappi provided the backbone of the defence. A tough, uncompromising stopper and a formidable striker of a dead ball Happel also starred for Rapid Vienna, the finest Austrian club side of their generation.

Already assured of greatness as a player, his management career increased his reputation still further. An early advocate of 'Total Football', he led Feyenoord to victory in the 1970 European Cup final, depriving Celtic of a second triumph. The trophy was magnetic for Happel; he reached the final with Bruges, losing to Liverpool in 1978, and won the competition again with Hamburg in 1983. Succeeding Rinus Michels as Holland coach, he emulated the great man by taking the Dutch to the final of the World Cup in 1978. And that was without Cruyff and Van Hanegem who, in typical Dutch style, chucked their toys from the pram on the eve of the tournament and refused to play in it.

☞ He played for a FIFA World XI in 1953.

⚽ He scored a hat-trick in the European Cup in 1957 against Real Madrid – two free-kicks and a penalty.

👎 In the 1954 World Cup for Austria his defence conceded three goals in three minutes against Switzerland, but went on to win 7-5, despite missing a penalty. Typically, they lost 6-1 to West Germany in the next round.

👎 Happel returned to the Finals in Sweden in 1958, but the team were past their best and went out early.

☞ Rapid Vienna renamed their Prater stadium the 'Ernst Happel-Stadion' in his honour when Happel died in 1992.

VITAL STATISTICS

		MANAGER		PLAYER	
Place of Birth:	Vienna, Austria				
Date of Birth:	29 June 1925 **Died:** 14 November 1992				
Caps:	51 (Austria) **Goals (International):** 5				
Clubs:	As Player: Rapid Vienna, Racing Club de Paris;	Achievement	9	Achievement	6
	As Manager: Rapid Vienna, Feyenoord,	Tactical Awareness	9	Skill	8
	Sevilla, Club Bruges, Standard Liege,	Motivation	6	Teamwork	8
	Hamburg, Innsbruck, Dutch national coach	Team Selection/Transfers	7	Passion	8
Trophies:	ALT 1946, 1948, 1951–52, 1954,	Personality	7	Personality	6
	1957, (1960, 1989–90); DLT (1969);				
	BLT (1976–78); BLG (1982–83);				
	EC (1970, 1983)	**TOTAL**	**38**	**TOTAL**	**36**

LEGEND RATING

Hard Men
The Not-So-Beautiful Game

THERE IS A DIFFERENCE between hard and dirty. A genuinely hard player can freeze an opponent out of the game purely on his reputation, whereas a dirty player who fancies himself simply gets wound up and sent off (think Dennis Wise or Alan Smith).

Higuita's conviction for kidnapping demands his inclusion; we're talking serial nutter here. Ron 'Chopper' Harris was the daddy of 1970s thuggery, and Ron Yeats easily eclipsed Tommy Smith as the hard man of Liverpool (Smith talked too much). Monti was the granddaddy, a ball-playing thug long before it was cool, and Gentile is the modern game's greatest man-marker, a man who turned wingers' bowels to water. Mackay was a legend – he would captain this side. Benetti was a vicious, cynical assassin who stood out even in a brutal Italian team. Neeskens was a great player but he wasn't afraid to leave a foot in, and Giles edges out Souness as the sly, provocative element. Up front we have Joe Jordan, all flailing elbows and tungsten head, toothless only in the literal sense. And Lineker. A decade of being hacked and harassed by the toughest defences in the world and never booked. That's hard.

☞ Unlucky omissions (defenders): Norman 'Bites Yer Legs' Hunter, Antonio Rattin, Dmitri Kuznetsov and Karl-Heinz Schnellinger.

☞ Deserved omissions: Terry Hurlock (hirsute pedestrian laughing stock), Neil Ruddock (Phil Mitchell in shorts), Robbie Savage (can't see Ron Yeats tolerating that hairstyle).

☞ Unlucky omissions (others): Andy Gray, Ted Drake, Bruce Rioch and John Fashanu.

☜ What, no place for Vinnie Jones? Sorry, not good enough. With the exception of Harris this lot are all quality internationals.

Manager: Lorenzo (Argentina)

4-4-2

Rene Higuita (G)

Ron Harris (D)   Ron Yeats (D)   Luis Monti (D)   Claudio Gentile (D)

Dave Mackay (M)   Romeo Benetti (M)   Johan Neeskens (M)
Johnny Giles (M)

Joe Jordan (F)   Gary Lineker (F)

Haynes, Johnny
Fulham, England

IT IS RARE FOR ONE PERSON to dominate a club's history so totally, but the bar-room discussions in Fulham begin and end with a collective nod: Johnny Haynes was the greatest player ever to pull on the black and white. An inside forward of immense technique, his confidence on the ball made him a London role model for a later generation of pretenders, including Terry Venables, Rodney Marsh and Stan Bowles.

Until the return of the Cottagers to the Premier League in 2001 the era of Haynes represented Fulham's only golden age and, while today's team is good to watch, it pales compared to the one of Haynes, Hill and Jezzard. Good enough to represent England at the 1958 World Cup when still a Second Division player, Haynes remained at Fulham throughout his career. It was a measure of his importance to them that, despite modest revenues, they were always prepared to meet his salary demands following the abolition of the maximum wage (Haynes was the first £100-a-week footballer). Successive relegations in 1968 and 1969 were a sad end to his career, but even while the team around him floundered, Haynes could never do any wrong in the eyes of Fulham fans.

- 1954. Scored on his England debut in a 2-0 win over Northern Ireland in Belfast.
- 1958. Hit an international hat-trick as USSR were thrashed 5-0.
- 1961. The first player to earn £100 per week at a British club.
- 1962. Seriously injured his knee in a road accident and is never picked again for England.
- His 594 league appearances for Fulham are a club record.

VITAL STATISTICS

Place of Birth:	London, England		
Date of Birth:	17 October 1934	**Died:** n/a	
Caps:	56 (England)	**Goals (International):** 18	
Clubs:	Fulham, Durban City		
Appearances:	Club (League): 594		
Goals:	Club (League): 145		
Trophies:	None		

Achievement	4.0
Skill	9.0
Teamwork	8.0
Passion	8.0
Personality	8.0
TOTAL	**37.0**

LEGEND RATING

Henry, Thierry
Arsenal, France

WHEN THE TROUBLESOME and disruptive Nicolas Anelka left Arsenal in 1998, Arsène Wenger turned to another quick French attacker to replace him. Thierry Henry had emerged as a wide attacking player at Monaco under Wenger's tutelage, and won a league title there in 1997. A lucrative move to Juventus followed, but, like many others in Serie A, Henry spent more time on the bench than the pitch, and left after less than a year.

So to Arsenal, and a difficult start, when both manager and player seemed unsure as to the most satisfactory use for all that skill and speed. Only when Wenger consistently used Henry in a central striking role, an opportunity afforded by Dennis Bergkamp's injuries and loss of form, was his true potential unearthed. Henry's second and third seasons at Arsenal brought him a torrent of goals in a classy side. The discovery that he could play as an orthodox front man was of equal benefit to France, for whom the addition of a world-class striker proved to be the missing piece in their attacking jigsaw.

The 2002 World Cup and Euro 2004 suggest Henry has still to find his place in the international arena, but his league form since 2002 has been simply sensational.

☞ He made his Monaco debut aged 17 and still looks as if he is about 17.

👍 Scored three goals in six games at the 1998 World Cup, but never wholly convinced, remaining on the bench for the final.

👎 Henry has a fiery streak, his browbeating of an official after a home defeat by Newcastle late in 2001 resulted in an FA disrepute charge.

👍 Intelligent and articulate, Henry is another player who adds substance to the notion that the best English spoken in the Premiership is by the overseas players.

👍 Won the PFA's Player of the Year award for 2002/3.

VITAL STATISTICS

Place of Birth: Paris, France

Date of Birth: 17 August 1977   **Died:** n/a

Caps: 62 (France)   **Goals (International):** 27

Clubs: Monaco, Juventus, Arsenal

Appearances: Club (All Matches): 318

Goals: Club (All Matches): 189

Trophies: WorC 1998; EuroC 2000; FLT 1997; LT 2002, 2004; FAC 2002, 2003

LEGEND RATING	
Achievement	9.0
Skill	9.0
Teamwork	7.0
Passion	8.0
Personality	7.0
TOTAL	**40.0**

Herbert, Herbert What's the Score?
Walsall 2 Arsenal 0, 1933

AFTER MORE THAN 70 years this match is still talked about in Walsall. Like all Cup upsets it defied logic; Arsenal were in the first season of what was to be a championship winning hat-trick, while the Saddlers were muddling around in the Third Division and approached the match with little more than the hope of making some quick cash. Arsenal's line-up included the Scottish 'Wembley wizard' Alex James, Britain's costliest player David Jack and the winger who became the club's record goalscorer, Cliff Bastin. Their manager, Herbert Chapman, had already made his name by leading Huddersfield to three league title wins.

But reputations meant little to the Walsall players who were intent on proving they were the physical (if not footballing) equals of the Gunners. Two Arsenal players had already been kicked into the stand before Gilbert Alsop's header gave Walsall a second-half lead, then, illustrating that the Corinthian spirit wasn't always prevalent despite those Pathé newsreel images, a kick by Arsenal's Tommy Black on Alsop led to a mass brawl and a penalty to the home side. Bill Sheppard duly converted; a rattled Arsenal had been well and truly outgunned.

- Flushed with this goalscoring success, Gilbert Alsop scored 40 league goals in each of the next two seasons, a club record.
- Chapman, who was a strict disciplinarian, never picked Tommy Black again.
- Scorer Bill Sheppard had a keen sense of timing; it was his first goal for the club.
- Arsenal ended the season as League Champions, Walsall finished fifth in Division Three (North).
- Walsall's dream ended in round four, where they lost 2-0 at Manchester City.

SCORERS   **Walsall:** Alsop, Sheppard (pen.)
EVENT   FA Cup Third Round, Fellows Park, 14 January 1933

WALSALL   (Man: Sid Scholey)
              1. Cunningham 2. Bennett 3. Bird 4. Reed 5. Leslie 6. Salt 7. Coward
              8. Ball 9. Alsop 10. Sheppard 11. Lee
ARSENAL   (Man: Herbert Chapman)
              1. Moss. 2. Male 3. Black 4. Hill 5. Roberts 6. Sidley 7. Warnes 8. Jack
              9. Walsh 10. James 11. Bastin.

Heysel Stadium
A Bleak Night in Belgium

29 MAY 1985 SHOULD HAVE BEEN a red-letter day for fans of Liverpool and Juventus. More than 60,000 of them were massed in Brussels' Heysel stadium before the European Cup final. But misguided ticket arrangements had allocated Liverpool a terrace behind one goal separated only by a thin chicken wire fence from 'neutrals' in the other half. The majority of these 'neutrals' turned out to be Juve fans who had snapped up tickets from locals when their own allocation ran dry.

How it all started will always be debatable. Some Liverpool fans claimed they reacted to missile throwing, while the Italians talk of a drunken English charge. The outcome was all too apparent. Fans fleeing from the trouble attempted to scale a wall in the now infamous sector Z, which collapsed under increasing pressure.

Thirty-nine Italians and Belgians died in the carnage and hundreds were injured, their fear and pain going out live to horrified television audiences watching across the world. Recriminations continued for years. Fingers were pointed at fans, local bar-owners, ticket allocators, Belgian police and the stadium authorities. All were a factor but the lessons were not learned, as Liverpool fans were to discover only four years later at Hillsborough.

☞ The stadium's age was cited as a factor but, built in 1930, it was actually seven years younger than Wembley and not unusually old for the time.

☞ Following the tragedy UEFA banned English clubs from Europe indefinitely. Ironically, the first club prevented from entering the European Cup were Liverpool's rivals, Everton. The ban was lifted after five years.

☟ Disgracefully, no memorial or plaque commemorates the disaster. The only reminder is a gate left for posterity when the stadium was razed to the ground.

☞ After the chaos, UEFA officials insisted the game should take place that evening, fearing further disturbances if they cancelled.

'If I had known about the fatalities I wouldn't have wanted to play. You go along to watch a game.'

Kenny Dalglish

Hidegkuti, Nandor
MTK Bucharest, Hungary

IN WINNING THE WORLD CUP in 1966 Alf Ramsey deployed Bobby Charlton as a deep-lying centre-forward. It would not be overstating the case to say that, without Nandor Hidegkuti, the thought would probably never have entered his head. In 1953 Ramsey played in the England team that were slaughtered by the Hungarians at Wembley, and from his position at right-back he had the perfect viewpoint to admire the skills of the Hungarian striker.

It helped that Hidegkuti was a hugely gifted player. He used the space behind his forwards to probe at the opposition, always looking for opportunities to shoot with either foot. Teams simply did not know how to contain him. The rigid formations of the 1950s could not be easily adapted to negate his threat, nor that of his interchanging team-mates Puskas, Kocsis and Czibor. That said, Hidegkuti's achievements were limited – his side failed to take a golden opportunity to win the World Cup, and, unlike Puskas, Kocsis and Czibor, he stayed in Hungary after the Soviet revolution, eschewing the riches of Western Europe. But his legacy to the game endures. Cruyff might have patented his own turn, but Hidegkuti invented a whole new position.

- ✋ Hidegkuti scored a hat-trick in the mauling of England at Wembley.
- ☞ In the 'Battle of Berne' against Brazil in the 1954 World Cup, he scored after four minutes, losing his shorts in the process.
- ✋ Hidegkuti became a successful coach at Fiorentina, winning the 1961 European Cup Winners' Cup.
- ✋ Hidegkuti won an Olympic Gold medal in 1952, in the middle of the team's four-year unbeaten run.
- ☞ On Hidegkuti's death in 2002, his club, MTV Budapest, announced that their stadium would be re-named in his honour.

VITAL STATISTICS

Place of Birth:	Budapest, Hungary
Date of Birth:	3 March 1922 **Died:** 14 February 2002
Caps:	68 (Hungary) **Goals (International):** 39
Clubs:	MTK Bucharest (then known as Voros Lobogo)

LEGEND RATING	
Achievement	7.0
Skill	9.0
Teamwork	8.0
Passion	8.0
Personality	7.0
TOTAL	**39.0**

Hill, Jimmy
Coventry City, BBC TV

JIMMY HILL CAN LAY CLAIM to being the first renaissance man of English football. Player, linesman, employment-rights activist, PFA and club chairman, media pundit … there are few areas of the modern game in which Jimmy Hill has not exerted an influence. A competent player in average sides, his most lasting achievement came in his role as PFA chairman when, leading a case on behalf of George Eastham in 1961, he brought about the abolition of football's maximum-wage system.

As a manager and then chairman, Hill transformed Third Division Coventry City, laying the foundations for a 34-year membership of the league's elite and pioneering the movement for the abolition of terracing (Highfield Road was an all-seater stadium 15 years before the Taylor Report made them compulsory).

In the media, he embraced the new culture of television coverage and became a national figure as a presenter and summariser for both ITV and the BBC. He irritates many, the Football League has never quite forgiven him for taking them on over 40 years ago, but the shadow of the most famous chin in football has cast a lasting influence.

☞ 1961. First PFA chairman to call for a players' strike over the maximum wage.

☞ 1972. Deputised for an injured linesman at Highbury. Hill was originally attending as a commentator.

☞ 1978. Key negotiator in the threatened strike over freedom of contract. This nut didn't crack until the Bosman case nearly 20 years later.

☜ 1982. Organised a rebel tour to South Africa, infuriating the FA and breaching the Gleneagles agreement not to play sport with a land still under the apartheid regime.

☞ 'Jimmy Hill is to football what King Herod is to babysitting,' Tommy Docherty once said.

VITAL STATISTICS

Place of Birth:	London, England	
Date of Birth:	22 July 1928	**Died:** n/a
Caps:	0 (England)	**Goals (International):** 0
Clubs:	As Player: Brentford, Fulham; As Manager: Coventry City	
Trophies:	None	

LEGEND RATING

Achievement	7
Tactical Awareness	8
Motivation	8
Team Selection/Transfers	7
Personality	8
TOTAL	**38**

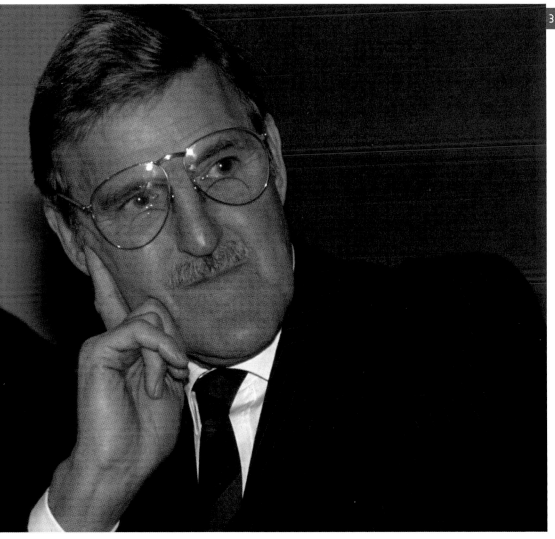

Hillsborough
The Day It All Had To Change

PERHAPS THE MOST sickening aspect of the worst disaster in British football was that it contained so many chilling echoes of previous tragedies. Like the crowd-related disasters at Ibrox and Heysel, it unfolded in a few minutes and was the result of sudden overcrowding. What made 15 April 1989 worse, apart from the unprecedented loss of 96 lives, were the terrifying images of fans – men, women, children and even whole families – struggling for life in the chaos. Reporting of a disaster normally contains scenes of the aftermath, the venue cleared and the dead removed, but with the media already gathered for the FA Cup semi-final between Liverpool and Nottingham Forest, the camera lenses quickly turned to the Leppings Lane terrace. The central pen was filling with Liverpool fans misdirected into an area too small to contain them, while outer sections remained relatively free. The pictures of helpless fans sparked a grief that went far beyond the boundaries of football. The following days were incredibly moving: the Kop was a sea of flowers, and players mingled with fans at funerals. The legacy was the Taylor Report, resulting in all-seater stadiums and an overhaul of crowd-control measures at all British events. The tragedy is that 96 innocent lives were lost before anyone would admit there was a problem.

- Although 95 people died as an immediate result of Hillsborough, the toll was to rise several years later after one young man's failure to recover from a coma.
- *The Sun* newspaper claimed outrageously that some Liverpool fans had stolen personal items from the dead. Copies of the paper were ritually burned on Merseyside.
- A national service of remembrance was held in Liverpool's Anglican Cathedral on 29 April 1989.
- The Hillsborough Justice Campaign still fights for the bereaved and their families. The authorities have escaped punishment and compensation for victims' families has been tiny, contrasting with the large awards given to police officers affected by 'stress'.

'Football is irrelevant now.'

Kenny Dalglish

'The only safe stadium in my view is an empty one.'

South Yorkshire coroner Stefan Popper, at the inquest

Himst, Pol van
Anderlecht, Belgium

AS BELGIUM EMERGED from the footballing wilderness in the late 1960s along with their neighbours Holland, Pol van Himst was the standard bearer for the new generation. A thoroughly modern type of footballer, his skill, elegance and vision marked him as a player ahead of his time – he was voted Player of the Year in Belgium at 17 years old.

Van Himst's long career with Anderlecht ended before the club's halcyon days in European competition, but he won a remarkable eight league titles and numerous awards.

At international level, he carried a heavy burden as the country's star player. A modest man, he was puzzled and hurt when he was personally vilified for Belgium's poor showing in the 1970 World Cup, and a two year absence from international football followed. Compensation arrived on his return to the squad in 1972 under Raymond Goethals. A creditable third place finish in the 1972 European Championships was achieved after a momentous 2-1 victory over a good Italian side in the quarter-finals, with van Himst notching the decisive second goal. Van Himst had an excellent tournament, and his standing in his home country was restored.

👍 In 2000, he was presented with an award as Belgium's Player of the Century, and inducted into FIFA's Hall of Fame.

👍 His 30 goals for Belgium remains a record which he shares with Bernard Voorhoof.

☞ As a coach, van Himst guided Anderlecht to successive UEFA Cup finals, winning the first against Benfica and losing to Tottenham on penalties the following year.

👍 He also enjoyed success after being appointed national coach in 1991, ensuring Belgium's qualification for the 1994 World Cup.

👎 His one crack at a European final ended in disappointment – after beating Arsenal 3-1 in the first leg of the Fairs Cup final in 1970, Anderlecht subsided weakly in the second leg.

VITAL STATISTICS

Place of Birth:	Sint-Pieters-Leeuw, Belgium	
Date of Birth:	2 October 1943	**Died:** n/a
Caps:	81 (Belgium)	**Goals (International):** 30
Clubs:	Anderlecht, RWD Molenbeek, Eendracht Aalst	
Appearances:	Club (League): 481	
Goals:	Club (League): 236	
Trophies:	BLT 1962, 1964–68, 1972, 1974	

	LEGEND RATING
Achievement	7.0
Skill	9.0
Teamwork	7.0
Passion	8.0
Personality	6.0
TOTAL	**37.0**

Hoddle, Glenn
Tottenham Hotspur, Monaco, Chelsea, England

GLENN HODDLE WAS A continental footballer who had to overcome the misfortune of being born in Hayes, Middlesex. Not overly concerned with pace and aggression, Hoddle rose above the hurly-burly of English football. The radar-equipped right foot bent and curled some classic goals in a long career.

Hoddle spent 12 years at Tottenham before he tried his luck abroad with Monaco, where he was hugely appreciated. His performances for England were patchy – occasionally inspired, too often anonymous. To be fair to him, no one built a side around his talent, which was what he needed. He was lured back to England as player-manager of Swindon Town. His understanding of the game and tactical acumen were immediately evident as he took an ordinary side into the top flight for the first time in their history. Those instincts served him equally well at Chelsea, and the FA appointed him England manager as successor to Terry Venables. He made a decent fist of the job, and it was his strong, and sometimes quirky, personal views that saw him eased out. His abilities as a manager seem to have been confirmed by sound work at Southampton but he was a disappointment at his alma mater, Spurs, where his remoteness from his players was exposed.

- He scored the only goal (a penalty) in the 1982 Cup Final replay against QPR.
- He started Chelsea's rush of foreign imports when he persuaded Ruud Gullit to join Chelsea. Gullit succeeded him as manager.
- Hoddle's debut for England against Bulgaria was awesome; he scored in a 2-0 win and looked a million dollars.
- A bizarre trust in Eileen Drewery, a faith healer, started the decline in Hoddle's relationship with the FA and the media whilst England manager.

VITAL STATISTICS

Place of Birth: Hayes, Middlesex, England

Date of Birth: 27 October 1957 **Died:** n/a

Caps: 53 (England)

Goals (International): 8

		MANAGER		PLAYER	
Clubs:	As Player: Tottenham, Monaco, Swindon	Achievement	8.0	Achievement	7.0
	Town, Chelsea (player-manager); As Manager:	Tactical Awareness	8.0	Skill	9.0
	England, Southampton, Tottenham,	Motivation	6.5	Teamwork	6.5
	Wolverhampton Wanderers	Team Selection/Transfers	8.5	Passion	8.5
Appearances:	Club (League for Tottenham): 377	Personality	7.5	Personality	7.0
Goals:	Club (League): 88				
Trophies:	FAC 1981, 1982; EUFAC 1984; FLT 1988	**TOTAL**	**38.5**	**TOTAL**	**38.0**

LEGEND RATING

Holy Trinity
Holland, 1988

THEIR FAILURE TO QUALIFY for the Finals of the 1982 and 1986 World Cups prompted Holland to call once again for the services of their greatest coach, Rinus Michels. Michels' 'Total Football' philosophy, born at Ajax in the late 1960s, was to serve Holland well yet again. The core of the team was Koeman, the captain, along with the Holy Trinity of Gullit, Rijkaard and Van Basten. Koeman was a decent defender who also happened to be a terrific attacking playmaker, and almost every Dutch move seemed to start with his precision passing from the back. Be it a short ball to the ever-willing Rijkaard or a longer pass to meet the run of an attacker, Koeman rarely missed his target. Gullit could attack or defend with equal aplomb, and Van Basten was a brutally efficient finisher. And for once a Dutch team delivered what it promised. At Euro 88 they produced the fluent, attacking football for which they were famous, and a first victory for 32 years over hosts West Germany won them a place in the final. A terrific game saw them wear down a skilful USSR team – a trophy had come home at last.

- Van Breukelen saved a penalty that would have brought Russia back into the game in the final – he was a superior keeper to any of the 1970s custodians.
- The second goal in the final was a masterpiece, Van Basten volleying a deep cross with stunning power past Rinat Dasaev.
- Even this squad had its internal ructions. There were rumours of a racial divide in the camp.
- The Dutch performance at the 1990 World Cup Finals was a sad coda to these heroics. With virtually the same team, they managed three dreary draws and were eliminated by Germany.

Manager: Rinus Michels

Key Players
Hans Van Breukelen (G) Jan Wouters (D) Ronald Koeman (D)
Frank Rijkaard (M) Ruud Gullit (M/F) Marco Van Basten (F)

Trophies
EuroC 1988

Home Internationals
We Want Them Back!

BY 1884 ENGLAND, Scotland, Wales and Ireland were all playing international football. So the idea that they should all play each other in an annual league was a logical step, and thus the Home Internationals were born. Scotland quickly gained the upper hand, winning three and sharing one of the first four tournaments, but it wasn't long before England rose to the challenge and, bar the occasional triumph for Wales and N. Ireland, it was the auld enemies that grew to dominate the event. For fans north of the border a visit to Wembley was always a trip to savour. Indeed, such was their enthusiasm for the fixture they were even known to outnumber the home fans on occasion. But after nearly a century, the Home Internationals began to fall apart. England and Wales refused to play in Belfast, wary of the political situation, and when Scotland and England cancelled games against the other home nations after 1984, the tournament was effectively over. Although the England/Scotland fixture continued for another five years, the extended season and the importance of other tournaments had finally taken its toll.

- Best English game? A 9-3 drubbing of Scotland in 1961. Jimmy Greaves helped himself to a hat-trick. Scottish keeper Frank Haffey never played for his country again.
- Best Scottish game? The 3-2 win at Wembley in 1967, England's first defeat since winning the World Cup.
- Best Welsh game? A 4-1 drubbing of England at Wrexham in 1980. Leighton James and Mickey Thomas put paid to Larry Lloyd's England career.
- Best Irish game? A 1-0 win against Wales in 1980 earned them their first outright championship victory for 66 years.
- The final tally of outright wins reads: England 34, Scotland 24, Wales 7, Northern Ireland 3.

'It meant more for the Scots to beat the English than it did for the English to beat the Scots.'

Bobby Charlton makes a dubious claim after the Scots win at Wembley in 1967

Hooligans
Mobs and Monsters

FOOTBALL HOOLIGANISM: a disease cultivated by the game itself or merely the reflection of a violent society? Your opinion on this subject tends to depend on whether you love or despise the game. One undeniable truth is that football violence is nothing new.

Rivalry, large crowds and a contact sport have provided a violent cocktail as long as the game has been played. In 1909, a major riot took place in Glasgow after officials unwisely refused to play extra-time to settle an Old Firm derby. The result was a burned stand, a ruined pitch and widespread damage to local property.

Even in the golden age of the 1940s, Millwall fans pelted the referee and linesmen during a routine match against Exeter. The late 1960s saw the dawn of organised gangs, with premeditated 'taking' of away ends and railway stations setting an unwelcome trend. As police tactics grew more sophisticated in the 1980s, so did the hooligans. Sharply dressed casuals with Stanley knives replaced the skinheads and their Dr Martens. Today the problem is controlled at league games with more season tickets and all-seater stadiums but away from the stadiums, in city centres, car parks and even on cross-channel ferries, the threat of hooliganism still lingers.

- 1972. Chelsea became the first British club to erect a perimeter fence. Although Hillsborough brought their eventual removal, they are still a common sight in grounds throughout the world.
- The scourge of racism against black players, particularly in Italy and Eastern Europe, is still a persistent stain that UEFA have been slow in erasing.
- In 1985 televised rioting at a match between Luton and Millwall led to the introduction of an ill-fated identity card scheme.
- February 2002. A reconciliatory football match in Kabul following the Afghan War sparked a riot. The stadium had a more grisly recent history as a Taliban execution venue.

'These people are society's problems and we don't want your hooligans at our sport.'

FA Secretary Ted Croker bites back at Prime Minister Thatcher, 1985

Hoop Heroes
The Celtic Dream Team

WITH A CLUB LIKE CELTIC, who have been winning domestic trophies hand over fist ever since their formation, the list of potential Dream Team candidates is far too long. One could easily select a squad that would require a convoy of team coaches to get to away games.

Inevitably, the Lisbon Lions feature heavily: McNeill, Gemmell, Johnstone, Murdoch and Lennox are all represented. The most devastating combination is up front. Henrik Larsson has proved himself one of the most consistent and prolific finishers in the history of the game in Scotland, while his striking partner, Kenny Dalglish, is one of the most complete forwards Britain has produced since the war. The midfield is as perfect as they come, a unit capable of turning from intricate ball-juggling to biting tackles at the flick of a tactical switch.

As manager, only Martin O'Neill as Celtic boss can touch Jock Stein's hem. Not only did Stein win nine championships in a row and win the 1967 European Cup, he also tilted the balance of power that had been weighted in Rangers' favour for a decade.

- John Thomson may well have become Celtic's greatest-ever keeper. Sadly, aged just 22, he died from injuries sustained in an Old Firm game.
- Tom Boyd deserves a place on the bench for loyalty during the 1990s, a decade dominated by Rangers.
- Frank McAvennie wins the cheeky chappie award ahead of Charlie Nicholas: he could drain a mini-bar quicker.
- Unluckiest omissions: Collins and Auld. Celtic's midfield is so strong that even these club legends from the 1950s and 1960s fail to be included.
- These boys would surely add a second European Cup to their 1967 success in Lisbon.

Manager: Jock Stein

4-4-2

Pat Bonner (80s/90s)

Danny McGrain (70s) Billy McNeill (60s/70s)
John Clark (60s) Tommy Gemmell (60s)

Jimmy Johnstone (60s/70s) Paul McStay (80s/90s)
Bobby Murdoch (60s) Bobby Lennox (60s)

Kenny Dalglish (70s) Henrik Larsson (90s/00s)

Subs: John Thomson (G) (20s/30s) Tom Boyd (D) (90s) Paul Lambert (M) (90s) Jimmy McGrory (F) (20s/30s) Frank McAvennie (F) (80s)

Howlers

How High Do You Want the Goal?

WE'VE ALL DONE IT. Fortunately for the rest of us, the repercussions of shanking an open goal or letting a tiddler through the legs are restricted to the banter of team-mates in the pub after the game.

Imagine if you can the misery of making the same error in front of a 30,000 crowd and a sniggering armchair audience of millions. How Villa's Peter Enckelman must look forward to visiting St Andrew's again. In 2002, during the first Birmingham derby for 16 seasons, he let a throw-in from one of his own players gently caress his studs as a near air-shot trickled past him and into the net.

Goalkeepers are in a unique position regarding howlers but strikers too have their own hall of infamy. Ryan Giggs can point to a groaning, personal trophy cabinet as proof of his talent but his pass into the Stretford End, when an open-goal beckoned during an FA Cup tie against Arsenal in 2003, will be replayed on out-take compilations for years to come. The bigger they are…

The blooper of the 2003–04 Premiership season is reserved for Ian Walker, whose mishandling of a gently trundling effort from Kevin Davies handed Bolton an equaliser. And so the first physical requirement for a keeper was demonstrated: a thick skin.

- David Seaman. Being beaten by Nayim from the halfway line in 1995 had finally become a distant memory. Then Ronaldinho approached an innocuous-looking free kick in Shizuoka seven years later…
- Paul Gascoigne. Fame and fortune in Italy should have awaited Gascoigne after the 1991 FA Cup final, his last appearance for Tottenham. The worst tackle of the decade left him the poorer by one cruciate ligament and with a career that never recovered.
- Gary Sprake. But for the ex-Leeds and Wales keeper, Elland Road would have bulged with trophies in the 1960s and 1970s. The jewel in his tarnished crown was an own goal caused by his throwing the ball backwards.

'David James. Superstar. Drops more
b******s than Grobbelaar'

**Manchester United fans at Anfield point
out 'Calamity' James' propensity for
dropping the occasional clanger.**

Hughes, Mark
Wales, Manchester United, Chelsea

WITH HIS FEARLESS, lion-hearted approach to striking, Mark Hughes could have easily made his mark in the eras of Dean or Lawton. A powerful forward with legs like tree-trunks, he was less than 6 ft tall but huge in stature. To judge him by his goalscoring record alone is a mistake, as his phenomenal work rate made him a favourite of fans and colleagues alike wherever he has played. His shielding of the ball brings grateful tributes from fellow strikers, while his waist-high volleys and control of a bouncing ball have produced countless goals from half-chances.

Despite his frequent later moves, he remains a son of Manchester United, who performed canny business by buying him back from Barcelona for a profit. His combative nature has inevitably brought dismissals, but he was never a dirty player. It is unlikely that anyone else would have been appointed Welsh national boss with no previous managerial experience, his inspiration as Red Dragon as well as Red Devil made him a popular choice. A promising start to the qualification campaign for Euro 2004 petered out, and it was no surprise when Hughes accepted the lure of the Premiership at Blackburn Rovers.

☞ Hughes' physique inspired the epithets 'Sparky' (the battery boy) in England and 'El Toro' (the bull) at Barcelona.

👆 1990. Scores twice in the FA Cup final against Crystal Palace.

👆 1994. Scores another Cup final goal against Chelsea, whom he joins and leads to another Cup victory in 1997, his fifth winners medal.

👆 1998. Awarded an MBE for services to football.

👆 1999. Appointed manager of Wales whilst still a player at Southampton.

VITAL STATISTICS

Place of Birth:	Wrexham, Wales
Date of Birth:	1 November 1963 **Died:** n/a
Caps:	72 (Wales) **Goals (International):** 16
Clubs:	Manchester United, Barcelona, Bayern Munich, Chelsea, Southampton, Everton, Blackburn
Appearances:	Club (League): 646
Goals:	Club (League): 164
Trophies:	FAC 1985, 1990, 1994, 1996, 1997; CWC 1991; LC 1992; LT 1993, 1994

LEGEND RATING	
Achievement	7.0
Skill	7.5
Teamwork	10.0
Passion	8.0
Personality	6.5
TOTAL	**39.0**

Hurst, Geoff
West Ham United, England

THE SIGHT OF an airborne Geoff Hurst smashing his hat-trick to seal England's World Cup final victory is one of the country's indelible post-war images. Inevitably, it dwarfed the rest of his career, but at the beginning of the tournament Hurst was a squad player, drafted in by Sir Alf Ramsey merely as cover for the more experienced Roger Hunt and Jimmy Greaves (Hurst had only made his debut for England earlier that year). But an injury to Greaves in the group stage provided Hurst with his opportunity. It was one he seized, scoring the only goal against Argentina in the quarter-finals.

Hurst was groomed as a striker by Ron Greenwood at West Ham; along with England team-mates Martin Peters and skipper Bobby Moore, he was a graduate of the Upton Park academy. After tasting the ultimate success at 24, Hurst's career rather stagnated and by the time he left the Hammers for Stoke at the age of 30 it was all but over. Like nearly all the 1966 England team, he was a managerial failure and excused himself from football for 15 years before returning as a promotional figurehead for England's successful Euro 96 bid. More recently he was part of the team that fought Germany for the right to host the 2006 World Cup Finals. On this occasion he lost.

👍 Hurst is still the only man to score a hat-trick in a World Cup final. It was Hurst's third different winner's medal at Wembley in successive seasons, having earlier won the FA Cup and European Cup Winners' Cup with West Ham.

👎 In the 1964 FA Cup final Hurst scored via the underside of the crossbar, a Wembley precursor to his more famous effort two years later in the World Cup final.

👍 1998. Hurst was made a Knight of the Realm.

☞ In 2001 Hurst finally published his long-awaited autobiography, *1966 And All That*.

☞ A talented all-round sportsman, Hurst considered becoming a professional cricketer.

VITAL STATISTICS

Place of Birth:	Ashton, England		
Date of Birth:	8 December 1941	**Died:** n/a	
Caps:	49 (England)	**Goals (International):** 24	
Clubs:	West Ham, Stoke, West Bromwich		
Appearances:	Club (League for West Ham): 410		
Goals:	Club (League for West Ham): 180		
Trophies:	FAC 1964; CWC 1965; WorC 1966		

LEGEND RATING	
Achievement	8.0
Skill	8.0
Teamwork	7.0
Passion	7.0
Personality	6.0
TOTAL	**36.0**

Hwan Nation Under A Groove
Korea 2 Italy 1, 2002

DEFENDING ONE-NIL LEADS, this one courtesy of Vieiri's near-post header from an 80th-minute corner, is the Italians' stock-in-trade. After 88 minutes, their defence filed back in textbook fashion to repel a final Korean attack before taking their accustomed place in the quarter-finals. A seemingly harmless cross rebounded from the flailing Panucci; Seol-Ki-Hyeon picked his spot from 10 yards and the game was turned on its head.

Extra time continued the air of unreality. Korea were possessed, Italy were rattled. With penalties three minutes away, Lee Young-Pyo's hopeful cross was apparently aiming for Maldini's head. The ageing maestro's legs finally failed, and he scarcely left the turf as Ahn Jung-Hwan's glancing header edged past Buffon into the far corner.

The reaction in Italy was one of disbelief and fury at Ecuadorean referee Byron Moreno. His erratic performance and harsh dismissal of Totti for alleged diving brought the fury of the Italian media on his head. It was partly justified. Moreno was handed a 20-match ban by FIFA after adding on a conveniently long period of extra-time during a league game in Ecuador. He now has a row of toilets named after him in Italy.

☞ South Korea could afford the luxury of a 5th-minute penalty miss. Ahn Jung-Hwan's low kick to Buffon's right lacked power, and the Italian keeper made an excellent save. Ahn made amends.

☞ Italy had Totti sent off for a nonsensical second offence. Tommasi was pulled back for a dubious offside when clear. Cue moaning. In the end they were the victims of their own negative approach; at 1-0 up they had the players to roast Korea, but not the will.

☞ Guus Hiddink became the toast of Korea. He had a street named in his honour, and amongst the many gifts showered upon him was four years of first-class air travel from Korean Air.

SCORERS	**South Korea:** Seol Ki-Hyeon, Ahn Jung-Hwan
	Italy: Vieri
EVENT	Second Round, World Cup Finals, Seoul, 18 June 2002

S. KOREA	(Man: Guus Hiddink)
	1. Lee Woon-Jae 2. Choi Jin-Chul 3. Hong Myung-Bo (Du Ri Cha)
	4. Kim Tae-Young (Hwang Sun-Hong) 5. Kim Nam-Il (Lee Chun-Soo)
	6. Yoo Sang-Chul 7. Lee Young-Pyo 8. Park Ji-Sung 9. Song Chong-Gug
	10. Seol Ki-Hyeon 11. Ahn Jung-Hwan
ITALY	(Man: Giovanni Trapattoni)
	1. Buffon 2. Panucci 3. Iuliano 4. Coco 5. Maldini 6. Zanetti 7. Zambrotta
	(Di Livio) 8. Tommasi 9. Totti 10. Del Piero (Gattuso) 11. Vieri

Immovable Object
Bayern Munich, 1970s

PRIOR TO 1974 the closest a German team had come to winning the European Cup was in 1960, when Eintracht Frankfurt were walloped by a rampant Real Madrid. Atletico Madrid were their opponents in the 1974 final and the Spaniards put up stern resistance, holding them to a 1-1 draw in the first game before succumbing 4-0 in the replay. Once Bayern had taken possession of Europe's biggest prize they were not keen to let go. Cajovski's team won the next two finals, overcoming Don Revie's Leeds in 1975, and then seeing off the challenge of St Etienne in 1976, emulating Ajax and Real Madrid in the process.

The team was gradually dismantled after the 1976 win at Hampden Park; Beckenbauer and Maier retired and Breitner tried his luck abroad. As they faltered the Borussia Monchengladbach team of Vogts, Bonhof and Simonsen took control in Germany, while Liverpool became the new masters of Europe. A domestic revival saw Bayern win the Bundesliga fairly regularly in the 1980s, but the wait for another European Cup would last longer, defeats in the finals of 1982 and 1987 adding to their frustration before their triumph in 2001.

- The 1975 final was played to a backdrop of appalling crowd trouble in Paris, as riot police struggled to contain Leeds fans in the stadium. Leeds were later banned from Europe for four years.
- Aston Villa beat Bayern 1-0 in the 1982 European Cup final; Breitner, Hoeness and Durnberger were still in the team, but past their best.
- Coach Cajovski was the man who led Bayern out of the darkness in the 1960s, building a team around Franz Beckenbauer.
- A young Karl-Heinz Rummenigge played in the 1976 European Cup final.
- Six Bayern players played in the 1974 World Cup final; all the seven listed below except Roth, a winger with a vicious shot.

Manager: Tschik Cajovski

Key Players
Sepp Maier (G) Franz Beckenbauer (D)
Georg Schwarzenbeck (D) Paul Breitner (D)
Uli Hoeness (M) Franz Roth (W/F) Gerd Müller (F)

Trophies
BLG 1972, 1973, 1974 EC 1974, 1975, 1976 WCC 1976

Impossible!
P38 W26 D12 L0

ARSENE WENGER SUGGESTED in November 2002 that his team were strong enough to go a season unbeaten. They were, but not that year. Some uncharacteristically brittle defending and a late surge by Manchester United cost them the title.

In 2003–04 the weaknesses of the previous campaign had been erased. Young Kolo Toure's strength and assurance had replaced the indecision of Pascal Cygan, and Ashley Cole's defending had tightened. Sol Campbell was a colossus. In midfield the slightly muted displays of Ljungberg were compensated by the surprising improvement in the form of Edu; Pires and Vieira remained outstanding influences. Ahead of them Bergkamp's divine touch and vision allowed him to defy advancing years, and the purchase of Jose-Antonio Reyes left the disappointing Wiltord looking for a new club. Oh, and there was Henry, the best player in the world.

After the pivotal encounter at Old Trafford, Arsenal looked a team with a mission, but also a team at peace. The anger and sense of injustice seemed to vanish, replaced by a firmness of purpose and self-belief. There were ordinary performances (at home to Birmingham and Fulham) and tough encounters (at Bolton and Liverpool), but the last few games were negotiated with a certainty and inexorability that their rivals reflected on over the summer. With some justification as it turned out – the Gunners roared into the 2004–05 season with a similar run of success.

☞ The Old Trafford game was a key. Van Nistelrooy's penalty miss meant the Gunners had negotiated their hardest game of the season with a point.

☞ The suspensions as a result of the shenanigans during that game were lighter than the club may have feared, and the replacements performed admirably to maintain the team's momentum.

☝ The identical fixture the following season saw Arsenal's run end. In their 50th game since defeat at Leeds in 2003, they went down 2-0 in another fractious and unedifying encounter.

☝ Perhaps the team's finest performance came in Europe against Inter in their Champions League group. A 5-1 thrashing of a team which had beaten them 3-0 at Highbury was a monumental result.

Manager: Arsene Wenger

Best XI:

Jens Lehmann (G)

Lauren (D) Kolo Toure (D) Sol Campbell (D) Ashley Cole (D)

Edu (M) Patrick Vieira (M) Robert Pires (M) Freddie Ljungberg (M)

Dennis Bergkamp (F) Thierry Henry (F)

Indiscipline

Cards and Chaos

THERE ARE FAR MORE RED CARDS these days, so football must be a dirtier game, right? Nothing could be further from the truth.

Yes, we know that neither Stanley Matthews or Bobby Charlton were cautioned during their careers, but in those days the referee sharpened his pencil just about once every 10 years. In the days of black-and-white TV, a player had to clock up two falls and a submission to warrant a red card. Nowadays, a dozen red cards is a standard haul on any given Saturday. And yet there are still players with unblemished records. In a recent season at Spurs Sol Campbell managed to complete an entire campaign without collecting a single booking, while Gary Lineker, like Matthews and Charlton, kept his nose clean throughout his career.

Of course there are players whose middle names might as well be Trouble. In the modern era Mark Dennis, Vinnie Jones and Alan Smith have all periodically forgotten what it feels like to shower with the rest of the team. But do footballers behave any worse today than they did 40 years ago? Not in our view.

- Take a bow Vinnie Jones. His booking for Chelsea after three seconds remains the quickest ever in the game's history.
- It was 96 years before a player was sent off while playing for England. Alan Mullery achieved this distinction against Yugoslavia in 1968.
- Red and yellow cards were invented by an ex-referee, Ken Aston. He must have got the idea after taking charge of Brazil versus Chile in the 1962 World Cup. The 'Battle of Santiago' was one of the dirtiest games ever played.
- 2003. Sheffield United's First Division league game with West Brom was abandoned after a combination of red cards and injuries reduced them to six players. Rules state that a team must number at least seven.

'The lad was sent off for foul and abusive language, but he swears blind he didn't say a word.'

Oldham manager Joe Royle tries unsuccessfully to explain his player's dismissal

Injuries

Ow!

INJURY is a professional footballer's greatest dread, even worse than being a full-back and discovering that Ryan Giggs has passed a fitness test. At their worst, they can make even spectators wince. Coventry's David Busst, sandwiched in a tackle at Old Trafford, snapped a leg at such a hideous angle that it made Peter Schmeichel physically sick and moved him to attend a post-match counselling session. But not all injuries are career threatening. Dave Beasant once missed several games after dropping a bottle of salad cream on his foot. (Sadly for Chelsea, his handling didn't improve noticeably on his return to the first team.)

It is one of the quirks of the game that some players can tackle their way through seasons of campaigning without collecting a scratch, while others can limp off after a pre-match kickabout with the club mascot. For his frequent absences from the first team during his spell at Aston Villa, Dalian Atkinson acquired the unenviable nickname of 'Sick Note' from sections of the Holte End. This tag has recently been inherited by Tottenham's Darren Anderton. Any career can be ended at a stroke by a mistimed tackle or an awkward landing. Despite the money, adulation and glamour, job security is not one of the benefits offered by professional football.

- Injuries can cost a team in more ways than one. In 1996 Middlesbrough were deducted three points after cancelling a fixture against Blackburn. Boro claimed most of their players were injured or had flu.
- Wembley acquired a hoodoo after players were badly injured in Cup finals during the 1950s and 1960s. In these pre-substitute times, they often changed the course of the match.
- 1980. Proving that danger lurks round many corners, Charlie George lost one finger and mangled two more after a run-in with a lawn mower.
- An injury crisis once forced Man City to name Tony Book and Glyn Pardoe as 'A' team substitutes. Their combined age was 92.

'He'll probably injure himself getting off the bus.'

TV summariser Brian Clough has harsh words for Stuart Pearson before the 1977 FA Cup final

Jairzinho
Brazil

BORN JAIR VENTURA FILHO, the young Jairzinho cut his footballing teeth as a dashing left winger with Botafogo. Less tricky, but more direct than his great predecessor Garrincha, his weapons were a deceptive change of pace and a fierce shot, but it was only when he emerged from Garrincha's shadow and moved to the right that Brazil got the best from him. A key member of the fabulous 1970 World Cup winning side, Jairzinho was an ideal outlet for the Brazilians, bringing the ball forward at high speed and feeding passes inside to Pelé and Gerson. He was also a consistent goal threat, and scored in every round of the tournament including the final (one of only two players to do so in the history of the game). Four years later Brazil were no longer the beautiful team and Jairzinho failed to make the same impact. A spell in European football with Olympique Marseille wasn't a great success and Jairzinho returned to his homeland, where he earned the last of his 98 caps for Brazil aged 38.

- He scored the winner in Cruzeiro's 1976 Copa América win.
- The 1966 World Cup saw Jairzinho playing on his less-favourite left side to accommodate Garrincha. He was twice the player on the right.
- Jairzinho recovered from a twice-broken leg to play in the 1970 World Cup Finals.
- Jairzinho had a somewhat ungainly running style, appearing never to be quite in control. Trust us, he was.
- The other player to score in every round at a World Cup Finals tournament was Alcide Ghiggia for Uruguay in 1950 – but his streak spanned just four games.

VITAL STATISTICS

Place of Birth:	Rio de Janeiro, Brazil
Date of Birth:	25 December 1944 **Died:** n/a
Caps:	98 (Brazil) **Goals (International):** 37
Clubs:	Botafoga, Marseille, Cruzeiro, Portuguesa, Caracas
Trophies:	WorC 1970

LEGEND RATING

Achievement	9.0
Skill	9.0
Teamwork	8.0
Passion	8.0
Personality	7.0
TOTAL	**41.0**

James, Alex
Arsenal, Scotland

THE ARSENAL SIDE of the 1930s was brimming with fantastic players, but Alex James was probably its most gifted. James was short and wiry and the baggy shorts of the day made him look almost Chaplinesque, but there was nothing slapstick about his football. Like his manager, the legendary Herbert Chapman, James was ahead of his time and, as a natural reader of the game, he adapted well to Chapman's innovative tactics. Arsenal fought off fierce competition to sign him from Preston, beating Liverpool, Aston Villa, Birmingham and Manchester City, although initially they may have wondered if it had been worth the trouble; James struggled to settle and was even dropped for a spell. Then one day, in a typically unconventional move, Chapman turned up at James's house and hauled him out of bed to play in an FA Cup replay at Birmingham. From thereon James never looked back, forming a successful partnership with the prolific Cliff Bastin on the left side of Arsenal's 3-4-3 formation. Both were consistently inspirational as Arsenal walked away with trophy after trophy. Eight caps for Scotland was a scandalous waste of his talent, especially as he was one of the architects of their finest pre-war hour: the 5-1 thrashing of England by the 'Wembley Wizards' in 1928.

☞ Arsenal paid Preston £8,750 for James in 1929 – a huge fee at the time.

☞ Preston were frequently referred to as 'Alex James and 10 others'.

✍ James's eight Scotland caps were spread over seven years, and included four goals, two of them in the annihilation of England in 1928.

☞ James's obituary appeared in *The Times*, a rare accolade for a footballer in 1953.

✍ James scored a cracking goal in the 1930 FA Cup final. Taking a free-kick quickly, he played a one-two with Bastin and smashed the ball into the roof of the net.

VITAL STATISTICS

Place of Birth:	Mossend, Scotland	
Date of Birth:	14 September 1901	**Died:** 1 June 1953
Caps:	8 (Scotland)	**Goals (International):** 4
Clubs:	Raith Rovers, Preston North End, Arsenal	
Appearances:	Club (League for Arsenal): 231	
Goals:	Club (League for Arsenal): 26	
Trophies:	FAC 1930, 1936; LT 1931, 1933, 1934, 1935	

Achievement	8.0	
Skill	9.0	
Teamwork	8.0	
Passion	7.0	
Personality	7.0	
TOTAL	**39.0**	

LEGEND RATING

Jargon and Gibberish
Thoughts From The Box

FOOTBALL IS NOT UNIQUE in having its own 'trade' vocabulary. All professions like to shroud themselves with an air of mystery by inventing a language that confuses and belittles outsiders. Computer programmers, financiers, doctors – all rely on our fear of their superior knowledge to protect their interests. Football is unique in having a language that is lacking in poetry and invention, but what it lacks in these departments it makes up for in sheer and utter nonsense. Without further ado, here are some favourites:

'*Well we got nine … and you can't score more than that.*' Bobby Robson.

'*When a player gets to 30, so does his body.*' Glenn Hoddle

'*I think we just ran out of legs.*' David Pleat

'*You half fancied that to go in as it was dipping and rising at the same time.*' Ron Atkinson

'*Hagi could open a tin of beans with his left foot.*' Ray Clemence

All masterpieces of verbal effluvium, but these individuals are only competing for the best-supporting role. Not even Atkinson's bizarre pronouncements threaten the pre-eminence of Keggy Keegle (as he was once dubbed by Brian Moore). Always ready with a cliché or banality, Our Kev is the nonpareil of football jargon-merchants.

The Very Best of Kev:

- 'Shaun Wright-Phillips has got a big heart. It's as big as him, which isn't very big, but it's bigger.'
- 'In some ways, cramp is worse than having a broken leg.'
- 'You get bunches of players like you do bananas, though that is a bad comparison.'
- 'It's like a toaster, the ref's shirt pocket. Every time there's a tackle, up pops a yellow card.'
- 'I know what is round the corner, I just don't know where the corner is. But the onus is on us to perform and we must control the bandwagon.'

'We must have had 99 per cent of the game. It was the other three per cent that cost us the match.'

The normally coherent Ruud Gullit forgets his calculator

Jennings, Pat
Tottenham Hotspur, Arsenal, Northern Ireland

WHEN TOTTENHAM sold the 32-year-old Pat Jennings for a paltry £40,000 in 1977 their fans were deeply unhappy. So imagine how they felt when, shortly after, it was revealed that the team who had bought him were Arsenal. On second thoughts, don't even go there....

Jennings played for a further seven seasons at Arsenal, and continued playing for Northern Ireland for a couple of years after that, before returning to Spurs in 1993 as goalkeeping coach.

In an era when British football was littered with great goalkeepers (except Scotland, of course), Jennings was up there with the best of them. A big man, with almost comically large hands, he exuded a comforting presence behind the defence not unlike Peter Schmeichel, although he was less inclined to fits of apoplectic rage than the excitable Dane. 'Big Pat' was perhaps marginally less acrobatic than one or two of his contemporaries, but his handling was impeccable. Jennings was a fixture in the Northern Ireland team in an international career spanning an amazing 22 years. He played in two World Cup finals, making his final appearance in the 1986 Finals against Brazil in Mexico – on his 41st birthday.

- Probably his finest moment was a brilliant performance in Northern Ireland's 1-0 win over hosts Spain at the 1982 World Cup Finals.
- Jennings scored a freak goal in the 1967 Charity Shield, a huge punt bouncing over Alex Stepney into the Manchester United goal.
- He was Football Writers' Player of the Year, 1973 and PFA Player of the Year in 1976.
- Undoubtedly, Jennings' most embarrassing moment was being dressed as a car battery in a ludicrous 1970s TV advertisement.
- He received an MBE in 1976 and an OBE in 1987.

VITAL STATISTICS

Place of Birth:	County Down, Northern Ireland		
Date of Birth:	12 June 1945	**Died:** n/a	
Caps:	119 (N. Ireland)	**Goals (International):** 0	
Clubs:	Watford, Tottenham, Arsenal		
Appearances:	Club (League): 757		
Goals:	Club (League): 0		
Trophies:	FAC 1967, 1979; LC 1971, 1973; EUFAC 1973		

LEGEND RATING	
Achievement	7.0
Skill	9.0
Teamwork	8.0
Passion	9.0
Personality	7.0
TOTAL	**40.0**

Jock's Delight
Celtic 2 Internazionale 1, 1967

IN THE TUNNEL it looked like a mismatch. Favourites Internazionale stood tall, tanned and experienced, and numbered Facchetti, Mazzola and Domenghini amongst their team of European all-stars. Celtic, in comparison, appeared pale, undersized and more used to scrapping in a frost-bound Glasgow than the Portuguese sunshine, and when Mazzola converted a penalty on six minutes after Craig had fouled Cappellini, few gave the Scots an earthly chance against Inter's famous catenaccio ('doorbolt') defence. Led by the peerless Facchetti, the Milan side were pioneers of the cagey game, defending in numbers and countering with speed.

But the turning-point came on the hour; making amends for his earlier indiscretion, Craig combined with Murdoch to create a chance that Gemmell converted with aplomb. A rattled Inter had been hustled into altering their game plan, but couldn't raise the pace. The match was heading for extra-time when a speculative cross-shot from the edge of the box was swept in by Chalmers with six minutes to go. Lucky perhaps, but no more than the Bhoys' performance merited. Inter had been sunk by Glaswegian passion, the Cup belonged to Celtic.

- Celtic were the first British team ever to win the European Cup, beating Manchester United to it by a year.
- Tommy Gemmell also scored in the 1970 final, but Celtic lost 2-1 to Feyenoord
- The match proved to be third time unlucky for Inter (they had won the trophy in 1964 and 1965).
- A genuine triumph for the city: all of Celtic's team were born within 15 miles of Glasgow.
- For Celtic the match completed a clean sweep; they had already won a domestic treble.

SCORERS   **Celtic:** Gemmell, Chalmers
              Internazionale: Mazzola (pen.)
EVENT   European Cup final, Lisbon, 25 May 1967

CELTIC   (Man: Jock Stein)
              1. Simpson 2. Craig 3. Gemmell 4. Murdoch 5. McNeill 6. Clark
              7. Johnstone 8. Wallace 9. Chalmers 10. Auld 11. Lennox
INTER   (Man: Helenio Herrera)
              1. Sarti 2. Burgnich 3. Facchetti 4. Bedin 5. Guarneri 6. Picchi
              7. Bicicli 8. Mazzola 9. Cappellini 10. Corso 11. Domenghini

Johnstone, Jimmy

Celtic, Scotland

IF JOCK STEIN was the architect of Celtic's greatest-ever team and Billy McNeill its keystone, then Jimmy 'Jinky' Johnstone was its magician-in-chief. A small, mercurial winger from a rich Scottish tradition of natural ball-players, Johnstone could win a game in a moment and was dubbed the 'flying flea' by a laudatory French press after a European tie against Nantes.

Although a member of the 1967 European Cup winning team, his most memorable games were Celtic's most infamous, namely the two ties against Racing Club in the 1967 World Club Championship. Johnstone's reputation saw him cynically hacked and abused in the first-drawn game (he had to wash opponents' spittle from his hair at half-time) and, determined to give as good as he got in the replay, he eventually received a red card for elbowing an opponent.

His greatest game came in 1970 when, against Leeds in a European Cup semi-final, he teased and tormented the English team's defence in a famous victory. He was ineffective in the final though, well shackled by an impressive Feyenoord rearguard. Despite his success, the game failed to make him his fortune and he was later forced to take jobs as a lorry driver and construction worker.

- Johnstone would have won more than 23 Scottish caps but for a lifelong fear of flying.
- His debut in 1963 was also his heaviest defeat as a player; a 6-0 trouncing by Kilmarnock.
- Johnstone once scored twice in a 5-1 drubbing of Red Star Belgrade. Before the match Jock Stein had promised him he would not have to fly to the return leg if Celtic won easily.
- Johnstone wasn't the only player sent off against Racing Club – three Celtic players were dismissed along with two opponents.

VITAL STATISTICS

Place of Birth:	Viewpark, Lanarkshire, Scotland		
Date of Birth:	30 September 1944	**Died:** n/a	
Caps:	23 (Scotland)	**Goals (International):** 4	
Clubs:	Celtic, San Jose Earthquakes, Sheffield United,		
	Dundee		
Appearances:	Club (League): 332		
Goals:	Club (League): 84		
Trophies:	SLT 1966–1974; SFAC 1965, 1967, 1969,		
	1971, 1972, 1974, 1975; EC 1967		

LEGEND RATING	
Achievement	7.0
Skill	9.0
Teamwork	6.0
Passion	8.0
Personality	7.0
TOTAL	**37.0**

Jules Rimet Trophy
World Cup

THE WORLD CUP was the brainchild of the president and the secretary of FIFA, Jules Rimet and Henri Delaunay. The only global tournament at the time was the strictly amateur Olympics, so Rimet persuaded FIFA to fund its own tournament. On their formation in 1904, FIFA had reserved the right to organise just such an event. Uruguay was the venue for the first tournament in 1930, but only four European teams travelled (due to a dispute with FIFA none of the British home nations bothered turning up). It would be 1950 before England competed in a Finals tournament, and it was not until 1958 that all four home nations reached the Finals. Qualification has become more difficult since the early days, largely because of the improvements made by some of the so-called lesser nations. Wales and Northern Ireland no longer enjoy success at international level, while the likes of Denmark and Turkey, once no-hopers, are now among the top seeded teams in Europe. Many observers were critical of the expansion of the Finals from 16 to 24, and then 32 teams. True, the reasons were principally commercial, and it has led to the inclusion of a higher proportion of weak sides, but the developing nations will only improve from exposure to a high level of competition.

- 👍 Brazil were allowed to keep the original trophy after winning for the third time in 1970.
- ☞ In a table based on results in World Cup Finals, the top sides are Brazil, Germany, Italy, Argentina and England.
- ☞ The 2002 World Cup in Japan and Korea was the first tournament outside Europe or the Americas. The 2010 finals will take place in South Africa.
- ☞ In 1986 Morocco became the first African team to get beyond the initial groups at the Finals. Cameroon went one better in 1990, reaching the quarter-finals and scaring England before losing on penalties.

'To say that these men paid their shillings to watch twenty-two hirelings kick a ball is merely to say that a violin is wood and catgut, that *Hamlet* is so much paper and ink.'

J. B. Priestley, a rare example of a literary giant with a good word for the beautiful game

Juventus
The Dream Team

STRANGELY, given that they were one of the dominant sides of the 1990s, none of Juventus' 1996 European Cup winning side makes it into our Dream Team. This is largely down to the rapidity with which players have come and gone in recent years; great players like Zidane, Baggio and Ravanelli have passed fleetingly through Turin. To be fair, Gianluca Vialli stayed a little longer but the competition for places up front means that even he fails to make the grade. Boniperti is the club's leading scorer, and leaving Bettega out of any Juve side would be considered a lynching offence by fans of the Old Lady.

The midfield is made up of the 1980s trio, supplemented by the Argentinian genius, Sivori. The moustachioed winger, Causio, and Ferrari, one of the greats from Juve's pre-war successes, keep the likes of Brady and Dino Baggio on the bench. Defensively, in true Italian tradition, this team is formidable. In goal the great Dino Zoff would probably be bored, hoping for a rare error from Scirea or Cabrini to help keep his fingers warm. Then again, with the merciless Gentile and Monti kicking lumps out of their opponents in front of him, he would inevitably have the occasional free-kick to deal with.

- Manager Carlo Carcano set the tone for future decades by winning five consecutive championships in the 1930s.
- Even in the 1930s Juve were known for importing players; Monti was Argentinian, as was his colleague Raimundo Orsi. In the 1950s and 1960s this trend was continued with the purchase of John Charles and the Danes Karl and John Hansen.
- Sivori, who scored nearly 150 goals for Juve, was named European Footballer of the Year in 1961. Internationally he played for both Argentina and his adopted Italy.
- Juventus' record of 25 championships puts them a distance ahead of their rivals in Italy; the Milan sides have 29 between them (AC 16 Inter 13).

Manager: Carlo Carcano

4-4-2

Dino Zoff (70s/80s)

Claudio Gentile (70s/80s) Gaetano Scirea (70s/80s) Luis Monti (30s)
Antonio Cabrini (80s)

Zbigniew Boniek (80s) Michel Platini (80s) Marco Tardelli (80s)
Omar Sivori (50s/60s)

Roberto Bettega (70s) Giampiero Boniperti (40s/50s)

Subs: Gianluigi Buffon (G) (00s) Carlo Parola (D) (50s) Franco Causio (M) (70s) Giovanni Ferrari (M/F) (30s) John Charles (F) (50s/60s)

Kanu, Nwankwo
Ajax, Arsenal, Nigeria

WHEN A PLAYER ACHIEVES so much at an early age, there is a danger that the rest of his career will be an anti-climax. When, aged 21, the player is diagnosed with a life-threatening heart condition, the rest of his career becomes a luxury. A luxury, fortunately, that Kanu is now enjoying, having made a complete recovery with the aid of an operation to repair a heart valve. Kanu was lured to Europe along with Finidi George, having been spotted playing in Nigeria. His natural touch and balance were surprising in such a big youth, and he possessed good vision and passing. He was still 18 when he came on as a substitute in the European Cup final. He wasn't yet 21 when he captained Nigeria in their successful campaign at the 1996 Olympics.

A dream move to Inter Milan turned into a personal nightmare, but the return to fitness was testimony to great strength of character. The form at Arsenal has been fitful, with only rare moments of genius like his hat-trick against Chelsea in 1999, the last curled in from a nigh-impossible angle. Inconsistency and the strength of the Arsenal squad saw his opportunities diminish, so he moved to West Brom in the summer of 2004, still only 29 years old.

- A year after picking up his winner's medal in the European Cup, Kanu played in a second final, but a disappointing performance from Ajax meant no second medal.
- Nigeria beat a full Brazilian team 4-3 in the semi-finals at the Olympics, Kanu scoring the Golden Goal winner. The opposition in the final was equally intimidating, but Argentina, too, were sent packing, this time 3-2.
- The African Nations Cup has proved elusive for Nigeria's eagles. They pulled out of the 1996 tournament, lost on penalties to Cameroon in 2000, and lost in the semi-finals to Mali in 2002.
- Kanu has twice won African Footballer of the Year, in 1996 and 1999.

VITAL STATISTICS

Place of Birth:	Owerri, Nigeria
Date of Birth:	1 August 1976 **Died:** n/a
Caps:	39 (Nigeria) **Goals (International):** 12
Clubs:	Federation Works, Iwuanyanwo Nationale, Ajax, Inter Milan, Arsenal, West Brom
Appearances:	Club (League): 258
Goals:	Club (League): 61
Trophies:	DLT 1994, 1995, 1996; LT 2002, 2004; FAC 2002, 2003; EC 1995

Achievement	7.0
Skill	8.0
Teamwork	7.0
Passion	8.0
Personality	6.0
TOTAL	**36.0**

LEGEND RATING

Keane, Roy
Manchester United, Republic of Ireland

ROY KEANE WAS PLAYING for Cobh Ramblers when he was spotted by a Nottingham Forest scout and brought to England by Brian Clough in 1990. Three years later Forest turned their £10,000 investment into £3.75 m from Manchester United. What seemed an extraordinary fee in 1993 now looks a snip, as Keane has been the driving force behind the Old Trafford club's recent run of success.

In the 2000–01 season Keane was vociferous in his criticism of his team-mates, accusing them of failing to maintain their hunger for success after the treble-winning season. Keane could lay claim to being the most complete midfielder in the modern era – only Patrick Vieira runs him close and, like Vieira, Keane has a dark side to his game. Fans will remember sendings-off for vicious tackles and violent outbursts alongside the dominant, driving performances. Keane's influence was also strong at international level. In a team big on passion but short on world-class players, it is the United man who was frequently asked to stand tall in crucial games. Unlike club colleague Ryan Giggs, Keane has always been there for his country, before his ill-judged outburst in the 2002 World Cup final and apparent retirement from international football. He made a surprise return to the Ireland team in 2004.

☞ A new United contract in 2000 worth £52,000 per week made him – for a brief spell – the highest paid player in the Premiership, and destroyed Old Trafford's established wage structure.

👆 He was the 2000 PFA and Football Writers' Player of the Year.

👆 In 1999 Keane missed United's famous Champions League final triumph over Bayern Munich through suspension.

☞ 1996–2001. United won the league title every year, except the one Keane spent sidelined with cruciate knee ligament damage.

☞ Keane has been critical of United's passionless corporate fans, once famously dismissing them as the 'prawn sandwich brigade'.

👆 2004. He set a modern-era record, playing in six FA Cup finals; Lord Arthur Kinnaird played in nine between 1873 and 1883.

VITAL STATISTICS

Place of Birth:	Cork, Ireland	
Date of Birth:	10 August 1971	**Died:** n/a
Caps:	62 (R. Ireland)	**Goals (International):** 9
Clubs:	Nottingham Forest, Manchester United	
Appearances:	Club (League): 430	
Goals:	Club (League): 60	
Trophies:	EC 1999; LT 1994, 1996, 1997, 1999, 2000, 2001, 2003; FAC 1994, 1996, 1999, 2004	

LEGEND RATING	
Achievement	9.0
Skill	7.5
Teamwork	9.0
Passion	9.5
Personality	6.0
TOTAL	**41.0**

Keegan, Kevin

Liverpool, Hamburg, Southampton, Newcastle United, England

HUGELY COMMITTED, deeply passionate – and, at times, comically naive – Kevin Keegan is one of the great characters of the modern game. Plucked from obscurity at Scunthorpe by Bill Shankly, Keegan became the focal point of Liverpool's attack, and his almost telepathic understanding with John Toshack proved to be one of the club's most successful striking partnerships. Never afraid of a new challenge, Keegan later moved to Hamburg, where his enthusiasm won colleagues and fans over after a shaky start. Back to England and another successful spell at Southampton under Lawrie McMenemy, and a final flourish at Newcastle.

Twenty-one goals in 63 internationals was a decent return for a striker, but Keegan rarely got the opportunity to shine in major tournaments – a 20-minute stint as a substitute against Spain in 1982 was his only appearance at a World Cup Finals. As a club manager Keegan has always sent out teams with one objective in mind: to attack. This approach has made his teams popular but has not seen him collect any major silverware. He was an absurd choice as England manager, clearly lacking the tactical wherewithal for international football, but he does deserve credit for reviving the fortunes of Newcastle, Fulham and Manchester City.

- He was Footballer of the Year, 1976 and European Footballer of the Year, 1978 and 1979.
- He is famous for emotional outbursts, most notably when wound up by Alex Ferguson in the race for the 1997 league title.
- He retired from international football when he was left out of Bobby Robson's first squad in 1982.
- His song, '*Head Over Heels*', was a minor hit in both England and Germany.
- He resigned as England manager after a home defeat by Germany in 2000, and was honest enough to admit to his tactical shortcomings.

VITAL STATISTICS

				MANAGER		PLAYER	
Place of Birth:	Armthorpe, Yorkshire, England						
Date of Birth:	14 February 1951	**Died:** n/a					
Caps:	63 (England)	**Goals (International):** 21					
Clubs:	Scunthorpe United, Liverpool, Hamburg,			Achievement	5	Achievement	9
	Southampton, Newcastle			Tactical Awareness	5	Skill	7
Appearances:	Club (for Liverpool): 323			Motivation	9	Teamwork	9
Goals:	Club (for Liverpool): 100			Team Selection/Transfers	9	Passion	9
Trophies:	LT 1973, 1976, 1977; FAC 1974;			Personality	8	Personality	8
	EUFAC 1976; EC 1977; BLG 1979;						
	European Player of the Year 1978, 1979			**TOTAL**	**36**	**TOTAL**	**42**

LEGEND RATING

Kempes, Mario
Argentina

THERE HAVE ALWAYS been players whose flames have flickered brilliantly one minute, only to be put out with an industrial-strength fire extinguisher the next. Mario Kempes fits into this category. A short purple patch elevated what would have been a worthy career into a memorable one, when Kempes fired Argentina to victory in the 1978 World Cup.

Kempes broke through into the national team early, but showed little sign of the success to come; in the 1974 World Cup Finals he failed to score a single goal. A move to Valencia in Spain helped improve his game against better defenders, and he succeeded in adding more disciplined finishing to the pace, balance and close control he already possessed. Suitably honed, Kempes cut a dash at the 1978 World Cup, his six goals in a tight tournament proving decisive, especially his excellent brace in the final against Holland. The winning goal, the finale to a burst through the Dutch defence, epitomised his determination, persistence and exquisite balance. Thereafter though, Kempes retreated into mediocrity, flitting between Europe and Argentina and failing to make an impact, or even score a goal, in the 1982 World Cup.

- He scored a penalty in the shoot-out against Arsenal in Valencia's 1980 European Cup Winners' Cup victory.
- He was South American Footballer of the Year in 1978.
- Kempes scored 24 goals in his first season in La Liga, and 28 the following year, the highest return since the great Di Stefano in 1957.
- He is known as 'El Matador' for his Latin good looks and fashionable long hair.
- He was the only player in Argentina's 1978 squad playing outside South America.

VITAL STATISTICS

Place of Birth:	Bellville, Cordoba, Argentina	
Date of Birth:	15 July 1952	**Died:** n/a
Caps:	43 (Argentina)	**Goals (International):** 20
Clubs:	Instituto de Cordoba, Rosario Central, Valencia, River Plate	
Appearances:	Club (League): 494	
Goals:	Club (League): 276	
Trophies:	CWC 1980; WorC 1978	

LEGEND RATING

Achievement	8.0
Skill	8.0
Teamwork	6.0
Passion	7.0
Personality	8.0
TOTAL	**37.0**

Klinsmann, Jurgen
Tottenham Hotspur, Germany

JURGEN KLINSMANN has always been keen to embrace new challenges, and when he returned to Tottenham Hotspur for a second spell in December 1997 he faced one of his biggest. Under the inept management of Christian Gross, an unpopular appointment by an unpopular chairman, Alan Sugar, the club were facing relegation. That they avoided this fate was largely down to the German striker who, repeating his success of the 1994–95 season, lit up White Hart Lane with his leggy athleticism and, more crucially, goals.

Klinsmann's appetite for new adventures is evidenced by his willingness to play in Italy, France and England, as well as his native Germany. Quick and incisive in the box, as well as good in the air, Klinsmann has been a consistent goal scorer at every one of his clubs, even maintaining an impressive ratio in the notoriously defensive Serie A with Inter. Adaptable and intelligent (while at Spurs he spoke English more eloquently than most of his colleagues), he appeared in three World Cups, scoring 11 goals in 17 games. Sometimes criticised for diving, it was a foul on him that won the penalty from which Andreas Brehme scored to win the 1990 World Cup final for Germany.

☞ The much-travelled Klinsmann spent 15 years in search of a league title before he finally won one – in the Serie A with Inter Milan in 1989.

☞ He arrived at Spurs in 1994 amidst media furore about his penchant for diving. A headlong plunge towards the corner flag on scoring his first goal for the club revealed a sense of humour.

👍 Klinsmann ended the 1994–95 season having turned the media around sufficiently for the Football Writers' Association to vote him their Player of the Year.

VITAL STATISTICS

Place of Birth:	Goppingen, Germany		
Date of Birth:	30 July 1964	**Died:** n/a	
Caps:	108 (Germany)	**Goals (International):** 47	
Clubs:	Stuttgart Kickers, VfB Stuttgart, Inter Milan,		
	Monaco, Tottenham, Bayern Munich, Sampdoria		
Appearances:	Club (League): 491		
Goals:	Club (League): 194		
Trophies:	SA 1989; WorC 1990; BLG 1997; EuroC 1996;		
	UEFAC 1996		

Achievement	9.0
Skill	8.0
Teamwork	9.0
Passion	8.0
Personality	7.0
TOTAL	**41.0**

LEGEND RATING

Koeman, Ronald

Ajax, PSV Eindhoven, Barcelona, Feyenoord, Holland

WITH A SOUBRIQUET of The Fourth Dutchman, applied in deference to team-mates Gullit, Van Basten and Rijkaard, one might raise an eyebrow at the prospect of Ronald Koeman's inclusion in a list of all-time greats. That is, until one looks at his record. From appearing as a prodigious 17-year-old at Groningen, his move upwards was only a matter of time. Aged 20, Ajax duly obliged. From then on, a league winner's medal, whether Dutch or Spanish, could seemingly be minted pre-season with his name already inscribed.

Ajax's lapse in letting him go to PSV proved their loss alone, as Koeman continued to pile on the silverware. After his appearances in the victorious shop window that was the 1988 European Championship squad, Cruyff's sizeable cheque book took him to Barcelona (one of the quixotic coach's smarter moves).

He became a Catalan treasure, whose name became a first-pick for any fan compiling their team of Barcelona all-stars. Neither tall for a central defender, nor a great tackler, Koeman's asset was his slide-rule distribution and instant ability to not only turn defence into attack but apply its coup de grace as well. In the nation of Total Football, he was arguably its purest executioner.

👍 Finest footballing moment: Wembley, 1992. Koeman's free-kick, deep into extra-time, won Barcelona their only European Cup.

👍 Koeman's goalscoring ratio is one of the finest-ever for a defender and the envy of some strikers. A dead-ball specialist, his free-kicks and penalties brought him much of his impressive total.

☞ Koeman is the first player to win the European Cup with different clubs; PSV in 1988 and Barcelona four years later.

👍 January 2000 – after spells as assistant coach at Barcelona and Vitesse Arnhem, Koeman landed his first role as head coach when taking the helm at Ajax. A League and Cup double followed in 2002. His contract runs until 2006.

☞ Koeman was assistant to Dutch national coach Gus Hiddink at the 1998 World Cup Finals.

VITAL STATISTICS

Place of Birth:	Zaandam, Holland	
Date of Birth:	21 March 1963	**Died:** n/a
Caps:	78 (Holland)	**Goals (International):** 14
Clubs:	As Player: FC Groningen, Ajax, PSV Eindhoven,	
	Barcelona, Feyenoord; As Head Coach: Ajax	
Appearances:	Club (All Matches): 533	
Goals:	Club (All Matches): 193	
Trophies:	OLT 1985, 1987–89; PLA 1991–94; EC 1988,	
	1992; EuroC 1988	

LEGEND RATING	
Achievement	9.0
Skill	8.0
Teamwork	10.0
Passion	8.0
Personality	7.0
TOTAL	**42.0**

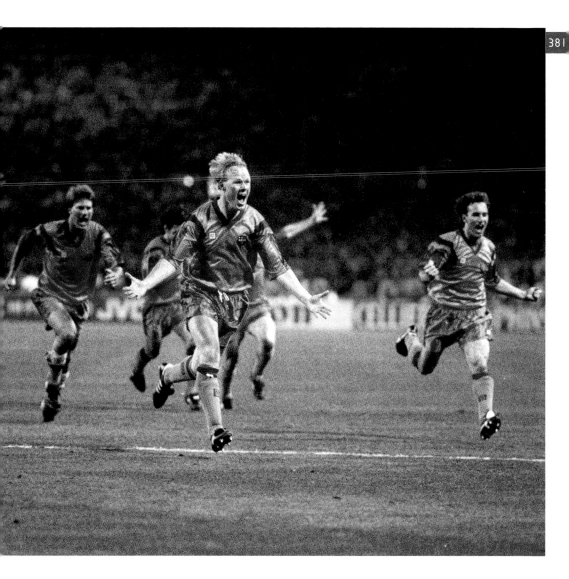

Krol, Ruud

Ajax, Holland

THE AJAX AND HOLLAND TEAMS of the 1970s will always be remembered for their fluid attacking football. What is often forgotten is their propensity for winning games whilst keeping a clean sheet.

Going into the 1974 World Cup final, Holland had conceded only a single goal in six group games. The orchestrator of that mean defence was Ruud Krol, the Ajax left-back. Already an international star after performing well in Ajax's European Cup successes, Krol cemented his reputation as a world class performer in that 1974 tournament.

Quick and direct, Krol's surging runs were a feature of the Dutch attacking play, and he could unleash a ferocious shot. In common with many of his colleagues, he was uncompromising in the tackle; footage exists of Krol leaving opponents writhing on the ground with perfectly fair tackles.

By the time the 1978 tournament came around, Krol's intelligent use of the ball and reading of the game saw him playing at sweeper in a Dutch team without the mesmeric influence of Cruyff or van Hanegem. Again Krol excelled, but again the Holy Grail evaded him.

☞ 'Football is not art, but there is an art to playing good football.' Ruud Krol on the Beautiful Game.

👍 Krol's 83 caps remained a Dutch record until broken by Aron Winter in 2000.

☞ After leaving Ajax for a spell with Vancouver Whitecaps, Krol spent four years with Napoli in Italy.

👍 Like Holland, Ajax also built their success on a sound back four. They kept clean sheets in all three of their European Cup final wins.

VITAL STATISTICS

Place of Birth:	Amsterdam, Holland	
Date of Birth:	24 March 1949	**Died:** n/a
Caps:	83 (Holland)	**Goals (International):** 4
Clubs:	Ajax, Vancouver Whitecaps, Napoli, Cannes	
Appearances:	Club (All Matches for Ajax): 457	
Goals:	Club (All Matches for Ajax): 30	
Trophies:	DLT 1970, 1972, 1973, 1977, 1979, 1980;	
	EC 1971, 1972, 1973; WCC 1972; ESC 1972	

Achievement	9.0
Skill	7.0
Teamwork	9.0
Passion	8.0
Personality	8.0
TOTAL	**41.0**

LEGEND RATING

Larsson, Henrik
Celtic, Sweden

SWEDEN'S FINEST EXPORT since Abba got a boyhood taste for football watching English league matches live on television, but it is north of the border where Henrik Larsson has made his name, becoming the biggest Celtic icon of the past 10 years.

Eye-catching both for his striking ability and fashionable dreadlocks, his 16 goals were a major factor in the title coming home to Parkhead after nine years of Rangers domination. It nearly ended there. After breaking his leg during a UEFA Cup match against Lyon in October 1999, there were fears that Larsson would never play again. But he battled back and, after a gradual comeback programme, soon began to find the net again. Following the arrival of Martin O'Neill as manager, Larsson's 42-goal season helped Celtic sweep all before them in 2001, and he followed that with near-identical campaigns in the following two seasons.

A seasoned international, he was one of the scorers in Sweden's quarter-final defeat of Romania in USA 94, and did his reputation no harm in the Far East in 2002, before announcing his retirement from internationals. 2003–04 was the last season of his contract with Celtic. After an emotional farewell, Barcelona won the race for his signature. For Celtic fans, he will always be a son of Glasgow.

- His 2001 European Golden Boot award was the first made to a Scottish-based player since Ally McCoist in 1993.
- He scored on his international debut as Sweden qualified for USA 94.
- Larsson was signed twice by Wim Jansen, for Feyenoord and Celtic.
- His son Jordan is named after his hero, basketball star Michael Jordan.
- Scores twice for Celtic in the 2003 UEFA Cup final, only for the Bhoys to succumb 3-2 to Porto.
- His impressive form in Euro 2004 made a mockery of his international 'retirement' two years earlier.

VITAL STATISTICS

Place of Birth:	Helsingborg, Sweden
Date of Birth:	20 September 1971 **Died:** n/a
Caps:	77 (Sweden) **Goals (International):** 28
Clubs:	Hogabog BK, Helsingborgs BK, Feyenoord, Celtic, Barcelona
Appearances:	Club (League): 448
Goals:	Club (League): 275
Trophies:	SLT 1998, 2001, 2002, 2004; SFAC 2001, 2002, 2004

LEGEND RATING	
Achievement	7.0
Skill	8.0
Teamwork	8.0
Passion	7.0
Personality	6.0
TOTAL	**36.0**

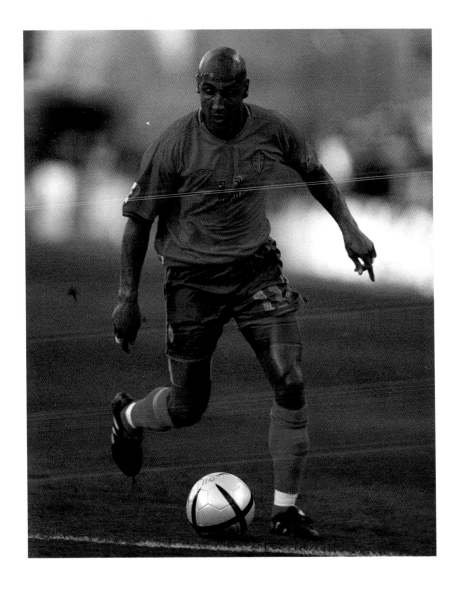

Last Gasp Title
Liverpool 0 Arsenal 2, 1989

IT REMAINS THE MOST dramatic finish to a championship race in history. A rearranged fixture had inadvertently brought the top two together for the season's final game. Liverpool held all the aces; only a two-goal Arsenal victory would bring the title to Highbury.

A goalless first-half suited Liverpool, but the home crowd's celebrations were put on ice at 52 minutes, when Alan Smith, applying the faintest of touches to a Nigel Winterburn free-kick, gave Arsenal the lead. The goal made Liverpool edgy, and as the final whistle drew closer they retreated towards their own goal, inviting pressure from the Gunners.

Deep into injury time the score remained 1-0 and the Kop's volume was increasing. Steve McMahon rallied the Liverpool ranks, gesturing frantically to his team-mates that there was just one minute to go. But a minute was all Arsenal needed. Dixon pumped a hopeful last effort to Smith, who spotted the desperate gallop of Michael Thomas. The pass was precise, the flick over Grobbelaar ice-cool. On 91 minutes and 22 seconds, Arsenal had won it.

- Ray Kennedy's goal at White Hart Lane to clinch the 1971 title and Alan Sunderland's winner in the FA Cup final eight years later had brought Arsenal fans to the brink. This result reduced them to gibbering wrecks.
- Both teams finished with virtually identical records: W22 D10 L6 GD +37. Arsenal won by scoring 73 goals to Liverpool's 65.
- Arsenal's task had looked impossible after Liverpool beat West Ham 5-1 in their previous home game to create a two-goal cushion. The *Daily Mirror* headline the following day was typical: 'You Haven't Got A Prayer, Arsenal'.
- Brian Moore's commentary is familiar to Arsenal fans: 'Thomas … it's up for grabs now … Thomasss!'

SCORERS	Smith, Thomas
EVENT	Division One, Anfield, 26 May 1989
LIVERPOOL	(Man: Kenny Dalglish) 1. Grobbelaar 2. Ablett 3. Staunton 4. Nicol 5. Whelan 6. Hansen 7. Houghton 8. Aldridge 9. Rush 10. Barnes 11. McMahon
ARSENAL	(Man: George Graham) 1. Lukic 2. Dixon 3. Winterburn 4. Thomas 5. O'Leary 6. Adams 7. Rocastle 8. Richardson 9. Smith 10. Bould 11. Merson

Lato, Grzegorz
Stal Mielec, Poland

STOCKY AND BALDING, Grzegorz Lato cut an unlikely looking sporting hero, but his three World Cup Finals and 10 goals made him one of Poland's most celebrated sons. Lato's whippet-like pace and tireless running proved a handful for most defenders, including Norman Hunter, whose missed tackle resulted in Lato's assist for Poland's goal at Wembley in 1973 – a goal that ensured their qualification for the Finals at England's expense.

In Germany a year later, where his combination with the dashing Andrej Szarmach was a feature of the tournament, Lato (who spent most of his career with Polish outfit Stal Mielec) finished as top scorer, his seven goals ensuring little-fancied Poland took third place.

Four years later the Poles disappointed, but 1982 provided Lato with a swansong as he and Szarmach were reunited alongside the new superstar, Zbigniew Boniek. Older, and with even less hair, he helped Poland to yet another third-place finish. Lato briefly played alongside his compatriot Wlodek Lubanski, for KSC Lokeren in Belgium, before a spot of belated globetrotting saw him wind up his career in Mexico and Canada.

- Lato's 10 World Cup Finals' goals have been bettered only by Pelé, Gerd Müller and Just Fontaine.
- Lato won his 100th cap in Poland's Boniek-inspired destruction of Belgium in the 1982 tournament.
- In 1976 a crowd of 106,000 in Warsaw saw Poland beat the mighty Dutch team of Cruyff and Neeskens 4-1 in a European Championship qualifier. Lato was among the scorers.
- His final goal tally (42) for Poland was second only to Lubanski.
- Lato has recently renewed his links with football, becoming a FIFA ambassador for childrens' charities.

VITAL STATISTICS

		Achievement	7.0
		Skill	8.0
Place of Birth: Malbork, Poland		Teamwork	8.0
Date of Birth: 8 April 1950 **Died:** n/a		Passion	9.0
Caps: 100 (Poland) **Goals (International):** 42		Personality	6.0
Clubs: Stal Mielec, KSC Lokeren, Atlante			
Trophies: PLT 1973, 1976		**TOTAL**	**38.0**

LEGEND RATING

Laudrup, Brian & Michael
Denmark

DENMARK'S EMERGENCE as a major force in European football is a relatively recent phenomenon, roughly starting around 25 years ago with the arrival of Allan Simonsen. Since then they have produced a string of talented players, not least the brothers Michael and Brian Laudrup. Michael, the elder by nearly five years, was the bright young thing in the side that helped illuminate Mexico 86 before their disappointing capitulation to Spain in the second round. A modern attacking midfielder with pace and touch, Michael's list of clubs (Juventus, Barcelona, Real Madrid, Ajax) bears witness to his quality. And yet, ironically, he was to miss his country's finest hour; a dispute with coach Richard Moller Nielsen led to him being left out of Denmark's stunning victory at Euro 92.

His brother, Brian, did win a medal at that tournament and went on to follow in his brother's footsteps, enjoying spells at several of Europe's finest club teams. His best days were probably at Ibrox where, after a spellbinding first season, he won over a sceptical Rangers crowd. It was often said that the brothers rarely played well together but on Michael's international finale, a memorable quarter-final at France 98 that Denmark narrowly lost 3-2 to Brazil, they made a mockery of this theory. Both played out of their proverbial skins.

☞ Between them the Laudrup brothers have turned out for most of the great European clubs.

👍 Brian is the first foreign player to be voted Scottish Footballer of the Year.

👎 Unlike the Rangers faithful, Chelsea fans do not have fond memories of Brian Laudrup. He left the club in bizarre circumstances to return to Denmark after only a few games.

☞ After the quarter-final with Brazil at France 98 Michael threw his boots into the crowd to signal his retirement. Brian's retirement from internationals followed soon after.

VITAL STATISTICS
BRIAN LAUDRUP

Place of Birth:	Vienna, Austria
Date of Birth:	22 February 1969 **Died:** n/a
Caps:	82 (Denmark) **Goals (International):** 21
Clubs:	Brondby, Bayer Uerdingen, Fiorentina, AC Milan, Rangers, Chelsea, Copenhagen, Bayern Munich
Appearances:	Club (League): 342
Goals:	Club (League): 84
Trophies:	SLT 1995, 1996, 1997; SFAC 1996; DLT 1987, 1988; SA 1994; EuroC 1992; ESC 1998

LEGEND RATING	
Achievement	8.0
Skill	9.0
Teamwork	8.0
Passion	6.0
Personality	7.0
TOTAL	**38.0**

VITAL STATISTICS
MICHAEL LAUDRUP

Place of Birth:	Copenhagen, Denmark
Date of Birth:	15 June 1964 **Died:** n/a
Caps:	104 (Denmark) **Goals (International):** 37
Clubs:	KB Copenhagen, Brondby, Juventus, Lazio,
	Barcelona, Real Madrid, Vissel Kobe, Ajax
Appearances:	Club (League): 464
Goals:	Club (League): 117
Trophies:	EC 1992; PLA 1991, 1992, 1993, 1994, 1995;
	SA 1986; DLT 1998

LEGEND RATING	
Achievement	8.0
Skill	9.0
Teamwork	8.0
Passion	6.0
Personality	7.0
TOTAL	**38.0**

Law, Denis
Manchester United, Scotland

HE SQUINTED, was scrawny and his unkempt, spiky hair gave him the appearance of a toilet brush. Yet, all this appeared little hindrance to Denis Law, who emerged as one of Manchester United's and Scotland's finest-ever strikers. The 'flying Scot' was as quick as a greyhound and with an aerial game few have surpassed.

He owes a huge debt to Bill Shankly, his first manager at Huddersfield, who moulded a novice schoolboy into an 18-year-old international. Like Jimmy Greaves, he failed to settle in Italy and it was only his return to Manchester, swapping a blue shirt for a red one, that revived his career. His forward combination with George Best and Bobby Charlton was the finest in English club football. Law left Old Trafford after being kicked out of the club by Tommy Docherty who, keen to assert his authority on his arrival in 1972, made an example of him. Law joined Man City and came back to haunt Docherty the following season when his back-heeled goal for City in the Manchester derby contributed to United's relegation to Division Two. Famously, Law did not celebrate the goal. Head bowed, he simply turned round and walked solemnly back to the centre circle. Since his retirement, his partnership with former team-mate Paddy Crerand, has made him one of the circuit's most popular after-dinner speakers.

☞ Law broke three transfer records: £35,000 to Man City (UK); £100,000 to Torino (world); £115,000 to Man United (world).

✎ He was voted European Footballer of the Year, 1964.

☝ 1968. Missed United's European Cup final victory through injury.

☞ His 30 goals for Scotland set a national record, now jointly held with Kenny Dalglish.

☞ Law retired with over 300 goals in club football.

VITAL STATISTICS

Place of Birth:	Aberdeen, Scotland
Date of Birth:	24 February 1940 **Died:** n/a
Caps:	55 (Scotland) **Goals (International):** 30
Clubs:	Huddersfield Town, Manchester City, Torino, Manchester United
Appearances:	Club (All Matches): 566
Goals:	Club (All Matches): 301
Trophies:	FAC 1963; LT 1965, 1967

Achievement	7.0
Skill	9.0
Teamwork	8.0
Passion	8.0
Personality	9.0
TOTAL	**41.0**

LEGEND RATING

League Cup
It Seemed A Good Idea At The Time

IT TOOK AN AGE to get going, and but for the persistence of league secretary Alan Hardaker it would never have got off the ground. The idea of a Cup purely for the top four divisions had been mooted for years but it didn't exactly arrive with a fanfare.

Most top clubs viewed 'Hardaker's folly' as an irrelevance and refused to enter, and Rochdale's appearance in the second final was indicative of its lack of cachet.

It was not until the final was switched to Wembley in 1967 that the tournament acquired the respect it so desperately needed, and QPR and Swindon provided further interest by winning it as Third Division sides, both beating First Division opposition in their respective finals against WBA and Arsenal. The award of a UEFA Cup place for the winners has helped maintain its importance over the years, but the recent growth of the Champions League has eroded its importance to the big clubs who now regularly field weakened teams in the competition.

In 2003–04 the competition, with its new sponsors Carling, received a shot in the arm thanks to a keenly-contested final. Bolton and Middlesbrough provided a welcome change, the latter's 2-1 victory earning them their first major silverware in over a century of trying.

☞ The League Cup has been through several incarnations. Bizarrely known as the Milk Cup for a while, it has also lent its name to sponsors Rumbelows, Coca-Cola, Littlewoods and Worthington's.

👆 The 1967 and 1969 finals were the making of Rodney Marsh and Don Rogers. Both scored winners and moved to bigger clubs.

👆 Liverpool fans were particularly scathing about the League Cup, mainly because it took them 20 years to win it. After four straight wins (1981–84) the 'tea kettle' jibes disappeared.

☞ The Aston Villa v Everton final went to a third game in 1977. After two dull encounters, Villa won 3-2 after extra time.

☞ Oxford and Luton won the trophy in the late 1980s. Both subsequently played in the bottom division.

Q: What is taken to Wembley every year and never used?

A: Malcolm McDonald

Sunderland quip after the 1976 League Cup final; it was his second Wembley disappointment in three seasons

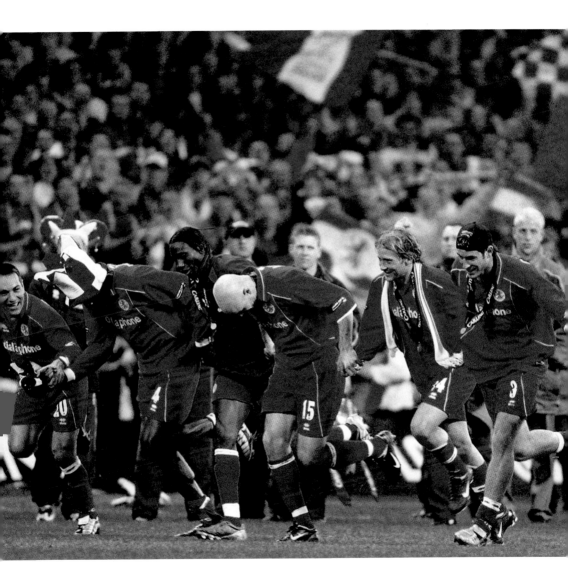

Leeds United – The Revie Years
Leeds, 1968–75

THE WORD PROFESSIONAL has several shades of meaning, and Don Revie's Leeds knew them all. Fit, organised and skilful they were the epitome of mechanical excellence but, at Revie's behest, they were also hard, ruthless and prone to bending the rules when it suited them. None of this should disguise their ability, though. Leeds lost only twice in winning the league in 1969, the lowest total in a 42-game season, and when they won the league again five years later it was with essentially the same team – togetherness was undoubtedly a factor in their success. Yet, at times, they could be their own worst enemy, and often failed at the final hurdle. They were league runners-up five times and blew two FA Cup finals, notably against Second Division Sunderland in 1973. They weren't always the prettiest or most popular team, but few sides got the better of them.

- Harvey's emergence as a replacement for the error-prone Gary Sprake was a major improvement to the side.
- The downside of the close-knit team was that they aged together; Leeds fell into sharp decline after this team broke up, and only re-emerged as a force in the early 1990s.
- Cooper was a great attacking full-back who ought to have won more than his 20 caps. He scored the goal that won the 1968 League Cup, bringing the squad their first trophy.
- Even in their title winning seasons Leeds weren't prolific scorers; Jones top scored in both campaigns with just 14.

Manager: Don Revie

Key Players

David Harvey (G) Jack Charlton (D) Norman Hunter (D)
Paul Reaney (FB) Terry Cooper (FB) Billy Bremner (M)
Johnny Giles (M) Peter Lorimer (F) Eddie Gray (W)
Allan Clarke (F) Mick Jones (F)

Trophies
LT 1969, 1974 FAC 1972 LC 1968 UEFA 1968, 1971

Lenstra, Abe
Heerenveen, SC Enschede, Holland

IN THE 1940s AND 1950s Abe Lenstra was the Golden Boy of Dutch football. A wilful and charismatic figure, he had great technique, a rasping shot and good vision. Lenstra was one of the early proponents of bending the ball with the outside of his foot. He was quick, but pace was not a prerequisite in those days.

At 16, Lenstra's father barred him from moving to Huddersfield with his mentor, Syd Castle, the former Herenveen coach. In spite of lucrative offerings from Inter Milan, Fiorentina and the like, Lenstra opted to remain in Holland, mainly as an amateur, although he played a few years as a pro in the twilight of his career.

A 19-year international career was hampered by frequent run-ins with the conservative authorities in Dutch football. Lenstra's habit of declining to play for the national team if he wasn't in the mood didn't help, either. Despite this, the inside forward finished his career as one of Holland's leading scorers, behind Kluivert, Bergkamp and Wilkes, and level with the great Cruyff.

Like Faas Wilkes, it is a shame Lenstra never got the opportunity to play in a more competitive era.

- Heerenveen v Ajax 1950. With half an hour to go Heerenveen were 1-5 down to Ajax. Lenstra scored two goals and made four more; Ajax lost the the game and the championship.
- Heerenveen's stadium is named after Abe Lenstra.
- A play was performed in the stadium in 1995, celebrating the legendary Ajax game.
- Being accused of being a lazy player Lenstra retorted famously: 'A good football player is like a pike; you don't have to do much, just snap at the right time.'

VITAL STATISTICS

Place of Birth:	Heerenveen, Holland
Date of Birth:	27 November 1920 **Died:** 2 September 1985
Caps:	47 (Holland) **Goals (International):** 33
Clubs:	SC Heerenveen, SC Enschede, Enschedese Boys
Appearances:	Club (All Matches): 730
Goals:	Club (All Matches): 700
Trophies:	None

LEGEND RATING	
Achievement	5.0
Skill	9.0
Teamwork	7.0
Passion	7.0
Personality	6.0
TOTAL	**34.0**

Leonidas

Brazil

WHEN LEONIDAS DA SILVA appeared in the 1934 World Cup Finals for Brazil, he was the only black player in the side and scored his country's only goal as a transitional team were easily brushed aside by Spain. His next appearance was at the 1938 Finals, in the extraordinary 6-5 extra-time win over Poland. Leonidas scored a hat-trick and scored in both games against Czechoslovakia in the next round. For the semi-final against Italy, Brazil made one of the most bizarre selection decisions in football history and left him out, a ploy designed to keep him fit for the final. Bet you can guess what happened next. Sure enough, they lost (2-1 to Italy), and Leonidas' chances of ever playing in a World Cup final were swept away by Hitler's armies just a few months later.

Leonidas was a major draw in his home country, appearing for many of the great sides, as well as for Penarol in Uruguay.

Diminutive and pugnacious, he was a well-balanced player with a reputation for scoring with extravagant bicycle kicks. In many ways he was the forefather of the great Brazilian sides to come – an early hint to the white-dominated footballing authorities that the black population harboured their game's true soul.

☞ Many accounts credit Leonidas with four goals in the win over Poland, but this is inaccurate. The Polish centre-forward Willimowski did score four, but in vain.

☞ He became known as 'The Black Diamond' in Brazil, and sometimes 'The Rubber Man' due to his acrobatic attempts on goal.

☌ Leonidas scored twice on his international debut against the powerful Uruguayans.

☞ Leonidas started a World Cup match in socks on a boggy pitch, but was told by the referee to put on some boots.

☝ Leonidas' replacement Peracio missed two sitters in the 1938 World Cup semi-final.

VITAL STATISTICS

Place of Birth:	Sao Cristovao, Brazil
Date of Birth:	11 November 1912 **Died:** 24 Januray 2004
Caps:	25 (Brazil) **Goals (International):** 25
	(Top scorer in 1938 World Cup Finals with 8 goals)
Clubs:	Havanesa, Barroso, Sul Americano, Sirio Libanes,
	Bomsucesso, Nacional, Vasco da Gama, Botafogo,
	Flamengo, Sao Paulo

Achievement	6.0
Skill	9.0
Teamwork	7.0
Passion	8.0
Personality	7.0
TOTAL	**37.0**

LEGEND RATING

L'Equipe
La France: Les Meilleux

THE STORY OF FRENCH FOOTBALL begins at the 1958 World Cup when, inspired by Just Fontaine's 13-goal burst (still a Finals record) *Les Blues* finally emerged from the shadows of their illustrious European neighbours, Italy and Germany. But it took them a further 26 years to claim their first international honour, the European Championship in 1984.

The peerless Platini and Giresse, two-thirds of that team's irresistible midfield, are included here. Jean Tigana, the third member of that celebrated midfield triumvirate, must wait on the bench though, forced out by Kopa and Zidane.

The backline is almost exclusively drawn from the team that won the 1998 World Cup and Euro 2000 titles. The exception is Marius Tresor, who is good enough to relegate Laurent Blanc to the bench.

Up front, the diminutive Papin will open up defences with his pace for the forward surges of Platini and Zidane. In the unlikely event of everyone else firing blanks, they could just give the ball to Henry and watch him run rings around the world's finest defenders, as he has done for the past few years.

- Platini has performed the roles of midfield general, captain, player-manager and French ambassador to FIFA, all of which he has fulfilled with the utmost competence.
- Fontaine's scored 30 goals in only 21 internationals for France, the best strike-rate in international football history.
- Both goalkeepers are noted for their eccentricity, combining flashes of brilliance with occasional dashes outside the box.
- Despite founding FIFA and the World Cup, France have taken their time to establish their international dominance. But, for their fans, the wait has been worth it. No other nation has held the World Cup and the European Championship simultaneously.

Player-Manager: Michel Platini

4-4-2

Fabien Barthez (90s)

Lilian Thuram (90s) Marcel Desailly (90s)
Marius Tresor (70/80s) Bixente Lizarazu (90s)

Raymond Kopa (50s) Patrick Vieira (90s/00s)
Zinedine Zidane (90s) Michel Platini (C) (80s)

Thierry Henry (90s/00s) Jean-Pierre Papin (80s)

Subs: Joel Bats (G) (80s) Laurent Blanc (D) (90s) Alain Giresse (M) (80s)
Dominique Rocheteau (F) (80s) Just Fontaine (F) (50s)

Lineker, Gary

Leicester City, Everton, Tottenham Hotspur, England

THE GOLDEN BOY. Lineker is a man it is hard to dislike, even if you find his personality a little anodyne. A model professional with all his clubs, not a season went by without Lineker delivering his quota of goals; he was top scorer in England three times, each time with different clubs. Despite recent gags regarding a longstanding toe problem, Lineker was rarely injured until moving to Japan and, incredibly for a player who regularly suffered intense provocation, went through his entire career without receiving a yellow card.

Following success in England with Leicester and Everton, Lineker moved to Barcelona, and soon proved he was capable of rising to the challenges of life in a foreign country. Indeed, but for a disagreement with Johan Cruyff who, bafflingly, decided that Lineker's best position was on the right wing, he could well have spent the rest of his career at the Nou Camp. As it was he returned to England to play for Terry Venables at Spurs with whom, at the age of 30, he finally collected his first domestic trophy, the FA Cup in 1991.

Since retiring, Lineker has enjoyed a successful media career, succeeding Des Lynam as the anchor on *Match Of The Day*. He had an outstanding 2002 World Cup in this capacity.

- He scored 10 goals in two World Cup Finals, winning the Golden Boot at Mexico 86 with six goals.
- He scored after four minutes of the first all-Merseyside FA Cup final in 1986, but Everton lost.
- He scored all four goals for Barcelona against Real Madrid in 1987.
- Lineker was controversially substituted by Graham Taylor during England's defeat to Sweden at the 1992 European Championships. It was to be his last appearance for his country.
- He was voted PFA Player of the Year, 1986 and 1992.

VITAL STATISTICS

Place of Birth:	Leicester, England		
Date of Birth:	30 November 1960	**Died:** n/a	Achievement 8.0
Caps:	80 (England)	**Goals (International):** 48	Skill 9.0
Clubs:	Leicester City, Everton, Barcelona, Tottenham,		Teamwork 8.0
	Nagoya Grampus		Passion 9.0
Appearances:	Club (All Matches): 447		Personality 7.0
Goals:	Club (All Matches): 236		
Trophies:	CWC 1989; FAC 1991		**TOTAL 41.0**

LEGEND RATING

Lisbon Lions
Celtic, 1966–74

GREAT SIDES TODAY are usually the product of a large chequebook and a worldwide scouting network. What made Celtic special was that their great teams were all home-grown, a collection of local lads with local roots; nearly all the players had stepped from the terraces to the pitch. Their mentor was manager Jock Stein. In Scottish footballing terms, Celtic were a big club with large resources when Stein joined them in 1965. But they were not successful. At the time the Scottish league belonged to the Rangers team of Greig and Baxter. Not only did Stein make them league champions within a year, he took the team beyond their parochial confines to make them Champions of Europe. The local lads became the 'Lisbon Lions' in 1967.

Like the great Liverpool teams, Celtic's continuity ensured a decade of success, including nine consecutive league titles. Players left and retired without disrupting the club's rhythm, a testimony to the conveyor belt of talent the club had created. Craig became McGrain and Auld became Dalglish. The result was the same: total domination.

- Stein had also been a Celtic player, winning the league and Cup double in 1954.
- In 1970 Celtic reached a second European Cup final, losing 2-1 to Feyenoord.
- In 1967 Celtic won every competition they entered. The European Cup, the Scottish Cup, the Scottish League Cup and the Glasgow Cup.
- Celtic declined after Stein's departure in 1978, and the manager's only venture into English club management lasted 44 days at Leeds.
- Before Stein's first title in 1966, Celtic had not won the league for 11 years.

Manager: Jock Stein

Key Players
Billy McNeill (D) Tommy Gemmell (D) Danny McGrain (D)
Bobby Lennox (M) Jimmy Johnstone (W) Bobby Murdoch (M)
Steve Chalmers (M) Kenny Dalglish (F)

Trophies
SLT 1966, 1967, 1968, 1969, 1970, 1971, 1972, 1973, 1974; SFAC 1967, 1969, 1971, 1972, 1974; EC 1967

Litmanen, Jari
Ajax, Finland

ONE CAN SAY without fear of contradiction that Jari Litmanen is the best thing to come out of Finland since roll-mop herring. During his international career Finland have gone from being cannon fodder to dangerous floaters, albeit without making the major breakthrough and qualifying for a major tournament. Litmanen is an ideal player to build a team around. A subtle, deep-lying forward, his vision and passing ability are perfect assets for bringing others into the game, and his goal-scoring record is none too shabby either.

After several successful years in Finland, Litmanen made the switch to Ajax where, following the departure of Dennis Bergkamp to Inter, he won a regular starting place in his preferred role as a slightly withdrawn front man. Once established he became a revelation, inspiring Ajax to three successive titles and successive European Cup finals in 1995 and 1996, winning the first. A move to Barcelona proved disappointing as Litmanen spent most of his time on the bench. Liverpool, too, chose to squander his talents, and in 2003 Litmanen moved back to Ajax. Not successful there, he returned to FC Lahti in April 2004.

- Injuries have hampered Litmanen in recent years – he was devastated to miss out on Liverpool's Cup treble in 2001.
- Thirty-four goals in his first full season solidified his reputation at Ajax, and his 24 goals in Europe is a club record.
- Litmanen scored Ajax's goal in the 1996 European Cup final, but Juventus triumphed on penalties.
- He was voted Finnish Footballer of the Year for seven successive years (1992–98).
- Gerard Houllier's reluctance to pick Litmanen is strange; whenever he plays he adds a creative edge to a largely unimaginative side.

VITAL STATISTICS

Place of Birth:	Lahti, Finland		
Date of Birth:	20 February 1971	**Died:** n/a	
Caps:	82 (Finland)	**Goals (International):** 22	
Clubs:	Reipas Lahti, HJK Helsinki, MyPa, Ajax, Barcelona, Liverpool		
Appearances:	Club (All Matches): 370		
Goals:	Club (All Matches): 156		
Trophies:	DLT 1994, 1995, 1996, 1998, 2004; EC 1995		

LEGEND RATING	
Achievement	8.0
Skill	9.0
Teamwork	8.0
Passion	6.0
Personality	6.0
TOTAL	**37.0**

Loadsabentmoney
Corruption

IN A PROFESSIONAL GAME where millions, and now billions, change hands in transfer fees and sponsorship deals, it was always hoping against hope to assume that a sporting spirit would prevail.

The maximum-wage system has got a lot to answer for. During its existence players would routinely supplement their income with under-the-counter cash payments, often surreptitiously placed in a pocket or shoe after the game. And old habits die hard. Even in the modern era, several clubs and individuals have been relegated, fined or expelled for conducting their financial business in a less than honest fashion.

Betting has brought the most severe problems. In 1964 tabloid revelations exposed three Sheffield Wednesday players in a match-fixing scandal. This proved to be the tip of a decidedly sleazy iceberg. The spiralling transfer fees and use of third-party agents in recent times have also led to some high-profile cases of skulduggery, the most notorious example being that of George Graham and agent Rune Hauge. For every one found guilty, you can be almost certain there are at least a dozen getting away with it.

- Match officials are not whiter than white. In 1979, a Scottish referee and both linesmen were banned for three years after accepting gifts from Milan before taking charge of their UEFA Cup tie against Levski Spartak.
- 1982. A major Italian betting scandal claimed several high-profile casualties, including Paolo Rossi.
- In a 1990s match-fixing scandal, Bruce Grobbelaar and Hans Segers faced court action after they were alleged to have accepted cash for conceding goals. Grobbelaar's case started a legal storm as his acquittal was quashed by an appeal court.
- Corruption isn't a modern preserve. In 1919 Leeds City were expelled from the league for making irregular payments.

'What I know most surely about morality and the duty of man I owe to sport.'

Albert Camus, novelist and Philosopher (1913–60); Camus briefly played professional football as a goalkeeper

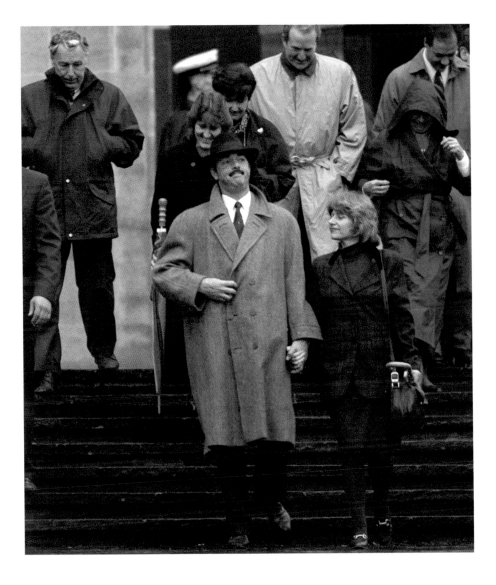

Loadsamoney
Celebrity Chairmen

CHAIRMEN TEND TO FALL into two categories. The first are the local businessmen who, made wealthy by their acumen in scrap metal or toilet paper, wish to realise a childhood dream, while the second are a disparate bunch of entertainers and media puppies who have nothing better to do with their money.

That said, many are genuine fans whose input is far more than financial; Elton John racks up enormous international phone bills and charters private jets in his desire to follow Watford, while Jasper Carrott stood on the St Andrews terraces for years before his fame brought him greater influence in the affairs of Birmingham City. Delia Smith, although a director rather than chairwoman, brings more than a decent half-time pie to Norwich City. Some of them are in it simply for the dough, though. Take Stan Flashman, whose principal interest at Barnet was never anything other than to turn a fast buck. 'Why sleep when you can make money,' reflected an attitude that many of his peers share but dare not utter in public.

- 'He's fat, he's round, he's never in the ground, Cap'n Bob.' Like their fanzine's editors, Derby fans fail to join the Robert Maxwell fan club.
- Elton John has always retained a philosophical attitude to some unacceptable homophobic chanting from opposing fans.
- Uri Geller's 'positive energy' had the opposite effect on Reading, who finished bottom of Division One in 1998. If he'd bent the goalposts instead of spoons they might have scored more often.
- Visiting fans at Craven Cottage collectively wave British passports at Mohamed al Fayed. It takes more than ownership of Fulham to obtain one, apparently.

'Maxwell Chairman? We may as well have Max Wall.'

Derby County fanzine The Sheep gets justifiably splenetic

LoadsaMurdochmoney
Sky TV

WHEN RUPERT MURDOCH'S satellite network joined the TV rights arena the rules suddenly changed. Here was a multi-billion dollar organisation prepared to use football as a loss-leader to accelerate subscription. How could the BBC, or even the commercial channels compete with that kind of spending power? Answer: they couldn't. Overnight we entered an era of saturation coverage. Live games were shown on Friday, Sunday and Monday. Now even Saturday morning games have begun to creep in. On top of the matches, endless magazine programmes have also been rolled out, featuring the exclusive insights of opinionated has-beens like Rodney Marsh and overweight tabloid journalists. Thank heavens for Andy Gray. Complete with his state-of-the-art graphics, Gray has brought boundless enthusiasm and optimism to Sky's live broadcasts. Yes, he tries to talk up a dour stalemate as a minor classic, but here is a man who earned respect for his achievements in the game talking to the viewer as an equal, another fan. Gray's computers were a bit of a standing joke at first, but the technology is excellent – those extra camera angles and graphics enhance, rather than detract from, the armchair experience.

☞ Sky feature great graphics and camera angles. But does anyone really care about 'player-cam'?

👍 'The biggest advance in TV football since the invention of the camera.' David Hill, 1992.

👎 'The most ludicrous and backward step football has taken in a long time.' Alex Ferguson, 1992.

☞ Thus far Sky hasn't had the negative effect on attendances many expected; beware pay-per-view.

👍 For all the criticism heaped upon them, Sky have given audiences significantly more opportunity to watch teams outside the Premiership than the terrestrial channels ever did.

'The governing body of football: television.'

Mike Ingham, 1991

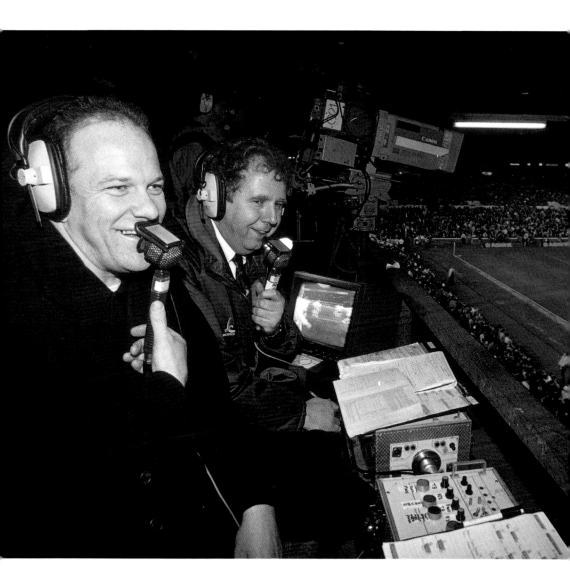

Lofthouse, Nat
Bolton Wanderers, England

'LA BANDIERA' is an Italian expression used to describe a player whose career is so intertwined with the fortunes of his club he becomes a symbol of its very soul. Nat Lofthouse is the 'Il Bandiera' of Bolton Wanderers. By far their most famous and successful player, he was the inspiration behind their most recent success, and as president still retains close ties with the Trotters.

Bolton were a robust Division One club in the 1950s and Lofthouse's battering-ram style suited them; powerful and dominant in the air he was the sort of player that coaches and pundits like to describe as 'a real handful'. In the 1958 FA Cup final against Manchester United, who were fielding a team weakened by the Munich air crash, he was able to put sentiment aside and scored both goals in a 2-0 win.

In a fine England career Lofthouse's greatest moment came in a 3-2 win against an Austrian team who were one of the best in Europe. A scratch England team had done well to stay level and, with just 10 minutes left, Lofthouse broke from inside his own half and finished in style. From that day forward he was universally referred to as 'The Lion of Vienna'.

- Lofthouse scored the opening goal in the 1953 'Matthews Final'.
- The second goal in the 1958 FA Cup final was highly controversial; Lofthouse barged United keeper Harry Gregg into the net with the ball.
- Lofthouse was the First Division's top scorer with 33 goals in 1956.
- He scored twice in a 2-2 draw on his England debut against Yugoslavia in 1950.
- Lofthouse displaced Jackie Milburn in the England team, and his impressive scoring rate saw him retain his place until the emergence of Tommy Taylor.

VITAL STATISTICS

Place of Birth:	Bolton, England	
Date of Birth:	27 August 1925	**Died:** n/a
Caps:	33 (England)	**Goals (International):** 30
Clubs:	Bolton Wanderers	
Appearances:	Club (for Bolton): 485	
Goals:	Club (for Bolton): 285	
Trophies:	FAC 1958	

LEGEND RATING	
Achievement	6.0
Skill	8.0
Teamwork	9.0
Passion	9.0
Personality	6.0
TOTAL	**38.0**

Losing it in Leon
England 2 West Germany 3, 1970

HARD DONE BY after the 1966 World Cup final when, but for the intervention of that famous Russian linesman, they would have almost certainly taken home the trophy, Germany were eager for revenge against England. And, in the sweltering heat of Leon in 1970, they extracted it with great relish.

England approached the game confidently. They were, after all, defending champions and had progressed through a group in which they were only narrowly defeated by the brilliant Brazilians. With 21 minutes left they were comfortably holding a 2-0 lead and their progress to the semi-finals looked assured but, proving that a chain is only as strong as its weakest link, stand-in keeper Peter Bonetti dived over a speculative effort from Beckenbauer and the match was suddenly back in the balance. Then, with the hapless Chelsea keeper a stranded spectator, Uwe Seeler's bizarre back-header looped agonisingly into the net with eight minutes remaining to send the match into extra-time. The German swagger had returned, while England looked exhausted. Gerd Müller had had a quiet game thus far, so quiet that it's doubtful if he had even broken sweat, but, great striker that he was, 'Der Bomber' took his only chance and England were out.

- With England 2-0 up, Alan Mullery missed a sitter and the chance to put the game beyond Germany's reach.
- For the substituted Bobby Charlton, it was to be a sad end to his 106th and final England game.
- Peter Bonetti was also never to play for England again.
- It has been claimed that England's loss altered the mood of the nation and contributed to Labour's defeat in the British General Election that took place a few weeks later.
- This match helped set up an Italy versus West Germany classic in the semi-final that the Germans lost.

SCORERS   **England:** Mullery, Peters
               West Germany: Beckenbauer, Seeler, Müller
EVENT   World Cup quarter-final, Leon, Mexico, 14 June 1970

ENGLAND   (Man: Sir Alf Ramsey)
               1. Bonetti 2. K Newton 3. Cooper 4. Mullery 5. Labone 6. Moore 7. F Lee
               8. Ball 9. R Charlton 10. Hurst 11. Peters
W. GERMANY (Man: Helmut Schoen)
               1. Maier 2. Schnellinger 3. Vogts 4. Fichtel 5. Höttges 6. Beckenbauer
               7. Overath 8. Seeler 9. Libuda 10. Müller 11. Löhr

Lucky (?) Arsenal
Arsenal: 1971

NOT WISHING TO BE OUTDONE by their neighbours, Arsenal became the fourth English team to win the League and Cup double 10 years after Spurs achieved the feat in 1961. Unlike Tottenham, who sauntered through the season without a hitch, Arsenal's double required every ounce of their famous resilience; they overhauled Leeds United's huge lead to win the title in the last game of the season, and twice came back from the dead in the FA Cup.

Man for man, Arsenal were not the best team in Division One, but their team spirit and organisation made up for their technical shortcomings, much in the way Ipswich had done in winning the title nine years earlier. The assured McLintock was the pick of the defence, Radford was a tireless worker up front, George Armstrong provided pace and width, while Ray Kennedy was their youthful spark, linking attack with midfield. Their sole concession to fancy dan-dom was local lad Charlie George, a maverick genius long on talent and sideburns. Arsenal's constant ability to extricate themselves from the mire led to them being tagged 'lucky Arsenal'. But that was unfair. In truth, no side could have been that lucky for that long.

- Arsenal's Fairs Cup win of 1970 laid the foundations and ended a long drought: their first trophy since the league title of 1953.
- Arsenal won the 1971 FA Cup the hard way. They were drawn away in every round, snatched a replay in the semi-final with an injury-time penalty, then came from behind in extra-time to beat Liverpool in the final.
- In 1970/71 Arsenal played 64 matches. When Preston won the first double in 1889, they wrapped up both trophies in just 27.
- Bertie Mee had been a reluctant manager in 1966. He asked for a get-out clause in his contract, allowing him to return to his previous position of physio if he wasn't successful.

Manager: Bertie Mee

Key Players
Bob Wilson (G) Frank McLintock (D) Charlie George (F)
John Radford (F) George Armstrong (W) Ray Kennedy (M)
George Graham (M)

Trophies
LT 1971 FAC 1971

Machine Dream
The Germany Dream Team

LIKE ALL THE BEST German teams it is strong in every position. Schoen was a disciplined manager with great tactical ability and a habit of getting the best out of his players. The balance of the side is tremendous – no midfield packed with fancy dans for Germany. We start with a world-class keeper in Sepp Maier, and a simply superb defence. The flair and brilliance of Franz Beckenbauer, with the taller, physically imposing Matthias Sammer alongside him is a partnership made in heaven. Outside them we have two conventional full-backs: on the right the tough-tackling Bertie Vogts and on the left the unflappable Andreas Brehme.

Lothar Matthaus is in his best position, that of a ball-carrying midfielder not ponderous sweeper. Walter, captain of the 1954 World Cup winning side, was a complete player – hard and skilful – and Rahn and Overath add pace and power to the flanks.

Up front the skills and industry of the durable Seeler sit well alongside the rapier thrusts of Gerd Müller, and Karl-Heinz Rummenigge provides back up on the bench alongside a certain J. Klinsmann.

☞ Only Matthias Sammer hails from the former East Germany.

☞ Beckenbauer made a strong case for player/manager, but we spared him the agony of having to leave out team-mate Paul Breitner.

☞ Gunther Netzer only made it to the bench, just like in 1974. Considering West Germany appeared in every Finals, it is extraordinary that such a good player played only 20 minutes in a World Cup tournament.

☞ Only Oliver Kahn of the current squad features in the 16 – a reflection of the current poverty of talent in German football. Hassler, Moller (Andreas), Voller and Scholl are just not in this league.

Manager: Helmut Schon (60s/70s)

4-4-2

Sepp Maier (70s)

Berti Vogts (70s) Franz Beckenbauer (C) (70s)
Matthias Sammer (90s) Andreas Brehme (80s)

Helmut Rahn (50s) Lothar Matthaus (80s/90s)
Franz Walter (50s) Wolfgang Overath (70s)

Uwe Seeler (60s) Gerd Müller (70s)

Subs: Oliver Kahn (G) (90s) Paul Breitner (D) (70s) Gunter Netzer (M) (70s) Karl-Heinz Rummennigge (F) (80s) Jurgen Klinsmann (F) (90s)

Mackay, Dave

Tottenham Hotspur, Derby County, Scotland

EVERY TEAM NEEDS a hard man and Dave Mackay filled that role with distinction for his various clubs, and for Scotland. Indeed, the image of Mackay taking exception to a tackle by a young Billy Bremner is one of the most enduring football photographs.

Mackay shot to fame in the midfield of the Hearts side that won the Scottish League in 1958, before moving to Spurs, where he became the cornerstone of the side that won the double in 1961.

After nearly a decade at White Hart Lane, Brian Clough persuaded Mackay to move to Derby County, where he captained the side that won promotion to the First Division. He then enjoyed spells as a manager at Swindon and Nottingham Forest, before returning to the Baseball Ground to help his old side through the aftermath of Clough's sudden departure to Leeds. With Mackay at the helm Derby won a second league title in 1975, but the suspicion that he was merely enjoying the fruits of Clough's earlier groundwork were borne out by his inability to start rebuilding the team effectively, and he was dismissed in 1976.

- He was joint (with Tony Book) Football Writers' Player of the Year in 1969.
- He had a reputation as a fearsome drinker, matched only by Alan Gilzean at Spurs.
- Battled back from two broken legs in 1963–64 (not so easy then, no micro-surgery).
- Missed the European Cup Winners' Cup final in 1963 with a stomach upset.
- Mackay played in the Hearts team that won the title with 132 league goals (a Scottish record), and a Spurs side that won the title with 115 goals (a joint English record).

VITAL STATISTICS

Place of Birth:	Edinburgh, Scotland
Date of Birth:	14 November 1934 **Died:** n/a
Caps:	22 (Scotland) **Goals (International):** 4
Clubs:	As Player: Heart of Midlothian, Tottenham Hotspur, Derby County, Swindon Town; As Manager: Swindon Town, Nottingham Forest, Derby County, Walsall, Birmingham City
Appearances:	Club (All Matches): 669
Goals:	Club (All Matches): 88
Trophies:	SFAC 1956, 1957; SLT 1958, 1959; LT 1961, (1975); FAC 1961, 1962, 1967

LEGEND RATING	
Achievement	8.0
Skill	6.0
Teamwork	8.0
Passion	10.0
Personality	7.0
TOTAL	**39.0**

Magyar Magic

Hungary, 1950s

GOING INTO the 1954 World Cup, Hungary had the footballing world at its feet. They were unbeaten since 1950 and had left a trail of strong sides in their wake, many of whom were still coming to terms with the humiliating nature of their defeats.

Like most great teams, the key to their success lay in the quality of their personnel. They had the best goalkeeper in the world in Grosics, a decent defence, a good prompter in half-back Bozsik and the best forwards the planet had ever seen. Kocsis, the bull-headed bomber, Hidegkuti, a subtle and deep-lying centre forward, and Czibor their flying winger were all outrageous technicians. And then there was Puskas, the dumpy maestro, tormenting defenders with his trademark drag-backs, and scoring goals for fun.

They were the best side in the tournament in 1954, surviving a 22-man battle in the quarter-final against Brazil and a classic semi-final against Uruguay, to reach their first and only major final. They blew it, throwing away a 2-0 lead to hand a workaday West German team the trophy. Two years later the Soviets invaded Hungary and within a year Puskas, Kocsis and Czibor had all fled to Spain, never to be reunited in the colours of their country.

☞ Having hammered South Korea 12-0 in the 1952 Olympics, Hungary restricted themselves to nine goals in the 1954 World Cup. One of the Korean players, suffering from cramp, was given a massage by the Hungarian full-back, Buzansky.

☝ Puskas went on to European Cup fame with Real Madrid as a member of their all-conquering side, and Kocsis played in a European Cup final for Barcelona.

☝ The World Cup final against Germany was painful; Hungary were 2-0 up, but Morlock and Rahn got Germany back level, then Rahn settled the game with a late breakaway.

☝ Puskas missed most of the 1954 World Cup Finals. He was injured in the first game against Germany.

Manager: Gustav Szebes

Key Players

Gyula Grosics (G) Jozef Bozsik (H/B) Sandor Kocsis (F)
Ferenc Puskas (F) Nandor Hidegkuti (F) Zoltan Czibor (F)

Trophies

They did not win a professional trophy (surprisingly they were beaten in the 1954 World Cup final by West Germany), but they did win the 1952 Olympic title in Helsinki and were also the first overseas country to beat England at home (they won 6-3 at Wembley on 25 November 1953). To prove that was not a one-off, they beat England 7-1 in Budapest on 23 May 1954.

Maier, Sepp
Bayern Munich, West Germany

THANKS TO the widening influence of television during the 1960s and 1970s, Josef-Dieter Maier was one of the most recognisable footballers in the world. His enormous black shorts belonged to another age, while his outsize gloves made him a hero to sportswear manufacturers and set a trend. (Today, it is unbelievable to think that goalkeepers once played with their bare hands.)

His 19 years as a member of Bayern Munich's greatest-ever side brought him 13 major trophies, including three consecutive European Cups, but it was as national goalkeeper that 'die Katze' caught the eye, and not always for the right reasons; TV viewers of the 1970 World Cup Finals were as maddened by his habit of falling over at the slightest contact as they were impressed by his spectacular agility. Maier's crowning glory was during the 1974 World Cup when, despite conceding the Final's quickest-ever goal (a Neeskens penalty), he helped West Germany claim the world crown with victory over Holland. A car accident in 1979 brought an untimely end to a career that might otherwise have reaped him a century of international caps.

- 👍 Maier was an ever-present at Bayern for 11 years and nearly 400 games.
- 👍 He was a squad member in four World Cup Finals, but failed to start a match in 1966.
- 👍 He was three-time German Player of the Year.
- ☞ Still a Bayern man, Maier remains on the coaching staff.
- 👍 At the 1974 World Cup Finals, Maier conceded just four goals in seven matches.

VITAL STATISTICS

Place of Birth:	Haar, Germany
Date of Birth:	28 February 1944 **Died:** n/a
Caps:	95 (W. Germany) **Goals (International):** 0
Clubs:	TSV Haar, Bayern Munich
Appearances:	Club (League): 473
Goals:	Club (League): 0
Trophies:	CWC 1967; BLG 1969, 1972, 1973, 1974;
	EC 1974, 1975, 1976; EuroC 1972; WorC 1974

LEGEND RATING	
Achievement	9.0
Skill	8.0
Teamwork	8.0
Passion	8.0
Personality	6.0
TOTAL	**39.0**

Maldini, Paolo
AC Milan, Italy

ARGUABLY THE FINEST LEFT-BACK ever to play the game, Paolo Maldini's class was emphasised early when, at 16, he became one of Serie A's youngest-ever debutants in 1985. Accomplished on the ball and decisive in the tackle, Maldini has been the immovable object of world football, equally comfortable on the left or in the centre where he has spent much of the latter part of his career. Unusually for someone who could have commanded huge signing-on fees, he has played his club football only with Milan. His seven league titles, four Italian Cups and four European Cups are a deserving reflection of his talent and loyalty.

Ultimate international success eluded Maldini, though. He was a member of the Italian teams that failed to secure the world crown at Italia 90, USA 94 and France 98, each time going out on penalties (most crushingly in 1994 when they were beaten by Brazil in the final). Maldini has played in some of the tightest defences the game has known, the foursome he made up with Antonio Benarrivo, Franco Baresi and Alessandro Costacurta in USA 94 being perhaps the finest. Despite pressure to remain, he bowed out of the international scene after World Cup 2002. In 2003 he lifted the European Cup at Old Trafford as Milan's captain. His father, Cesare, performed the same task for the same club in the same country 40 years earlier.

- Maldini's international caps are an Italian record to which he is still adding.
- He was World Player of the Year in 1994.
- In the 1994 World Cup Finals, when Franco Baresi was injured, Maldini moved into the middle for the first time, and immediately looked as accomplished as any centre-half in the tournament.
- Maldini's loyalty to Milan stemmed from his father, Cesare, who captained the team and was Paolo's boyhood coach.
- Cesare and Paolo formed a unique father-son, manager-captain combination at the 1998 World Cup Finals; no one complained about Cesare picking Maldini junior.

VITAL STATISTICS

Place of Birth:	Milan, Italy		
Date of Birth:	26 June 1968	**Died:** n/a	Achievement 9.0
Caps:	126 (Italy)	**Goals (International):** 6	Skill 10.0
Clubs:	AC Milan		Teamwork 8.0
Appearances:	Club (All Matches): 608		Passion 9.0
Goals:	Club (All Matches): 26		Personality 8.0
Trophies:	SA 1988, 1992, 1993, 1994, 1996, 1999,		
	2004; EC 1989, 1990, 1994, 2003		**TOTAL 44.0**

LEGEND RATING

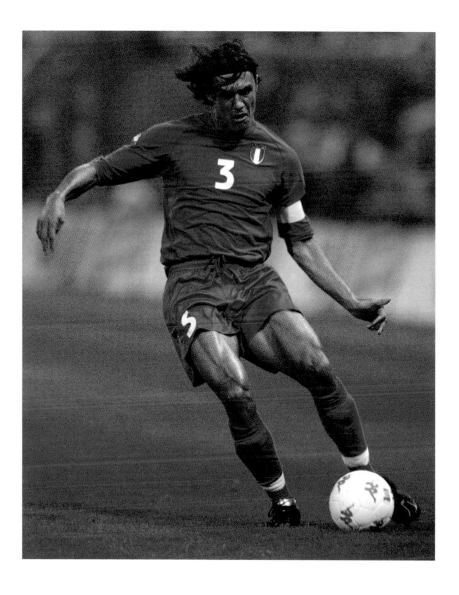

Maracana
Rio De Janeiro, Brazil

THE ONCE-MAGNIFICENT Maracana in Rio de Janeiro is officially the biggest football stadium in the world, and still holds the record for the largest-ever officially counted attendance.

The stadium was built in readiness for the 1950 World Cup and it was the deciding fixture at the Finals between Uruguay and Brazil that attracted the landmark crowd, a colossal 199,854. Due to modern safety regulations it's a crowd record that is unlikely to be beaten.

In its time, the Maracana set a procession of records and innovations. The cantilevered roof was the world's largest. The lifts to the VIP boxes, the luxurious dressings rooms, complete with oxygen masks, set standards that dingy wooden English grounds took two generations to match.

Sadly the stadium, which will be forever associated with the great days of Brazilian soccer, is now in a poor state of repair and major refurbishment work is urgently required. At present, much of the stadium, which still has a capacity of 80,000, has been declared unsafe and crowds of less than 10,000 are now common.

☞ Originally called Estadio Municipal, it was renamed in 1964 after Mario Filho, the mayor of the city who masterminded the project. It became known as the Maracana after the little river that runs close by the stadium.

☞ The famous 1950 World Cup encounter with Uruguay proved Brazil's most bitter defeat. Their national team fell to a shock 2-1 defeat and Uruguay were crowned champions.

☞ The temperature in the dressing rooms is regulated to reflect precisely the air temperature at pitch level. In many cases this is over 35˚ C.

✍ The Maracana also holds the world record for a club game, Flamengo and Fluminese drew 177,656 in August 1963.

VITAL STATISTICS

Location:	Rio De Janeiro, Brazil
Local Clubs:	Botofago, Vasco da Gama, Flamengo, Fluminense
Date Built:	1950
Current Capacity:	120,000
Max. Capacity:	199,854

Maradona, Diego
Napoli, Argentina

THE MOST NATURALLY GIFTED PLAYER football has ever seen, or a despicable drug-ridden cheat? Whatever your opinion, Maradona's talent was undeniable. After emerging in his native Argentina with Argentinos Juniors, for whom he made his league debut aged only 15, Maradona quickly attracted the attention of European scouts.

A move to Spain for £4.2 m should, in theory at least, have made him the jewel in Barcelona's star-studded crown, but the young and immature Diego failed to settle and, in 1984, joined Napoli in Italy's Serie A for £6.9 m. Maradona brought unprecedented success to Naples, single-handedly shifting the powerbase of Italian football from north to south, but he also fell in with the wrong crowd. Throughout his time at the club he was repeatedly seen in the company of local mobsters, and rumours of his cocaine addiction were rife.

The 1986 World Cup quarter-final versus England provided an insight to his personality: a flagrant punch past Peter Shilton for Argentina's first goal was followed by a 60-yard run and wonder-goal minutes later. Maradona's personal flaws make him an unattractive figure, but should not obscure his vast talents as a footballer. His poor origins and volatility made him susceptible to bad advice off the pitch and provocation on it, compounded by his failure to ignore either.

- Maradona was the subject of three world-record transfer fees, and was the first £1 m teenager.
- Maradona inspired Napoli to their first Scudetto. When he left, their fortunes immediately declined.
- Maradona was banned twice for drug use and is still battling against cocaine addiction.
- He was South American Player of the Year in 1979 and 1980 and was voted FIFA's Player of the 20th Century.
- A tackle, by the 'Butcher of Bilbao' Andoni Goicochea, that ruled Maradona out for four months, sparked an attempted storming of Bilbao's team hotel by enraged Catalans.

VITAL STATISTICS

Place of Birth: Lanus, Argentina
Date of Birth: 30 October 1960 **Died:** n/a
Caps: 91 (Argentina) **Goals (International):** 34
Clubs: Argentinos Juniors, Boca Juniors, Barcelona, Napoli, Seville, Newell's Old Boys
Appearances: Club (All Matches): 749
Goals: Club (All Matches): 311
Trophies: WorC 1986; SA 1987; EUFAC 1988

LEGEND RATING	
Achievement	9.0
Skill	10.0
Teamwork	8.0
Passion	10.0
Personality	6.0
TOTAL	**43.0**

Masters of the Maracana

Brazil: The Team

THIS BEING BRAZIL, the defence is not particularly impressive (we certainly weren't agonising over who to leave out). Julio Cesar and Edinho got the vote because they were the only proven combination we could find. The Branco we selected is the fulminating attacking back of the 1986 and 1990 World Cups, not the has-been who turned out for Middlesbrough. Djalma Santos was scary and aggressive, and adds serious bite. The goalkeeper, Gylmar, was the best of a pretty ordinary bunch.

'Not that amazing' could not be said of the midfield – numerous world-class players didn't even make the 16 (Zagallo, Falcao, Dunga, Didi, Cerezo). We went for Zico for a bit of bite and movement as well as skill, as Socrates wasn't overfond of running.

The 1950s' legends Ademir and Leonidas, both on the bench, got the vote up front as big, powerful strikers and would score truck-loads with the service from Garrincha and Jairzinho. Ronaldo, after his comeback in the 2002 World Cup Finals, gets a place ahead of Romario, Tostão and 1950s legend Vava.

But then, does it really matter how good the rest of them are? Any team containing Pelé has to be awesome.

- ☝ No space for Bebeto (that baby-cradling nonsense was unforgivable).
- ☞ Gylmar was the goalkeeper in the 1958, 1962 and 1966 World Cups.
- ☞ Socrates and Gerson would have to be kept apart in training to stop them nicking each others cigarettes.
- ☟ Julio Cesar and Edinho were the excellent central defensive combination in the dour 1986 side.
- ☝ No substitute goalkeeper, most of the recent ones have been pretty awful – odd that such a fabulous team has such a dearth of decent goalkeepers.

Manager: Mario Zagallo

4-4-2

Gylmar (50s)

Cafu (90s/00s) Junior Cesar (80s)
Edinho (80s) Branco (80s/90s)

Garrincha (50s/60s) Socrates (80s)
Zico (80s) Jairzinho (60s/70s)

Pelé (C) (50s/60s) Ronaldo (00s)

Subs: Nilton Santos (D) (50s/60s) Rivaldo (M) (90s/00s)
Rivelino (M) (70s) Ademir (F) (50s) Romario (F) (90s) Leonidas (F) (30s)

Matthaus, Lothar
Bayern Munich, Internazionale, Germany

A CENTRAL FIGURE in German football for two decades, Lothar Matthaus was the natural successor to Franz Beckenbauer. Though not as good a defensive player as Beckenbauer, he possessed the same ability to launch attacks from deep, and scored more goals than 'The Kaiser'. Matthaus also had admirable durability and stamina, was rarely injured and tremendously fit. He played at the highest levels of the game until the age of 38 without looking silly.

Matthaus enjoyed a club career that saw him win countless trophies in Germany, with Bayern Munich, and with Inter Milan in Italy, although the closest he came to European Cup success was the heart-stopping 1999 final against Manchester United. For all his club achievements, though, it was in the international arena that Matthaus marked himself out as an all-time great. He was the lynchpin of the German national team for the best part of a decade, and scored the penalty that won them the World Cup final against Argentina in 1990. Possessed of a self-belief that often spilled over into arrogance, Matthaus has never been the most popular player and has been involved in several run-ins with team-mates, including the normally docile Jurgen Klinsmann.

- He played in a record 25 games at the World Cup Finals, and jointly holds the distinction of playing in five Finals' tournaments with Antonio Carbajal of Mexico.
- He had retired from international football, but returned to the squad for France 1998 when Mattias Sammer was injured.
- He was voted European Player of the Year in 1990 and was named as the first World Player of the Year in 1991.
- In the 1999 European Cup final, Matthaus was substituted after 80 minutes, and watched in horror as Man United scored the two late goals that denied him a full set of European medals.
- Matthaus has managed Rapid Vienna and Partizan Belgrade, and was appointed Hungarian national coach in December 2003.

VITAL STATISTICS

Place of Birth:	Erlangen, Germany	
Date of Birth:	21 March 1961	**Died:** n/a
Caps:	144 (Germany)	**Goals (International):** 22
Clubs:	Borrusia Monchengladbach, Bayern Munich,	
	Inter Milan, New Jersey Metrostars	
Appearances:	Club (League): 581	
Goals:	Club (League): 160	
Trophies:	BLG 1985, 1986, 1987, 1994, 1997; SA 1989;	
	UEFAC 1991, 1996; WorC 1990	

LEGEND RATING	
Achievement	9.5
Skill	7.5
Teamwork	9.0
Passion	8.5
Personality	6.5
TOTAL	**41.0**

Matthews' Final
Blackpool 4 Bolton Wanderers 3, 1953

ONE OF WEMBLEY'S most sentimental occasions, the 'Matthews Final', saw the nation's favourite balding winger with baggy shorts finally win an FA Cup final at 38.

The drama was perfectly scripted. Blackpool, 3-1 down after an hour, were heading for their third final defeat in six seasons when, as if on cue, Stanley Matthews embarked on a trail of destruction down the right wing, setting up Stan Mortensen to score. With only three minutes left, it still looked like mere consolation, but a Mortensen free-kick to complete his hat-trick set up the FA Cup's most memorable finale. Again, it was a dribble from Matthews, who seemed to lose his footing before squaring for Bill Perry to smash the winner.

For the nation it was all part of the 1953 pageantry that inspires images of the Coronation, Everest and Compton's Ashes. For Bolton, it could have been so different had an injury not reduced England left-back Banks to the role of passenger for the last, vital half an hour. But the enduring image is that of Matthews standing proud, finally holding the FA Cup.

- This was Matthews' third FA Cup final; he was a loser in 1948 and 1951.
- Blackpool nearly didn't make it to Wembley. Outplayed by Spurs, they won their semi-final in the last minute.
- Hat-trick hero Stan Mortensen scored in every round.
- Mortensen later managed the club, from 1967–69.
- Like many north-west clubs, both Blackpool and Bolton faded in the 1960s.

SCORERS   **Blackpool:** Mortensen 3, Perry
               Bolton Wanderers: Lofthouse, Moir, Bell

EVENT   FA Cup final, Wembley, 2 May 1953

BLACKPOOL (Man: Joe Smith)
               1. Farm 2. Shimwell 3. Garrett 4. Fenton 5. Johnston 6. Robinson 7. Matthews
               8. Taylor 9. Mortensen 10. Mudie 11. Perry

BOLTON   (Man: Bill Ridding)
               1. Hanson 2. Ball 3. Banks 4. Wheeler 5. Barrass 6. Bell 7. Holden 8. Moir
               9. Lofthouse 10. Hassall 11. Langton

Matthews, Stanley

Blackpool, Stoke City, England

ASK ANY LEFT-BACK between 1930 and 1965 who was the opponent they most feared and the answer would have been instant: Stanley Matthews. One of the quickest players ever over 10 yards, Matthews defined modern wing play and pioneered standards of fitness that enabled him to play beyond his 50th birthday. Pointless arguments still rage about how he would have fared in the modern game, but there have been few bigger draws. Stoke's attendance leapt from 8,000 to 35,000 when he re-signed in 1961, returning to his hometown club after 13 years away. His defining match was with Blackpool, whom he joined after a clash with management at Stoke in 1947. The sight of Matthews transforming the 1953 FA Cup final by laying on three late goals for a 4-3 win is now as much a part of Wembley folklore as the twin towers and Billy the white horse. Yet, for all his ability, that game produced his only major trophy. Still, trophies and medals were not what made Matthews popular. He won his acclaim as the people's champion for his innate modesty and sportsmanship. His death, in February 2000, solicited immaculate one-minute's silences at grounds throughout the country.

- Matthews was the inaugural European Footballer of the Year in 1956 and Football Writers' Player of the Year in 1948 and 1963.
- 1965. He became the first footballer to be knighted.
- He was the oldest ever First Division player at 50 years, 5 days.
- He never earned fortunes, taking home a basic £50 per week on his retirement.
- The ultimate gentleman, Matthews was never booked in a 35-year career.

VITAL STATISTICS

Place of Birth:	Stoke-on-Trent, England
Date of Birth:	1 February 1915 **Died:** 23 February 2000
Caps:	54 (England) **Goals (International):** 11
Clubs:	Stoke City, Blackpool
Appearances:	Club (League): 698
Goals:	Club (League): 71
Trophies:	FAC 1953

LEGEND RATING	
Achievement	6.0
Skill	10.0
Teamwork	8.0
Passion	9.0
Personality	7.0
TOTAL	**40.0**

Maximum Wage
No One's Worth That Much!

ROY KEANE IS REPORTED to earn £200,000 every month. Yet, just over 40 years ago, players nearly came out on strike over the less than princely sum of £20 per week. The argument had been rumbling for years. The legendary Billy Meredith had led a players' revolt as early as 1907 over a £4 per week ceiling and a contract that tied players to a club effectively for an entire career. He succeeded in establishing a players' union, but the maximum wage remained. It was not until 1961 that the next instalment of this saga erupted. PFA Chairman Jimmy Hill had successfully managed to get the maximum wage abolished when he took up the case of George Eastham. Eastham's contract had expired at Newcastle and though Arsenal were keen to sign him the Magpies refused to release him. The case went to the Ministry of Labour, who ruled in Eastham's favour. The days of the tied contract were over. Today's complaint that all players earn too much misses an important point. For every Keane, there are 10 YTS lads at Halifax scraping a living.

☞ The first beneficiary of the maximum wage's demise was Johnny Haynes. Fulham made him the country's first £100 per week player.

☞ 1950. Following the post-war boom in attendances, players threatened to strike unless their pay was increased. They won a rise but the maximum wage was to remain for another 11 years.

☞ The rise of agents has helped inflate players' pay packets. Some, like Eric Hall, admit only a passing interest in football.

☞ Most former players are philosophical about the riches they missed out on. As Stanley Matthews remarked in 1987: 'People say the wages are too high, but it's a short career.'

☞ For top players today, merchandising rights are as important as salary. 'Image rights' is the latest phrase in contract negotiations.

'A slave contract.'

Jimmy Hill defines the maximum wage system

Mazzola, Sandro & Rivera, Gianni
Italy

TWO GREAT PLAYERS born less than a year apart, the careers of Alessandro Mazzola and Gianni Rivera ran almost in parallel. Which of them was the better player remains a source of debate even today amongst Italian football followers. Rivera was the first to shine, earning himself the nickname *Bambino d'Oro* ('Golden Boy') when he first shot to prominence playing for AC Milan in the early 1960s. Handsome and cavalier, he immediately became the darling of the Italian football press, a status he enhanced when, aged just 19, he was a member of the Milan side that won the European Cup in 1963. Rivera went on to collect a sackful of medals, picking up his final *Scudetto* at the age of 35 in 1979. Milan's great rivals Inter had also forged a European Cup winning side based around their great homegrown talent. Though Sandro Mazzola did not break through with the fanfare of Rivera, he nonetheless developed into an equally gifted and influential playmaker.

At international level again it was Rivera who shone first, but Mazzola forced his way into the side in the late 1960s, and from thereon most judges agree he made the greater impact. Curiously, no coach ever attempted to build a side around them both.

- Mazzola's father, Valentino, played for Italy, but was killed along with the rest of his Torino colleagues in an air crash in 1949.
- In the 1970 World Cup, Italian coach Valcareggio could not decide who to pick, so played Mazzola and Rivera 45 minutes each. But Mazzola played so well in the final Rivera was only given a paltry six minutes to shine.
- Rivera's feats for Milan led to him being voted European Footballer of the Year in 1969.
- Mazzola scored Inter's goal in the 2-1 defeat by Celtic in Lisbon in the 1967 European Cup final.
- One of the few occasions both appeared in a World Cup game was in 1966, when the *Azzurri* were eliminated by North Korea.

VITAL STATISTICS
SANDRO MAZZOLA

Place of Birth:	Torino, Italy		Achievement	9.0
Date of Birth:	8 November 1942	**Died:** n/a	Skill	8.0
Caps:	70 (Italy)	**Goals (International):** 22	Teamwork	8.0
Clubs:	Inter Milan		Passion	7.0
Appearances:	Club (for Inter): 561		Personality	6.0
Goals:	Club (for Inter): 157			
Trophies:	EC 1964, 1965; SA 1963, 1965, 1966, 1971; EuroC 1968		**TOTAL**	**38.0**

LEGEND RATING

VITAL STATISTICS
GIANNI RIVERA

Place of Birth:	Allessandria, Italy
Date of Birth:	8 August 1943 **Died:** n/a
Caps:	60 (Italy) **Goals (International):** 14
Clubs:	Allessandria, AC Milan
Appearances:	Club (League): 527
Goals:	Club (League): 128
Trophies:	EC 1963, 1969; CWC 1968, 1973; SA 1962, 1968, 1979; EuroC 1968

Achievement	8.0
Skill	8.0
Teamwork	7.0
Passion	8.0
Personality	7.0

LEGEND RATING

TOTAL 38.0

McNeill, Billy
Celtic, Scotland

ON HIS 17TH BIRTHDAY in 1957, Billy McNeill began a 34-year association with Celtic that eventually made him the club's most decorated captain and one of its most popular figures. McNeill was the centre-half keystone around which Jock Stein built Celtic's famous 'Lisbon Lions', the European Cup winners of 1967. He won his first league title with Celtic in 1966, and went on to win it a further eight years in a row, setting a record that remained in tact until Rangers enjoyed an identical period of domination in the 1980s and 1990s.

Like his mentor Jock Stein, he won the double with Celtic both as player and manager. Unlike Stein, however, he lasted longer in English management, although his four years with Aston Villa and Manchester City were undistinguished. Rejoining his alma mater, he was fired unsentimentally in 1991 after two trophy-less seasons. A triple heart bypass has since curtailed his public appearances, but the family-run McNeill's bar in the city centre stands both as a testament to his Glasgow roots and a museum to his achievements.

- On McNeill's international debut Scotland lost 9-3 to England.
- McNeill's 486 league appearances are a Celtic record.
- He scored the opening goal in a 4-0 thrashing of Rangers in the 1969 Scottish Cup final.
- McNeill also scored the winner in the 1965 Scottish Cup final.
- He earned the nickname 'Caesar' (presumably due to his commanding leadership rather than fondness for wearing a toga).

VITAL STATISTICS

Place of Birth:	Blantyre, Scotland	
Date of Birth:	2 March 1940	**Died:** n/a
Caps:	29 (Scotland)	**Goals (International):** 3
Clubs:	Celtic	
Appearances:	Club (League): 486	
Goals:	Club (League): 22	
Trophies:	EC 1967; SLT 1966–74; SFAC 1965, 1967, 1969, 1971, 1972, 1974, 1975	

Achievement	8.0	
Skill	7.0	
Teamwork	9.0	
Passion	9.0	
Personality	7.0	
TOTAL	**40.0**	LEGEND RATING

Meazza, Giuseppe

Internazionale, Italy

GIUSEPPE MEAZZA WAS THE FIRST international footballer to shine on the world stage. The original World Cup Finals in 1930 had fired the imagination of the elite nations – England apart – and Italy seized the European initiative by winning the 1934 and 1938 competitions. The brawny 'Peppino' Meazza was their attacking focal point and goalscorer, although his versatility meant he was comfortable at either centre or inside-forward.

Good enough to play for Inter at 17, he scored 33 goals in the 1929–30 season while still a teenager, and his athleticism and fitness meant that Inter continued to rely on him until way past his 35th birthday. His most successful period was during the 1930s; following his international debut at the start of the decade he remained Italy's undisputed first-choice striker until the outbreak of the Second World War. After wartime spells with Milan, Juventus and Varese, he later returned to his spiritual home at Inter as player-manager. His death, at 69 in 1979, united fans of the rival Milanese teams in common grief.

- Thirty-three goals in 53 internationals made him Italy's leading scorer until Luigi Riva.
- 1930. Scored twice on his international debut versus Switzerland.
- 1938. Captained Italy to a second successive World Cup final triumph.
- Italy scored six goals in the two World Cup finals of the 1930s. Surprisingly, not one came from Meazza.

VITAL STATISTICS

Place of Birth:	Milan, Italy
Date of Birth:	23 August 1910 **Died:** 21 August 1979
Caps:	53 (Italy) **Goals (International):** 33
Clubs:	Ambrosiana, AC Milan, Juventus, Varese,
	Atalanta, Inter Milan
Appearances:	Club (League): 439
Goals:	Club (League): 264
Trophies:	WorC 1934, 1938; SA 1938, 1940

Achievement	8.0
Skill	8.0
Teamwork	7.0
Passion	9.0
Personality	7.0
TOTAL	**39.0**

LEGEND RATING

Mercer, Joe
Everton, Arsenal, Manchester City, England

AS A PLAYER Joe Mercer was the heartbeat of two formidable sides. He played left-half in the Everton team that won the last pre-war championship and, at the end of the war when Arsenal were looking to shore up their ranks with some experience and know-how, he added to his medal collection as the Gunners claimed league titles in 1948 and 1953. Mercer had been expected to stay at Arsenal for no more than a couple of seasons, but eventually stayed eight years, only retiring in 1953 when, after skippering them to the title, he received a rousing final ovation from the Highbury faithful.

Managerial spells with Sheffield United and Aston Villa were followed by a successful period at Manchester City, where he teamed up with Malcolm Allison. Mercer's genial man-management and Allison's tactical inventiveness proved to be a potent combination, and they duly delivered the FA Cup and the club's first and only league title. When England sacked Alf Ramsey after he failed to take England to the 1974 World Cup Finals, Mercer was appointed caretaker boss. But he had no desire to inherit the job permanently, and his brief tenure served as little more than light relief before the appointment of Don Revie.

- City axed Mercer in 1972. Allison stayed, amid rumours of political dirty tricks.
- England lost only one of Mercer's seven games in charge, despite his apparently carefree approach.
- He was voted PFA Player of the Year in 1950.
- Joe Mercer to newly-appointed Stoke boss, Tony Waddington: 'My advice is never to trust anyone in the game, and when I put down this phone, don't trust me either.'

VITAL STATISTICS

Place of Birth: Ellesmere Port, Cheshire, England
Date of Birth: 9 August 1914   **Died:** 9 August 1990
Caps: 5 (England)
Goals (International): 0
Clubs: As Player: Everton, Arsenal;
As Manager: Sheffield United,
Aston Villa, Manchester City,
Coventry City
Trophies: LT 1948, 1953, (1968); FAC 1950, (1969); LC (1970)

	MANAGER		PLAYER	
Achievement	7	Achievement	8
Tactical Awareness	8	Skill	6
Motivation	8	Teamwork	8
Team Selection/Transfers	6	Passion	9
Personality	8	Personality	7
TOTAL	**37**	**TOTAL**	**38**

LEGEND RATING

Meredith, Billy

Manchester United, Wales

ONE OF WALES' greatest internationals, the original 'wizard of the wing' dazzled crowds in an amazing career lasting 30 years. An adopted son of Manchester, his two spells with City and one for United made him the forerunner of Ryan Giggs, Peter Barnes and co. Not surprisingly, since he played until he was nudging 50, most of Meredith's records surround his incredible longevity, although his own claim to have played in over 1,500 games and scored 470 goals has never been convincingly validated.

However, the stocky ex-miner's legacy was more enduring than his mighty playing career. As a feisty chairman of the maverick player's union, Meredith and his United sidekick, Charlie Roberts, eventually persuaded the FA to recognise them as an official body in 1908 and, though their fledgling union collapsed following a revolt a year later, their work is now acknowledged to have been a significant step in the advancement of player's rights.

- His 48 caps for Wales was an astonishing total for a team playing scarcely more than home internationals.
- 1920. He became the oldest man to play international football at 45 years and 229 days.
- 1924. Became the oldest player to play in the FA Cup aged 49.
- Meredith's maximum wage was £4 per week in 1907. Roy Keane earns the same today in just over 46 seconds.
- He captained Wales to their first Home International title in 1907.

VITAL STATISTICS

Place of Birth:	Black Park, Chirk, Wales
Date of Birth:	30 July 1875 **Died:** 19 April 1958
Caps:	48 (Wales) **Goals (International):** 11
Clubs:	Northwich Victoria, Manchester City, Manchester United
Appearances:	Club (League for Man Utd): 303
Goals:	Club (League for Man Utd): 35
Trophies:	LT 1908, 1911; FAC 1904, 1909

Achievement	7.0
Skill	8.0
Teamwork	7.0
Passion	8.0
Personality	9.0
TOTAL	**39.0**

LEGEND RATING

Milburn, Jackie
Newcastle United, England

JOHN EDWARD THOMPSON MILBURN, or 'Wor Jackie', was the son of Alec Milburn. Alec's brother Tanner had four sons, all of whom played league soccer, while Tanner's daughter, Cissie, had two more sons, Jackie and Bobby Charlton. On these grounds, it is probably safe to say that Jackie Milburn came from decent footballing stock.

In his long career at St James's Park, Milburn's name became synonymous with Newcastle United. On his death, thousands poured on to the streets to pay their respects, and a statue has been erected in his memory in the city centre. Milburn started his professional career late due to the war, and played initially as an inside-forward, then on the wing before moving to centre-forward in 1947. He wasn't tall, but he terrorised defences with his speed and quick feet, and his 13 England caps were a meagre reflection of his ability. Had he been a little more selfish, his goals tally may have been even more impressive than the 177 league goals he notched for the Magpies.

Upon his retirement Milburn briefly tried his hand as a manager, notably taking over an ageing Ipswich team from Alf Ramsey. They were relegated two years after winning the title, and Milburn moved back to the north-east to work in the local media.

☞ 46,000 turned out for Milburn's testimonial – 10 years after he left Newcastle.

👍 His tally of 177 league goals for Newcastle remains a record.

👍 He scored both goals in a 2-0 FA Cup final defeat of Blackpool in 1951, and after 45 seconds in the 1955 final against Manchester City.

👍 He scored on his debut for England and got one hat-trick, against Wales.

☞ Milburn left Newcastle for a successful spell as player-manager at Linfield in Northern Ireland. He even appeared in the European Cup for the club.

VITAL STATISTICS

Place of Birth:	Ashington, England		
Date of Birth:	11 May 1924	**Died:** 9 October 1988	
Caps:	13 (England)	**Goals (International):** 10	
Clubs:	Newcastle United		
Appearances:	Club (League): 354		
Goals:	Club (League): 177		
Trophies:	FAC 1951, 1952, 1955		

Achievement	6.0
Skill	9.0
Teamwork	7.0
Passion	9.0
Personality	7.0
TOTAL	**38.0**

LEGEND RATING

Milla, Roger
Cameroon

ALTHOUGH ROGER MILLA'S World Cup goal scoring exploits for Cameroon are a matter of record, reliable information regarding his date of birth and even his name is harder to come by. The family name is written Miller, so Roger's own spelling is baffling while his age has proved so difficult to pin down journalists have been forced into guesswork. Even Joan Collins has guarded her date of birth less zealously than this player.

After nine years with top Cameroon side Tonerre Yaounde, Milla moved to France, where he entertained fans across the country with his brio and humour. The 1982 World Cup Finals in Spain eventually provided him with an international stage 15 years after his professional debut, and he was still around for the 1994 Finals in the USA despite being well over 40. His, and Cameroon's, best tournament was Italia 90, where the outsiders stunned the world in the opening game by beating holders Argentina, and eventually forced their way through to the quarter-finals where they were only despatched by Gary Lineker's penalties. His style, enthusiasm and trademark corner flag dance brought some levity to what was largely a brutal and disappointing tournament.

- ☞ Aged 42 (allegedly) at USA 94, Milla became the oldest player in World Cup Finals history.
- ☝ Twice African Footballer of the Year, his 1976 award wasn't repeated until 14 years later.
- ☞ Fittingly, the 42-year-old scored in his 1994 swansong appearance, albeit in a 6-1 thrashing by Russia.
- ☝ Milla scored two goals against Romania to take Cameroon past the group stage for the first time in 1990.
- ☝ He followed that with two more, as Cameroon became the first African side to reach the quarter-finals with a 2-1 win over Colombia.

VITAL STATISTICS

Place of Birth: Yaounde, Cameroon
Date of Birth: 20 May 1952 **Died:** n/a
Caps: 81 (Cameroon) **Goals (International):** 42
Clubs: Leopaerd Douala, Tanerre Yaounde, Valenciennes, Monaco, Bastia, Saint Etienne, Montpellier, Saint Pierre
Trophies: African Player of the Year 1976, 1990

Achievement	5.0
Skill	7.0
Teamwork	7.0
Passion	9.0
Personality	10.0
TOTAL	**38.0**

LEGEND RATING

Mine's A Treble!
Manchester United 2 Bayern Munich 1, 1999

IT WAS FAR FROM the greatest European Cup final, and a much inferior game to Man United's previous final appearance in 1968. But for late, jaw-dropping drama there will probably never be another game like it. Bayern scored after six minutes and after 90 minutes United were still 1-0 down. The referee's assistant held up a board showing three minutes of injury time. Up in the stand the ribbons of Bayern Munich were being attached to the giant trophy. Then, a minute later, United won a corner. Maybe Bayern were distracted by the sight of Peter Schmeichel haring into the penalty area. If so the great Dane proved to be an ideal decoy, leaving Sheringham to sweep the ball past Oliver Kahn for the equaliser. It was more than United had dared hoped for, and a minute later their wildest dreams had been realised. Beckham curled in another corner, Sheringham flicked on and supersub Ole Gunnar Solskjaer volleyed past a disbelieving Kahn. The Bayern team sank to their knees as United capered back to the half-way line.

☞ The game was won on the 90th anniversary of Matt Busby's birth.

✎ United played poorly. To cover the loss of Keane and Scholes (both suspended) Beckham was forced inside and Giggs played on the right, where he failed to offer his customary threat.

☞ The referee was Pierluigi Collina, who would witness another English triumph over German opposition in Munich in 2001.

☞ There was sympathy for most of the German team, but not for Mario Basler, whose triumphal exit as he was substituted in the last minute was premature and presumptuous.

☟ Consolation came two years later for Bayern, as they beat Valencia on penalties to win the Cup, having beaten Man United home and away in the quarter-finals.

SCORERS	**Manchester United:** Sheringham, Solskjaer
	Bayern Munich: Basler
EVENT	European Champions League final, Nou Camp, Barcelona, 26 May 1999
MAN UTD	(Man: Alex Ferguson)
	1. Schmeichel 2. Neville (G) 3. Irwin 4. Butt 5. Johnsen 6. Stam 7. Beckham
	8. Blomqvist (Sheringham) 9. Cole (Solskjaer) 10. Yorke 11. Giggs
BAYERN	(Man: Ottmar Hitzfeld)
	1. Kahn 2. Babbel 3. Tarnat 4. Linke 5. Matthaus 6. Kuffour 7. Jermies
	8. Effenberg 9. Jancker 10. Basler 11. Zickler

Modern Classic

Liverpool 5 Alaves 4, 2001

LIVERPOOL WERE HUNTING a unique treble. They had already won the Worthington Cup, and Michael Owen had stolen the FA Cup from under Arsenal's noses the previous Saturday. Alaves provided almost unknown opposition. They had been Spain's surprise package for a couple of seasons and, in striker Javi Moreno, boasted the top scorer in La Liga.

The entire game was played at breakneck pace. Liverpool seemed to sense a weakness in the Alaves defence and went for the jugular, while Alaves, perhaps mindful of their defensive frailties, went for all-out attack. But then, after going two goals behind in the first 16 minutes they didn't really have much choice. Coach 'Mane' abandoned three at the back early, adding an extra forward and moving to 4-3-3. The substitute, Ivan Alonso, scored almost immediately. After coming on for Emile Heskey, Robbie Fowler looked to have scored the winner but Jordi Cruyff popped up with a last-gasp header to tie the scores at 4-4.

Alaves had two players sent off in extra-time but fought doggedly until, with just three minutes remaining, Geli put through his own net to hand victory, and a unique Cup treble, to Liverpool. They had won it with a Golden Goal.

☞ There were some curious substitutions in this match. Alaves withdrew their best player, Moreno, after he had scored twice while Liverpool took off Henchoz, whom Moreno had tormented, and used Steven Gerrard at right-back.

☞ Alaves came into the tournament with no European pedigree, but they beat Rosenborg, the perennial Norwegian champions, Inter Milan and Kaisersalautern on the way to the final.

☞ Spain had seven quarter-finalists, four semi-finalists and two finalists in the two European competitions in 2001. Italy's teams were all knocked out before the quarter-finals.

☞ Westerveld's performance suggested he wasn't quite up to the mark. He, too, was replaced the following year.

SCORERS	**Liverpool:** Babbel, Gerrard, McAllister (p), Fowler, Geli (og)
	Alaves: Ivan Alonso, Moreno, Moreno, Cruyff
EVENT	UEFA Cup Final, Dortmund, 16 May 2001
LIVERPOOL	(Man: Gerard Houllier)
	1. Westerveld 2. Babbel 3. Carragher 4. Hamann 5. Hyypia 6. Henchoz
	7. Murphy 8. Gerrard 9. Heskey 10. Owen 11. McAllister
ALAVES	(Man: Jose Manuel Esnal)
	1. Herrera 2 Karmona 3. Tomic 4. Geli 5. Contra 6. Eggen 7. Tellez
	8. Desio 9. Javi Moreno 10. Astudillo 11. Cruyff

Monti, Luis
Juventus, Italy

LUISITO MONTI WAS BORN in Buenos Aires and played most of his early football in South America. He appeared for Argentina in the inaugural World Cup, playing in the ill-tempered final that saw his team defeated 4-2 by the ruthless Uruguayans. Four years later, and playing for Juventus, Monti, along with many other *Oriundi* (foreigners of Italian descent), was invited to represent Italy in the 1934 tournament. This time he won a winner's medal as the hosts, aided by some supine refereeing, battered their way to victory.

Monti personified the Italian team. Though a gifted player, his talents included a great ability to spread the play with raking passes, he was more than happy to mix it when necessary. In the semi-final he intimidated the Austrian playmaker Sindelar, and handed out similar bad office to the Czech, Nejedly, in the final.

The tournament, intended as a showpiece for Mussolini's Italy, instead became a symbol of its ugliness and corruption. In a different era Monti may have been encouraged to show more of his footballing skill and less of his cynicism, but as it is he will be remembered as the prototype brutal footballer – a Vinnie Jones in baggy shorts.

- 👍 He won four successive Italian league titles at Juventus (1932–35).
- 👍 Monti won a major trophy before the World Cup was even invented, leading Argentina to the South American championship in 1927.
- 👉 Monti played in the 1930 World Cup final despite receiving a death threat before the match; the police searched all spectators for revolvers at the gates.
- 👉 Monti was instrumental in turning a friendly against England into the 'Battle Of Highbury.' When he limped off after a tackle by Ted Drake, the Italian team went berserk.
- 👉 Monti is the only player to have appeared in World Cup Finals for two different nations.

VITAL STATISTICS

Place of Birth:	Buenos Aires, Argentina
Date of Birth:	15 May 1901 **Died:** 9 September 1983
Caps:	18 (Italy) He also played for Argentina in the 1930 World Cup
Goals (International):	1 (for Italy)
Clubs:	Huracan, Boca Juniors, San Lorenzo, Juventus
Appearances:	Club (League for Juventus): 225
Goals:	Club (League for Juventus): 24
Trophies:	ALT 1923–24, 1927; SA 1932–35; WorC 1934

Achievement	9.0
Skill	6.0
Teamwork	7.0
Passion	8.0
Personality	6.0
TOTAL	**36.0**

LEGEND RATING

Moore, Bobby
West Ham United, England

'WORDS CANNOT SUM UP the grief I feel for my great friend. He was one of the world's finest defenders and a great sportsman.' So said Pelé after the sudden death, from cancer, of Bobby Moore in 1993.

Moore was the ultimate example of mind over body. He appeared to possess few of the physical attributes required in a great defender, but made up for his lack of muscle with an ability to read the game that bordered on the psychic. Moore took the ball by stealth rather than power and, though he rarely needed to resort to tackling, when he did so it was always surgical and clean. Rattling bones wasn't his style. He was loyal too; with the exception of a swansong alongside George Best and Rodney Marsh at Fulham, Moore spent his entire career at West Ham. Upton Park now has a stand named after him, and the ground is home to a bust and plaque honouring his achievements.

His England career started in 1962, and continued almost unbroken until his retirement from internationals in 1973. He competed in three World Cups, winning the Player of the Tournament award in 1966 when he captained England to a 4-2 victory over Germany in the final.

☞ Moore was outstanding in the 1970 World Cup Finals, despite having spent four days in a Colombian jail after a woman falsely accused him of stealing a bracelet.

☞ Moore nearly missed the 1966 World Cup as he was in contractual dispute with West Ham. Under FA rules this made him ineligible for England, so a temporary contract was arranged to see him through the tournament.

☞ Moore was not the saint he is often made out to be. He was twice reprimanded for breaking pre-match curfews for West Ham and England.

☞ He was PFA Player of the Year in 1964, and received an OBE in 1967.

VITAL STATISTICS

Place of Birth:	Barking, Essex, England	
Date of Birth:	12 April 1941	**Died:** 24 February 1993
Caps:	108 (England)	**Goals (International):** 2
Clubs:	West Ham United, Fulham, Seattle Sounders,	
	San Antonio Thunder	
Appearances:	Club (All Matches): 823	
Goals:	Club (All Matches): 29	
Trophies:	WorC 1966; FAC 1964; CWC 1965	

Achievement	9.0
Skill	10.0
Teamwork	9.0
Passion	9.0
Personality	6.0
TOTAL	**43.0**

LEGEND RATING

Müller, Gerd
Bayern Munich, West Germany

GERD MÜLLER, 'Der Bomber', was arguably the most lethal finisher in the history of the game. Like many out-and-out goal scorers, he did little outside the penalty area, and looked unremarkable in open play, but in the box his reflexes were cobra-like. Powerful, and with terrific balance, he was always in the right position to receive the ball, his body always shaped in readiness for a strike on goal.

Müller was drafted into the German team in 1966 immediately after the World Cup final, and surprisingly retired after scoring the winner against Holland in the 1974 final, aged only 28. The eight years in between were a one-man goal-fest as Germany swept aside lesser opposition, and even proved themselves a match for the inspired Dutch. At club level Müller spent 15 years with Bayern Munich, scoring at a ratio of better than one goal per game for a remarkable seven seasons.

- He was European Footballer of the Year in 1970, and twice winner of the Golden Boot.
- He scored a phenomenal 14 goals in 13 games in two World Cup final tournaments, including successive hat-tricks in 1970.
- Müller was top scorer at the World Cup in 1970 and the European Championships in 1972.
- Hampered by an injury in 1978, Müller saw out his career in the NASL with Fort Lauderdale.
- He won a hat-trick of European Cups with Bayern Munich.

VITAL STATISTICS

Place of Birth:	Zinsen, Bavaria, Germany
Date of Birth:	3 November 1945 **Died:** n/a
Caps:	62 (Germany) **Goals (International):** 68
Clubs:	TSV Nordlingen, Bayern Munich, Fort Lauderdale Strikers
Appearances:	Club (League for Bayern Munich): 427
Goals:	Club (League for Bayern Munich): 365
Trophies:	WorC 1974; EC 1974, 1975, 1976; BLG 1969, 1972, 1973, 1974; CWC 1967

LEGEND RATING	
Achievement	10.0
Skill	10.0
Teamwork	6.0
Passion	8.0
Personality	8.0
TOTAL	**42.0**

Munich Air Disaster
End of an Era

6 FEBRUARY 1958 is a date that will remain a black-letter day in the world of football. A plane crash with fatalities was a tragic event in itself, but that the airliner involved should also include most of English football's finest post-war club side was headline news that numbed fans across the globe. In the freezing conditions at Munich airport the plane had already made one abortive attempt at a take-off but, undeterred, the pilot made the decision to try again. On the second attempt the plane left the ground but could not climb high enough to avoid hitting a fence and airport building, whereupon it broke in two and burst into flames.

Although eight players died, some miraculously managed to escape the wreckage alive. They included manager Sir Matt Busby and a young Bobby Charlton, who was to continue playing for another 15 years after the crash. Charlton's long career served as a poignant reminder of what may have lain ahead for his less fortunate colleagues. The names of the dead are a roll-call of unfulfilled talent:

Geoff Bent; Roger Byrne; Eddie Colman; Duncan Edwards; Mark Jones; David Pegg; Tommy Taylor; Bill Whelan.

☞ Duncan Edwards was not killed in the crash, but died from his injuries on 21 February 1958.

✎ Seven of the dead were 25 or younger; Busby's famous Babes had been almost totally wiped out.

✎ Three members of United's staff also died, plus the journalist Frank Swift, an ex-Manchester City and England goalkeeper.

☞ A memorial clock was erected at Old Trafford. It contains the date of the crash and is a popular meeting point for fans.

☞ The programme for United's next league match contained 11 blank spaces where the players' names would normally have been inserted.

'People still haven't forgotten. Strangers come up and tell me: "He were a good 'un."'

Anne Edwards, mother of Duncan, 1993

Mussolini's Muscle
Italy, 1930s

VITTORIO POZZO COACHED the Italian squad at the 1912 Olympics as a young man. He was hugely impressed by what he saw of the great Austrian coach, Hugo Meisl, and when he was given control of the Italian national side, he determined to build a side to match Meisl's 'Wunderteam'.

Pozzo introduced a discipline not previously seen in a national team, along with some deeply innovative tactics. By the time the 1934 World Cup Finals came along, the Italians had a strong squad. Add to this their home advantage, and a propensity for intimidating both opponents and weak referees, and it was little surprise to see them emerge as winners of a deeply unsatisfactory tournament. They won again four years later – same manager, same tactics and yet more aggro. But we shouldn't be too cynical; Schiavio, Meazza, Ferrari and Piola were super players and Monti, however brutal, was a card-carrying colossus. Still, for many their 1938 victory will always be tarnished; not because of their underhand approach, but because of Giuseppe Meazza's unfortunate decision to celebrate with a fascist salute after being presented with the trophy.

☞ Pozzo used Monti as an attacking centre-half, an innovation to help combat the changes made to the offside laws in 1926.

👍 Between their two World Cup triumphs, Italy also won at the Olympics.

☞ Pozzo fortified the team with the *oriund*, nationalised South Americans like Monti and Orsi (both former Argentines).

☞ Tactics were very rigid in the 1930s; Pozzo confounded the Czechs in 1934 by simply asking his wide players to swap wings.

👍 Pozzo remains the only manager to have won two World Cups.

Manager: Vittorio Pozzo

Key Players

Gianpero Combi (G) Luis Monti (D) Giovanni Ferrari (F)
Raimundo Orsi (W) Gino Colaussi (W) Giuseppe Meazza (F)
Angelo Schiavio (F) Silvio Piola (F)

Nedved, Pavel
Juventus, Czech Republic

WHEN THE RESULTS of the poll for European Player of the Year in 2003 were announced, it was a surprise to many in Britain that the award went to Pavel Nedved, playmaker at Juventus and for the Czech Republic. Look at the facts and it's less of an eye-opener.

When the old lady sold Zinedine Zidane to Real Madrid in 2001, it was generally agreed that he was irreplaceable. That Juve won the Serie A title in the following two seasons and reached the Champions League final in 2003 was due in no small part to the decision to bring in the Czech, then at Lazio, as Zidane's replacement.

A two-footed attacking midfielder with an eye for goal and excellent work rate, he was able to take on Zidane's creative mantle, perhaps not with the same guile, but with huge industry and drive and no small amount of flair. Nedved's suspension for that Champions League final was surely crucial; he had been the inspiration behind Juve's defeat of Real Madrid in the semis.

With Nedved at the heart of a hard-working and free-scoring team, the Czech Republic played some of Euro 2004's best football. The bitter disappointment of his early injury in the 1-0 defeat to Greece prompted his retirement from international football.

- Even before his triumphs at Juventus, Nedved had won a league and cup double in Italy with Lazio.
- Nedved scored in the last ever Cup Winners' Cup final, as Lazio beat Mallorca.
- Nedved won three Czech league titles with Sparta Prague before his move to Italy.
- The last Czech player to win European Footballer of the Year was Jozef Masopust, 31 years before.
- Nedved was one of the stars of the Czech team that reached the final of Euro 96, losing to Germany by way of a Golden Goal.

VITAL STATISTICS

Place of Birth:	Prague, Czech Republic
Date of Birth:	30 August 1972 **Died:** n/a
Caps:	81 (Czech Republic) **Goals (International):** 17
Clubs:	Marila Pribram, Sparta Prague, Lazio, Juventus
Appearances:	Club (League): 336
Goals:	Club (League): 78
Trophies:	OLT 1993, 1994, 1995; SA 2000, 2002, 2003; CWC 1999

Achievement	7.0
Skill	8.0
Teamwork	7.0
Passion	8.0
Personality	6.0
TOTAL	**36.0**

LEGEND RATING

Neeskens, Johan
Ajax, Holland

JOHAN CRUYFF WAS THE CUTTING EDGE of the great Holland team of the 1970s, but Johan Neeskens (or 'Johan Two' as he became known) was the conductor of the orchestra. An ideal midfield fulcrum, his accurate passing and shooting underpinned the movement and pace of his colleagues.

Neeskens made the transition from Ajax star to international star in 1970, and went on to play in both the 1974 and 1978 World Cup Finals. By the time the latter came he had left Ajax for Barcelona, spending five years with the Catalan club. Perhaps Neeskens' defining moment came against Brazil in 1974 when, ignoring all his colleagues, he casually chipped the goalkeeper like a golfer holing out from a bunker.

Like many other stars of his generation, Neeskens finished his career in the NASL with New York Cosmos. He has assisted later Dutch teams in a coaching capacity and remains active in the game.

👍 In 1974 Neeskens scored with a second-minute penalty in the World Cup final.

👍 Scored five times from midfield in World Cup 1974: impressive for a player not known for getting into the opposition box.

👎 In 1976 Holland lost to Czechoslovakia in a violent European Championship semi-final. Again Neeskens showed his dark side and was one of two Dutch players sent off.

☞ Although talented, Neeskens was no angel. In a notoriously bitter match against Brazil in 1974 he played the role of midfield hard-man to great effect.

☞ Neeskens' move to Barcelona was orchestrated by former Dutch coach Rinus Michels, anxious to reunite him with Cruyff.

VITAL STATISTICS

Place of Birth: Heemstede, Holland

Date of Birth: 15 September 1951   **Died:** n/a

Caps: 49 (Holland)   **Goals (International):** 17

Clubs: Haarlem, Ajax, Barcelona, New York Cosmos, Groningen, Fort Lauderdale Strikers, Baar

Appearances: Club (League): 481

Goals: Club (League): 92

Trophies: DLT 1972, 1973; EC 1971, 1972, 1973; CWC 1979

LEGEND RATING	
Achievement	7.0
Skill	9.0
Teamwork	9.0
Passion	7.0
Personality	6.0
TOTAL	**38.0**

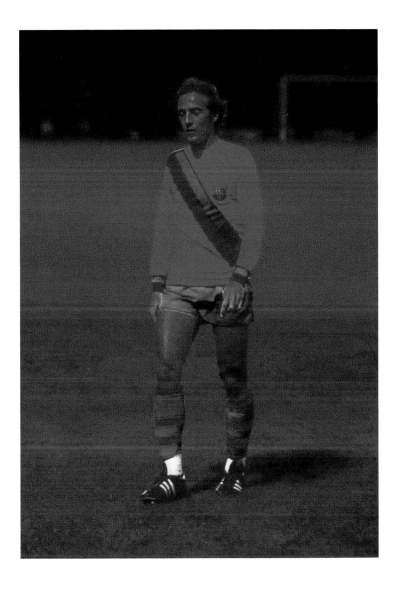

Nerazzurri – The Finest

The Internazionale Dream Team

IN 1930 the first national championship of Italy was won by Ambrosiana-Inter, as Internazionale were first known. Their leading scorer, and the top scorer in the country that year, was Giuseppe Meazza. Inter have continued to win trophies throughout their history, but only one of their teams has enjoyed total domination of Serie A.

In the 1960s, led by their controversial coach Helenio Herrera, Inter, with a team built on a rock-like defence including Burgnich, Guarneri and the formidable attacking back Facchetti, were out on their own. Yet, while their defence might have taken most of the plaudits, their midfield, boasting the talents of Sandro Mazzola, the Spaniard Suarez and the young Angelo Domenghini, was not short on ability either. Try as they might, subsequent Inter coaches have failed to match that synthesis of efficient defending and rapid counter-attack. Perhaps the problem is that players in the modern Serie A come and go too fast; Inter have had great players like Baggio, Matthaus, Ronaldo, Bergkamp and Klinsmann, but no great team.

- 1950s goalkeeper Ghezzi was known as Kamikaze. Brave and agile, he is a legend at Inter.
- Facchetti remains Inter's most capped player, with 94 appearances for Italy.
- Bergomi is Inter's most loyal player of recent years. No flitting about for him, as just over 750 appearances show.
- Meazza remains Inter's top scorer with 264 goals from 439 matches.
- Three UEFA Cup wins in the 1990s merely offered tantalising glimpses of the European success the club craves. Two of the final victories were over Italian opposition.

Manager: Helenio Herrera

4-3-1-2

Walter Zenga (80s/90s)

Tarcisio Burgnich (60s/70s) Riccardo Ferri (80s)
Giuseppe Bergomi (80s/90s) Giacinto Facchetti (C) (60s/70s)

Sandro Mazzola (60s) Luis Suarez (60s) Angelo Domenghini (60s/70s)

Roberto Baggio (90s)

Roberto Boninsegna (60s/70s) Giuseppe Meazza (30s)

Subs: Giorgio Ghezzi (G) (50s) Aristide Guarneri (D) (50s/60s)
Lothar Matthaus (D/M) (90s) Jair (M/F) (60s) Jurgen Klinsmann (F) (90s)

Netzer, Günther

Borussia Mönchengladbach, West Germany

A GERMAN GASCOIGNE without the boozing, belching and domestic violence; for a brief period Günther Netzer could lay claim to being the finest midfield player in the world. After missing out on the 1970 World Cup, Netzer came to the fore in the 1972 European Championships when he was instrumental in his country's victory over England in the quarter-final. Despite being several players short, West Germany won at a canter. Beckenbauer was magnificent at the back, Müller unstoppable in the box, and Netzer, long hair flowing, linked the two with aggression and immaculate distribution. The Germans went on to win the tournament with ease. For years the mainstay of a strong Borussia Mönchengladbach team, Netzer later made a high profile move to Real Madrid in 1973, only to suffer a grievous loss of form that impacted on his international career. At the 1974 World Cup Finals he made just one appearance, briefly figuring as a substitute against East Germany. Few players looked as good as Netzer did for those few years, but few have faded so dramatically either.

👍 Netzer was in Hennes Weisweiler's Mönchengladbach side that won the club their first Bundesliga title in 1970.

☞ Netzer's replacement in the German team, Mönchengladbach team-mate Rainer Bonhof, was a strong, hard-running player, less skilful than Netzer, but an easier player to fit into Helmut Schoen's pattern.

👎 Mönchengladbach lost the 1973 UEFA Cup final to Liverpool. Shankly's team were grateful for a 3-0 lead from Anfield, as Mönchengladbach pummelled them in the return, winning 2-0.

👍 Netzer became manager of Hamburg on his retirement, inheriting a strong team including Kevin Keegan. He duly brought them their first Bundesliga title for 19 years.

VITAL STATISTICS

Place of Birth:	Mönchengladbach, West Germany
Date of Birth:	14 September 1944 **Died:** n/a
Caps:	37 (W. Germany) **Goals (International):** 6
Clubs:	Borussia Mönchengladbach, Real Madrid, Grasshopper
Appearances:	Club (League for Borussia): 230
Goals:	Club (League for Borussia): 82
Trophies:	BLG 1970, 1971, (1979 as manager of Hamburg); EuroC 1972; PLA 1975, 1976

LEGEND RATING

Achievement	8.0
Skill	9.0
Teamwork	8.0
Passion	7.0
Personality	7.0
TOTAL	**39.0**

New Power
Ajax 5 Liverpool 1, 1966

BY THE MID-1960s, Dutch club football had barely caused a ripple in Europe. No achievement, no pedigree, no nothing. This result changed everything. At a stroke, Holland was on the footballing map.

It wasn't simply arrogance that did for Liverpool. Any team managed by Shankly were hardly likely to lack application. Compared to the finely tuned Ajax, whose intricate and innovative Total Football was to tear up existing coaching manuals, the famous 'red machine' puffed and blowed in their wake like a badly oiled traction engine.

Ajax began in a blur. After three minutes, De Wolf's cross was met by Groot's head to power them into the lead. By half-time it was 4-0, with a goal from 19-year-old Cruyff and a brace in five minutes from Nuninga. The dense fog, which made half the crowd reliant on the roars from the rest to keep up with the score, only added to what was fast becoming a surreal occasion.

Liverpool regrouped somewhat after the break, but the damage limitation exercise was weakened by Groot's strike 15 minutes from time. A consolation from Lawler with two minutes left proved one of the tournament's less vital away goals. For Ajax and Dutch football, things would never be the same again.

☞ Italian referee Sbardella justified starting a game in such foggy conditions by claiming he could see both goals from the centre spot. He must have overdosed on carrots.

☞ Despite their away strip of blue, Ajax played in all white for the only time in their history.

👃 After 44 minutes, Sjaak Swart disappeared down the tunnel, having mistaken the referee's whistle as the signal for half-time. He trotted back on to the field and crossed for Nuninga to score Ajax's fourth.

☞ A disbelieving Shankly claimed Liverpool would win 7-0 in the return leg at Anfield. The game finished 2-2, with two goals for the emerging Cruijff.

👎 Ajax blew it in the next round, losing to Dukla Prague.

SCORERS	**Ajax:** de Wolf, Cruijff, Nuninga (2), Groot
	Liverpool: Lawler
EVENT	European Cup, Second Round, Olympic Stadium, Amsterdam, 7 December 1966
AJAX	(Man: Rinus Michels)
	1. Bals 2. Suurbier 3. Pronk 4. Soetekouw 5. van Duivenbode 6. Müller 7. Groot
	8. Swart 9. Cruijff 10. Nuninga 11. de Wolf
LIVERPOOL	(Man: Bill Shankly)
	1. Lawrence 2. Lawler 3. Smith 4. Yeats 5. Graham 6. Callaghan 7. St John
	8. Stevenson 9. Hunt 10. Strong 11. Thompson

New Theories

England 3 Hungary 6, 1953

A PACKED HOUSE arrived at Wembley confidently expecting an easy England victory. A bullish press had led the nation to believe that England were unbeatable, largely on the basis that no overseas team had won at Wembley before. The England team, ageing and complacent in their heavy boots, scoffed at the men wearing 'carpet slippers,' especially the 'little fat chap' leading them out. It is unthinkable that a modern coach would be so badly prepared (England's opponents were a highly dangerous outfit, unbeaten for 20 games). Hungary scored in the first minute, a precise angled strike from Nandor Hidegkuti. An England equaliser offered false hope before Hidegkuti scored again and 'the little fat chap,' Ferenc Puskas, added two more.

The rest of the detail is irrelevant. Hungary went into cruise mode, giving the impression they could score at will. Their passing triangles and sudden sprints forward into space completely flummoxed an unimaginative England defence. Puskas had breezed past Billy Wright, England's best defender, on numerous occasions, and the use of the deep-lying centre forward Hidegkuti had given prosaic England untold problems.

☞ The headlines the next day compared Hungary to the Scottish 'Wembley Wizards' of 1928, who had embarrassed England at Wembley in much the same fashion.

☞ The England side featured Matthews and Mortensen fresh from their heroics at the FA Cup final. Mortensen got a consolation but Matthews hardly saw the ball.

☜ The sides played again six months later as a last warm-up for Hungary's World Cup campaign. England made seven changes in an effort to counter the Hungarian tactics. The plan failed dismally as Hungary won 7-1. Back to the drawing board, chaps.

SCORERS **England:** Sewell, Mortensen, Ramsey (pen)
Hungary: Hidegkuti (3), Puskas (2), Bozsik

EVENT Friendly International, Wembley, 25 November 1953

ENGLAND (Man: Walter Winterbottom)
1. Merrick 2. Ramsey 3. Eckersley 4. Wright 5. Johnston 6. Dickinson 7. Matthews 8. Taylor 9. Mortensen 10. Sewell 11. Robb

HUNGARY (Man: Jimmy Hogan)
1. Grosics 2. Buzansky 3. Lantos 4. Bozsik 5. Lorant 6. Zakarias 7. Budai 8. Kocsis 9. Hidegkuti 10. Puskas 11. Czibor

Nicholson, Bill
Tottenham Hotspur, England

WHEN BILL NICHOLSON RESIGNED as manager of Spurs in 1974, it brought a 36-year love affair to an end. With Bill Shankly retiring the same year it also marked the passing of the last remaining manager from the old school. 'I am abused by players, there is no longer respect,' lamented Nicholson, announcing his decision to step down.

If anyone deserved respect it was Nicholson. As a player he had served the club well in the post-war years; starting at full-back, he later switched inside to centre-half, then moved again, this time to half-back, in the 1951 league title winning side. As manager he brought success and consistency to the club, while always remaining mindful of his obligation to play exciting football. The 1961 double-winning team scored over 100 goals, playing scintillating football at odds with Nicholson's dour, uncompromising demeanour.

Under his tutelage, after a difficult first season, Spurs only once finished in the bottom half of the First Division. They were a notable cup team, too, becoming the first British side to win a European trophy. Nicholson was incensed when the club appointed an Arsenal man, Terry Neill, to replace him, arguing that Danny Blanchflower would have been a better choice. His instincts proved right. Neill took Spurs into Division Two within three years.

- In Nicholson's first game as a manager, Tottenham was a 10-4 winner against Everton.
- Nicholson scored after 19 seconds of his England debut, but was never picked again.
- He won a PFA merit award in 1984 for his services to the game.
- In 1961, the Spurs double-winning team had just one player booked all season.
- Nicholson was a contributor to *Soccer – The Fight For Survival, A Blueprint For The Future*, a 1980–81 review of a game in crisis.

VITAL STATISTICS

Place of Birth:	Scarborough, England
Date of Birth:	26 January 1919 **Died:** 23 October 2004
Caps:	1 (England) **Goals (International):** 1
Clubs:	As Player: Tottenham Hotspur; As Manager: Tottenham Hotspur
Trophies:	LT (1951), 1961; FAC 1961, 1962, 1967; LC 1971, 1973; CWC 1963; UEFAC 1972

LEGEND RATING	
Achievement	9
Tactical Awareness	8
Motivation	8
Team Selection/Transfers	9
Personality	8
TOTAL	**42**

Nistelrooy, Ruud van
Manchester United, Holland

WHEN MANCHESTER UNITED unveiled £19 m Ruud van Nistelrooy from PSV Eindhoven in April 2000, only for him to fail a medical, the snigger from their rivals was almost audible. When the same player ruptured cruciate ligaments a few weeks later during routine training in Holland, they could hardly contain themselves. To paraphrase the chant, they're not laughing anymore.

Since recovering from injury the Dutchman has become one of Europe's most complete and feared strikers. Strong, skilful, with acute positional sense and a deadly finish, the footballing world lies at van Nistelrooy's feet.

His impact was immediate. A goal on his debut in the 2001 Charity Shield was followed by two more on his first Premiership appearance. So began a season that was to finish with 36 goals, an incredible total in these days of squad rotation. Even though his fee was a British record, albeit a short-lived one, it already looks judicious compared to the £58 m lavished by United on Veron and Ferdinand.

Holland's failure to qualify for the 2002 World Cup Finals robbed the world stage of his talents.

- Van Nistelrooy was leading scorer in the Dutch League for two successive seasons.
- 2001–02. Voted PFA Player of the Year. Van Nistelrooy also won the Dutch equivalent whilst at PSV.
- Biggest disappointment – knee injury not only scuppers his United transfer but robs him of the entire Euro 2000 tournament.
- 2002–03. Van Nistelrooy breaks the Premiership record by scoring in nine consecutive League games.
- In February 2004 he scored his 100th United goal in only his 131st game. Only Denis Law reached his United century quicker.

VITAL STATISTICS

Place of Birth:	Oss, Holland	
Date of Birth:	1 July 1976	**Died:** n/a
Caps:	24 (Holland)	**Goals (International):** 11
Clubs:	Den Bosch, SC Heerenveen, PSV Eindhoven,	
	Manchester United	
Appearances:	Club (League): 273	
Goals:	Club (League): 167	
Trophies:	DLT 2000; LT 2003; FAC 2004	

LEGEND RATING	
Achievement	6.0
Skill	9.0
Teamwork	8.0
Passion	8.0
Personality	7.0
TOTAL	**38.0**

Nou Camp
Barcelona, Spain

THE NOU CAMP is rightly regarded as one of the great stadiums of world soccer and enjoys the rare and coveted UEFA five-star rating.

Home to Barcelona and its passionate fans, the stadium opened in 1957 and is seen as a monument to Catalan pride. It is regularly packed to capacity. Even today, with a slightly reduced capacity of 109,000, the stadium is the biggest in Europe and attendances for league matches regularly top the 100,000 mark.

The pitch is built eight metres below street level and its towering stands make it one of the most intimidating theatres in the game. The word cauldron has been used to the point of cliché by commentators but it describes the shape and atmosphere of the Nou Camp in a nutshell.

The Nou Camp underwent a major refurbishment in readiness for the 1982 World Cup Finals, increasing the capacity from a scarcely snug 90,000 to an immense 120,000. It played host to the opening game of the competition between Argentina and Belgium. Due to the Bernabeu's lure in the nation's capital, the Nou Camp remains the finest ground never to have staged the final.

- Despite the increased capacity, the curtain-raiser of the 1982 World Cup is the only time that the opening match has not been watched by a capacity crowd. A mere 85,000 turned up.
- The first-ever match in 1957 at the Nou Camp was a curious choice. Barcelona's opponents were Poland – the home side winning 4-2.
- The formal name is El Nou Estadi del Futbol Club Barcelona. No wonder they stick to Nou Camp.
- The Nou Camp has staged four major European club finals; the European Cup in 1989 and 1999, plus the Cup Winners' Cups of 1972 and 1982.

VITAL STATISTICS

Location:	Barcelona, Spain
Local Club:	Barcelona
Date Built:	1957
Current Capacity:	109,000
Max. Capacity:	120,000

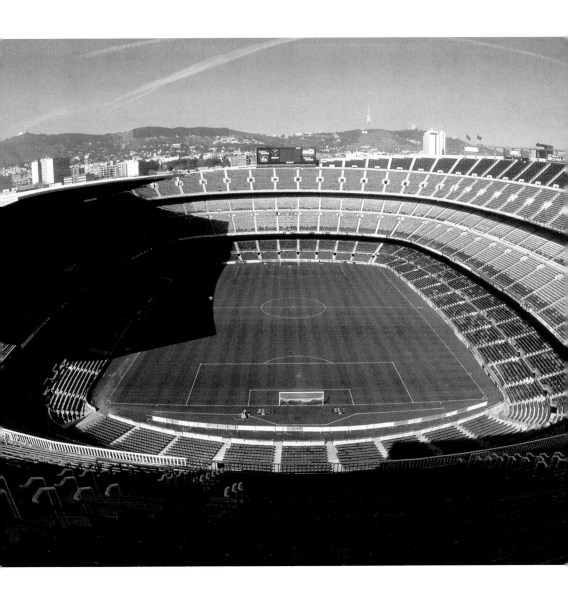

Now Listen To Me, Young Man!
Nottingham Forest, late 1970s

WHEN BRIAN CLOUGH and Peter Taylor joined Nottingham Forest in 1975, no one could have anticipated the success the next five years would bring. Upon winning promotion in 1977 they added the great Peter Shilton to their side, went top of the First Division after three opening wins, and stayed there. A tight defence, a midfield with an unparalleled work rate, and mobile strikers were the key ingredients – plus a little bit of that Cloughie *je ne sais quoi* sprinkled on top.

Even greater things followed in Europe, courtesy of two contrasting European Cup finals. The first in 1979, won by a single Trevor Francis goal, was reward for a sparkling performance against Malmo while the second, another 1-0 win over Kevin Keegan's Hamburg in 1980, showed the more dogged side of their nature. Despite unceasing pressure from the German team Forest stood firm, with Kenny Burns outstanding at the heart of their defence. That was the last of their major titles, but under Clough they remained a significant force in the top flight for another decade, as new stars like Neil Webb, Stuart Pearce and Clough's own son, Nigel came to the fore.

- Trevor Francis made the goal in the 1979 European Cup final, and John Robertson scored the winner in 1980.
- Forest ousted reigning champions Liverpool in the first round of the 1979 European Cup.
- Forest also won the League Cup in 1979, Gary Birtles scoring twice in a 3-2 win.
- Forest won the League Cup twice more under Clough, in 1989 and 1990. Alas though, the FA Cup eluded him.
- Birtles is best remembered for a nightmare spell at Man United, but his performance as a lone striker in the 1980 European Cup final for Forest was outstanding.

Manager: Brian Clough

Key Players
Peter Shilton (G) Larry Lloyd (D) Viv Anderson (D)
Kenny Burns (D) John McGovern (M) Ian Bowyer (M)
Archie Gemmill (M) Martin O'Neill (W) John Robertson (W)
Trevor Francis (F) Tony Woodcock (F)

Trophies
LT 1978 EC 1979, 1980 LC 1978, 1979

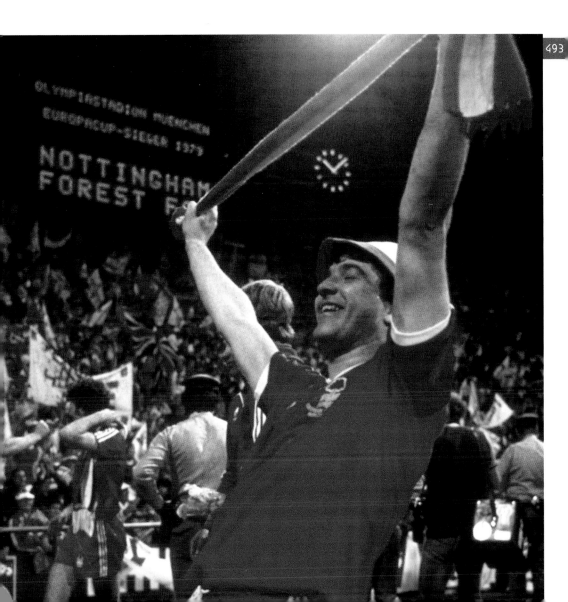

Numbers

And coming on for the last five minutes, No 73....

AT THE START of the 1928–29 season, the players of Chelsea and Arsenal wore shirt numbers for the first time. The experiment proved popular, not least because it was a crude ploy to make fans buy the match programme. In 1933 numbers made their first appearance at the FA Cup final, and six years later they were voted in as a permanent fixture. This meant that, for the first time, players' positions became synonymous with the numbers they wore; the centre-forward became simply 'the number nine,' while it was unthinkable that the number seven would not hug the right touchline for most of the game.

In 1993–94 numbering was replaced by the squad system in the Premier League. This saw players keep their number for an entire season and, in most cases, even longer, usually until they move to another club. This has enabled the introduction of the players' names to be printed above the number; a feature that clubs quickly learned the value of when selling replica shirts. Who wants a plain old number nine jersey when you can have 'Lua Lua 20' instead?

☞ In the 1933 FA Cup final, the teams were numbered one to 22, each player having his own number. The goalkeepers wore one and 22.

☞ Some players are synonymous with their numbers. Who can imagine Pelé without the number 10 shirt on his back, or Bobby Moore walking out in anything but his famous number six?

☞ The number 13 remains unpopular for superstitious reasons. If used at all, it usually goes to the substitute goalkeeper.

☞ Ade Akinbiyi selected the preposterous 55 as his squad number after moving to Crystal Palace in 2002. Denied his favourite number 10 shirt, he selected a sum of 10 instead.

'When he gets mine home he'll wonder who the bloody hell's it is.'

Ireland's Mick McCarthy after swapping shirts with Ruud Gullit at the 1988 European Championships

Offside

Oi, linesman, get that flag up!

FOOTBALL IN THE 1920s was becoming defensive and stale, with as many as 40 offside decisions per game, so the authorities introduced a simple but effective antidote. They decided, from that point on, that an attacker needed just two (rather than three) players between him and the goal to be called onside. Teams immediately had to rethink their tactics, with many sides introducing a withdrawn centre-half as a third defender to combat the new ruling. Recently the offside law was once again changed in favour of the attacking side; where previously an attacking player who was level with the opposition's last defender was considered offside, he is now free to continue (in other words he's onside). This makes defending against players with the pace of Ronaldo, Thierry Henry or Michael Owen very difficult.

Less satisfactory is the 'not interfering with play' rule affecting players in 'secondary' and 'non-active' areas. This is blurred and confusing, and leads to the sort of inconsistency that gives managers premature heart attacks.

☞ Combined with the back-pass rule, the 'level' ruling has spawned a generation of goalkeepers adept at coming off their line and playing the ball with foot or head. Shay Given and David James, for example, are adept at operating as sweeper when required.

☞ The ability to stay onside is a good measure of a striker's awareness and timing, and a handy guide to the intelligence of a footballer. Alan Shearer hardly ever gets caught offside. Craig Bellamy does. We rest our case.

👎 Arsenal are the masters of the offside trap. Their 'fab five' of Seaman, Dixon, Winterburn, Adams and Bould were great defenders, and played the tactic to near-perfection.

☞ Pet hate #1: braying buffoons in the stand who berate the linesman for an offside decision when they are 100 yards away behind the goal.

☞ Pet hate #2: said buffoon who howls at the linesman for not raising the same flag when the opposition striker reaches the ball beyond the centre half, ignoring the fact that said striker was five yards behind the pedestrian stopper when the ball was played.

'There's a big misconception. We never actually played offside. You'll see countless pictures of us standing in a line with our hands up appealing, but we were not actually going out to get sides offside.'

Lee Dixon talking crap

ONSIDE

OFFSIDE

Okocha, Augustin 'Jay-Jay'
PSG, Bolton Wanderers, Nigeria

JAY-JAY. So good they named him twice. So say supporters of Bolton Wanderers; a homage to the enormous talent of their Nigerian captain, and his part in keeping this unfashionable club in the Premiership during 2003 and 2004.

Nigerian supporters wouldn't disagree. Okocha rethought his retirement from international football to lead his country in the 2004 African Nations Cup; despite elimination in the semi-finals Jay-Jay was voted the tournament's most valuable player. Victory in that competition in 1994, in the Olympics in 1996 and appearances in three World Cup Finals tournaments add up to a significant international career.

Okocha came to prominence as a precocious teenager with Eintracht Frankfurt; a move to Fenerbahce prefaced a high-profile transfer to Paris Saint-Germain. When the PSG contract expired, Sam Allardyce spent hours persuading the Nigerian captain that the Reebok Stadium should be his next destination. After a slow start Okocha blossomed in early 2003, and his joyful skills and powerful shooting were instrumental in keeping Wanderers in the Premiership. A further two year contract at Bolton will please Premiership watchers everywhere, not just at the Reebok.

☞ Okocha played in Fenerbahce's 1996–97 win at Old Trafford in the Champions League; probably the club's finest moment in Europe.

👍 A brace of goals in a 5-2 win over Aston Villa secured Bolton's place in the 2004 Carling Cup final; the second was a stunner, bent with power around the 'wrong' side of the wall, but Okocha struggled to make an impact in the final.

☞ Okocha hit the bar three times in a Premiership match at Spurs in 2003 – at least Wanderers won.

👍 Okocha scored in the 2000 African Nations Cup final, but Nigeria lost to Cameroon on penalties. Jay-Jay's revenge came in 2004 when his curling free-kick saw Nigeria defeat their rivals in the quarter-final.

VITAL STATISTICS

Place of Birth:	Enugu, Nigeria	
Date of Birth:	14 August 1973	**Died:** n/a
Caps:	59 (Nigeria)	**Goals (International):** 8
Clubs:	Eintracht Frankfurt, Fenerbahce, Paris Saint-	
	Germain, Bolton Wanderers	
Appearances:	Club (League): 313	
Goals:	Club (League): 74	
Trophies:	None	

	LEGEND RATING
Achievement	7.0
Skill	9.0
Teamwork	6.0
Passion	8.0
Personality	7.0
TOTAL	**37.0**

Old Gold

Wolves, 1950s

THE GREAT WOLVES TEAM of the 1950s nearly ended the decade by winning the double; had they done so they would have emulated the feats of Huddersfield and Arsenal in winning three consecutive titles. That they stumbled just short shouldn't obscure the fact that this was a more than tidy team, and one that had dominated for the best part of 10 years despite formidable challenges from Blackpool, Manchester United and big-spending Arsenal.

They played in the uncompromising mould of their manager, Stan Cullis, their post-war captain and a fine defensive half-back. Cullis was an ex-military man and his team reflected his disciplinarian and simple views. An excellent keeper in Bert Williams, and a defence augmented in later years by Billy Wright's move to centre-half, gave them a solid base at the back. In midfield, their half-backs Eddie Clamp and Ron Flowers were industrious and tenacious, and wasted little time dwelling on the ball, preferring instead to release the wingers, Mullen and Hancocks. Once in the possession of the wide players the ball would be taken to the byline and crossed, hopefully finding the head or boot of Peter Broadbent. 'Total Football' it wasn't, but it worked, and few opponents had an answer to it.

☞ Apart from Wright and Flowers, few of these were great internationals; they were a team, not a collection of individuals.

☞ Cullis started the great post-war era as Wolves captain, but never won a major trophy as a player.

☞ Bill Slater was one of the last successful amateurs, mixing work at Birmingham University with football. He played for England as a semi-professional.

☞ Slater was voted Player of the Year in 1960, and later received an OBE and CBE for services to sport.

☞ Billy Wright and Jimmy Mullen were awarded a joint testimonial in 1962. Stan Cullis had to wait until 1992, when a new stand at Molineux was also opened in his honour.

Manager: Stan Cullis

Key Players
Bert Williams (G) Ron Flowers (HB) Billy Wright (HB/D)
Bill Slater (HB) Johnny Hancocks (W) Jimmy Mullen (W)
Peter Broadbent (F)

Trophies
LT 1954, 1958, 1959 FA Cup 1960

O'Leary, David
Arsenal, Leeds United, Republic of Ireland

WHEN HE FIRST APPEARED in Arsenal's first team as a skinny, gangling teenager, David O'Leary looked too fragile to last 90 minutes. But in a distinguished career at Highbury he eventually managed over 600 appearances for Arsenal, including 558 in the league. O'Leary became one of the best defenders in Europe during his 20-year career. An excellent reader of the game, he was the rock at the heart of the Arsenal team, much as Tony Adams has been in the last decade.

O'Leary picked up 67 caps for the Republic of Ireland, and would surely have played many more internationals but for a long spell in the wilderness following a row with Jack Charlton. But the two did patch up their differences sufficiently for O'Leary to be picked in the squad for the 1990 World Cup Finals in Italy.

O'Leary served his management apprenticeship under George Graham at Leeds, stepping into Graham's job after he left for Tottenham. Under him, Leeds quickly made progress. Despite building a strong side with a series of expensive purchases in the transfer market, O'Leary left the club, seemingly unsure what do when the team started to decline. His first season in charge at Aston Villa (2003–04) showed signs that he had learned from the Leeds experience and has the potential to be more than a 'cheque-book-manager'.

☞ David's brother Pierce was capped seven times by Ireland. He once came on for David in a Wembley international.

☞ Gangling appearance earned him the nickname 'Spider' at Arsenal.

☝ Leeds came through tough groups to reach the semi-final of the 2001 Champions League. They beat Milan, Lazio and Deportivo La Coruna, and eliminated Barcelona in the initial group stages.

☝ O'Leary scored the winning penalty in a play-off against Romania to qualify for the 1990 World Cup Finals.

☟ He irritated many football followers with his avowal that his team are merely boys, and his Wenger-like defence of their indiscipline.

☟ His departure from Leeds in 2002 was followed by months of dispute over his severence pay.

VITAL STATISTICS

Place of Birth:	Dublin, Ireland			Achievement	7.5
Date of Birth:	2 May 1958	**Died:** n/a		Skill	6.5
Caps:	67 (R. Ireland)	**Goals (International):** 1		Teamwork	8.0
Clubs:	As Player: Arsenal; As Manager: Leeds United,			Passion	8.5
	Aston Villa			Personality	7.5
Appearances:	Club (League): 558				
Goals:	Club (League): 10				
Trophies:	LT 1989, 1991; FAC 1979; LC 1987			**TOTAL**	**38.0**

LEGEND RATING

O'Neill, Martin

Nottingham Forest, Leicester City, Celtic, Northern Ireland

ONE OF THE MORE ENTERTAINING features of Leicester City and Celtic matches in recent years has been the sight of a slender, curly-haired man hopping up and down maniacally on the touchline. Martin O'Neill wears his heart on his sleeve; if a referee or player has incurred his wrath, there's no need to wait for the press conference.

O'Neill was a fine player, winning trophies at home and in Europe under Brian Clough at Nottingham Forest. The width provided by O'Neill and John Robertson were crucial to that side's success. Playing for Northern Ireland his chances of winning international trophies were limited, but he captained the side in one of their proudest moments when they defeated hosts Spain in the 1982 World Cup. O'Neill as manager was able to combine the spirit of that Irish side with the tactical wiles and subtle motivation of Brian Clough. An excellent record in the lower divisions with Wycombe took him eventually to Leicester, where he made the club competitive in the Premier League. Then the big one, Celtic, and the restoration of pride for the green half of Glasgow. O'Neill is rapidly building a reputation that allows his name to be spoken in the same sentence as Jock Stein.

- O'Neill has earned respect for the honourable way he has approached moves in his career; he turned down a huge job at Leeds in respect of his commitments at Leicester.
- O'Neill took Wycombe Wanderers into the league for the first time in their history, overcoming huge local apathy in commuter-belt Buckinghamshire.
- Immense player loyalty is one of the key's to O'Neill's success; witness the ease with which Leicester's best player, Neil Lennon, was prised away from Filbert Street.
- O'Neill won the title in his first season at Celtic, his purchase of Chris Sutton providing the perfect foil for the lethal Henrik Larsson.

VITAL STATISTICS

Place of Birth:	Kilrea, County Derry, N. Ireland		
Date of Birth:	1 March 1952	**Died:** n/a	
Caps:	64 (N. Ireland)	**Goals (International):** 8	
Clubs:	As Player: Distillery, Nottingham Forest, Norwich City, Manchester City, Notts County; As Manager: Wycombe Wanderers, Norwich City, Leicester City, Celtic		
Trophies:	EC 1979–80; LT 1978; LC 1978–79, (1997, 2000); SLT (2001–02, 2004); SFAC (2001)		

MANAGER		PLAYER	
Achievement	8	Achievement	9
Tactical Awareness	7	Skill	7
Motivation	9	Teamwork	8
Team Selection/Transfers	8	Passion	7
Personality	9	Personality	8
TOTAL	**41**	**TOTAL**	**39**

LEGEND RATING

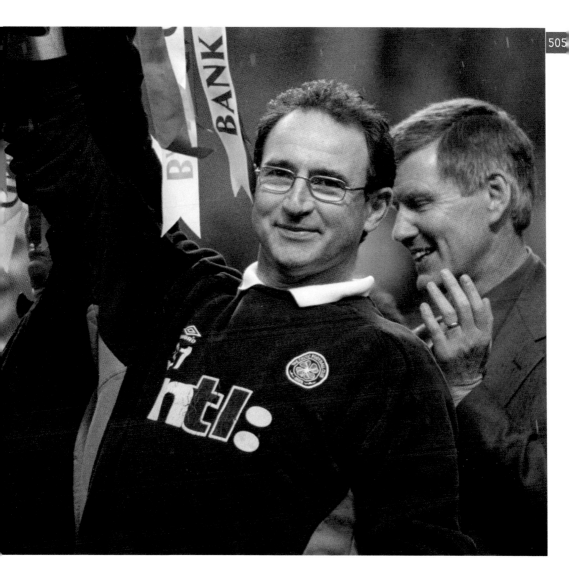

Orange Order Restored
Holland 2 USSR 0, 1988

HISTORY SEEMS TO have diminished this victory by the Dutch. The class of 1988 is remembered as a great side who only had to turn up to win the tournament. The truth is they were a side with a handful of gifted players who gelled better as the tournament progressed and discovered a secret weapon in Marco Van Basten.

The central defence, with a midfield player (Rijkaard) and a ball-playing sweeper with no pace (Koeman) was decidedly flaky, and the main source of goals in qualifying was the pedestrian Johnny Bosman. The flowering of Van Basten in the second match against England, when he scored a memorable hat-trick, added the edge Holland needed to supplement the craft of Vanenburg and Gullit's power and dominance. After scraping past Ireland in the decisive group match, Van Basten added to his tally with a text book late goal to win the semi-final against Holland's old nemesis, West Germany.

So to the final; the Dutch were expected to win but not easily. In the event the Soviets never really showed. The game is remembered for Van Basten's decisive goal. Mühren's long cross seemed to be drifting too deep for a strike on goal, but the Dutch maestro met it with a ferocious dipping volley that Dasaev, a world class goalkeeper, never saw.

- USSR had actually beaten Holland 1-0 in the opening group game, with a goal from Vassily Rats.
- This was a Soviet team that had illuminated the World Cup two years earlier and still based itself around the formidable unit of Dinamo Kiev players.
- Van Breukelen saved a late penalty from Belanov – he had saved a penalty in that season's European Cup final as well.
- Under today's legislation, Van Basten's opening goal against England would have gone down as a Trevor Steven own goal; churlish, but true.
- Former Ipswich star Arnold Mühren was 37 years old when the game was played; a fitting coda to the career of one of the finest imports into the English game.

SCORERS	**Holland:** Gullit, Van Basten
EVENT	European Championships final, Munich, 25 June 1988

HOLLAND	(Man: Rinus Michels)
	1. Van Breukelen 2. Van Aerle 3. Van Tiggelen 4. Wouters 5. Koeman, R
	6. Rijkaard 7. Vanenburg 8. Gullit 9. Van Basten 10. Mühren 11. Koeman, E
USSR	(Man: Valeri Lobanovski)
	1. Dasaev 2. Helveg 3. Khidiatulin 4. Aleinikov 5. Mikhailichenko 6. Demianenko
	7. Belanov 8. Gotsmanov (Baltacha) 9. Protasov (Pasulko) 10. Zavarov 11. Rats

Over The (Blue) Moon
The Manchester City Dream Team

ALTHOUGH OFTEN IN THE SHADOW of their neighbours, this team would give the current Manchester United side a run for its money.

Few teams in the history of the game can boast a stronger goalkeeping duo; Frank Swift was the finest keeper of his generation and relegates Joe Corrigan to the familiar role of understudy, a position he filled so often for England, covering for Shilton and Clemence in the 1970s.

In defence, Book and Doyle are obvious candidates from the side that won the Championship, FA Cup and Cup Winners' Cup in the 1960s, while Dave Watson was England's finest centre-half of the 1970s. In midfield, Kinkladze and Summerbee would stretch opponents wide, leaving Bell and Revie to surge forward into the gaps. Up front, Lee justifies his place on the grounds that City, and later Derby, enjoyed their most successful spells with him leading the line. Tilson fired the bullets in City's other championship-winning side in 1937. The bench is conspicuous by its lack of defenders, so in the event of a back-four injury this team would have to revert to 3-5-2. This shouldn't pose a problem; attack has always been City's preferred form of defence.

- Frank Swift became a distinguished football journalist after retiring. Tragically, he died in the 1958 Munich air crash.
- Dennis Tueart would be encouraged to attempt as many overhead kicks as possible. His effort won the 1976 League Cup and remains one of Wembley's most eye-catching goals.
- Colin Bell could stake a claim for inclusion in a post-war England side. His pace over short distances earned him the nickname 'Nijinsky'.
- Steve Daley or Michael Robinson are not selected; despite their expensive price tags, neither justifies inclusion.
- Mercer and Allison formed a potent manager/coach team in the 1960s. Can Mercer forgive Allison for ruining his legacy?

**Managers: Joe Mercer and
Malcolm Allison**

4-4-2

Frank Swift (30s/40s)

Tony Book (C) (60s/70s) Mike Doyle (60s/70s) Dave Watson (70s)
Willie Donachie (70s)

Georgiou Kinkladze (90s) Don Revie (50s)
Colin Bell (70s) Mike Summerbee (70s)

Francis Lee (70s) Fred Tilson (30s)

Subs: Joe Corrigan (G) (70s) Asa Hartford (M) (70s) Peter Doherty (M/F) (30s)
Rodney Marsh (W) (70s) Dennis Tueart (F) (70s)

Owen, Michael
Liverpool, Real Madrid, England

FEW FOOTBALLERS ACHIEVE in a lifetime what Michael Owen had by the time he was 22. He became the youngest Liverpool player ever at the age of 17 years, 144 days. He became the youngest England player in the 20th century. Aged 18, in the 1998 World Cup Finals, he scored a sensational solo goal against Argentina, beating three experienced defenders before lashing the ball into the goal.

After a wobbly spell, when doubts emerged, Owen hit back late in the 2000–2001 season, leading the Liverpool line as they won a unique treble of cups, and scoring two late goals to steal the FA Cup from Arsenal. Early the following season he scored a quite brilliant hat-trick as England slaughtered Germany 5-1.

The injuries resurfaced in 2003, and a shocking record from the penalty spot allowed the doubters to find their voices again. Owen approached the end of the 2003–04 season at a crossroads. After an ordinary Euro 2004, he was used as a liquid asset by Liverpool, and sold to Real Madrid.

Owen's principal asset is his blistering pace, but to dismiss him as simply quick would be to take him lightly. He is able to use either foot, has a good first touch, good balance, and takes a high percentage of his chances.

- Voted PFA Young Player of the Year in 1998.
- Voted BBC Sports Personality of the Year in 1998, and third in the same poll in 2001.
- Like Liverpool icons Dalglish and Hansen before him, Owen is a class golfer.
- Owen scored his 100th goal for Liverpool early in 2002, still aged only 22.
- After a few games on the bench Owen started to find his touch at Real Madrid, with four goals in successive games in October 2004.

VITAL STATISTICS

Place of Birth:	Chester, England	
Date of Birth:	14 December 1979	**Died:** n/a
Caps:	65 (England)	**Goals (International):** 28
Clubs:	Liverpool, Real Madrid	
Appearances:	Club (All Matches): 273	
Goals:	Club (All Matches): 164	
Trophies:	FAC 2001; LC 2001, 2003; UEFAC 2001	

Achievement	7.5
Skill	9.0
Teamwork	7.5
Passion	8.5
Personality	7.5
TOTAL	**40.0**

LEGEND RATING

Own Goal

Oops!

SOME OWN GOALS are just down to plain bad luck. A defence can hardly legislate for a cruel deflection or unavoidable ricochet. Gary Mabbutt could hardly be blamed for the goal that won the FA Cup for Coventry in 1987, as his outstretched leg diverted a cross over Ray Clemence.

Other instances are simply inexplicable. Des Walker's combination of a cushioned defensive header and a clearance placed the ball neatly in the top corner to give Spurs the trophy they had handed to Coventry four years earlier. You'll never beat Des Walker? On this occasion he did it all by himself.

Spare a thought for Sunderland, whose wretched form and luck in 2003 were never better illustrated than in their home match against Charlton. Three down in half an hour was dire enough. The fact that two own goals from Michael Proctor and two wicked deflections were the cause summed up their season.

The best, however, are those moments that, had they occurred at the other end, would be lauded as pieces of sublime skill achieved only after months of work on the training ground.

- The start of the 1999–2000 season brought a rash of own goals in the Premier League. Frank Sinclair became Leicester's top scorer in reverse with two in successive games, both in the last minute.
- Occasionally, goalkeepers have obliged the opposition by throwing the ball into the net. Gary Sprake can take a bow for this: his video of gaffes would run to several hours.
- Pat Kruse got Cambridge United off to a flyer in 1977, scoring after only eight seconds. Unfortunately he was playing for Torquay, thus making history with the quickest-ever own goal.
- Chelsea's championship-winning season of 1954–55 was helped with a bizarre own goal at Leicester. It entered the records as 'Froggatt and Milburn, shared own goal', a unique achievement.

Gary Mabbutt's Knee.

Title of a Coventry City fanzine, named after the cause of their only piece of silverware

Paisley, Bob

Liverpool

BOB PAISLEY MADE HIS DEBUT as a professional footballer for Liverpool in 1939, and retired as the most successful manager in the club's history in 1983 after 44 years of service. Although never a glittering international star, as a player Paisley was good enough to win a championship medal with Liverpool in 1947. When his playing career came to an end he joined the Anfield back-room staff, becoming a redoubtable deputy to the legendary Bill Shankly. When Shanks quit, Paisley took over as manager reluctantly, believing he was no more than a stop-gap for a bigger name. How wrong he was. Building on Shankly's legacy, Paisley remained at the helm for nine seasons, during which time Liverpool dominated both domestic and European soccer, winning six league titles, three European Cups and three league Cups – a haul of silverware that made this shy, quietly-spoken old man in a cardigan the most successful manager in the history of the English game.

☞ Paisley was the first Liverpool manager to lift the European Cup.

☞ He never won the FA Cup, either as a player or manager.

👍 Between January 1978–81, Liverpool were unbeaten at Anfield for a staggering 85 games (63 in the league).

👍 In 1978–79 Liverpool coasted to the title using only 15 players, two of whom played four games between them.

👍 He was voted Manager of the Year six times.

VITAL STATISTICS

Place of Birth: Hetton-le-Hole, England

Date of Birth: 23 January 1919   **Died:** 12 February 1996

Caps: 0 (England)   **Goals (International):** 0

Clubs: As Player: Bishop Auckland, Liverpool;
As Manager: Liverpool

Trophies: LT (1947), 1976, 1977, 1979, 1980, 1982, 1983; LC 1981, 1982, 1983; EC 1977, 1978, 1981; UEFAC 1976

Achievement	10
Tactical Awareness	9
Motivation	9
Team Selection/Transfers	9
Personality	6
TOTAL	**43**

LEGEND RATING

Passarella, Daniel
Argentina

IN A NATION BETTER KNOWN for hatchet-men defenders, Daniel Passarella broke the mould. The first Argentine to lift the World Cup was a cultured sweeper who, by and large, eschewed the brutal and often violent tactics deployed by some of his team-mates.

After nine years in the Argentine national league with Sarmiento and then River Plate, Passarella was eventually lured to Serie A where he enjoyed seven distinguished seasons (with Fiorentina and Internazionale) before returning for a second spell with River Plate.

A move from player to manager in 1989 brought further success. Four domestic titles in the 1990s saw him promoted to national team boss, and he led Argentina to the quarter-finals at France 98 before retiring. For such a fine player, his tally of domestic honours was modest, but it was a different story at international level. In 1978 Passarella famously skippered Argentina to victory in the World Cup, his promptings from the back providing the ammunition with which Mario Kempes was to shoot down Holland in the final.

- Passarella had an incredible goal-scoring record for a defender (143 goals in 486 appearances).
- Passarella was not averse to bouts of nastiness. In the 1978 final he 'caught' Johan Neeskens in the face with an elbow.
- The memory of Passarella receiving the World Cup was tarnished by the image of General Jorge Videla, murderer of children, smiling at his country's triumph.
- Passarella's style of play bore an uncanny resemblance to Stuart Pearce, right down to the thunderous shooting imparted by vast muscular thighs.
- Passarella was an unpopular manager of Argentina before the 1998 World Cup Finals, due to his reluctance to pick Batistuta.

VITAL STATISTICS

Place of Birth:	Buenos Aires, Argentina	
Date of Birth:	25 May 1953	**Died:** n/a
Caps:	71 (Argentina)	**Goals (International):** 21
Clubs:	Sarmiento, River Plate, Fiorentina, Inter Milan	
Appearances:	Club (League for River Plate): 298	
Goals:	Club (League for River Plate): 99	
Trophies:	WorC 1978	

LEGEND RATING	
Achievement	8.0
Skill	7.0
Teamwork	8.0
Passion	9.0
Personality	6.0
TOTAL	**38.0**

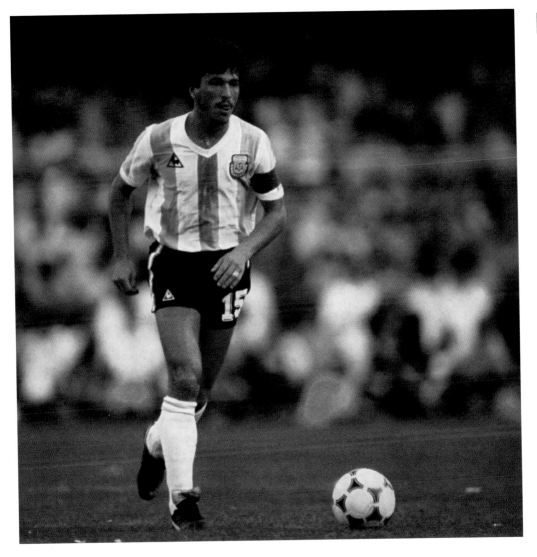

Pearce, Stuart
Nottingham Forest, England

THERE CAN BE FEW better examples of a player making the most of modest natural ability than Stuart Pearce; what he lacked in pace he made up for in sheer will and an almost clairvoyant ability to read the game, and what he missed in skill he overcame with brute strength. Those thunder thighs meant Pearce rarely lost a tackle, and his crossing and powerhouse shooting made him a potent weapon in attack, especially from set-pieces.

Pearce spent time in non-league soccer before signing for Coventry, from where, having been spotted by Brian Clough, who was quick to recognise his leadership qualities, he moved on to Nottingham Forest, making 522 appearances in over 10 years at the City Ground. As it appeared his career was ending, Pearce had a flirtation with the manager's job at Forest but, quickly realising a struggling Premiership club was no place for a beginner, he stood down and elected to further his playing career at Newcastle. Spells at West Ham and Manchester City followed and he remained at the latter as coach. His passion and naked aggression made 'Psycho' first choice for England for a decade, and they have struggled to find an adequate replacement since. Football fans love a trier, and no one gave more for his country than Stuart Pearce.

- Pearce was distraught to have missed a crucial penalty in the shoot-out at the 1990 World Cup. His fierce exultation when he made amends at Euro 96 became an iconic image.
- The 'Psycho' nickname comes not just from his raw playing style, but also from the intensity of the stare in his clear eyes.
- Pearce was awarded an MBE in 1999.
- In 1999 Pearce was involved in a horrific accident in which his car was crushed by a lorry: the lorry came off worst.
- Pearce's fondness for crunching punk rock has caused much mirth amongst press and team-mates. He claims that the more conventional music favoured by his colleagues gives him a headache.

VITAL STATISTICS

Place of Birth:	London, England		
Date of Birth:	24 April 1962	**Died:** n/a	
Caps:	78 (England)	**Goals (International):** 5	
Clubs:	Coventry, Nottingham Forest, Newcastle United,		
	West Ham, Manchester City		
Appearances:	Club (League): 570		
Goals:	Club (League): 72		
Trophies:	LC 1989, 1990		

		LEGEND RATING
Achievement	6.0	
Skill	6.0	
Teamwork	8.0	
Passion	10.0	
Personality	8.0	
TOTAL	**38.0**	

Pelé
Santos, Brazil

EDSON ARANTES DI NASCIMENTO is the greatest footballer of all time. No arguments.

Born in Tes Coracoes, a small provincial town in the Brazilian state of Minas Gerais, Pelé (as he is better known) began his career at Santos, forcing his way into the first team by the age of 16, and made his debut for Brazil a year later in 1958 when, at 17, he collected his first World Cup winner's medal in Sweden. Pelé went on to play in three more World Cup tournaments; he struggled with injuries in 1962, and again in 1966, but in 1970, playing in a deeper role, he was the architect of some of the finest football the game has ever known. Surrounded by players who were in tune with his alert mind and quick feet, Brazil produced unforgettable, almost perfect football.

Pelé played all his domestic football in his beloved white shirt for Santos, a career that spanned nearly 20 years. He retired in 1974, but was persuaded to return to the game a year later when, like Franz Beckenbauer, Bobby Moore and many other of his old adversaries, he signed a $4.5 m contract to play in the newly-formed NASL with New York Cosmos. Pelé has remained in football as an ambassador for the game, and has served a spell as Brazil's Minister for Sport.

☞ Only Ferenc Puskas of Hungary has bettered Pelé's tally of 77 international goals.

☞ When Pelé retired from Brazilian soccer, Santos also 'retired' his No. 10 shirt.

�✎ Pelé scored a hat-trick in the 1958 World Cup semi-final, then two more in the final, including a mesmerising, acrobatic volley.

☞ Pelé's record as the only man to have played in three World Cup winning squads is unlikely to be matched.

�✎ Pelé scored in excess of 1,200 first-class goals in his career.

VITAL STATISTICS

Place of Birth:	Tres Coracoes, Brazil		
Date of Birth:	21 October 1940	**Died:** n/a	
Caps:	91 (Brazil)	**Goals (International):** 77	
Clubs:	Santos, New York Cosmos		
Appearances:	Club (All Senior Matches): 1363		
Goals:	Club (All Senior Matches): 1283		
Trophies:	WorC 1958, 1970; BLT 1956, 1958, 1960–62, 1964, 1966–68; WCC 1962, 1963		

LEGEND RATING	
Achievement	10.0
Skill	10.0
Teamwork	10.0
Passion	10.0
Personality	9.0
TOTAL	**49.0**

Penalty Shoot-Outs
Despair and Derring-Do

THEY MAY BE A TERRIBLE WAY to lose a game, but they make for great theatre. Penalty shoot-outs made their debut in 1970, a device introduced to settle the mind-numbing tedium of something called the Watney Cup. Since then of course, they have gone on to settle some of the world's most important matches.

For England fans, memories of high-profile failures are fresh. At Italia 90, the team were just a few kicks away from the World Cup final, but with the scores locked at 3-3, Stuart Pearce and Chris Waddle missed to send Bobby Robson's team home. Lightning struck for a second time at Euro 96 with Germany again proving to be England's nemesis from 12 yards. Gareth Southgate was the culprit this time. Then in France 98 it was Argentina's turn to expose England's vulnerability from the spot, David Batty making it a hat-trick of shoot-out failures with a feeble effort in St Etienne. It was David Beckham – of all people – whose missed penalty sent hosts Portugal through to the semis in Euro 2004.

The prospect of penalties has even entered some teams' pre-match thinking. In the 1986 European Cup final, Steaua Bucharest, figuring they had little chance of beating Barcelona in open play, shamelessly played for 0-0 in the hope of pinching victory in the lottery of a penalty shoot-out. Incredibly it worked. Barcelona missed all their penalties and Steaua were crowned champions of Europe.

☝ Pearce, Waddle and Southgate turned their failure to financial advantage, starring in a TV advertising campaign for Pizza Hut.

☞ Controversially, penalties replaced second replays in the FA Cup in 1991. Exeter beat Colchester 4-2 in the first shoot-out.

✎ In 1994 Italy's Roberto Baggio blazed over the bar to hand Brazil victory in the 1994 World Cup final. The other errant Italian was the great Franco Baresi.

☞ David Batty volunteered to take a penalty against Argentina in France 98, even though he had never taken one in a game before.

☞ 1997. Marlow beat Littlehampton 11-10 on penalties in the FA Cup first qualifying round. The first 21 spot-kicks were scored.

'Maybe they were kicking the s**t out of O'Leary for missing it.'

Roddy Doyle misinterprets the reaction of David's team-mates after he scores the winning penalty against Romania during Italia 90, in *The Van*

Peters, Martin
West Ham United, England

THE THIRD OF THE 'HOLY TRINITY' of West Ham players in the 1966 World Cup winning side, alongside Bobby Moore and Geoff Hurst, Peters had forced his way into the England reckoning the previous season, making his debut only weeks before the tournament began. An extremely versatile player – appearing in virtually every position for West Ham – he was a good tackler and passed the ball well with either foot, but his real gift was his ability to steal into the penalty area and score vital goals, a knack that earned him the nickname 'The Ghost'. His overall scoring record was better than nearly one in three games, an exceptional return for a midfield player. Unlike Moore and Hurst, Peters left West Ham while still in his prime, and won further trophies with Tottenham. Like many of his England contemporaries, he wasn't a success as a manager. It would have been interesting to see Peters in the modern game – his style would have suited the Premiership.

- Peters scored 'the other goal' in the 1966 World Cup final, and one of England's goals in the 3-2 defeat by Germany in the 1970 World Cup quarter-final.
- Peters teamed up with his England colleague Geoff Hurst after their playing careers were over – selling car insurance.
- The £200,000 Bill Nicholson paid West Ham for Peters was a British record.
- Peters even appeared in goal for West Ham, deputising as a substitute in only his third appearance for the club.
- As Spurs captain in 1975, Peters led a deputation to try and persuade Bill Nicholson to rescind his resignation.

VITAL STATISTICS

Place of Birth: London, England
Date of Birth: 8 November 1943   **Died:** n/a
Caps: 67 (England)   **Goals (International):** 20
Clubs: West Ham, Tottenham, Norwich City, Sheffield United
Appearances: Club (All Matches): 882
Goals: Club (All Matches): 220
Trophies: WorC 1966; CWC 1965; LC 1971, 1973; UEFAC 1972

LEGEND RATING	
Achievement	8.0
Skill	8.0
Teamwork	8.0
Passion	7.0
Personality	6.0
TOTAL	**37.0**

Pinch Me...
Germany 1 England 5, 2001

ALL THOSE YEARS of angst and frustration at England's inability to beat Germany were washed away in one glorious evening. Only a year before, England had given an abject performance at home to the same opponents, losing to a soft Dietmar Hamann free-kick. There were five changes to the team from the previous October; Adams, Keown, Le Saux, Andy Cole, and Gareth Southgate all giving way to younger legs. England played with the exuberance of youth and, even after going a goal down in the early stages, remained determined to set the agenda. Gerrard crunched his Liverpool team-mate Hamann to remind him he wasn't going to dictate this game. The Germans were inept (they weren't very good in 2000, but Keegan was scared to have a go at them). Poor at the back, unimaginative in midfield and ponderous up front, they carried no threat. On this occasion England did what a good team should do and destroyed vastly inferior opponents. A team with four world-class players beat a team with (maybe) one.

OK, that's enough critical analysis. WASN'T IT GREAT!?

☞ German goalkeeper Oliver Kahn, one of the greats of the last decade, flapped about like a baboon in a straitjacket.

☞ The Germans were missing key players like Scholl and Jeremies. Tough.

☞ Canadian-born Owen Hargreaves, substitute for Gerrard, was playing on his home ground. He had impressed for Bayern in the European Cup final against Valencia.

☞ Eriksson exploited the space behind the German wing-backs to great effect, Beckham and Gerrard dropping balls in for the excellent Gary Neville and Ashley Cole to pick up.

☞ Ferdinand was at fault for the German goal, but was near flawless after that.

SCORERS	**Germany:** Jancker
	England: Owen (3) Gerrard, Heskey
EVENT	World Cup qualifier, Munich, 1 September 2001
GERMANY	(Man: Rudi Voller)
	1. Kahn 2. Worns 3. Linke 4. Nowotny 5. Boehme 6. Hamann
	7. Rehmer 8. Ballack 9. Jancker 10. Neuville 11. Deisler
ENGLAND	(Man: Sven-Goran Eriksson)
	1. Seaman 2. Neville, G 3. Cole 4. Gerrard 5. Campbell 6. Ferdinand
	7. Beckham 8. Scholes 9. Heskey 10. Owen 11. Barmby

Pires, Robert
Arsenal, France

DESPITE THEIR PERIODS of success and the consistent emergence of Double winning teams, only the current Arsenal squad has shaken off the club's reputation for producing dour, efficient sides. 'Boring Arsenal' was always the last resort of the envious. The jibes have been rammed down critics' throats in the last two years. At the heart of this flair renaissance is Robert Pires.

Contrary to popular opinion; fast, exciting wing play is not an innovation at Highbury. It is simply that the likes of George Armstrong and Brian Marwood can not hold a candle to the Frenchman, whose arrival for £6 m in July 2000 from Marseille as a direct replacement for Marc Overmars relegated even the talented Dutchman to the role of yesterday's man.

Pires could hardly have failed to catch the eye. As a member of the French squad that held World and European championships simultaneously, he proved too valuable a prize to remain in the backwater of the French league. The only unanswered question was whether he could shine in top-class European domestic competition. The answer, as Arsenal fans will testify, has been an emphatic yes.

- ☞ 2000. Sets up the Golden Goal for David Trezeguet that wins Euro 2000 for France.
- 👍 2001–02. Wins the Football Writers' Player of the Year award.
- 👎 March 2002. Damages cruciate ligaments in an FA Cup 6th round tie v Newcastle. Pires is sidelined for six months but a makes full recovery.
- 👍 2000–01. Scores away to Lazio to clinch Arsenal's place in the Champions League's second phase.
- 👍 2001. Scores winner in FA Cup semi-final v Spurs.
- 👎 Pires' only blot is a tendency to fall too easily in the penalty area. Sadly, he is not alone.

VITAL STATISTICS

Place of Birth:	Reims, France		Achievement	9.0
Date of Birth:	29 October 1973	**Died:** n/a	Skill	9.0
Caps:	73 (France)	**Goals (International):** 14	Teamwork	7.0
Clubs:	Metz, Marseille, Arsenal		Passion	7.0
Appearances:	Club (All Matches): 444		Personality	7.0
Goals:	Club (All Matches): 118			
Trophies:	LT 2002, 2004; FAC 2002; WorC 1998; EuroC 2000		**TOTAL**	**39.0**

LEGEND RATING

Platini, Michel
Juventus, France

THE FINEST EUROPEAN MIDFIELDER of the past 30 years, Michel Platini combined sublime skill with a goalscoring record that would put many international forwards to shame. Touch, vision and great accuracy with either foot made him a divine playmaker, but he added the virtue of a constant flow of goals, both from set-pieces and open play. After 10 years in the French league, he turned down a move to Arsenal in 1982 claiming, perhaps justifiably, that English clubs played too many games. The Gunners' loss was Juventus' gain, as trophies followed for the Italian giants. Platini's high point came in the 1984 European Championships when, teaming up with Jean Tigana and Alain Giresse in midfield, he skippered France to a famous victory on home soil. Platini's astonishing return of nine goals in five games, including two hat-tricks, made him the tournament's top scorer. His business interests brought about a shock retirement in 1987, but he was tempted by the French national manager's job three years later. An uneasy tenure, Platini resigned after France's premature exit from Euro 92 but became president of the France 98 World Cup committee and continues to enjoy a high profile as a special advisor to FIFA.

☞ Platini's penalty won the European Cup at Heysel in 1985, but the evening's earlier tragedy overshadowed everything.

🖐 Platini remains a strong critic of English club football, particularly its reliance on foreign players.

☞ His three World Cups included two as French captain, both of which brought semi-final defeats in 1982 and 1986.

✍ He scored the winner a minute before the end of a ding-dong-do against Portugal in the semi-final of Euro 84.

✌ Platini is the only player to have been voted European Player of the Year in three consecutive years – 1983, 1984 and 1985. Even the great Johan Cruyff had a year off!

VITAL STATISTICS

Place of Birth:	Joeuf, France		
Date of Birth:	21 June 1955	**Died:** n/a	
Caps:	72 (France)	**Goals (International):** 41	
Clubs:	AS Joeuf, Nancy, St Etienne, Juventus		
Appearances:	Club (All Matches): 576		
Goals:	Club (All Matches): 307		
Trophies:	EuroC 1984; FLT 1981; SA 1984, 1986;		
	CWC 1984; EC 1985		

LEGEND RATING	
Achievement	9.0
Skill	10.0
Teamwork	9.0
Passion	9.0
Personality	8.0
TOTAL	**45.0**

Play-Offs
All That Way For This

DERIDED BY MANY at their inception in 1987, the play-offs have become an integral part of the season, adding tension to matches that previously would have been meaningless. Initially the play-offs involved the top division side immediately above automatic relegation, and the three sides immediately beneath automatic promotion in the division below. This system was discarded after two years, and since 1989 the play-offs have involved only sides jostling for promotion, with relegation being automatic. The system still has its critics (Swindon Town's promotion in 1993, when they finished 12 points behind Portsmouth in Division One, is often cited as an example of the iniquities of the system). The first beneficiaries were Charlton, Swindon and Aldershot. Charlton edged out Leeds 2-1 in a replay after the two-legged final finished level, thus preserving their status in Division One. There have been one or two classic confrontations since. In 1995 Bolton reversed a two goal deficit to overcome Reading 4-3, while Sunderland and Charlton battled out a memorable 4-4 draw in 1998, the Addicks eventually winning 7-6 on penalties to retain their place in the Premiership.

- Sunderland had a ball in 1990. They scraped into the play-offs in sixth place in the Second Division, beat their great rivals Newcastle and lost 1-0 to Swindon at Wembley. The gods were shining on the Wearsiders though; Swindon were demoted for financial irregularities, and Sunderland got their promotion.
- In 1999, Manchester City were 2-0 down to Gillingham with a minute to go. They drew level and won on penalties. Not untypical of City's ups and downs in recent years.
- Ipswich lost to Sheffield United on away goals in 1997, Charlton in 1998 and Bolton after a 4-3 ding-dong-do at Portman Road in 1999. Revenge was sweet in 2000 as they battled past Bolton (5-3 this time) and beat Barnsley in the final.

'Not only have I had to give up chess because I don't have time anymore, but I'm also smoking myself to death. If we go through and win the play-offs at Wembley, I'll be smoking more than my old boss Menotti.'

Ossie Ardiles, then manager of Swindon, 1990

Pride and Passion

Local Derbies

NOTHING RAISES SUPPORTERS' passions more than a match against local rivals. Some of the game's most atmospheric occasions are derby days, whether in Liverpool, Manchester, North London, Glasgow or Milan. Although an Old Firm derby is no place for the faint-hearted, these games aren't necessarily the ones where feelings run highest. Provincial areas can spurn rivalries as heated as any found in big cities.

Local rivalry is often at its most intense at clubs where success is evasive. Absurd as it seems, supporters can often get more pleasure from seeing a rival fail than watching their own team win. This usually stems from envy – witness the 'Stand Up If You Hate Man U' factor in recent seasons. Sometimes one local team lords it over another, leading to resentment, and occasionally mutual dislike between twin towns intrudes on football. These intense rivalries are not always geographical; Chelsea and Leeds are still carrying around baggage from the 1970 FA Cup final, and Tottenham and Southampton have been doing their best to nurture ill feeling over the last few years.

☞ West Bromwich Albion and Wolves have a bitter enmity. Both top sides in the 1950s, they have only flirted with the big time since, and it clearly rankles.

☞ Stoke City were top flight for years, but their fall from grace coincided with John Rudge's successful stewardship of local rivals, Port Vale, and the battle for Potteries pre-eminence was resumed.

☝ Cardiff and Swansea share a mutual loathing that may even transcend their dislike of the English. Some recent encounters have been blood-curdling affairs.

☝ Suggestions that Hearts and Hibs merge to form one Edinburgh club saw the men behind the scheme bombarded with hate mail and death threats.

'I sometimes think you love Norwich more than you love me,' moans the wife.

'Aye,' husband replies, 'And I sometimes think I love Ipswich more than I love you.'

PSV

The Dream Team

THE TOUGHEST CALL HERE may well be the manager. Guus Hiddink did bring home the treble in 1988, but it was Kees Rijvers who broke the hegemony of Ajax and Feyenoord in the mid-1970s and established PSV as one of the top three sides in Dutch football.

Van Beveren was probably the best Dutch goalkeeper ever, stylish and athletic; apologies to European Cup winning van Breukelen. The defence – typically has only one Dutch player, Koeman, the sweeper-playmaker behind the treble in 1988. The imperturbable Nordqvist would cover Koeman's occasional aberrations; neither Heintze nor Gerets took any prisoners. The name of Ruud Gullit in midfield needs no comment. Van der Kuijlen was a main man in the 1970s, with 394 goals in 648 official matches. The van der Kerkhofs add speed and body to the midfield – the twins were PSV to the core and to separate them would be heartless. The towering Edström, with his aerial ability, excellent technique and sound vision, played a key role in the mid-1970s team, both with PSV and Sweden. Romario heads off some awesome candidates for the position alongside him; maybe we were swayed by his amazing last goal in the 1989 game against Steaua Bucharest – footballing poetry.

- ✍ Van der Kuijlen was two-footed, could pass and had a rasping shot. Goal keepers would duck when they saw one of his canonballs coming.
- ✍ Missing from this dream team is Ronaldo. He was great, but was frequently injured.
- ✍ Also missing is striker Luc Nilis. He had six memorable years with PSV, before a tragic move to Aston Villa. He broke his leg in one of his first matches, and his career was over.
- ☞ The only current player in this selection is van Bommel, the big-hearted leader of PSV, who has been waiting for some years now for a well deserved big transfer.
- ✍ Edström was a bit of a pin-up – it is no coincidence that Ralf became a popular name in Holland while he was with PSV.

Manager: Kees Rijvers

4-3-3

Jan van Beveren (70s)

Eric Gerets (80s) Ronald Koeman (80s) Björn Nordqvist (70s)
Jan Heintze (80s/90s/00s)

Ruud Gullit (80s) Willy van der Kuijlen (60s/70s/80s)
Willy van der Kerkhof (70s/80s)

René van de Kerkhof (70s/80s) Romario (80s) Ralf Edström (70s)

Subs: Hans van Breukelen (G) (80s) Berry van Aerle (D) (80s) Mark van Bommel (M) (90s/00s) Ruud van Nistelrooy (F) (90s/00s) Coen Dillen (F) (40s/50s/60s)

Puskas, Ferenc
Real Madrid, Hungary

SHORT AND BARREL-CHESTED, slightly overweight, one-footed and useless in the air, nonetheless Ferenc Puskas is rightly regarded as one of the best attacking players in history. His pace and blistering left foot shot took Puskas straight into the Hungarian side after the war, still aged only 18. His success with Hungarian army side Honved led Real Madrid to lure him to Spain, where he teamed up with Alfredo Di Stefano in arguably the greatest attacking pairing, well, er, ever. The duo led Real to unprecedented domestic and European success. 'The Galloping Major' won the award for Spain's top goal scorer four times, and when he didn't win it Di Stefano did.

Internationally Puskas played in another remarkable team, the great Hungarian side that went unbeaten for four years between 1950 and 1954, before losing out in the World Cup final to Germany. Critics and crowd could only watch and admire as Puskas, Czibor, Hidegkuti and Kocsis thrashed England 6-3 at Wembley – the first-ever home defeat for England. The side broke up in 1956 after the revolution in Hungary, and Puskas was later to make four appearances for his adopted country, Spain.

- Injured for the quarter-final and semi-final, Puskas insisted on playing in the 1954 World Cup final, even though only half-fit. Typically he scored, but Germany recovered from 2-0 down to win 3-2.
- Scored four times in Real's legendary 7-3 annihilation of Eintracht Frankfurt in the 1960 European Cup final.
- Puskas' 83 goals for Hungary is a world record (and in only 84 matches).
- In 1993 Puskas made an emotional return to a more liberal Hungary as caretaker-manager of the national side.
- Even at 35 Puskas managed a hat-trick in the European Cup final against Benfica in 1962. Sadly for him, Real lost 5-3.

VITAL STATISTICS

Place of Birth:	Budapest, Hungary	
Date of Birth:	2 April 1927	**Died:** n/a
Caps:	84 (Hungary); 4 (Spain)	
Goals (International):	83 (Hungary)	
Clubs:	Kispest, Honved, Real Madrid	
Appearances:	Club (All Matches): 1300	
Goals:	Club (All Matches): 1176	
Trophies:	PLA 1961, 1962, 1963, 1964, 1965;	
	HLT 1950, 1952, 1954, 1955; EC 1960	

Achievement	8.0
Skill	10.0
Teamwork	9.0
Passion	9.0
Personality	8.0
TOTAL	**44.0**

LEGEND RATING

Race, Roy
Melchester Rovers, England

WITH A CAREER spanning five decades, Roy Race's evergreen qualities put even Roger Milla and Peter Shilton to shame. Signing for his local club Melchester Rovers, he carried the dreams of every British schoolboy with a career that brought a string of league titles and European Cups. Unlike Bobby Moore, he never had the distinction of lifting the World Cup, but it was one of the few honours that eluded him. A blonde, dashing centre-forward he wore the red and yellow of Melchester for nearly 40 years, first as player, then as player-manager. In 1993 Roy cheated death in a helicopter crash that forced the amputation of his left foot. He left Melchester for a short spell as boss of Italian legends AC Monza, but his heart was never in it. Surviving by the skin of his teeth, he suffered a crushing blow with the closure of *Roy Of The Rovers Monthly* in 1994, but rallied briefly with *Roy Race: The Playing Years* (1995). A comeback in *Match Of The Day* magazine ended when it ceased publication in 2001. Oh, and did we mention he was a cartoon character?

☞ 1954. He appeared on the front cover of boy's magazine *Tiger*, but it was a year before he made his debut, scoring twice in a 3-3 draw.

☞ 1959–60. Roy is endorsed by Bobby Charlton, who lent his name to the writing of the Race saga.

🖐 1974–75. Appointed player-manager of Melchester Rovers. After a chequered career he resigned live on TV 18 years later, only to be reinstated the same season.

🖐 1981–82. Survives a shooting. Five years later Race survives a terrorist bomb attack that kills eight team-mates.

🖐 1994–95. In an increasingly desperate plot twist, Roy's wife Penny is killed in a car crash as the Races become the most tragic family since the Kennedys.

VITAL STATISTICS

		LEGEND RATING
Place of Birth:	Melchester, England	
Date of Birth:	Unknown, Roy is timeless **Died:** n/a	Achievement 9.0
Caps & Goals (International): Unknown, but Roy has played for		Skill 10.0
	England for over 25 years	Teamwork 10.0
Clubs:	Melchester Rovers (player-manager from 1974);	Passion 10.0
	As Player/Manager: Walford Rovers	Personality 10.0
Appearances & Goals: Club (League): Lost count over 35 years		
Trophies:	Too many to list – he is very successful	**TOTAL 49.0**

THE PAPER FOR ALL FOOTBALL FANS!

ROY OF THE ROVERS

15th OCTOBER, 1977
EVERY MONDAY

8p

ROY RACE

Roy Race

Racism
Don't Pretend It's Gone Away

ONE OF SOCIETY'S LARGEST BARNACLES has been attached to the game for decades. It was 1884 when Arthur Wharton turned out for Darlington to become Britain's first black footballer. One can only wonder what reception awaited him.

In the 1970s the rise of the National Front brought chanting inside grounds and the selling of racist literature at the gates. Clubs were not only ignorant of the problem but contributed to it, perpetuating the stereotype that black players lacked bottle or commitment. One popular theory also suggested they couldn't play in cold weather.

The situation today is much improved. Black players have successfully integrated all over Europe, although the problem has not disappeared. Attitudes have improved in Britain but worrying hotbeds remain in Italy, Iberia and the Balkans. Today's challenge for the British game lies in increasing the number of black people operating in football across the board. Black executives, referees, coaches, managers and board members are still an exception (the only current black member of England's set-up is Hope Powell, coach of the national women's team). Asian players and fans need to be similarly welcomed. Verdict? Much improved, but must try harder.

- April 2004. Ron Atkinson fires an on-air racist outburst against Marcel Desailly after Chelsea's Champions League defeat at Monaco. Rightly, it costs him all his media contracts.
- Prejudice extending into religious bigotry, Rangers' policy of signing only Protestants proved ignorance is not only skin deep.
- In 1995, followers of the racist group Combat 18 caused the abandonment of England's friendly in Dublin.
- October 2004. Spanish coach Luis Aragones racially abuses Thierry Henry in an attempt to 'motivate' Arsenal team-mate Jose Antonio Reyes. Are you Big Ron in disguise? The following month, Spanish fans racially abuse England's black players during a friendly in Madrid.
- October 2004. Courageous referee Rene Temmink abandons a league match between ADO Den Haag and PSV Eindhoven following fans' racist chanting.

'When I came into the assembly hall in South Africa it was full of blackies and it was getting f*****g dark when they were all sitting together.'

UEFA boss Lennart Johansson.
(If you find this amusing, please take the book back to the shop, we don't want your money.)

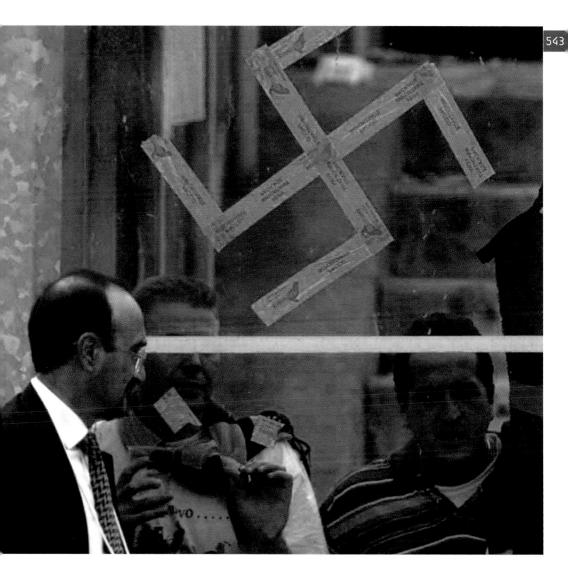

Rahn, Helmut
Rot-Weiss-Essen, West Germany

THE WEST GERMAN SIDE that won the World Cup for the first time contained two great players; their captain and playmaker, Fritz Walter, and the winger, Helmut Rahn.

A natural athlete and sprinter, Rahn was a relative unknown before the 1954 World Cup Finals. His first impact came against Yugoslavia, when he seemed to beat the entire team before ramming the ball home, but his speed and directness were also a major factor in the final as West Germany, with two goals from Rahn, came from behind to beat favourites Hungary 3-2.

Four years later Rahn went to Sweden, having stirred up German club football with his unfashionable team Rot-Weiss-Essen. He was a star of the German side again, showing great skill for such a big, imposing man, but after getting his team into the semi-finals with a brilliant solo goal against Yugoslavia, he was finally subdued by Sweden in the semis. A man for the big occasion, Rahn scored 21 goals in 40 games for Germany, a fantastic strike rate for a winger.

- ☞ Unstoppable in full flight, he is known as 'The Train' in Germany.
- 👍 In the 1954 final, with Germany 2-1 down, Rahn scored with a sharp volley. Then, six minutes from the end, he ran through the Hungarian defence to strike the winner.
- 👍 Rahn's club, Rot-Weiss-Essen won the German cup in 1953 and the league in 1955 (the only time in their history).
- 👎 Rot-Weiss-Essen didn't make much impact in the inaugural European Cup, going out to Hibernian in the first round.
- ☞ Before the 1958 tournament Rahn had been out of the German side. He was drinking heavily and overweight. Coach Herberger worked some magic, and a fit and motivated Rahn arrived at the Finals.

VITAL STATISTICS

Place of Birth:	Essen, Germany	
Date of Birth:	16 August 1929	**Died:** 14 August 2003
Caps:	40 (W. Germany)	**Goals (International):** 21
Clubs:	Rot-Weiss-Essen, MSV Duisburg, SC Enschede	
Trophies:	WorC 1954; WGLT 1955	

LEGEND RATING	
Achievement	8.0
Skill	8.0
Teamwork	7.0
Passion	7.0
Personality	8.0
TOTAL	**38.0**

Ramsey, Alf
Ipswich Town, England

'ENGLAND WILL WIN the World Cup in 1966.' In 1963, this was a rare boast from a reserved and modest manager named Alf Ramsey. And yet, amazingly, it came true. The sight of Ramsey still seated impassively on the bench as the final whistle blew to signal England's victory over West Germany was in stark contrast to the outpourings of joy around him, but inside you can be sure his heart was stirring. Thirty minutes before he had roused an England team, shattered by Germany's injury-time equaliser to force the game into extra time, with the words: 'You've won it once, now you've got to win it again.'

Ramsey's motivational skills had been proven even before 1966. Four years earlier, in charge of what was a modest array of talent at Ipswich, he brought the First Division title to Portman Road for the first and only time in their history. His style was pragmatic rather than entertaining, and was a reflection of a playing style that brought him 32 England caps and a league title with Spurs. Knighted in 1967, he seemed untouchable, but England's capitulation to Germany and their failure to qualify for the 1974 Finals cost him his job. A brief managerial flurry at Birmingham notwithstanding, it was the end for Ramsey.

- Won the Second and First Division titles in successive seasons as player and manager.
- Furiously dubbed Argentina 'animals' following the 1966 World Cup quarter-final.
- Ramsey's innovative 4-4-2 formation led England to be dubbed the 'wingless wonders'.
- Ramsey was the FA's second choice for the England job; Burnley's Jimmy Adamson turned it down.
- Ramsey's first England game was a disaster. England lost 3-0 to France and were eliminated from the European Nations Cup.

VITAL STATISTICS

Place of Birth:	Dagenham, Essex, England	
Date of Birth:	22 January 1920	**Died:** 28 April 1999
Caps:	32 (England)	**Goals (International):** 3
Clubs:	As Player: Southampton, Tottenham;	
	As Manager: Ipswich Town, England national side,	
	Birmingham (caretaker)	
Trophies:	LT 1962; WorC 1966	

Achievement	9
Tactical Awareness	9
Motivation	9
Team Selection/Transfers	8
Personality	6
TOTAL	**41**

LEGEND RATING

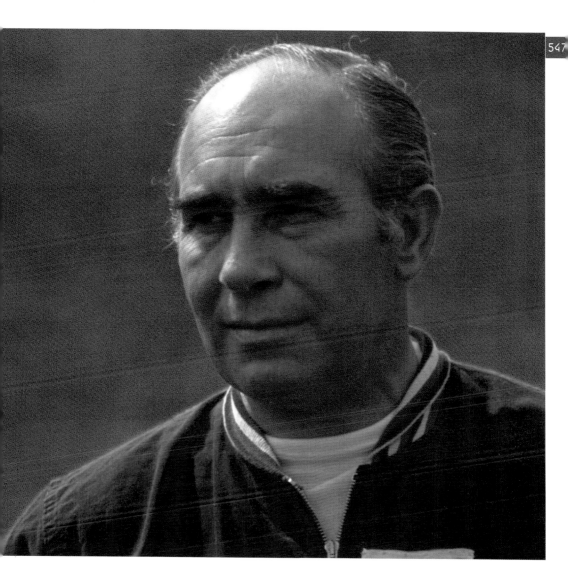

Rangers
The Dream Team

LIKE THEIR OLD-FIRM NEIGHBOURS, Rangers have a large pool of successful candidates to pick from. Yet, while it's tempting to select a team based on medals won, the quality control needs to be more stringent.

For all the tabloid revelations and weight problems, in his prime Andy Goram was probably Scotland's finest goalkeeper. George Young represents the 'Iron Curtain' defence in the immediate post-war era, and the twin legends of Greig and Gough are impossible to ignore in central defence. Sandy Jardine is not on his natural flank, but is a far classier option than the left-back alternatives. The midfield is not short of trickery: Baxter and Gascoigne's on-field skills were every bit as extravagant as their bar bills. The other half of midfield is tinged with sadness. Who knows the heights Ian Durrant would have scaled had one rogue tackle not put paid to his career, while memories of Davie Cooper's wing play are always tempered with the tragedy of his sudden and shocking death at 39. In attack, Brian Laudrup, Rangers' most gifted forward of all time, is paired with their most prolific goalscorer.

- 👍 Rangers' 49 league titles are a Scottish record.
- 👍 Graeme Souness led Rangers out of their longest barren spell, laying the foundations in the late 1980s for a side that equalled Celtic's record of nine successive titles.
- 👉 On the bench, Derek Johnstone is preferred to one-time team-mate Colin Stein. Johnstone's two spells with the club over more than a decade earned him hero status.
- 👉 Terry Butcher was the pick of Rangers' English signings of the late 1980s. Other notables included Trevor Steven, Ray Wilkins and Chris Woods.
- 👍 John Greig was voted Rangers' greatest player of the twentieth century in an end-of-millennium poll.

Manager: Graeme Souness

4-4-2

Andy Goram (90s)

George Young (40s/50s) Richard Gough (80s/90s) John Greig (C) (60s/70s)
Sandy Jardine (60s/70s)

Paul Gascoigne (90s) Jim Baxter (60s) Ian Durrant (80s) Davie Cooper (70s/80s)

Brian Laudrup (90s) Ally McCoist (80s/90s)

Subs: Peter McCloy (G) (70s/80s) Terry Butcher (D) (80s) Ian Ferguson (M) (80s/90s)
Jorg Albertz (M) (90s) Derek Johnstone (F) (70s/80s)

Rant

Norway 2 England 1, 1981

'LORD NELSON! Lord Beaverbrook! Sir Winston Churchill! Sir Anthony Eden! Clement Attlee! Henry Cooper! Lady Diana! (lapses into frenzied Norwegian, roughly translated as 'we have beaten them all!') Maggie Thatcher, can you hear me? Maggie Thatcher! Your boys took a hell of a beating! Your boys took a hell of a beating!'

The scene: Oslo, 9 September 1981. A hapless England looked to have blown their World Cup qualifying hopes for the third successive tournament by losing 2-1 to a Norwegian team considered to be cannon fodder. News enough in itself, but the match passed into footballing folklore thanks to this joyful rant at the final whistle from the Norwegian radio commentator, Bjorge Lillelien, who, in a few breathless seconds, outdid even the most frenzied Brazilian broadcaster with his random grasp of British celebrity. England would love to consign this banana skin to a permanently sealed archive, but thanks to our hero it will be mentioned in perpetuity whenever the teams meet. Henry Cooper has never been in such exalted company.

- Lucky England still qualified for Spain 82 thanks largely to Romania's home defeat by Switzerland.
- England had been vilified months earlier by also losing to Switzerland.
- The team in Oslo contained four all-conquering Liverpool players, plus Kevin Keegan and Bryan Robson.
- The rant may have inflicted lasting damage, as the commentator died prematurely a few years later.
- Although Lord Nelson had only a single eye and one arm, he may have performed better than many of England's players that night.

SCORERS	**Norway:** Albertsen, Thoresen
	England: Robson
EVENT	World Cup qualifier, Oslo, 9 September 1981
NORWAY	(Man: Tor Roste Fossen)
	1. Antonsen 2. Bernsten 3. Aas 4. Hareide 5. Grondalen 6. Giske 7. Albertsen
	8. Thorensen 9. Okland (Pedersen) 10. Jacobsen 11. Lund (Dokken)
ENGLAND	(Man: Ron Greenwood)
	1. Clemence 2. Neal 3. Mills 4. Osman 5. Thompson 6. Robson 7. Keegan
	8. Francis 9. Mariner (Withe) 10. Hoddle (P. Barnes) 11. McDermott

Rattin, Antonio
Argentina

UNFORTUNATELY FOR one of Argentina's most durable players, Antonio Rattin is best known for a single match in the 1966 World Cup Finals. An obdurate Argentine team were taking no prisoners against England in the quarter-final, with Rattin a persistent culprit. Eventually the referee's patience snapped and Rattin was ordered off. Initially he refused to go and it looked at one stage as though his team-mates may leave with him in protest, but he eventually departed and his team were not required to play again following England's 1-0 victory. At the final whistle, Alf Ramsey refused to allow his players to swap shirts with the opposition, and later described the Argentines as 'animals'. There can be little doubt he had Rattin in mind when his words were chosen.

The tough-tackling centre-half honed his skills in 14 seasons with Boca Juniors, where his height and strength allowed him to intimidate opponents. In the cynical Argentine league his bullying style was considered a prudent and legitimate survival technique, but at Wembley it brought him nothing but ignominy.

☞ As a teenager Rattin rejected overtures from several clubs in favour of his beloved Boca Juniors.

👍 He appeared in two World Cup Finals tournaments, 1962 and 1966.

☝ Became the first player to be sent off in Wembley's 43-year history.

☞ A knowledgeable all-rounder, Rattin directed gymnastics and fencing teams after his playing career ended.

☞ 1980. Appointed technical director of football at Boca Juniors.

VITAL STATISTICS

Place of Birth:	Tigre, Argentina		
Date of Birth:	16 May 1937	**Died:** n/a	
Caps:	34 (Argentina)	**Goals (International):** 1	
Clubs:	Boca Juniors		
Appearances:	Club (League): 353		
Goals:	Club (League): 26		
Trophies:	ALT 1962, 1964, 1965, 1969, 1970		

Achievement	6.0
Skill	6.0
Teamwork	8.0
Passion	9.0
Personality	7.0
TOTAL	**36.0**

LEGEND RATING

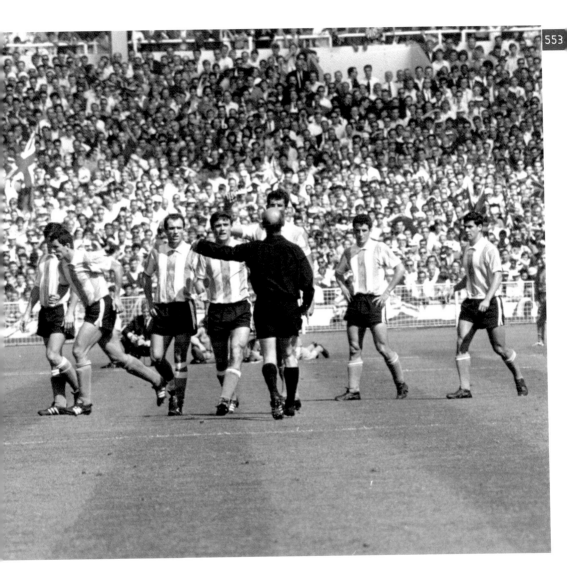

Raul, (Gonzalez Blanco)
Real Madrid, Spain

NO NEED FOR the full name. Just say 'Raul' and every football fan will know who you're talking about. The Spanish centre-forward, who turned 27 towards the end of the 2004 European Championships appears to have been haunting European defences for eons.

Madrid-born, Raul's entire club-footballing career to date has been with Real Madrid; he has remained the homebred heart of a team of expensively assembled glitterati. A quiet, self-effacing man content to let others take the headlines, Raul doesn't always get the respect his intelligence, aerial ability and finishing merit deserves. His performance against Manchester United in the 2003 Champions League quarter-final was as complete a display of centre-forward play as you could wish to see.

At international level, Raul, like Spain, remains a bridesmaid. Fancied strongly at Euro 2000 and the 2002 World Cup, they failed to progress beyond the quarter-finals in either. Nor did he get a chance to match his club success at Euro 2004 – even the quarter-finals proved elusive for Spain in Portugal.

☞ Raul's league debut was as a 17-year-old substitute for Emilio Butragueno, 'The Vulture', whom he was to replace as the focus of Real's attack.

👆 Raul is already Spain's fifth most-capped player; he may yet overtake Zubizaretta, Hierro, Camacho and Gordillo.

👆 Raul scored in the Champions League final against Valencia and in 2002 against Bayer Leverkusen.

👎 Missed a penalty as Spain crashed out of Euro 2000 to France.

👎 Spain lost their crucial quarter-final against Korea in the 2002 World Cup when Raul was absent due to injury.

VITAL STATISTICS

Place of Birth:	Madrid, Spain	
Date of Birth:	27 June 1977	**Died:** n/a
Caps:	79 (Spain)	**Goals (International):** 39
Clubs:	Real Madrid	
Appearances:	Club (for Real Madrid): 176	
Goals:	Club (for Real Madrid): 80	
Trophies:	PLA 1997, 2001, 2003; EC 1998, 2000, 2002; WCC 1998, 2002	

Achievement	8.0	
Skill	8.0	
Teamwork	8.0	
Passion	7.0	
Personality	6.0	
TOTAL	**37.0**	LEGEND RATING

Real Madrid
The Dream Team

THE GREATEST CLUB SIDE of the twentieth century has boasted some of the finest players in the history of football. Most of those included here date back to a more agreeable era when, to be permitted the honour of wearing the white shirt, meant you played for as long as was humanly possible (not two or three years until your agent fixed you up with a tidy signing-on fee in Milan, Rome or Turin).

Hence we've opted for durable, long-serving Spanish players, not the likes of Figo and Zidane. The overseas players featured are those who served their time, many of them risking the wrath of their native authorities by choosing club over country. The first great Real side from the 1930s is represented by the great goalkeeper, Zamora, and the full-back, Quincoces, while several others have been plucked from the team that dominated European football in the late 1950s. The rest are stalwarts of the 1970s and 1980s, when Real were less of a force in Europe, but remained powerful domestically, winning La Liga several times with a team peppered with Spanish internationals.

☞ Jorge Valdano, Raymond Kopa, Martin Vazquez, Hector Redondo, Luis Del Sol, Hector Rial, Carlos Santillana. All great international players. None of them make the bench.

✎ Pirri made 414 La Liga appearances for Real over 16 years, winning a European Cup aged 21 in 1966, and 10 league titles.

☞ The much-capped Jose Camacho, a mainstay of Real and Spain, throughout the 1980s, has had spells as manager of the club, including one of 22 days in 1998.

✎ Of the modern generation, Manolo Sanchis is the most decorated, having won two European cups, two UEFA cups and eight Spanish league titles.

Manager: Miguel Munoz

4-3-3

Ricardo Zamora (30s)

Quincoces Lopez (30s) Jose Santamaria (60s)
Jose Camacho (C) (70s/80s) Manolo Sanchis (90s)

Zinedine Zidane (90s/00s) Jose del Campo, "Michel" (80s)
Paco Gento (50s/60s)

Alfredo Di Stefano (50s/60s) Raul (00s) Ferenc Puskas (60s)

Subs: Miguel Angel (G) (80s) Uli Stielike (D/M) (80s)
Hugo Sanchez (F) (80s) Emilio Butragueno (F) (80s)
Jose Sanchez 'Pirri' (F) (60s/70s)

Red Devils
The Manchester United Dream Team

LOVE 'EM OR LOATHE 'EM, you can't deny that Manchester United have enjoyed the services of some fabulous footballers. Many international teams would struggle to assemble a squad like this.

In goal, the choice of Schmeichel brooks no argument, while the defence is built around the post-war era, with Irish international Carey ably supported by fellow Busby Babes Edwards and Byrne, and Martin Buchan, United's one truly class player from the team that struggled through the 1970s.

The midfield pays homage to the strength of the current team. Only an unlucky Paul Scholes misses out, but Beckham, Keane and Giggs all stand up to scrutiny. Add the power and shooting of Bobby Charlton, and you're in dreamland. Bryan Robson, upon whom England were almost exclusively dependent for inspiration during the 1980s, has to settle for a place on the bench. (Imagine a midfield with Paddy Crerand, Robson, Paul Scholes and Billy Meredith. They're the reserves). The forwards would be guaranteed to provide entertainment. Both volatile and intolerant of those less gifted, Best and Cantona would frustrate and fascinate in equal measure. And if it didn't work, Denis Law would enjoy playing alongside either of them.

☞ How do you choose between Matt Busby and Alex Ferguson, both knights of the realm? We couldn't.

👍 After the incomparable Charlton, Bill Foulkes' 682 appearances make him United's most loyal servant.

👍 Johnny Carey was an early example of the attacking full-back, a solid defender with good ball skills. He later became a successful manager of Blackburn Rovers.

☞ In the 1978 World Cup, Scotland manager Ally McLeod played Martin Buchan at full-back. Only when he returned him to the centre did their performances begin to pick up.

👍 Van Nistelrooy merits inclusion even after three seasons. Now we know why Fergie was prepared to wait to sign him.

Director of Football: Sir Matt Busby
Manager: Sir Alex Ferguson

4-4-2

Peter Schmeichel (90s)

Johnny Carey (40s/50s) Duncan Edwards (50s) Martin Buchan (C) (70s)
Roger Byrne (50s)

David Beckham (90s) Bobby Charlton (60s) Roy Keane (90s) Ryan Giggs (90s)

Eric Cantona (90s) George Best (60s/70s)

Subs: Alex Stepney (G) (60s/70s) Bill Foulkes (D) (60s) Bryan Robson (M) (80s/90s)
Denis Law (F) (60s/70s) Ruud Van Nistelrooy (F) (00s)

Referees
Who's The W****** In The Black?

REFEREES HAVE A TOUGH JOB, and media exposure has done them no favours. They make decisions without the benefit of seven cameras and slow-motion, and yet they still get far more right than wrong.

A good referee is like a well-behaved child or dog; all the more worthy of praise when their presence goes unnoticed. But in the modern game too many referees at the top level forget that people are there to watch the football, not them. Intoxicated by the fame offered by TV exposure, they go out of their way to make decisions based on fussy interpretations of rules that they would be better served ignoring altogether. Hang your head in shame Mr David Elleray. And Mike Riley. And Graham Poll. And Paul Durkin. And Paul 'Ballet Shoes' Alcock....

It seems nowadays that pandering to authority is more important than helping the game remain a good spectacle. Witness the treatment of Dermot Gallagher, an excellent referee, who was demoted for having the temerity to use common sense instead of wielding the FA whip.

- A dreadful offside decision probably cost Leeds United the League title in 1971. In a crucial end of season clash, West Brom scored a blatantly offside winning goal. Leeds went mad, as did their fans, resulting in Elland Road being closed for a spell.
- In a World Cup match between Brazil and Sweden, Clive Thomas awarded a corner in the dying seconds. Brazil scored from a header straight from the corner, but Thomas claimed he had already blown for full-time and disallowed the goal.
- A better, and braver, decision by a British referee was Jack Taylor's award of a penalty to Holland in the first minute of the 1974 World Cup final. Sadly he ruined it by giving West Germany the oft-seen tit-for-tat penalty later in the game.

'I wasn't sure whether the linesman was indicating the ball had crossed the goal line or whether he had spotted the same offence as me. It wasn't offside. I saw an offence, although I can't remember what it was. In fact there were about eight or nine infringements I could have blown for before the player shot.'

Having denied Chesterfield a place in the FA Cup final, Elleray compounds an abysmal decision by justifying it with a nonsensical rant

Renaissance for Rossi
Italy 3 Brazil 2, 1982

IF FIFA EVER DECIDE to award medals for the greatest matches in the World Cup, this one will be on the podium. The eventual winners knocked out the pre-tournament favourites in an absolute classic.

Brazil were defending a 24-game unbeaten record and needed only a draw to progress to the semi-finals while, by contrast, Italy had started the tournament in stuttering fashion, struggling in the first group stage with three draws.

The match twisted and turned throughout. Three times Italy led, only to be pegged back by Zico's brilliance in setting up Socrates and then Falcão who scored with a thunderbolt from the edge of the area. The difference between the teams proved to be the rejuvenated Paolo Rossi. None of his goals were exceptional, but a hat-trick against the world's best team was no mean feat. Admittedly, Brazil's back line was average at best, and their goalkeeper was just plain incompetent. Italy's back four, on the other hand, were immense. Marshalled by the evergreen Zoff in goal, they withstood everything Brazil could chuck at them in the last 15 minutes to win the day and break the hearts of neutral supporters around the globe.

- Bergomi showed impressive maturity after coming on as a first-half substitute. Most 18-year-olds would have shrunk from dealing with Zico and Eder.
- For Paolo Rossi, this was the day he came in from the cold. His ban following his part in a Serie A betting scandal was only lifted a few weeks before the tournament.
- 40-year-old Dino Zoff denied Brazil throughout. His save from Oscar with two minutes left won the game.
- It had been a torrid time for both of Italy's forwards. Antognoni had only recently recovered from a fractured skull.
- Rossi's goals against Brazil were his first of the tournament. He finished as its leading scorer with six.

SCORERS	**Italy:** Rossi (3)
	Brazil: Socrates, Falcão
EVENT	World Cup second round, Barcelona, 5 July 1982
ITALY	(Man: Enzo Bearzot)
	1. Zoff 2. Gentile 3. Cabrini 4. Tardelli 5. Collovati 6. Scirea 7. Oriali
	8. Conti 9. Rossi 10. Antognoni 11. Graziani
BRAZIL	(Man: Tele Santana)
	1. Waldir Peres 2. Leandro 3. Junior 4. Cerezo 5. Oscar 6. Luizinho
	7. Falcão 8. Socrates 9. Serginho 10. Zico 11. Eder

Revie, Don
Manchester City, Leeds United, England

WHETHER ONE REGARDS HIM as one of England's great club managers or the father of modern cynicism, Don Revie's influence on the domestic and national game is considerable. A competent, if unspectacular player, Revie was always a deep-thinking tactician, adapting his role as target man to a more deep-lying centre-forward in a copy of the tactic deployed by the Hungarian striker, Hidegkuti. But it was as a manager that he excelled, notably with Leeds United. A struggling Second Division outfit in 1961 Revie had transformed Leeds into runaway league champions by 1969. His team, comprised of gifted and ruthlessly determined players like Jack Charlton, Billy Bremner and Johnny Giles, became feared as much for their ruthless professionalism as for their talent. The natural choice as England manager in 1974 following the sacking of Sir Alf Ramsey, Revie turned from saviour to sinner in three years. England's failure to qualify for a second successive World Cup Finals – and the discovery that he had been secretly negotiating a deal to manage the United Arab Emirates – saw him pilloried in the press. His boats burned, Revie disappeared completely from public life. Obituaries on his death in 1989 showed old wounds were not easily healed, although, to a man, his Leeds team spoke in his defence.

- PFA footballer of the year in 1955.
- Despite Leeds' success, Revie's team should have won much more, finishing league runners-up five times and losing three Cup finals.
- Leeds lost only two games in the 1969 season, the fewest ever in a 42-game campaign.
- 1969. Leeds establish a record of 34 consecutive league games unbeaten.
- Bob Stokoe claimed that Revie offered him a bribe to throw a vital league game. Stokoe gained his revenge years later in 1973, as manager of the Sunderland side that upset Leeds to win the FA Cup final.

VITAL STATISTICS

Place of Birth: Middlesbrough, England

Date of Birth: 10 July 1927 **Died:** 28 May 1989

Caps: 6 (England) **Goals (International):** 4

Clubs: As Player: Leicester City, Hull City, Manchester City, Sunderland, Leeds United; As Manager: Leeds United, England national side, United Arab Emirates national side

Trophies: LT 1969, 1974; FAC 1972; LC 1968; UEFAC 1968, 1971

Achievement	8
Tactical Awareness	9
Motivation	8
Team Selection/Transfers	9
Personality	4
TOTAL	**38**

LEGEND RATING

Rijkaard, Frank

Ajax, AC Milan, Holland

THE DUTCH TEAM that won the European Championship final of 1988 – Holland's first major triumph – was built around the most talented trio of players they had produced since Cruyff, Rep and Neeskens. Their names? Ruud Gullit, Marco van Basten and Frank Rijkaard. If Gullit was their spokesman and leader and Van Basten their executioner and inspiration, then Rijkaard was their pendulum, the metronomic midfield force that made them tick. Utterly dependable, fit, strong and skilful, Rijkaard was the epitome of the modern midfield player, and it was his work that allowed the others to wreak their havoc. His copybook was blotted in the 1990 World Cup when he was sent off for spitting at Rudi Voller as the Dutch, tournament favourites, were beaten by Germany.

When AC Milan linked Rijkaard up with his two compatriots at club level, they continued to sweep all before them. Rijkaard even managed to steal the spotlight in 1990, scoring the winning goal against Benfica in the European Cup final. A return to Ajax brought yet more domestic trophies, and a third European Cup. Rijkaard was a surprising choice as Holland coach in 1998. He had no experience and, though his team rallied well to reach the semi-finals of Euro 2000, he resigned shortly after. Since taking over as coach of Barcelona, Rijkaard has achieved a sharp turnaround in the fortunes of the Spanish giants in a remarkably short space of time.

- In 1988 Rijkaard made a disastrous move to Real Zaragoza, playing only 11 games before moving to Milan.
- Seven league titles, one in each of his last four seasons (two at Milan, two at Ajax).
- The problems with racism in Dutch football have never been resolved – Gullit and Rijkaard, then later Davids, Kluivert and Seedorf have all complained about 'hidden agendas' within the squad.
- Rijkaard laid on Kluivert's goal in Ajax's 1995 European Cup success – against Milan of all teams....
- Rijkaard never played for a side that finished lower than third in the League.

VITAL STATISTICS

Place of Birth:	Amsterdam, Holland
Date of Birth:	30 September 1962 **Died:** n/a
Caps:	73 (Holland) **Goals (International):** 10
Clubs:	Ajax, Sporting Lisbon, Real Zaragoza, AC Milan
Appearances:	Club (All Matches): 415
Goals:	Club (All Matches): 74
Trophies:	CWC 1987; EuroC 1988; EC 1989–90, 1995; SA 1992–93; DLT 1982, 1983, 1985, 1994–95

LEGEND RATING	
Achievement	9.0
Skill	8.0
Teamwork	9.0
Passion	7.0
Personality	7.0
TOTAL	**40.0**

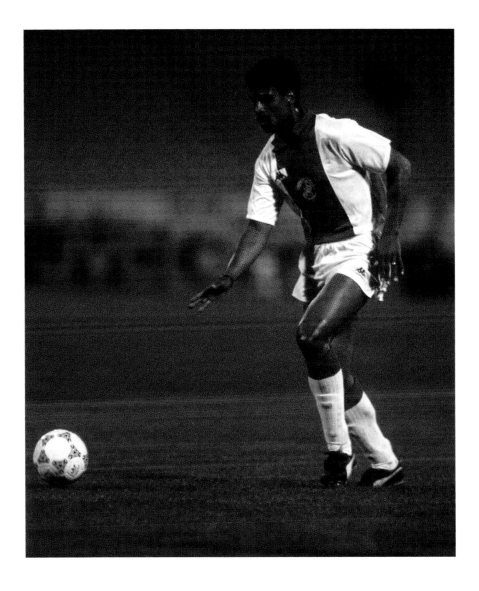

Riva, Luigi
Cagliari, Italy

ONE OF ITALY'S BRIGHTEST STARS in the 1960s, Luigi Riva emerged from humble beginnings with Legnano and Cagliari to become the hero of the *Azzurri* attack with seven goals in the 1970 World Cup qualifiers. He continued this form at the Finals, hitting the winner in the semi-final with Germany and finishing as Italy's top scorer, boosting his international tally to 22 goals in 21 games.

Riva approached the 1970s Finals on a high. He had finished the previous season at the top of the Serie A scoring charts (for the third time in four years), and his goals had helped Cagliari to their first ever *scudetto*.

A few months after the Finals, however, Riva broke a leg for the second time in his career. Initially there were fears he may never play again, but he defied the doubters and made a full recovery – they did not call him 'The Rumble Of Thunder' for nothing. Indeed, he alleviated fears about his fitness to such an extent that, in 1973, Juventus made a massive bid of £1.5 m for him. At that price Cagliari were tempted to sell, but Riva refused to budge, preferring to remain loyal to his native Sardinia. A disappointing swansong at the 1974 World Cup Finals was followed by his retirement, and elevation to the Cagliari boardroom.

☞ He made his international debut in 1965, aged 21, but it was another three years before he held down a regular place.

👎 Riva's thunderous shot once broke a spectator's arm during a pre-match warm-up.

👎 A few days later, he broke his leg and was out of action for six months.

👍 35 goals in 42 internationals; one of the highest ratios of the past 40 years.

👍 Riva came into the team for the replayed final in the 1968 European Championship, scoring the opener in a 2-0 win.

VITAL STATISTICS

Place of Birth:	Leggiuno, Italy		
Date of Birth:	7 November 1944	**Died:** n/a	
Caps:	42 (Italy)	**Goals (International):** 35	
Clubs:	Legnano, Cagliari		
Appearances:	Club (All Matches): 338		
Goals:	Club (All Matches): 170		
Trophies:	EuroC 1968; SA 1970		

Achievement	7.0
Skill	8.0
Teamwork	9.0
Passion	8.0
Personality	7.0
TOTAL	**39.0**

LEGEND RATING

Rivaldo, Vitor Barbosa Ferreira

Brazil, Deportivo La Coruna, Barcelona

RIVALDO EMERGED with Corinthians and Palmeiras as "the next big thing" in Brazilian football. Failure in the 1996 Olympics led to Rivaldo being pilloried in the press and prompted his departure for Spain. The 1998 World Cup was a better tournament for Rivaldo, and for Brazil. Rivaldo started every game as playmaker from the left hand side, running at defences and creating space for the lethal Ronaldo to exploit. His best game was in the 3-2 win over Denmark when he scored twice, and was at the heart of some scintillating football from Brazil. Victory in the 1999 Copa America confirmed Rivaldo's status, but even he has struggled to inspire a lacklustre Brazil side in the last two years.

It seemed Rivaldo's move to Spain had been the catalyst for his breakthrough as a world star. Given a free role at Deportivo La Coruna he had been a revelation, and Barcelona had to pay a massive £18 m to prise him away. The money was well-spent, as Rivaldo's dribbling and shooting skills were a major contributor to successive championships. A loss of form saw Rivaldo out of the Barca team in 2002, and rumours circulated of a move to the Premiership with Bolton. Instead he opted for Greece and Olympiakos.

- Rivaldo's ratio of a goal every other game is outstanding for a midfield player – 24 in 37 league games for Barca in 1998–99 was truly exceptional.
- Voted European and World Player of the Year in 1999.
- Rivaldo, and others, have invited huge criticism from Brazilian press for their lack of availability for internationals. This is nonsense, it hasn't stopped the Argentinians developing the strongest team in the world.

VITAL STATISTICS

Place of Birth:	Recife, Brazil		
Date of Birth:	19 April 1972	**Died:** n/a	
Caps:	68 (Brazil)	**Goals (International):** 33	
Clubs:	Paulista, Santa Cruz, Mogi-Mirin, Corinthians,		
	Palmeiras, Deportivo La Coruna, Barcelona,		
	AC Milan, Cruzeiro, Olympiakos		
Appearances:	Club (League): 324		
Goals:	Club (League): 157		
Trophies:	BLT 1994; PLA 1998–99; WorC 2002; EC 2003		

LEGEND RATING

Achievement	9.0
Skill	9.0
Teamwork	8.0
Passion	8.5
Personality	6.0
TOTAL	**40.5**

Rivelino, Roberto
Corinthians, Brazil

ONE OF THE ABIDING memories of the great 1970 World Cup Finals was Rivelino's shooting, especially from set-pieces. His ability to impart vicious swerve on the ball, while maintaining velocity on his shot, was a phenomenon the world had never witnessed before. He could place the ball seemingly wherever he wanted. And he didn't always bend it; sometimes he would simply instruct Jairzinho to stand in the wall, hit it straight at him, and hoped he remembered to duck.

Rivelino played for his local team, Corinthians, for 10 years without ever winning anything significant, although towards the end of his career he moved to the more fashionable Fluminense. In Brazil opponents grew wise to his free-kick expertise, but his international foes never seemed to learn their lesson. At the 1974 Finals, in a vastly inferior Brazil team, he continued to enjoy success; against Zaire he scored with a shot struck so hard the ball rebounded back out of the opponents' penalty area.

By the 1978 World Cup Rivelino was a peripheral figure, overshadowed by the emerging Zico, but with his famous left foot, missile free-kicks and magnificent gaucho moustache his mark on the game had already been made.

☞ Rivelino's end of career payola came, not in the USA like so many others, but in Saudi Arabia.

☞ Rivelino became a well-respected commentator on Brazilian TV on his retirement in 1981.

☝ Rivelino is credited with scoring the world's fastest goal, belting the ball from the kick-off over a goalkeeper who was still completing his pre-match prayers.

☞ Corinthians fans dubbed him 'Little King of the Park' – his loyalty to an unsuccessful club made him something of a folk hero.

☞ Rivelino's 'Zapata' moustache sparked a craze amongst South American footballers. Oh dear.

VITAL STATISTICS

Place of Birth:	Sao Paulo, Brazil		
Date of Birth:	1 January 1946	**Died:**	n/a
Caps:	92 (Brazil)	**Goals (International):**	26
Clubs:	Corinthians, Fluminense, El Helal		
Trophies:	WorC 1970		

LEGEND RATING	
Achievement	9.0
Skill	9.0
Teamwork	8.0
Passion	7.0
Personality	7.0
TOTAL	**40.0**

Roberto Carlos da Silva
Real Madrid, Brazil

TRADITIONALLY the most exciting Brazilian footballers have been their forwards, but over the last few years one of the superstars of their game has been a brilliant attacking full-back. Thrilling runs from left back have always been a feature of Brazilian football – Nilton Santos, Branco, Leonardo – but Roberto Carlos has taken the art of marauding to a new dimension. Whether overlapping the midfielders, or cutting in with the ball to attempt one of his outrageous, swerving strikes, Carlos commits himself wholeheartedly to attack. His ability to bend the ball makes him a real danger at set pieces – many a goalkeeper has scoffed as Carlos has lined up a 35-yarder, only to watch open-mouthed as the ball flies into the top corner. He and Cafu were an exciting combination at the 1998 and 2002 World Cup Finals.

Carlos moved to Europe from Palmeiras in 1995, and had an unproductive year at Inter Milan before enjoying a hugely successful spell at Real Madrid in a star-studded side where he collected winner's medals in La Liga and the Champions league.

Finally, in 2002, he found his Holy Grail, and Roberto Carlos booked his place in footballing history as a World Cup winner. He is one of the greats.

- He won two successive Copa America tournaments in 1997 and 1999.
- Cafu, his full-back partner, helped Roma win their first Italian league for nearly 20 years in 2001.
- At Inter, Roy Hodgson tried to move Roberto Carlos into midfield – a logical move, but not to the player's liking.
- Capped at 18 in the 1992 Olympic tournament, he was disappointed to miss the 1994 World Cup, where Leonardo and Branco filled the 'left-back who can't defend' slot.
- Roberto Carlos was Ronaldo's room-mate at the 1998 World Cup finals, and the first to witness the mystifying 'convulsion' that rendered Ronaldo such a passenger in the final.

VITAL STATISTICS

Place of Birth:	Garca, Brazil	
Date of Birth:	10 April 1973	**Died:** n/a
Caps:	98 (Brazil)	**Goals (International):** 8
Clubs:	Palmeiras, Inter Milan, Real Madrid	
Appearances:	Club (League): 385	
Goals:	Club (League): 46	
Trophies:	PLA 1997, 2001; EC 1998, 2000, 2002;	
	WorC 2002	

LEGEND RATING	
Achievement	8.0
Skill	9.0
Teamwork	6.0
Passion	7.0
Personality	6.0
TOTAL	**36.0**

Robson, Bobby

Ipswich Town, England, Newcastle United

EXCELLENT PLAYER. Great manager. Nice bloke. Few figures in football are treated with the universal respect accorded Bobby Robson. Robson's 35 years as a manager, eight of them with England, followed 17 years as a successful midfield player with West Brom and Fulham, where he played alongside the legendary Johnny Haynes. After retiring as a player Robson managed Ipswich for 13 years. During that time Robson bought and sold countless players but it was the signings of the Dutchmen Arnold Mühren and Frans Thijssen, two of the first overseas players to make a significant impact in English football, for which he is probably best remembered.

As England manager he survived an indifferent start, failing to qualify for the European Championships, but his record in two World Cups was impressive. In 1986 he took England to the quarter-finals and then, four years later, led them to the semis at Italia 90. On both occasions England lost out to the eventual tournament winners. After seven years abroad, he returned to his native North-East and revitalised a Newcastle United in sharp decline after ineffective management by Kenny Dalglish and Ruud Gullit. Chairman Freddie Sheppard's memory was short, though. His dismissal of Robson after an indifferent start to the 2004–05 campaign was shabby and ill-timed.

☞ He caused immediate controversy as England manager by omitting Kevin Keegan from his first squad in 1982.

☞ He enjoys good relations with the media these days, but was subjected to a vicious tabloid campaign to oust him as England manager in 1988 following a 1-1 draw with Saudi Arabia.

☞ He scored twice on his England debut in a 4-0 defeat of France, 1957.

☞ He has won only one English domestic trophy as a manager, the FA Cup with Ipswich in 1978.

☞ He left Ipswich for the England job after finishing second in the First Division in successive seasons.

VITAL STATISTICS

Place of Birth:	Sacriston, England	
Date of Birth:	18 February 1933	**Died:** n/a
Caps:	20 (England)	**Goals (International):** 4
Clubs:	As Player: Fulham, West Bromwich Albion;	
	As Manager: Vancouver Whitecaps, Fulham,	
	Ipswich, PSV Eindhoven, Sporting Lisbon,	
	FC Porto, Barcelona, Newcastle United	
Trophies:	FAC 1978; UEFAC 1981; CWC 1997; DLT 1991,	
	1992; PLT 1995, 1996	

Achievement	7
Tactical Awareness	8
Motivation	9
Team Selection/Transfers	8
Personality	9
TOTAL	**41**

LEGEND RATING

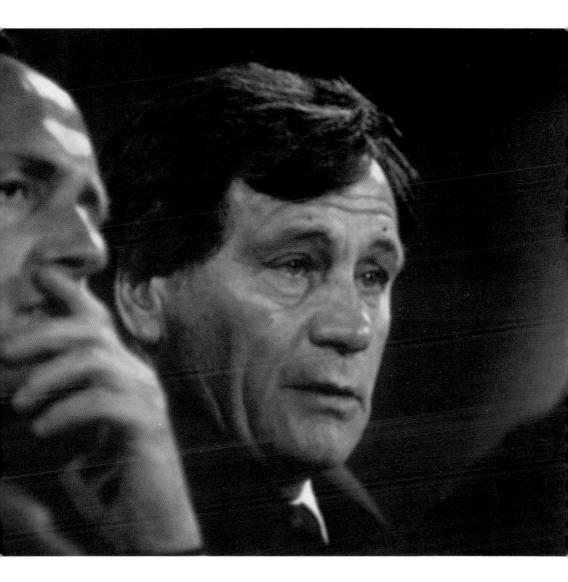

Robson, Bryan
West Bromwich Albion, Manchester United, England

ENGLAND'S FINEST PLAYER of the 1980s was also one of their unluckiest. Although 'Captain Marvel' brought a huge midfield presence to bear for club and country, his catalogue of injuries threatened to make him more celebrated in the *Lancet* than the back pages. Robson's first World Cup Finals in 1982 saw him come of age, but the sight of him limping prematurely out of the following two tournaments left England fans mouthing the words 'if only'.

The heartbeat of West Bromwich Albion's finest post-war side, Robson later moved to Manchester United in search of the major prizes. It worked. He won FA Cup winners' medals in 1983, 1985 and 1990 and picked up a European Cup Winners' Cup gong in 1991. It looked like a league championship was going to elude him but, in the latter stages of his Old Trafford career, United finally came good, picking up their first title in 26 years in 1993. Robson played in only five matches that season, but no one in the country begrudged him his medal. His self-motivation and determination seemed ideal qualities for management, but despite leading Middlesbrough to two Wembley finals, his record in the league was poor, and his record in the transfer market was even worse. He was replaced as Middlesbrough boss by Steve McLaren in 2001. After a brief spell at Bradford, Robson returned to his roots as manager of West Brom in November 2004.

- He captained England 65 times, second only to Bobby Moore.
- With 26 international goals he is the only non-striker in England's top 10.
- 1982. Scored after 27 seconds versus France, the quickest goal in World Cup Finals history.
- He lifted the FA Cup as captain three times (1983, 1985 and 1990).
- £1.5 m fee paid to West Brom by Man United in 1981 was a British record.

VITAL STATISTICS

Place of Birth:	Chester-le-Street, England
Date of Birth:	11 January 1957 **Died:** n/a
Caps:	90 (England) **Goals (International):** 26
Clubs:	West Brom Albion, Manchester United, Middlesbrough
Appearances:	Club (League): 568
Goals:	Club (League): 114
Trophies:	LT 1993, 1994; FAC 1983, 1985, 1990; CWC 1991

LEGEND RATING	
Achievement	7.0
Skill	7.0
Teamwork	10.0
Passion	9.0
Personality	7.0
TOTAL	**40.0**

Ronaldo, (Luis Nazario de Lima)

Inter Milan, Real Madrid, Brazil

IT WAS CLEAR from an early age that Ronaldo Luis Nazario de Lima had the lot. Playing in Brazilian football as a teenager he proved unstoppable, and was promptly shipped off to Europe to play for PSV Eindhoven in Holland.

The shaven-headed waif with the buck teeth isn't a complete striker by any means; he can't head the ball well and doesn't have the finishing of, say, Gerd Muller or Gary Lineker, but he has serious pace, great close control and impressive strength. In full flight he is a breathtaking sight and pretty much unstoppable, like Jimmy Greaves with a rocket up his shorts.

In Europe he has torn apart Dutch, Spanish and Italian club defences with equal relish, and had a brilliant Copa América with Brazil in 1997. He came into the 1998 World Cup billed as the world's greatest player and lived up to the hype with some fine performances, but the events surrounding his 'funny turn' prior to the final against France (and his subsequent insipid performance) meant fans came away discussing his health rather than his football. Not any more. The Golden Boot in Japan and Korea in the World Cup Finals in 2002 confirmed that the comeback kid had truly returned.

- Doubts first emerged over Ronaldo's fitness at PSV but Barcelona gambled £10 m on him and struck gold: 34 goals in La Liga and a winning goal in the Cup Winners' Cup final.
- April 2003: scores memorable hat-trick at Old Trafford as Real eliminate Manchester United from the Champions League.
- He was voted World Player of the Year in 1996 and 1997.
- For Cruzeiro, aged 18, he scored 58 goals in 60 games.
- He was European Footballer of the Year in 1997.

VITAL STATISTICS

Place of Birth:	Rio de Janeiro, Brazil	
Date of Birth:	22 September 1976	**Died:** n/a
Caps:	74 (Brazil)	**Goals (International):** 50
Clubs:	Cruzeiro, PSV Eindhoven, Barcelona, Inter Milan, Real Madrid	
Appearances:	Club (All Matches): 343	
Goals:	Club (All Matches): 267	
Trophies:	WorC 2002; CWC 1997; UEFAC 1998	

Achievement	8.0
Skill	9.0
Teamwork	7.0
Passion	8.0
Personality	6.0
TOTAL	**38.0**

LEGEND RATING

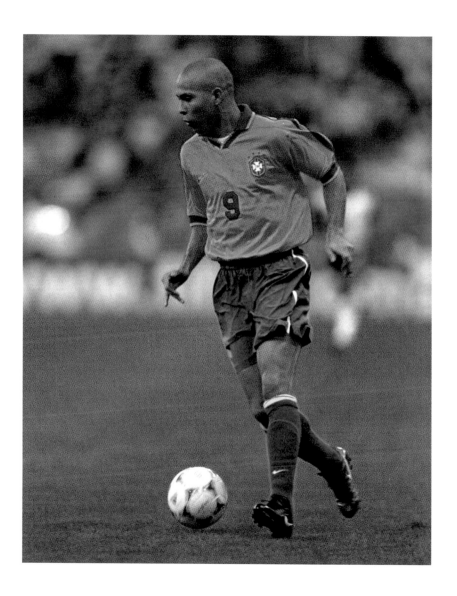

Ronnie's Rocket
Hereford United 2 Newcastle United 1, 1972

THE GAME THAT still keeps Ronnie Radford in personal appearances was notable for more than just non-leaguers scalping top-division opponents. Hereford had already produced a major surprise by drawing 2-2 at St James's Park.

Due to bad weather the replay had already been postponed several times and, when it was finally given the go-ahead, the pitch resembled a treacle pudding. The state of the playing surface was undoubtedly a factor, and made Malcolm MacDonald's pre-match boast that Newcastle would win by double figures seem even more foolhardy. The general perception is that this was a typical blood-and-thunder FA Cup tie. In fact, nothing much happened for 80 minutes, and when MacDonald rose at the far post to give Newcastle the lead the anti-climax appeared complete. But Radford had other ideas. His 40-yard screamer, replayed so frequently on TV it is often mistakenly believed to have been the winner, was in fact just the prelude to Ricky George's extra-time decider and the pitch invasion, a delirious mass of snorkel parkas and bad hair-cuts, that it prompted. Just four days later, Hereford held West Ham in the fourth round, before a Geoff Hurst hat-trick in the replay made Upton Park the final stop in a memorable ride.

☞ Commentator John Motson, previously second fiddle on *Match of the Day*, became a household name after this match.

🔔 Ronnie Radford's equaliser was *Match of the Day's* goal of the season, the only time a non-league player has won the award.

🔔 Hereford's third round in 15 years made it third time lucky.

☞ Hereford's scorers had more illustrious namesakes; double-holders Arsenal also played twin strikers called Radford and George.

☞ Hereford were elected to the Football League that season, largely on the strength of this game.

SCORERS **Hereford United:** Radford, George
Newcastle United: MacDonald
EVENT FA Cup third round replay, Edgar Street, 5 February 1972

HEREFORD (Man: Colin Addison)
1. Potter 2. Gough 3. Mallender 4. Jones 5. McLaughlin 6. Addison
7. George 8. Tyler 9. Meadows 10. Owen 11. Radford
NEWCASTLE (Man: Joe Harvey)
1. McFaul 2. n/k 3. n/k 4. n/k 5. Moncur 6. n/k 7. n/k 8. n/k
9. Macdonald 10. Tudor 11. n/k

Roonaldo, Ronaldo & Friends
The Stars of Euro 2008?

THE ESTABLISHED ORDER was threatened at Euro 2004. Of the major European stars, only Luis Figo, belatedly, Pavel Nedved and Michael Ballack did anything to further or justify their reputations. Instead, a new generation of superstars made their names, and pleasingly for English fans most of them will play in the Premiership in 2004–05.

England's Wayne Rooney was the first to stamp his presence on the tournament. Rampaging performances in the group matches, with two goals against both Switzerland and Croatia, marked him as England's major threat, and it was his injury, not the disallowed 'goal' that was the turning point of the match against Portugal.

Cristiano Ronaldo, after a super second half to the Premiership season, took that form into the championships. Ronaldo has bags of confidence, is comfortable on either side and carries a surprising aerial threat for a winger. Suggestions earlier in the season that he is merely a show-pony now look silly.

Maybe the most surprising performance was that of Milan Baros, who looked a potent threat alongside the man-mountain, Koller. Gerard Houllier must have watched and wondered what might have been as Liverpool's forgotten man took away the golden boot as the tournament's leading scorer.

☞ Two of Chelsea's new signings, Arjen Robben (Holland) and Petr Cech, the Czech goalkeeper, made highly promising debuts in a major tournament.

☞ The performances of Roma's Antonio Cassano, drafted into the Italian team after Totti's ban, were some compensation for the team's early exit.

☞ Rooney's record as the tournament's youngest scorer lasted only days as Switzerland's Johan Vonlanthen netted against France, aged 18 years and four months, three months younger than Rooney.

☞ Philip Lahm, the Stuttgart left-back, was one of Germany's best attackers, and the midfielder, Bastian Schweinsteiger, showed promise after making his international debut in the first game.

4-4-2

Petr Cech (Cz R)

Philipp Lahm (Ger) Giourkas Seitaridis (Gre) Ledley King (Eng)
Ashley Cole (Eng)

Cristiano Ronaldo (Por) Antonio Cassano (Ita) Tomas Rosicky (Cz R)
Arjen Robben (Hol)

Wayne Rooney (Eng) Milan Baros (Cz R)

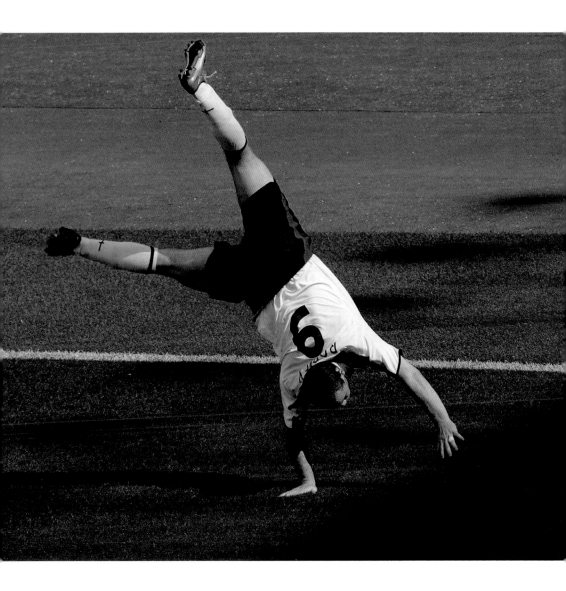

Rooney, Wayne
Manchester United, Everton, England

YOU'RE 18, you've had a high profile move to Britain's most famous club, but had to sit out the first few weeks with an injury. You get your chance; a big night, a Champions League game at Old Trafford. So what do you? Play safe and pass sideways? Freeze and have a minger? No. You score a hat-trick. At least that's what you do if you're Wayne Rooney.

Rooney is without doubt the most exciting English player to have emerged in this writer's adult lifetime. Gascoigne had chutzpah; Le Tissier was a divine talent without desire; Owen a lethal bullet. Rooney has elements of them all, and if the combination comes to fruition he could turn England into a genuine threat over the next decade. His performance in England's crucial 2-0 win over Turkey marked him as having the temperament to go with the talent, and goals against Macedonia and Liechtenstein confirmed him as a genuine international player while still a teenager. His performances at Euro 2004 confirmed him as world class.

Rooney was handled with kid gloves by Everton manager, David Moyes, often leaving Toffee's fans unhappy in the process. Ferguson, too, will be reluctant to over-use the teenager, so maybe Rooney will be spared the fatigue that seems to afflict many young stars.

☞ Rooney made his Premiership debut against Spurs in August 2002, two months shy of his 17th birthday.

👆 He became Everton's youngest-ever scorer when he netted twice against Wrexham in a Worthington Cup match on 1st October 2004.

👆 Shortly afterwards a sensational last-minute winner against Arsenal made Rooney the Premiership's youngest ever scorer, eclipsing Michael Owen.

👆 12th February 2003, Rooney became England's youngest-ever player, again eclipsing Owen.

👆 A first England goal followed in the 2-1 win in Macedonia – surprise, surprise, eclipsing Owen's record as England's youngest scorer.

VITAL STATISTICS

Place of Birth:	Liverpool, England			Achievement	6.0
Date of Birth:	24 October 1985	**Died:** n/a		Skill	9.0
Caps:	19 (England)	**Goals (International):** 9		Teamwork	8.0
Clubs:	Everton, Manchester United			Passion	8.0
Appearances:	Club (League): 82			Personality	6.0
Goals:	Club (League): 21				
Trophies:	None			**TOTAL**	**37.0**

LEGEND RATING

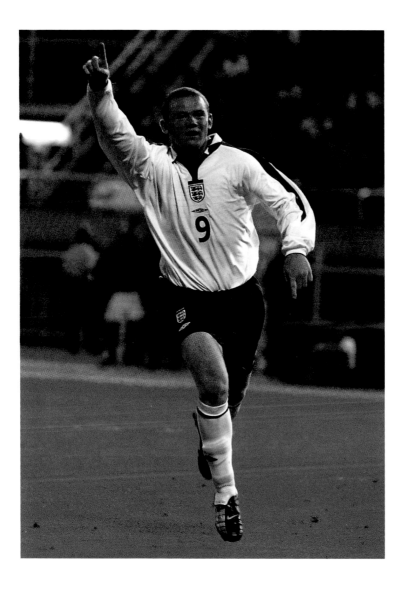

Rossi, Paolo

Juventus, Italy

THE HERO OF ITALY'S greatest post-war triumph was nearly on the scrapheap as a teenager. Two knee operations, the result of injuries picked up playing for Juventus' youth team, nearly strangled the career of one of Italy's most notable forwards. Offloaded by the Turin giants in 1975 after three years as a professional, he spent two seasons with Como before Vicenza offered him another chance. His reputation was made during a highly successful 1978 World Cup Finals, and prompted his £3.5 m world-record transfer to Perugia the following year. However, after only one season, Rossi found himself in serious bother after being implicated in a betting scandal that rocked Italian football, and was later banned for two years (Perugia were relegated for their part in the scam). His ban completed, Perugia got rid of him to Juventus for just £650,000, but within a year Rossi was the toast of the nation, firing Italy to the summit of world football at the 1982 World Cup Finals. Rossi was the tournament's top scorer with six, a haul that included a hat-trick against Brazil in the decisive group game, and the goal that set Italy on their way to a 3-1 win over West Germany in the final. His career came full circle in 1986, when that troublesome knee forced his early retirement at 29.

☞ Rossi had played only three games since the lifting of his ban before appearing at Spain 82.

☝ Rossi failed to score in the first four matches of the 1982 Finals. You know the rest…

☝ Like Perugia, AC Milan were also kicked out of Serie A for their part in the betting scandal.

🏆 He was World and European Footballer of the Year in 1982.

VITAL STATISTICS

Place of Birth:	Prato, Italy
Date of Birth:	23 September 1956 **Died:** n/a
Caps:	48 (Italy) **Goals (International):** 20
Clubs:	Prato, Juventus, Como, Lanerossi, Vicenza, Perugia, AC Milan
Appearances:	Club (League): 251
Goals:	Club (League): 103
Trophies:	WorC 1982; CWC 1984; EC 1985; SA 1982, 1984

LEGEND RATING	
Achievement	9.0
Skill	8.0
Teamwork	8.0
Passion	7.0
Personality	6.0
TOTAL	**38.0**

Rossoneri
The AC Milan Dream Team

WHAT A DEFENCE! Nils Liedholm was a superb all-round player, Cesare Maldini sound and intelligent, and the other three are simply fantastic: the steel and guile of Franco Baresi, speed and subtlety of Maldini, and 'The Rock', Marcel Desailly. Further insurance against an opposition raid is also provided by the midfield, notably Rijkaard and Gullit who, for all their ball-playing gifts, never shirked their defensive responsibilities. Those two, along with Milan icon Rivera, give this team a compact and efficient midfield. The one thing it possibly lacks is width, hence the inclusion of Swedish winger, Hamrin, on the bench. There is also the option of bringing Donadoni on for Rijkaard at half-time. (Gullit, Donadoni and Rivera – shall we play football or have a fashion shoot?)

Up front a steady supply of goals is guaranteed. Marco Van Basten, a three-time winner of the European Footballer of the Year award, is one of the greatest finishers of all time, and the powerful Swede, Nordahl, not far behind. Sadly, there is no room for the gifted Daniele Massaro, and only the bench for the moody genius of Dejan Savicevic. A fabulous team, but even Silvio Berlusconi might blanch at the wage bill.

☞ Fabio Cudicini is the father of Chelsea goalkeeper, Carlo Cudicini.

☞ Cesare and Paolo Maldini are also father and son. As manager of Italy, it was Cesare who persuaded Paolo to move to centre-half in the absence of Franco Baresi.

☞ More defensive talent sits on the bench in the shape of Alessandro Costacurta. An unlikely footballer, Costacurta collects art and owns a part share in a gourmet restaurant.

☜ Unlucky omissions? Gunnar Gren, Milan's other great Swede, Prati, scorer of a hat-trick in the 1969 European Cup final, and Demetrio Albertini, gifted midfielder in the 1990s.

☞ Only half this squad are Italian, evidence of Milan's reliance on overseas stars to bring them success.

Manager: Arrigo Sacchi

1-4-3-2

Fabio Cudicini (60s)

Franco Baresi (C) (70s/80s/90s)

Nils Liedholm (50s/60s) Cesare Maldini (60s) Marcel Desailly (90s)
Paolo Maldini (80s/90s)

Frank Rijkaard (80s) Ruud Gullit (80s) Gianni Rivera (60s/70s)

Marco Van Basten (80s) Andrei Schevchenko (00s)

Subs: Sebastiano Rossi (G) (90s) Alessandro Costacurta (D) (90s)
Roberto Donadoni (M) (80s) Dejan Savicevic (F) (90s) Gunnar Nordahl (F) (50s/60s)

Rough Justice
West Germany 3 (5) France 3 (4), 1982

THIS MATCH HAD EVERYTHING, including one of the great injustices a World Cup audience had ever witnessed. The game was delicately poised at 1-1 when France's Patrick Battiston burst clear onto the German goal, only to be cynically brought down on the edge of the area by a head-high challenge from German goalkeeper, Schumacher. Amazingly, Dutch referee Charles Corver failed to award even a foul – rough justice for the French full-back who was stretchered off with concussion and broken teeth.

With all neutrals baying for German blood, justice appeared to have been served as France swept into a 3-1 lead in extra-time with only 17 minutes left. But, settling for their two-goal advantage, the French sat back inviting German pressure. Germany seized the initiative and two goals in five minutes, the second a brilliant overhead kick from Fischer, saw them force a penalty shoot-out. Amazingly, France threw it away a second time. Schumacher saved Didier Six's kick to prevent a 4-2 lead, and repeated the trick to keep out Bossis's effort with the scores at 4-4. Then, as the shoot-out moved into sudden-death, Hrubesch applied the final, killer blow. The tears shed by French players were shared by football lovers everywhere.

☞ 'I'm convinced the world knows the best team lost. We only have ourselves to blame, though,' Michel Platini.

☞ Substitute Patrick Battiston had only been on the pitch for five minutes.

☞ 'He [Schumacher] is very sorry for what happened. It was an accident.' German coach Jupp Derwall, who even managed to keep a straight face.

☜ A French newspaper poll after the game revealed Schumacher to be the least popular man in French history, edging Adolf Hitler into second place.

☞ Justice finally prevailed as Italy beat Germany 3-1 in the final.

SCORERS	**W. Germany:** Littbarski, Rummenigge, Fischer.
	France: Platini (pen.), Tresor, Giresse
EVENT	World Cup semi-final, 8 July 1982

W. GERMANY (Man: Jupp Derwall)
1. Schumacher 2. Kaltz 3. K-H Förster 4. Stielike 5. Briegel (Rummenigge) 6. B. Förster
7. Dremmler 8. Breitner 9. Littbarski 10. Magath (Hrubesch) 11. Fischer

FRANCE (Man: Michel Hidalgo)
1. Ettori 2. Amoros 3. Janvion 4. Bossis 5. Tigana 6. Tresor 7. Genghini (Battiston)
(Lopez) 8. Giresse 9. Platini 10. Rocheteau 11. Six

Rummenigge, Karl-Heinz
Bayern Munich, West Germany

AS THE GREAT GERMAN SIDE of the early 1970s broke up, manager Helmut Schoen looked around in vain for stars to replace Beckenbauer, Netzer, Overath and Müller. How he must have rejoiced at the emergence of Karl-Heinz Rummenigge. Quick and mobile, with distinctive blonde hair and a typically Bavarian swagger, Rummenigge was a hard player to mark, always seeming to find a yard in which to fashion a shot at goal.

However, fortune never smiled on Rummenigge in the World Cup. He played in a poor side in 1978, and had the unique misfortune to captain two losing finalists, in 1982 and 1986. In both those tournaments Rummenigge was hampered by injuries, and Germany were a blunt edge without him. He had better luck in the European Championships though, winning the tournament in 1980 when, with the young playmaker Bernd Schuster feeding him with passes, he performed with customary vivacity. In 10 years at Bayern Munich, Rummenigge won a full set of domestic honours and two European Cup winner's medals. He tried his luck at Inter for three seasons, but they never really hit the heights, and he later played out his career in the relative obscurity of the Swiss league with Servette.

☞ The £2.5 m fee paid to Bayern Munich by Inter was a German record.

🍃 He was European Footballer of the Year, 1980 and 1981.

🎨 His 1982 World Cup hat-trick against Chile was a masterclass in finishing – one with each foot and a textbook header.

☞ Had the talented Schuster not absented himself from international football, Rummenigge's goal tally would surely have been higher. For most of his career Germany lacked both a quality playmaker and a quality target man for Rummenigge to feed off.

☞ The decision to play the injured Rummenigge in the 1982 World Cup final is alleged to have prompted a fierce row in the West German dressing room at half-time.

VITAL STATISTICS

Place of Birth:	Lippstadt, Germany
Date of Birth:	25 September 1955 **Died:** n/a
Caps:	95 (Germany) **Goals (International):** 45
Clubs:	Bayern Munich, Inter Milan, Servette
Appearances:	Club (All Matches): 424
Goals:	Club (All Matches): 220
Trophies:	EC 1975, 1976; EuroC 1980; BLG 1980, 1981

LEGEND RATING	
Achievement	9.0
Skill	8.0
Teamwork	9.0
Passion	9.0
Personality	6.0
TOTAL	**41.0**

Rush, Ian
Liverpool, Wales

ONE OF THE GREAT instinctive finishers, Rush broke a stack of goal-scoring records in his time with Liverpool. Discovered at Chester as a teenager, he was bought by the Anfield club in 1979 for £300,000.

As well as great poise in front of goal, Rush's best asset was his movement. Blessed with great stamina, he constantly dragged defenders out of position and deceived them with late feints and runs – the perfect foil for the spontaneous creativity of Kenny Dalglish. A defender once claimed that keeping tabs on him was 'like marking a ribbon'.

Rush never achieved the recognition he deserved abroad. This was due in part to being Welsh, which meant he never had the opportunity to shine in a good international team, and to his unhappy season with Juventus. Bought by the Italians for £3.2 m, Rush was sold back to Liverpool for £2.8 m the following year, observing, profoundly, that the experience had been 'like being in a foreign country'. Rush should have retired at Liverpool, as lacklustre spells at Leeds and Newcastle did nothing for his reputation. Better to remember him as the highest scorer in Liverpool's history.

- He scored a record 44 FA Cup goals, including five in finals (also a record).
- He scored 49 League Cup goals (this is a record held jointly with Geoff Hurst).
- Rush the record breaker: 'I am proud and privileged to have beaten the record of a great player like Roger Hunt.'
- Rush had played only 33 games in the Fourth Division for Chester when Liverpool stepped in.
- He was PFA and Football Writers' Player of the Year, 1984.

VITAL STATISTICS

Place of Birth:	Flint, Wales
Date of Birth:	20 October 1961 **Died:** n/a
Caps:	73 (Wales) **Goals (International):** 28
Clubs:	Chester, Liverpool, Juventus, Leeds United, Newcastle United
Appearances:	Club (All Matches): 584
Goals:	Club (All Matches): 253
Trophies:	LT 1982–84, 1986, 1988, 1990; FAC 1986, 1989, 1992; LC 1981–83, 1994, 1995; EC 1981, 1984

LEGEND RATING	
Achievement	8.0
Skill	9.0
Teamwork	9.0
Passion	8.0
Personality	6.0
TOTAL	**40.0**

San Siro
Milan, Italy

THE SPECTACULAR SAN SIRO was built in 1925. Remodelled to the tune of £50 m for the 1990 World Cup Finals, it superseded even the original to remain one of the world's great sporting venues.

Originally home to AC Milan, they were joined after the Second World War by their local rivals Internazionale; the two have been happily co-habiting ever since. One can only imagine parochial outrage if Manchester City were rehoused at Old Trafford or Rangers became tenants at Celtic Park.

Today the ground is known as the Giuseppe Meazza Stadium, after it was renamed before Italia 90 in honour of the legendary Inter and Italian star of the 1920s and 1930s (he later played a swansong for Milan).

As a result of the improvements, the stadium has a unique system of spectator access, ramps running around its perimeter, an additional third tier of seating extending the capacity to 82,000, and a new roof enhancing the already intimidating atmosphere. Its spiralling towers corner give the impression of a modern-day fortress. The psychological advantage to its two home teams is immense.

☞ The original stadium was funded from an unlikely source. Tyre magnate Piero Pirelli provided much of the funding.
☞ The San Siro has hosted two European Cup finals. Internazionale enjoyed home advantage in 1965 to beat Benfica. In 1970, Feyenoord overcame Celtic.
☞ One of the great World Cup shocks occurred at the San Siro. The opening match of Italia 90 saw holders Argentina succumb 1-0 to Cameroon.
☞ The San Siro was so named after a local saint.
☞ The addition of the roof has restricted the amount of sunlight reaching the pitch. In recent years millions of pounds have been spent keeping the playing surface up to standard.

VITAL STATISTICS

Location:	Milan, Italy
Local Club:	AC Milan, Internazionale
Date Built:	1926
Current Capacity:	83,107
Max. Capacity:	83,107

Sanchez, Hugo
Real Madrid, Mexico

MEXICO'S BEST PLAYER wasn't the greatest servant to his home nation. Absent in Europe for most of his career and with a habit of crying off for all but the most important internationals, he was in frequent dudgeon with the authorities. This was a shame because an ordinary Mexican team needed his inspiration. Lively and mobile, Sanchez could shoot with either foot, and was exceptional in the air for a smallish, slim man. He is probably best remembered by European audiences for his trademark goal celebration, an acrobatic handspring he had perfected long before that sort of thing became de rigeur.

He appeared in two World Cup tournaments, although his first – as a 19-year-old prodigy in 1978 – was a disaster; the team were abject and Sanchez failed to live up to his pre-tournament billing. 1986 was much better. On home soil the Mexicans put on a decent show, reaching the quarter-finals. Sanchez enjoyed a sensational career in Spain with Real Madrid where his partnership with Emilio Butragueno was the spearhead of a team that collected five consecutive Spanish titles.

☞ The closest Sanchez got to a European Cup final was in 1989, when Real were beaten by AC Milan in the semi-final.

☞ Sanchez's famous goal celebration was inspired by his sister, an Olympic gymnast.

🖐 Sanchez was top scorer in La Liga from 1985–88.

☞ Sanchez scored the opener in Real Madrid's 5-1 first-leg win in their UEFA Cup final victory over Cologne. Surprisingly, this was his only success in Europe.

🖐 Butragueno, 'The Vulture' was one of Spain's finest strikers – he scored 4 goals in a 5-0 mauling of Denmark at the 1986 World Cup Finals.

VITAL STATISTICS

Place of Birth:	Mexico		
Date of Birth:	11 June 1958	**Died:** n/a	
Caps:	57 (Mexico)	**Goals (International):** 26	
Clubs:	UNAM, Atletico Madrid, Real Madrid, Rayo Vallecano		
Trophies:	PLA 1986, 1987, 1988, 1989, 1990; UEFAC 1986		

Achievement	7.0
Skill	9.0
Teamwork	7.0
Passion	8.0
Personality	8.0
TOTAL	**39.0**

LEGEND RATING

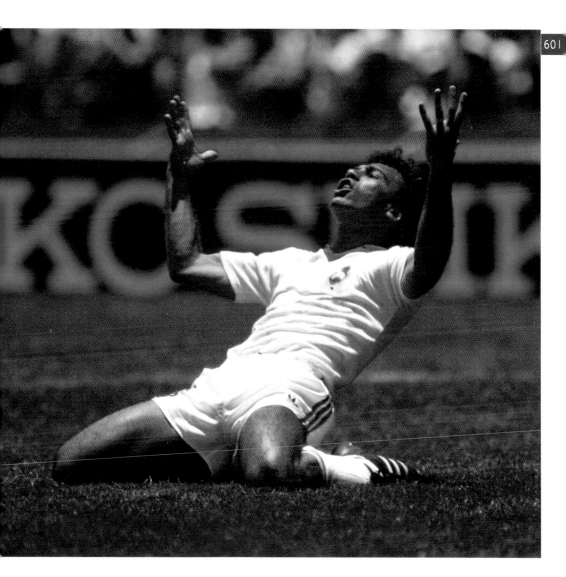

Saturday Night Fever
Match Of The Day

Until the BBC tried an experiment with its fledgling minority channel BBC2 in 1964, the only way to watch a league game was to turn up at the ground. That experiment was called *Match Of The Day*, and became a national institution and staple ingredient of Saturday-night viewing. Its first commentator, Kenneth Wolstenholme, was of the old school, a master of understatement and circumspect pronunciation. The programme was to eventually rely on Barry Davies and John Motson for its real colour, two men whose voices became synonymous with the show over a period of 30 years. In the early days only edited highlights from one or two games were transmitted but, following the arrival of Sky to the marketplace, the format was overhauled to include highlights of all matches from the top division. Presenters have come and gone down the years, the analytical approach of Jimmy Hill giving way to the smoothness of Des Lynam. More recently Gary Lineker was promoted to the anchor role, and it is he who currently introduces the show's coverage of FA Cup and international matches. Whatever the personnel, the signature tune has remained the same, acting as a musical comfort blanket to armchair fans for nearly four decades.

☞ The first broadcast on 22 August 1964 attracted only 20,000 viewers, less than half the crowd at Anfield as Liverpool beat Arsenal 2-0. First ever *MOTD* goal is scored by Roger Hunt.

👆 1966. Promoted to regular Saturday-night slot following success of the BBC's World Cup coverage.

☞ 1980–82. *MOTD* yo-yoed between Saturday night and Sunday afternoon as ITV muscled in on the BBC monopoly.

👆 1983. Live deal agreed with ITV, but a strike left screens football-free. Two years later *MOTD* lost league games for seven years to ITV.

👆 1992. Deal with Sky returned league action to *MOTD*. A nine-year run ended on 19 May 2001.

👆 August 2004. *MOTD* returns to our screens after a three year absence.

'Those who participate provide the poetry. Those who commentate provide the prose – and not very good prose at that. That's why so many ex-players have taken up commentating. It's called missionary work.'

Gary Lineker addressing the Oxford Union in 1990 in a debate on the motion that 'this house believes it is better to commentate than participate'

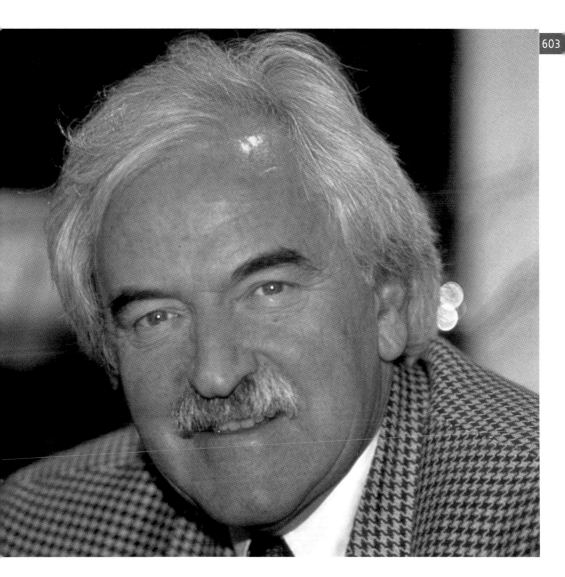

Savo's Day
AC Milan 4 Barcelona 0, 1994

THE 1994 EUROPEAN CUP FINAL brought together two genuine heavyweights. Barcelona had won the tournament two years before, and Milan didn't fancy becoming the first team to lose consecutive finals, having lost 1-0 to Marseille in 1993. Both sides had registered 3-0 wins in their semi-final matches, Barcelona against Porto and Milan against Monaco. So both were bullish about their chances. Before the match Barcelona coach Johan Cruyff had told anyone who would listen that his team was superior, and with the gifted Hristo Stoichkov in his ranks he had a right to feel upbeat. But Milan had confidence in their wonderful defence, where Capello used Marcel Desailly to compensate for the loss of Franco Baresi. In the end it was no contest. Barcelona were not awful, they were simply blown away by some of the most accomplished football ever played. The Italians were compact and organised, and in Dejan Savicevic they had the man for the occasion. While Stoichkov pouted ineffectually, Savicevic ran rings around Ronald Koeman and the Barcelona defence, making two first-half goals for Daniele Massaro and adding an outrageous third. Desailly scored a fourth before the hour, and the game was over.

☞ Desailly had won the European Cup with Marseille the year before, but the French club were later stripped of their title.

☞ Milan returned to the final the following year, but Savicevic was left out. A late Patrick Kluivert goal saw Ajax rob their title.

☞ Savicevic was a memeber of the Red Star Belgrade team that won a sterile 1991 final on penalties.

☞ The third goal was outstanding, Savicevic lobbing Zubizarreta from close to the touchline.

☞ Cruyff set about rebuilding his team the following season, off-loading Koeman and Zubizarreta among others.

SCORERS	Massaro 2, Savicevic, Desailly
EVENT	European Cup final, 18 May 1994, Athens

AC MILAN (Man: Fabio Capello)
1. Rossi 2. Tassotti 3. Maldini 4. Albertini 5. Galli 6. Panucci 7. Donadoni
8. Boban 9. Massaro 10. Savicevic 11. Desailly

BARCELONA (Man: Johan Cruyff)
1. Zubizarreta 2. Ferrer 3. Koeman 4. Nadal 5. Berguiristan 6. Bakero
7. Guardiola 8. Amor 9. Sergi 10. Stoichkov 11. Romario

Schiaffino, Juan

Uruguay

THE FIRST POST-WAR WORLD CUP, held in Brazil in 1950, saw the re-emergence of Uruguay as a powerful force. Built around a solid defence with an excellent goalkeeper in Maspoli, this attritional side wore down their opponents to claim the trophy. What creative spark they had came from inside-forward Schiaffino and the lively winger, Ghiggia. Fittingly these two scored the goals against Brazil that clinched the Cup.

Four years later Ghiggia had 'become' Italian, but Schiaffino remained as the main playmaker. Gaunt to the point of being emaciated, his physique concealed a rare determination and supple strength. An inventive passer and fine dribbler, Schiaffino was the orchestrator of Uruguay's finest displays at the 1954 World Cup, where the *Azzurri* proved too good for Scotland (7-0) and England (4-2), but bowed out 4-2 to Hungary in one of the classic semi-finals. That Juan Alberto Schiaffino stood tall against Hidegkuti, Czibor and the rest is testimony to his talent. His displays led AC Milan to invest in the talented Uruguayan. And it was money well spent as they won three of the next five Italian championships, and reached the 1958 European Cup final, where they went down narrowly to Real Madrid.

☞ Though Uruguayan, Schiaffino won four caps as a nationalised Italian.

☞ He later managed Penarol and, briefly, the Uruguayan national team.

✎ He scored the equaliser in the 1950 World Cup's deciding match against Brazil. He was set up by the brilliant Ghiggia, who scored the winner himself.

☞ Schiaffino played in the 1958 European Cup final for Milan against the mighty Real Madrid, scoring in a 3-2 defeat.

☞ AC Milan smashed the world-record transfer fee to land Schiaffino, paying a staggering £72,000.

VITAL STATISTICS

Place of Birth:	Montevideo, Uruguay
Date of Birth:	28 July 1925 **Died:** 13 November 2002
Caps:	22 (Uruguay); 4 (Italy)
Goals (International):	12
Clubs:	Penarol, AC Milan, Roma
Appearances:	Club (for Serie A): 188
Goals:	Club (for Serie A): 50
Trophies:	WorC 1950; SA 1955, 1957, 1959

Achievement	7.0
Skill	9.0
Teamwork	8.0
Passion	8.0
Personality	6.0
TOTAL	**38.0**

LEGEND RATING

Schmeichel, Peter

Manchester United, Denmark

OF ALL SIR ALEX FERGUSON'S signings as a manager, few were as shrewd as his capture in 1991 of goalkeeping giant Peter Schmeichel. (Knowing what they know now Brondby would surely have charged and received 30 times the £500,000 fee they asked United to cough up for the great Dane.) A giant presence between the sticks, Schmeichel's arrival provided a defensive platform that launched United on a decade of dominance. Though famous for bellowing vocal 'encouragement' to his team-mates – outbursts to match even the hair-drying performances of his manager – he was far more than just a big gob. His starfish presence shrank the goal for any onrushing forward and made him the best one-on-one keeper in the world (some would say of all time), while his last-gasp charges into the opposing penalty area started a trend and brought him a European goal. The burdens of United's year-round schedule saw him depart at the top, weeks after winning the treble, but retirement was a long way off for this enthusiastic fitness fanatic. A surprise return to the Premiership has seen him past his best at Aston Villa, but the void left by his departure at Old Trafford has never been truly filled. The sight of him at Maine Road in 2002–03 was a strange one for United fans. He finally retired in May 2003.

- 👆 He was a member of the Danish 1992 European Championship team. They won despite being rank outsiders.
- ☞ In season 1996–97, after a highly-publicised row at Highbury, Ian Wright accused him of racism.
- 👆 He is the only goalkeeper to have scored with two English clubs, Manchester United and Aston Villa.
- ☞ 'People say we have the best goalkeeper in the world. I wonder why we didn't bring him.' Danish team-mate Fleming Povlsen lowers Schmeichel's popularity rating at the 1992 European Championships.
- ☞ Schmeichel's penalty save from van Basten won the semi-final for Denmark. Povlsen's comments went unrecorded.

VITAL STATISTICS

Place of Birth:	Gladsaxe, Denmark
Date of Birth:	18 November 1963 **Died:** n/a
Caps:	122 (Denmark) **Goals (International):** 2
Clubs:	Hidvovre IF, Brondby, Manchester United, Sporting Lisbon, Aston Villa, Manchester City
Appearances:	Club (League): 587
Goals:	Club (League): 9
Trophies:	DLT 1987, 1988, 1990, 1991; LT 1993, 1994, 1996, 1997, 1999; FAC 1994, 1996, 1999; EC 1999; EuroC 1992

LEGEND RATING	
Achievement	9.0
Skill	9.0
Teamwork	7.0
Passion	10.0
Personality	7.0
TOTAL	**42.0**

Schoen, Helmut
West Germany

AFTER A MIDDLING CAREER as an inside-forward either side of the war, Helmut Schoen turned to coaching. In 1955 he teamed up with the seasoned German national coach, Sepp Herberger, and served an eight-year apprenticeship at the feet of the master. This period saw the World Cup winning side of 1954 break up, and a new squad emerge, centred around the balding centre forward Uwe Seeler and a dynamic young star by the name of Franz Beckenbauer. It also saw West Germany reaffirm their reputation for durability and resolve. In the 1966 World Cup they gave some typically powerful displays, eventually losing to England in the final and, with the phenomenal Gerd Müller added to their squad, they showed commendable consistency in reaching the semi-finals in 1970.

The emergence of yet another great player, Gunther Netzer, saw West Germany win the European Championship in 1972; but it was the World Cup this squad really wanted. And sure enough, their time came in 1974. With two world-class full-backs in Vogts and Breitner now in their armoury, West Germany won through to the final where, against expectations, Holland were worn down in true German style, and Schoen was able to retire a happy man.

- The German penchant for diving forwards seemed to start under Schoen. Helmut Haller was a proficient early exponent, and Bernd Holzenbein's antics won penalties in the semi-final and final in 1974.
- In 1966 Schoen received some criticism for playing Beckenbauer in midfield instead of at the back. By 1970 'Der Kaiser' was *in situ* as the greatest attacking central defender of them all.
- Schoen accommodated the explosive Müller in 1970 by moving Seeler back into midfield, where his wiles compensated for his diminishing speed.
- West Germany only narrowly qualified for the 1970 tournament, a last-gasp win over Scotland seeing them home.

VITAL STATISTICS

Place of Birth:	Dresden, Germany	
Date of Birth:	15 September 1915	**Died:** 23 February 1996
Caps:	16 (Germany)	**Goals (International):** 17
Clubs:	As Player: Dresden SC, Hertha Berlin, Wiesbaden, Saar; As Manager: Saar, West Germany	
Trophies:	WorC 1974; EuroC 1972	

LEGEND RATING

Achievement	10
Tactical Awareness	8
Motivation	8
Team Selection/Transfers	8
Personality	6
TOTAL	**40**

Scifo, Enzo
Belgium

BELGIUM'S MOST STYLISH modern player was in fact born of Italian parents, and was the subject of interest by the *Azzurri's* scouts before finally settling for Belgian citizenship. A boy wonder, he debuted for Anderlecht at 17 and won full international caps while still a teenager. Belgium's gain became more apparent as Scifo went on to lead their midfield in four World Cups from 1986–98. Even with Scifo, though, the Red Devils were never more than bridesmaids, their best performance being a surprise semi-final appearance in 1986.

Scifo's obvious talents made a move inevitable and a transfer to Internazionale ended his five-year spell in Belgium. Unhappy in Milan, he later enjoyed a couple of spells in French football before a better spell in Italy with Torino brought a rare trophy, the Italian Cup. Things came full circle in 1998 with a return to his first major club, Anderlecht. Scifo as club footballer will not be remembered, but as the most talented member of a succession of good, if not exceptional, Belgian sides, he deserves his place in European football history.

- ☞ Although a teenage prodigy, Scifo only won one trophy after the age of 21.
- ✋ Best moment? Scoring one of the penalties as Belgium beat Spain to win a 1986 World Cup semi-final place.
- ☞ Scifo nearly retired at 23 after his experiences at Milan, but was persuaded to reconsider by Auxerre manager Guy Roux.
- ☞ A dead-ball specialist, Scifo scored a memorable free kick against Paraguay in the 1986 World Cup – only to realise it was indirect.
- ✋ Scifo is one of only a handful of players to have played in four World Cup Finals tournaments.

VITAL STATISTICS

Place of Birth:	Le Louvierre, Belgium
Date of Birth:	19 February 1966 **Died:** n/a
Caps:	84 (Belgium) **Goals (International):** 14
Clubs:	Anderlecht, Inter Milan, Bordeaux, Auxerre, Torino, Monaco
Trophies:	BLT 1985, 1986, 1987; FLT 1997

LEGEND RATING	
Achievement	5.0
Skill	9.0
Teamwork	8.0
Passion	7.0
Personality	6.0
TOTAL	**35.0**

Scottish Goalies
English Jokes

SCOTTISH GOALKEEPERS are not usually treated with as much respect as they deserve – an old footballing cliché. But clichés, whilst overused, are usually born out of fact. And the fact, in this instance, is that Scotland, particularly in the last 40 years, has not been well served for goalkeepers. Many times in their history they have had a team the equal of England's, but without an international-class goalkeeper, never mind truly great performers such as Banks and Shilton.

Forget the performances of Frank Haffey in 1961 and Stewart Kennedy in 1975; they were one-off bad games by two poor goalkeepers who never played again for Scotland. The real issue is selection. The sheer number of caps given to Alan Rough (53) and Jim Leighton (91) is mind-boggling. Rough, a decent shot-stopper but ordinary all-round goalkeeper kept out David Harvey, the excellent Leeds goalkeeper. Leighton, occasionally inspired but more often indecisive and nervy, won more than twice as many caps as Andy Goram. Outspoken and controversial Goram may have been, but he was a far better goalkeeper than Leighton.

- Haffey, in his second match, conceded nine goals in an avalanche at Wembley – odd, it had taken a Bobby Charlton penalty to beat him in his first game.
- Kennedy's performance against England in a 5-1 defeat at Wembley made him a figure of fun for years. He was a bag of nerves and was discarded afterwards.
- Leighton played in Alex Ferguson's excellent Aberdeen team in the 1980s. He briefly re-joined Ferguson at Manchester United, but left in acrimonious circumstances after being dropped for the Cup final replay. They are still not on speaking terms.
- Scotland's current custodian, Neil Sullivan is an excellent goalkeeper. He's a Londoner.

'Two Andy Gorams, there's only two Andy Gorams,'

Kilmarnock fans after Goram was diagnosed with mild schizophrenia

Seaman, David
Arsenal, England

DAVID SEAMAN cost Arsenal £1.3 m from QPR in 1990. Perhaps not a bargain on the same scale as Alex Ferguson's swoop for Peter Schmeichel, but not a bad bit of business. After joining the Gunners, Seaman helped the club to a succession of trophies, including the 1998 League and Cup double.

A usually reliable keeper, Seaman has been harshly pilloried for a couple of high-profile errors; in the 1995 European Cup Winners' Cup final he was lobbed by Real Zaragoza's Nayim from the half-way line and, against Germany in a World Cup qualifier in 2000, he was beaten from 35 yards by a Dietmar Hamann free-kick. But those who criticise him for this conveniently forget the countless hours of impeccable service he gave both Arsenal and England. Seaman was England's number one for most of the last decade, a period in which only Tim Flowers and Nigel Martyn seriously threatened to displace him. He was outstanding at both Euro 96, France 98 and the 2002 World Cup Finals, despite his over-publicised mistake against Brazil. His fantastic, last-minute save in the 2003 FA Cup semi-final was the perfect riposte to critics who thought he was past his best.

☞ Seaman flirted with professional cricket as a youngster; he was a powerful fast bowler in Yorkshire league cricket.

👌 Not bad in the kitchen, either, Seaman was winner of a celebrity *Ready Steady Cook* programme in 1998.

☞ In a 1997 World Cup qualifier against Moldova Seaman captained England for the first time.

👌 Seaman redeemed himself for the Hamann goal, making a fabulous save moments before England took a 2-1 lead in the return game in Munich.

👎 January 2004: after half a season in poor form at Manchester City, injury forced his retirement, not the best swansong for one of England's finest.

VITAL STATISTICS

Place of Birth:	Rotherham, England	
Date of Birth:	19 September 1963	**Died:** n/a
Caps:	75 (England)	**Goals (International):** 0
Clubs:	Peterborough United, Birmingham, Queens Park Rangers, Arsenal, Manchester City	
Appearances:	Club (League): 731	
Goals:	Club (League): 0	
Trophies:	LT 1991, 1998, 2002; FAC 1993, 1998, 2002, 2003; LC 1993; CWC 1994	

LEGEND RATING	
Achievement	8.0
Skill	8.0
Teamwork	7.0
Passion	7.0
Personality	7.0
TOTAL	**37.0**

Seeler, Uwe
Hamburg, West Germany

PELÉ IS ONE OF TWO PLAYERS to have scored in four World Cup Finals tournaments. The other is Uwe Seeler, who played and scored in the same four tournaments graced by the great Brazilian. Seeler first appeared for Germany as a precocious teenager in the World Cup of 1958, but by the time the next Finals came around he was the finished article – a powerful, mobile centre forward, two-footed and decent in the air.

In the 1966 World Cup Seeler, a little slower but still a potent goalscorer, led the Germans to the final – and we all know what happened next. Despite their failure in England, Germany stuck with Seeler for the next tournament in Mexico where, aged 34, he played in a midfield role that allowed Helmut Schoen to accommodate Gerd Müller. The satisfaction of gaining revenge over England was tempered by defeat in a great semi-final against Italy. Seeler won several trophies at club level with Hamburg, mainly a succession of regional championships prior to the formation of the joint Bundesliga in 1964. He was top scorer with 30 in the first season of the new national league, and remains Hamburg's most celebrated star. Even more popular than Kevin Keegan.

☞ Seeler was only 17 when he made his debut for Germany, with relatively few Bundesliga performances behind him.

☝ His 21 World Cup appearances remained a record until the arrival of Lothar Matthaus.

☝ Seeler scored 404 goals in 476 league appearances. In total he scored over 500 goals in over 700 games.

☞ Inter Milan offered the vast sum of £1 m for Seeler in 1961, but still he stayed at Hamburg.

☝ Seeler scored a hat-trick against reigning Bundesliga champions Borussia Dortmund, as Hamburg won the 1963 German Cup final 3-0.

VITAL STATISTICS

Place of Birth:	Hamburg, West Germany	
Date of Birth:	5 November 1936	**Died:** n/a
Caps:	72 (W. Germany)	**Goals (International):** 43
Clubs:	Hamburg	
Appearances:	Club (All Matches): 710	
Goals:	Club (All Matches): 551	
Trophies:	BLG 1960	

Achievement	9.0
Skill	8.0
Teamwork	9.0
Passion	7.0
Personality	7.0
TOTAL	**40.0**

LEGEND RATING

Shackleton, Len
Sunderland, England

ENGLAND MANAGERS have traditionally regarded talented individual players with suspicion, often ignoring them in favour of more workaday but malleable players. In recent times Glenn Hoddle and Matt Le Tissier were both victims of this peculiar mindset, while an earlier example is Len Shackleton. A plain-speaking Yorkshireman 'Shack's' blunt observations did not always go down well with managers and administrators, but plain was never an adjective to describe his play. He was the most skilful English player of the 1940s and 1950s. A small inside-forward, he cut swathes through opposing defences with instant ball control and supreme dribbling ability. Moving to Newcastle in 1946 proved an important step in his career, as his performances at St James's Park made him a crowd favourite. But a clash with management saw him sold to neighbours Sunderland. It is at Roker Park where he will be most fondly remembered. If Shackleton was on form, so were Sunderland. His performances made a struggling First Division side a competent one, and it was probably no fluke that the fading of the great man's powers coincided with the club being relegated in 1957–58. That was to be Shackleton's final season. Sunderland have never found another like him.

☞ In 1935–36 Shackleton became the shortest-ever English schoolboy international, standing at a Lilliputian 4 ft 0 in.

✎ He scored six times on his debut for Newcastle in a 13-0 win over Newport.

☞ In his autobiography, Shackleton headed one chapter 'The Average Director's Knowledge of Football'. The rest of the page was left blank.

☞ The British transfer record was broken twice to buy Shackleton. Newcastle paid Bradford Park Avenue £13,000 in 1946, receiving over £20,000 from Sunderland 16 months later.

☞ His five England caps are a scandalous under-use of his talent. Paul Mariner won 35.

VITAL STATISTICS

Place of Birth:	Bradford, England	
Date of Birth:	3 May 1922	**Died:** 28 November 2000
Caps:	5 (England)	**Goals (International):** 0
Clubs:	Bradford Park Avenue, Newcastle, Sunderland	
Appearances:	Club (for Sunderland): 348	
Goals:	Club (for Sunderland): 101	
Trophies:	None	

Achievement	5.0
Skill	9.0
Teamwork	7.0
Passion	8.0
Personality	9.0
TOTAL	**38.0**

LEGEND RATING

Shankly, Bill
Liverpool, Scotland

AFTER A PLAYING CAREER severely curtailed by the war, in which the highlight was an FA Cup winner's medal with Preston in 1938, Shankly entered football management with Carlisle, and started on his road to destiny. The apprenticeship was long and unglamorous; several years in the lower divisions with unfashionable clubs gave no indication of what was to come. Shankly seemed an odd choice for a struggling Liverpool in 1959, and their lean spell continued until 1964 when a league title finally came their way for the first time in 17 years. A further two championships, two FA Cups and a UEFA Cup followed before Shankly's retirement in 1974.

His contribution to Liverpool could never be measured in trophies alone, though. The wisecracking Scot laid the foundations of the 'boot-room' dynasty at Anfield, a think-tank of ideas and tactics that was to serve Liverpool well for 20 years. The continuity of playing style and management, and the philosophy of self-belief that characterised the club across that time were Shankly's legacy.

- Liverpool won the title in 1966 using only 14 players.
- Shankly never won the European Cup – the closest he came was a controversial defeat by Inter Milan in the 1965 semi-finals.
- An earthy humorist, Shankly's most famous observation was: 'Football is not a matter of life and death, I can assure you it is much more important than that.'
- 'The socialism I believe in is not really politics. It is a way of living. It is humanity. I believe the only way to live and be truly successful is by collective effort, with everyone working for each other, everyone helping each other, and everyone having a share of the rewards at the end of the day … it's the way I see football and the way I see life.' Bill Shankly

VITAL STATISTICS

Place of Birth:	Glenbuck, Ayrshire, Scotland	Achievement	9
Date of Birth:	2 September 1913 **Died:** 28 September 1981	Tactical Awareness	9
Caps:	5 (Scotland) **Goals (International):** 0	Motivation	10
Clubs:	As Player: Carlisle United, Preston North End;	Team Selection/Transfers	9
	As Manager: Carlisle United, Grimsby Town,	Personality	9
	Workington, Huddersfield Town, Liverpool		
Trophies:	LT 1964, 1966, 1973; FAC 1965, 1974;	**TOTAL**	**46**
	UEFAC 1973		

LEGEND RATING

Shearer, Alan

Blackburn Rovers, Newcastle United, England

NOT ESPECIALLY TALL, or particularly quick come to that, Alan Shearer is a striker who relies on strength and timing. He is also an exceptionally fine header of the ball – probably the best since Andy Gray – and possesses a thumping right foot.

Shearer emerged as a prodigy at Southampton, where he managed to shine in a mediocre side without making the breakthrough at international level. Then Jack Walker's cash, plus the promise of winning the sort of trophies that were always going to elude him at Southampton, lured him to Blackburn Rovers. At Ewood Park Shearer's scoring rate increased immediately, and his prolific partnership with Chris Sutton propelled Blackburn to the league title in 1995. Later he struck up a similarly fruitful partnership for England with Teddy Sheringham, a double-act that climaxed with the destruction of Holland at Wembley in the group stages of Euro 96.

That same year Shearer returned to Newcastle, his boyhood team. Since then he has been hampered by a series of injuries, but when fit has continued to score goals. Now retired from international football to protect his body from further punishment, Shearer has been touted as a managerial successor to Bobby Robson at St James's Park. Watch this space….

☞ Both Shearer's domestic transfers were record fees; his £15 m move to Newcastle was a then world record.

✍ He scored 37 goals in Blackburn's title-winning season. The following season he got 30 again, becoming the first player to reach the target in three consecutive seasons having scored 30 plus in the previous campaign.

✍ He was the youngest top-division player to score a hat-trick (17 years, 140 days, for Southampton in 4-2 win over Arsenal).

✍ He scored in normal time and in the shoot-outs in two of England's recent high-profile matches (against Germany at Euro 96 and Argentina at France 98).

✍ He is the joint fourth-highest England goal scorer.

VITAL STATISTICS

Place of Birth:	Newcastle, England		Achievement	8.0
Date of Birth:	13 August 1970	**Died:** n/a	Skill	8.0
Caps:	63 (England)	**Goals (International):** 30	Teamwork	9.0
Clubs:	Southampton, Blackburn Rovers, Newcastle		Passion	8.0
Appearances:	Club (League): 531		Personality	7.0
Goals:	Club (League): 302			
Trophies:	LT 1995		**TOTAL**	**40.0**

LEGEND RATING

Sheringham, Teddy

Tottenham Hotspur, Manchester United, England

'OH, TEDDY, TEDDY, he went to Man United and he won f*** all!' In 1998, following Teddy Sheringham's first and unsuccessful season at Old Trafford, this became a popular chant across the country. Having been in and out of the team all year (Yorke and Cole were Fergie's preferred combination), Sheringham, with a Premiership winner's medal already in the bag, came on as a ninth-minute substitute in the 1999 FA Cup final and scored as United beat Newcastle 2-0. The following week he again made a substitute appearance and hit the equaliser in the Red Devils' unforgettable 2-1 triumph over Bayern Munich. From 'f*** all' to a hat-trick of medals in just 12 months.

Recognition for Sheringham came relatively late. Regarded as a journeyman at Millwall and Nottingham Forest, he blossomed at Spurs, forming a deadly combination with Jurgen Klinsmann. Accusing Spurs of lacking ambition he then left for United, but returned to his spiritual home for a swansong in 2001, immediately adding another dimension to an otherwise prosaic side. A move, at 37, to Portsmouth saw a player past his best struggling to galvanise a poor team.

Sheringham's partnership with Alan Shearer was instinctive and awesome, and they inspired England to the semi-finals of Euro 96.

- ✋ 1999. Scored as a substitute for United in both the FA Cup final (after 90 seconds) and European Cup final.
- ✋ Repeats the feat in England's vital World Cup qualifier against Greece in 2001, scoring with his first touch to level at 1-1.
- ✋ Sheringham's finest international performance came during Euro 96 as he and Shearer scored two apiece in the 4-1 destruction of Holland.
- ☞ Sheringham played in the 2002 World Cup Finals, becoming the oldest outfield England player to appear in the Finals.
- ✋ Sheringham was both PFA and Football Writers' Player of the Year in 2001.

VITAL STATISTICS

Place of Birth:	Highams Park, England	
Date of Birth:	2 April 1966	**Died:** n/a
Caps:	51 (England)	**Goals (International):** 11
Clubs:	Millwall, Aldershot, Notthingham Forest,	
	Tottenham, Manchester United, West Ham United	
Appearances:	Club (League): 711	
Goals:	Club (League): 285	
Trophies:	LT 1999, 2000, 2001; FAC 1999; EC 1999	

LEGEND RATING	
Achievement	9.0
Skill	8.0
Teamwork	8.0
Passion	7.0
Personality	7.0
TOTAL	**39.0**

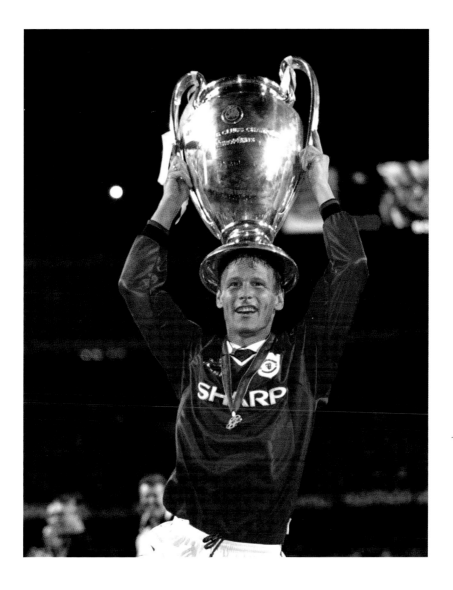

Shevchenko, Andrei

Dynamo Kiev, AC Milan, Ukraine

IN THE EARLY NINETIES, we thought Andrei Kanchelskis was the quickest and most skilful Ukrainian in the game. He was for a while, but the 'Ukraine train' was shunted into a siding on the arrival of Andrei Shevchenko. The star in a Milan team that is never short of them, Shevchenko has a winger's pace coupled with a centre forward's predatory instincts. A fearsome shot in either foot, often delivered on the run, make him a complete forward.

He came to prominence for Dynamo Kiev, where his performances in the shop window of the Champions League made a move inevitable. The bigger the opposition, the better he played. Shevchenko's displays against Barcelona and Real Madrid earned him rave notices but it was Italy, not Spain, who captured his signature. Although his own performances were never in doubt, finding the right attacking partner for Shevchenko proved difficult; he never clicked with Bierhoff or Weah. The key was the recruitment of fellow countryman Sergei Rebrov, allowing them to renew their fierce form for Kiev. Despite Rebrov's departure, he has continued to dominate the Milan forward line; six seasons with an Italian club is unusual for an overseas striker. The pinnacle of his career with the Italian giants was a Champions League winners' medal in 2003.

☞ In 1986, Shevchenko started with the Dynamo Kiev junior training scheme aged 10. Five years later, he was evacuated to avoid the radioactive fallout from Chernobyl.

☞ His value to Milan was emphasised when club president Berlusconi awarded Shevchenko a four-year contract worth a reported $64,000 per week.

👍 He is often compared with great Russian strikers Blokhin and Belanov. All three are great finishers, although Shevchenko is a more versatile player than either.

👍 Shevchenko scored the winning penalty when Milan eclipsed Serie A rivals in the 2003 Champions League final.

👍 December 2004: voted European Footballer of the Year.

VITAL STATISTICS

Place of Birth:	Dvirkivshchyna, Kiev, Ukraine	
Date of Birth:	29 September 1976	**Died:** n/a
Caps:	52 (Ukraine)	**Goals (International):** 22
Clubs:	Dynamo Kiev, AC Milan	
Appearances:	Club (League): 275	
Goals:	Club (League): 162	
Trophies:	ULT 1995–99; EC 2003; SA 2004	

Achievement	5.0
Skill	9.0
Teamwork	8.0
Passion	8.0
Personality	5.0
TOTAL	**35.0**

LEGEND RATING

Shilton, Peter

Nottingham Forest, Southampton, England

PETER SHILTON CONTINUED PLAYING for so long that it seemed the only thing likely to persuade him to hang up his gloves was the arrival of his bus pass in the post. Having made his debut for Leicester in 1966, aged 17, he was still playing league football aged 47. His best spell as a club footballer was in Brian Clough's Nottingham Forest that won the European Cup twice, but he also played in the Southampton side that contained five England captains – himself, Keegan, Watson, Mills and Channon.

For a number of years Shilton played second fiddle or alternated with Ray Clemence in the England goal; at times it seemed that everyone bar the managers could see he was the better of the two men. He later made the number one jersey his own, and though he went on to record a record number of England caps (125), one wonders what tally he may have reached if his international managers had been more decisive. Shilton played in three World Cups, conceding only one goal in the 1982 tournament as England were eliminated without losing. Once he had ironed out early gremlins in his technique, Shilton became the complete goalkeeper. A great shot-stopper, although perhaps not in the same class as Gordon Banks, dominant in the area, and fast off his line.

- Shilton played his 1,000th league game for Leyton Orient against Brighton. Fittingly, he kept a clean sheet.
- Surprisingly, he only ever played in one FA Cup final, finishing on the losing side with Leicester in 1969.
- The £325,000 Stoke paid Leicester for Shilton was a world record for a goalkeeper.
- Shilton filed for bankruptcy in the 1990s, amid reports he had accrued heavy gambling debts.
- Shilton received an MBE in 1986, and an OBE in 1991.

VITAL STATISTICS

Place of Birth:	Leicester, England
Date of Birth:	18 September 1949 **Died:** n/a
Caps:	125 (England) **Goals (International):** 0
Clubs:	Leicester City, Stoke City, Nottingham Forest, Southampton, Derby County, Plymouth Argyle, Wimbledon, Bolton Wanderers, Coventry City, West Ham, Leyton Orient
Appearances:	Club (League): 1005
Goals:	Club (League): 0
Trophies:	EC 1979, 1980; LT 1978; LC 1979

LEGEND RATING	
Achievement	9.0
Skill	9.0
Teamwork	8.0
Passion	9.0
Personality	7.0
TOTAL	**42.0**

Shirts Off

Charity Shield, 1974

THE CHARITY SHIELD is invariably billed as the season's 'curtain raiser'. In truth it's usually nothing of the sort; if watching two ring-rusty teams pussyfoot around each other for 90 minutes is raising the curtain then it might be better to keep it drawn. But not all Charity Shield matches are dull. Take 1974 for instance. After an hour of simmering ill-feeling, the flashpoint occurred on the hour. Billy Bremner and Kevin Keegan, neither with the longest of fuses, traded blows at the edge of the penalty area. Their dismissals were inevitable, and the pair compounded their shame by petulantly throwing off their shirts en route to the tunnel. The FA was particularly sensitive to accusations that it was failing to put its hooligan house in order. These were the dark days of the mid-1970s, and images of Spurs fans rioting in Rotterdam a few weeks earlier were still fresh in the mind. For Bremner and Keegan, Wembley 1974 was the wrong place and the wrong time. The FA felt compelled to act. The fine of £500 each was huge, the 11-week bans bigger still. Scapegoats they certainly were, but Bremner and Keegan had only themselves to blame.

☞ Niggle was usually in the air with Revie's Leeds, and wounded Merseyside pride at surrendering the title to them the previous season gave the occasion an extra dash of spice.

☜ Bremner and Keegan became the first British players to be sent off at Wembley. Only Argentina's Rattin had enjoyed the dubious honour before them.

☞ The Charity Shield was televised live for the first time that year, a fact that hardly lessened the outrage.

☞ Opportunistic MPs had a field day. Some called for a life ban and a civil prosecution, but they probably wanted to hang shoplifters as well.

'Players must learn that they cannot throw punches at each other.'

FA Secretary Ted Croker after throwing the book

Simply The Best
Brazil 4 Italy 1, 1970

IT WAS THE GAME that settled the argument as to the greatest-ever team. Brazil had saved the best until last, perpetuating a philosophy that simply believed in scoring more goals than the opposition.

Their opponents were hardly makeweights. A team with Facchetti at its defensive heart and Luigi Riva a spearhead had seen off Germany in an epic semi-final – but they had the misfortune to run into a forward line with every great player at his peak.

The main surprise was that after 65 minutes, the score was still 1-1. Pelé's opener inside 20 minutes appeared to set up a procession, but the Achilles' heel that was Brazil's defence handed Boninsegna an equaliser before half-time. Once Gerson had restored the lead with a trademark long-range strike though, normal service was resumed. The fourth goal was pure Brazil, Carlos Alberto joyously lashing home after a gorgeous build-up saw the ball rolled languidly into his path by Pelé. It remains one of the World Cup's most repeated goals – a glorious souvenir of a peerless team.

- The match that won Brazil their third World Cup saw them awarded the Jules Rimet trophy outright.
- Jairzinho's goal meant he scored in all six games of the tournament.
- Mario Zagallo was the first man to win the World Cup as both a player and a coach.
- Zagallo coached Brazil again at France 98. They failed to repeat the performance, falling ingloriously to the hosts in the final.
- Pelé's opener was Brazil's 100th goal in the World Cup Finals.

SCORERS **Brazil:** Pelé, Gerson, Jairzinho, Carlos Alberto
Italy: Boninsegna
EVENT World Cup Final, Estadio Azteca, Mexico City, 21 June 1970

BRAZIL (Man: Mario Zagallo)
1. Felix 2. Carlos Alberto 3. Brito 4. Piazza 5. Everaldo 6. Clodoaldo
7. Gerson 8. Jairzinho 9. Tostao 10. Pelé 11. Rivelino
ITALY (Man: Feruccio Valcareggi)
1. Albertosi 2. Cera 3. Burgnich 4. Bertini (Juliano) 5. Rosato 6. Facchetti
7. Domenghini 8. Mazzola 9. de Sisti 10. Boninsenga (Rivera) 11. Riva

Simulation

Or Cheating, as it's Commonly Known

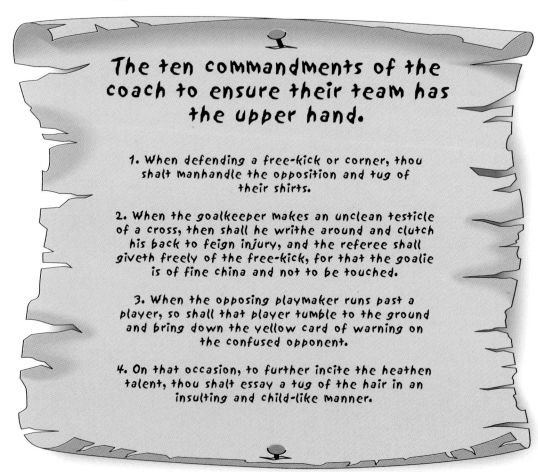

The ten commandments of the coach to ensure their team has the upper hand.

1. When defending a free-kick or corner, thou shalt manhandle the opposition and tug of their shirts.

2. When the goalkeeper makes an unclean testicle of a cross, then shall he writhe around and clutch his back to feign injury, and the referee shall giveth freely of the free-kick, for that the goalie is of fine china and not to be touched.

3. When the opposing playmaker runs past a player, so shall that player tumble to the ground and bring down the yellow card of warning on the confused opponent.

4. On that occasion, to further incite the heathen talent, thou shalt essay a tug of the hair in an insulting and child-like manner.

5. When the striker has pushed the ball too far past the defender, then shall he tumble to the ground in a melodramatic fashion, trusting in the inadequacy of the black-clad judiciary.

6. Whensoever a foul tackle is committed on a player, then shall that player wave his hand in supplication, demanding the yellow card of wrath for the pugilist.

7. Should, in the instance of commandment six, the tackled player be too busy rolling around in agony, then shall one of his nearby colleagues take upon themselves the onerous task of officious hand-waving.

8. Should a player be tackled in a robust and physical manner, so shall that player roll over to a count of five. The player shall them commence clutching a body part as if in agony, irrespective of whether any contact was made with that particular body part.

9. When a player's dramatic performance demands the attention of the physician, then shall that player be honour-bound to offend the opposition by skipping around like a lamb shortly after the departure of that physician.

10. Should a free-kick or penalty be awarded to the opposition, then shall the defenders undergo a routine of gamesmanship and delay until the moment the kick is struck.

Socrates
Brazil

SOCRATES' LAST KICK in a Brazilian shirt was missing one of the penalties in the quarter-final shoot-out defeat by France at the 1986 World Cup. It was a sad end for the tall, bearded midfielder who, much as he did four years earlier in Spain, had illuminated the tournament with his repertoire of impudent, lazy skills. No fitness fanatic – he smoked 20 cigarettes a day – Socrates appeared to stroll through games, spraying passes and shots like a merchant dispensing largesse to the less fortunate. The 1982 midfield of Socrates, Zico, Falcao and Cerezo would have won most World Cups, but the strikers were uncharacteristically lightweight for a Brazilian side. Four years later a generally lethargic Brazilian team failed to do themselves justice, and France's penalty win was deserved. Socrates played the majority of his club football for various sides in Brazil, apart from a disastrous season at Fiorentina in 1984 where the physical demands of European club football and the alien lifestyle quickly saw him scurry home. Socrates has remained an opinionated and intelligent observer of the game, and in recent years has been a fierce critic of the officials running Brazilian football. In October 2004, the 50-year-old Socrates dropped Lancastrian jaws by signing a month's contract with non-league Garforth Town. It isn't how we'll remember him.

- Socrates' goal against the USSR in 1982 was a classic, sidestepping two tackles and thrashing a missile of a shot into the top corner.
- In the 1986 World Cup Socrates scored with a cheeky penalty, without a run-up, against Poland. When he tried a repeat in the quarter-final shoot-out, French goalkeeper Bats saved easily.
- Known as 'The Doctor' due to his medical training, it is ironic that Socrates was a high-profile sporting smoker.
- Socrates younger brother played for Brazil under the pseudonym Rai.
- No boy-wonder, Socrates was 25 before he played for Brazil.

VITAL STATISTICS

Place of Birth:	Brazil		
Date of Birth:	19 February 1954	**Died:** n/a	
Caps:	60 (Brazil)	**Goals (International):** 22	
Clubs:	Botafogo, Corinthians, Fiorentina, Flamengo, Santos		
Appearances:	Club (for Corinthians): 302		
Goals:	Club (for Corinthians): 166		
Trophies:	None		

Achievement	7.0
Skill	10.0
Teamwork	8.0
Passion	8.0
Personality	9.0
TOTAL	**42.0**

LEGEND RATING

Somersaults and Salsa
The Fine Art of Goal Celebration

OLD BLACK-AND-WHITE newsreel shots of footballers scoring goals and trotting, stony-faced back to the centre circle seem to come from a different game. No kissing, no cuddling, no diving, no fist-clenching, no ripping the shirt off, no gymnastics, no mime, no tableaux vivants. How dull it all must have been.

However, the amateur dramatics of the modern goal scorer have become tedious. The obligatory cupping of the ear to mock a silenced home crowd, the plunge to the knees by the corner flag – no wonder referees were instructed to curb the worst excesses. Whole teams were charging towards the scorer, engulfing them in scrums of adulation.

Who knows where it all started? Charlie George lying flat out on the Wembley turf after firing in the winner against Liverpool? Others have refined and re-defined the art: Hugo Sanchez, Real Madrid's great Mexican, with his trademark somersault; Klinsmann plunging to the ground in self-mockery of his reputation as a diver; Roger Milla and Lee Sharpe posing around the corner flag. Entire teams got involved in complicated routines, the most bizarre being Chelsea's reproduction of a classical painting following a strike by Roberto di Matteo. Oh dear.

- The most athletic? Peter Beagrie, the much-travelled winger, has treated many a ground to a somersault worthy of Sanchez.
- The worst? Has to be the awful baby-cradling pantomime introduced by Brazilian Bebeto at the 1994 World Cup.
- The silliest? Aylesbury Town, after a cup goal, waddling around on their knees doing the Aylesbury duck.
- The most irresponsible? Robbie Fowler pretending to snort cocaine off the dead-ball line.
- The most ill-judged? Not strictly after a goal, but at the end of the 1993 League Cup final, Tony Adams threw goal scorer Steve Morrow over his shoulder. Morrow broke his arm and missed the FA Cup final as a result.

'I made a two-fingered gesture towards the fans to show that I had scored twice. It must have been misinterpreted.'

Paul Peschisolido

Souness, Graeme
Liverpool, Rangers, Scotland

AS A PLAYER Graeme Souness was a manager's dream. Possessed of great vision, passing ability and a tremendous shot, he was also blessed with a steel and aggression that set him apart from other playmakers. The downside was his short fuse, and seeming inability to curb his violent streak. It was Souness' form in a moderate Middlesbrough side that prompted Liverpool to shell out £325,000 for his signature – a British record that was to last only a month. He later left Anfield for a successful spell in Italy with Sampdoria before returning to Britain as player-manager of Glasgow Rangers. Souness' first season at Rangers saw them win their first Scottish title for nine years. An orgy of success at Ibrox was followed by a fraught period as Liverpool manager where, after some less-than-prudent transfer business, he was eventually forced into tending his resignation (the end came following an embarrassing FA Cup defeat by Bristol City in 1994). After a spell in Portugal as Benfica boss, Souness took charge at Blackburn Rovers, with whom he won promotion to the Premiership in 2001.

In a cloak-and-dagger move, Souness was announced as Newcastle's manager following the grubby dismissal of Bobby Robson. Tearaways such as Bellamy are already feeling the iron fist of his discipline.

🖐 He signed Paul Stewart from Tottenham with a view to using him as Liverpool's main striker – possibly one of the worst signings ever by a major club.

🖐 Souness was pilloried in Liverpool for his dealings with *The Sun* newspaper, the paper that earned the eternal enmity of the city for their crass coverage of the Hillsborough disaster.

VITAL STATISTICS

Place of Birth:	Edinburgh, Scotland
Date of Birth:	6 May 1953 **Died:** n/a
Caps:	54 (Scotland) **Goals (International):** 4
Clubs:	As Player: Tottenham, Middlesbrough, Liverpool, Sampdoria, Rangers; As Manager: Rangers, Liverpool, Benfica, Blackburn Rovers, Newcastle United
Appearances:	Club (All Matches): 528
Goals:	Club (All Matches): 78
Trophies:	LT 1979–80, 1982–84; LC 1981–84, (2000); EC 1981, 1984; FAC (1992); SLT (1987, 1989–91)

MANAGER		PLAYER	
Achievement	7	Achievement	9
Tactical Awareness	7	Skill	8
Motivation	7	Teamwork	8
Team Selection/Transfers	7	Passion	7
Personality	6	Personality	6
TOTAL	**34**	**TOTAL**	**38**

LEGEND RATING

Spot-Luck

Brazil 1 France 1, 1986 (aet) (France won 4-3 on penalties)

WOULD PLATINI'S GENIUS carry the day against a talented, but curiously defensive Brazil? The match proved to be a tight affair – technically excellent but with few clear-cut chances. Careca opened the scoring with a fine strike, but Platini, celebrating his 31st birthday, pulled the French level. The game came alive in the last 20 minutes. Two minutes after Zico's entrance as a substitute, Brazil were awarded a dubious penalty. Four years before, Zico had tucked away a penalty in similar circumstances, but history was not to repeat itself – he missed, and the game headed into extra-time.

France were denied an obvious penalty when Bellone was upended by the goalkeeper, and Socrates, of all people, spurned an easy chance a minute later. And so to penalties. Socrates attempted a repeat of his nonchalant chip earlier in the tournament, but succeeded only in effecting a back-pass to Joel Bats. Platini, with a chance to all but seal the result, then blazed high over the bar, but following a miss by Julio Cesar, his midfield colleague Luis Fernandez struck the winning penalty for France.

☞ Penalty Shoot-out: Brazil: Socrates (missed), Alemao, Zico, Branco, Julio Cesar (missed)
France: Stopyra, Amoros, Bellone, Platini (missed), Fernandez.

👎 France lost to Germany in the semi-final (again), and their team broke up after the tournament. They would win the next Finals tournament in which they competed, in 1998.

👎 Socrates and Zico never played for Brazil again – the end of an era.

☞ Careca vied with Gary Lineker as the best striker in the tournament. Brazil might have achieved more if they had found him a decent partner.

SCORERS	**Brazil:** Careca, 17
	France: Platini, 41
EVENT	World Cup quarter-final, Guadalajara, 21 June 1986
BRAZIL	(Man: Tele Santana)
	1. Carlos 2. Josimar 3. Branco 4. Elzo 5. Julio Cesar 6. Edinho 7. Junior
	8. Alemao 9. Socrates 10. Careca 11. Müller
FRANCE	(Man: Henri Michel)
	1. Bats 2. Amoros 3. Tusseau 4. Fernandez 5. Bossis 6. Battiston
	7. Giresse 8. Tigana 9. Stopyra 10. Platini 11. Rocheteau

Stein, Jock
Celtic, Scotland

JOCK STEIN'S EXPLOITS as a player merit more than a passing mention in the Celtic history books, having won the League and Cup in a five-year career at Parkhead. But it was his feats as manager that ensured his legendary status. Stein broke Rangers' domination of Scottish football in the 1960s, and presided over the most successful period in Celtic's history – a record run of nine consecutive league titles, including two domestic trebles.

Football and this son of a Lanarkshire miner nearly parted company in the early days, as he drifted from Albion Rovers to Llanelli before Celtic gave him his big break. Stein's most memorable accomplishment was bringing the European Cup to Glasgow in 1967 when, against an all-star Inter team, he masterminded a stunning 2-1 victory in Lisbon. In 1978, following a near-fatal car crash and a row over his appointment to the Celtic board, he left the club to take up the job of Scotland manager, where his eight-year tenure brought two successive qualifications for the World Cup. Tragically, Stein was not around to take his team to Mexico in 1986. During Scotland's final, victorious qualifying match against Wales in Cardiff he collapsed on the touchline and died of a heart-attack.

☞ Only one of his 26 managerial honours was not with Celtic (the 1961 Scottish Cup with Dunfermline).

☞ Stein managed Leeds United in 1978 for just 44 days, the same number as Brian Clough four years earlier.

☜ He reached the World Cup Finals as Scotland manager in 1982, but lost out to Brazil and the USSR in a strong group.

☞ Bill Shankly to Stein after Celtic's European Cup final win: 'John, you're immortal.'

☜ Alex Ferguson took temporary charge of Scotland after Stein's death, but failed to get them through the group stage at Mexico 86.

VITAL STATISTICS

Place of Birth:	Burnbank, Scotland
Date of Birth:	5 October 1923 **Died:** 11 September 1985
Caps:	0 **Goals (International):** 0
Clubs:	As Player: Albion Rovers, Llanelli, Celtic;
	As Manager: Dunfermline, Hibernian, Celtic,
	Leeds United
Trophies:	SLT 1966–74, 1977; SFAC 1961, 1965, 1967,
	1969, 1971, 1972, 1974, 1975, 1977; EC 1967

LEGEND RATING	
Achievement	10
Tactical Awareness	9
Motivation	9
Team Selection/Transfers	7
Personality	7
TOTAL	**42**

Stoichkov, Hristo
Barcelona, Bulgaria

ONE OF THE GREAT CHARACTERS of the 1990s, Stoichkov was in the news as much for his fiery outbursts as his brilliant football. Exceptionally quick for a big man, he was hard to dispossess when he got going and packed a vicious left-foot shot. As a youngster he played for CSKA Sofia, where some impressive goalscoring drew the attention of scouts from the big European clubs. A move to Barcelona in 1990, as a replacement for Gary Lineker, brought him copious rewards, including four consecutive Spanish titles, and the European Cup.

Stoichkov arrived at the 1994 World Cup in the USA at the height of his powers, but the Bulgarians were not expected to go far; except for Stoichkov, their captain Mikhailov, a world-class goalkeeper, and the balding Letchkov in midfield, their team was a collection of European journeymen. But, after surviving a tough group they saw off Mexico on penalties, came from behind to beat Germany, and were unlucky to lose to Italy in an entertaining semi-final. Stoichkov scored in every game except the first and finished as the tournament's joint-top scorer. It proved to be his finest moment. The fire later burned out and he retired in 2000.

- Stoichkov was given a lengthy suspension in his first season at the Nou Camp after stamping on a referee's foot.
- He also fell out with manager Johan Cruyff; like Lineker before him he didn't take kindly to being asked to play out wide.
- Stoichkov missed the 1985–86 season. He was banned for his part in a riot involving players and spectators at the 1985 Bulgarian Cup final. The league disbanded both clubs for four years.
- His goal against Mexico in 1994 summed up his game; running on to a through ball, he took it in his stride and lashed it over the goalkeeper. No frills, just great power and precision.
- He was voted European Footballer of the Year in 1994.

VITAL STATISTICS

Place of Birth: Plovdiv, Bulgaria

Date of Birth: 2 August 1966 **Died:** n/a

Caps: 83 (Bulgaria) **Goals (International):** 37

Clubs: CSKA Sofia, Barcelona, Parma, Kawisa Reysol, Chicago Fires

Appearances: Club (for Barcelona): 174

Goals: Club (for Barcelona): 83

Trophies: EC 1992; CWC 1997; BLT 1985, 1987, 1989, 1990; PLA 1991, 1992, 1993, 1994

LEGEND RATING	
Achievement	8.0
Skill	10.0
Teamwork	6.0
Passion	9.0
Personality	8.0
TOTAL	**41.0**

Strachan, Gordon
Aberdeen, Manchester United, Scotland

GORDON STRACHAN'S TENACITY while still a player has served him just as well as manager. His career in the dugout saw him rise in 1996 as the people's choice at Coventry, only to depart with his reputation tarnished a few months after the Sky Blues' relegation five years later.

Lesser men may have banked the cash and retired to the golf course. Weeks later, David Jones' misfortune at Southampton created an opening that Strachan was swift to seize. Eighteen months on, perennial strugglers Saints reached an FA Cup final in May 2003 while narrowly missing a UEFA Cup place through the league.

One need not look far for a mentor. As a ball-winning midfielder, Strachan was the pivot of Sir Alex Ferguson's Aberdeen which won domestic and European glory in the early 1980s. Reunited at Old Trafford, the League title was to elude both men but Strachan beat his manager by a season courtesy of a move to Leeds.

As captain, Strachan galvanised Leeds to the Second Division title in 1990, the League Championship following only two seasons later. Ferguson opened the floodgates the following season. For Strachan, Highfield Road provided an end to his playing career but the real learning curve was yet to come.

☞ Strachan played in the 1982 and 1986 World Cup Finals for Scotland. He scored against West Germany in the latter but, like his team-mates, never shone.

👍 He has won greater popularity than Ferguson due to blending Caledonian canniness with engaging humour.

👍 He was voted Scottish Footballer of the Year 1980 and English Footballer of the Year 1992.

☞ Made a surprise announcement that 2003–04 would be his last season with Southampton, despite their good start. He left in February 2004.

VITAL STATISTICS

		MANAGER		PLAYER	
Place of Birth:	Scotland				
Date of Birth:	9 February 1957 **Died:** n/a				
Caps:	50 (Scotland)				
Goals (International): 5		Achievement	5	Achievement	7
Clubs:	As Player: Aberdeen, Manchester United,	Tactical Awareness	6	Skill	7
	Leeds United, Coventry City;	Motivation	8	Teamwork	9
	As Manager: Coventry City,	Team Selection/Transfers	7	Passion	8
	Southampton	Personality	9	Personality	8
Trophies:	SLT 1980, 1984; SFAC 1982–84;				
	CWC 1983; FAC 1985; LT 1992	**TOTAL**	**35**	**TOTAL**	**39**

LEGEND RATING

Substitutes

Supersubs: A History

BEFORE THE MID-1960s you just had to be lucky. If a player lay writhing on the ground, his manager had to pray that the mysterious powers of the magic sponge would work their recuperative spell. If that failed, there was no bench to turn to – you were down to 10 men. Eventually the authorities realised the unfairness of the situation, not least because a succession of Cup finals had been ruined by injuries. And so it was that on 21 August 1965 Keith Peacock duly trotted on to the field as the league's first substitute, pressed into action for Charlton against Bolton Wanderers. Now the tables have turned completely. Three from five substitute choices are permitted today, making old-fashioned dugouts standing-room only. In friendly internationals the habit has reached epidemic proportions, with games fragmented by the replacing of entire teams. But whether enforced or tactical, substitutes still have the power to turn a game. Just ask Alex Ferguson. With United trailing 1-0 to Bayern Munich in the closing minutes of the European Cup final in 1999 he turned to the bench, had a brief chat with his assistant, Steve McClaren, and invited Teddy Sheringham and Ole Gunnar Solskjaer to strip for action. You probably know the rest....

- The 1970s saw the coining of the word 'Supersub'. It was invented for Liverpool striker David Fairclough, who had a happy knack of coming on late to score vital goals.
- In 1983, a league proposal to double the number of substitutes to two was rejected by clubs on grounds of expense. They were fearful of paying more appearance money and win bonuses.
- Substitutes had been permitted in friendly matches since 1922. It took the Football League 43 years to cotton on.
- Most effective substitute? Ole Gunnar Solskjaer. His catalogue of off-the-bench heroics include a four-goal salvo in 11 minutes against Nottingham Forest.

'He accepts the situation when he is on the bench ... very few players can come into the heat of a game and be so totally tuned in.'

Alex Ferguson on Ole Gunnar Solskjaer

Sunderland's Stunner
Arsenal 3 Manchester United 2, 1979

ACTUALLY, it wasn't a great match. But for exciting climaxes, no FA Cup final had witnessed drama like it since Stanley Matthews moved into overdrive in 1953. Arsenal had established a two-goal cushion by half-time and were content to run down the clock during the second half. United scarcely looked up to the task.

But with five minutes remaining, Gordon McQueen, still loitering in the penalty area after a badly-worked set-piece, turned in a speculative cross. Even now, Arsenal looked more than capable of holding their nerve. Enter Sammy McIlroy, who dribbled through a nervous and transfixed Gunners' defence two minutes later to toe-end the ball past the advancing Jennings. It squeezed tantalisingly inside his right-hand post, like a gently caressed snooker ball falling into a side pocket. In the stands the United fans lost it big time. Unfortunately for them, so did their team. From the restart, with just seconds to go, Arsenal moved the ball to Brady on the left wing, and the Irishman hit a wicked, curling cross over a flailing Gary Bailey on to the outstretched right boot of Alan Sunderland. The goal gaped, he scored, and the Cup was won at last.

☞ This was the second of Arsenal's hat-trick of successive Cup final appearances, and the only time they won. Ipswich and West Ham beat them in 1978 and 1980 respectively.

☞ This was Arsenal's 11th game of the competition, having taken five matches to overcome Sheffield Wednesday in the third round.

✍ This was Pat Rice's fourth final in an amazing run.

✎ For Dave Sexton, this was the nearest he came to a major trophy as United manager. He was sacked in 1981 after four barren seasons.

✎ Several hundred United fans left the stadium when their team were 2-0 down.

SCORERS	**Arsenal:** Talbot, Stapleton, Sunderland
	Manchester United: McQueen, McIlroy
EVENT	FA Cup Final, Wembley, 12 May 1979
ARSENAL	(Man: Terry Neill)
	1. Jennings 2. Rice 3. Nelson 4. Talbot 5. O' Leary 6. Young 7. Brady
	8. Sunderland 9. Stapleton 10. Price 11. Rix
MAN UTD	(Man: Dave Sexton)
	1. Bailey 2. Nicholl 3. Albiston 4. McIlroy 5. McQueen 6. Buchan 7. Coppell
	8. Greenhoff J 9. Jordan 10. Macari 11. Thomas

Tale of Two Maradonas
Romania 3 Argentina 2, 1994

ARGENTINA HAD STARTED the tournament with Maradona in fine form … until urine tests found his body to be crammed with drugs. Romania, meanwhile, had the man they called the 'Maradona of the Carpathians', Gheorghe Hagi, fit and hoping to show a world audience that he was as good as he thought he was. Romania had come through their group despite losing 4-1 to Switzerland and, allaying fears that they might adopt a cagey strategy, took the lead after just 12 minutes through a splendid Dumitrescu free-kick. A Batistuta penalty pulled Argentina level four minutes later, but Dumitrescu, collecting a subtle pass from Hagi, hit his second to make it 2-1 on 16 minutes.

Argentina pressed but Romania defended valiantly, and retained a constant threat on the break, thanks largely to Hagi whose exquisite close control and ability to launch passes from deep in his own half provided them with a reliable outlet. Supporting Dumitrescu on one such foray, he put Romania 3-1 up with a fine, rising strike from distance. Back came Argentina, a mistake by the otherwise sound Prunea letting in Balbo, but it was to prove no more than a consolation. Romania, inspired by Hagi and the commanding Belodedici, held on to clinch a famous and popular victory.

☞ If the match had gone to extra-time, Romania would have struggled. Their coach, Iordanescu, withdrew both Dumitrescu and Hagi to help protect his lead.

☞ Dumitrescu only played at centre forward because Florin Raducioiu was suspended. His goals earned him a move to Spurs, where his performances ranged from the sublime to the downright risible.

☞ Romania lost their quarter-final with Sweden. An entertaining game ended 2-2, both goals from the returning Raducioiu.

☞ Argentina's flair players disappointed. Batistuta worked hard as usual, but the talented Ortega failed to fill the gap left by Maradona, and Redondo, terrific for Real Madrid, was anonymous.

SCORERS	**Romania:** Dumitrescu 12, 18 Hagi 56
	Argentina: Batistuta (pen) 16 Balbo 75
EVENT	World Cup Second Round, Pasadena, 3 July 1994
ROMANIA	(Man: Angel Iordanescu)
	1. Prunea 2. Petrescu 3. Prodan 4. Belodedici 5. Lupescu 6. Popescu
	7. Selymes 8. Munteanu 9. Hagi 10. Dumitrescu 11. Mihali
ARGENTINA	(Man: Alfio Basile)
	1. Islas 2. Sensini 3. Caceres 4. Ruggeri 5. Chamot 6. Basualdo
	7. Simeone 8. Redondo 9. Ortega 10. Balbo 11. Batistuta

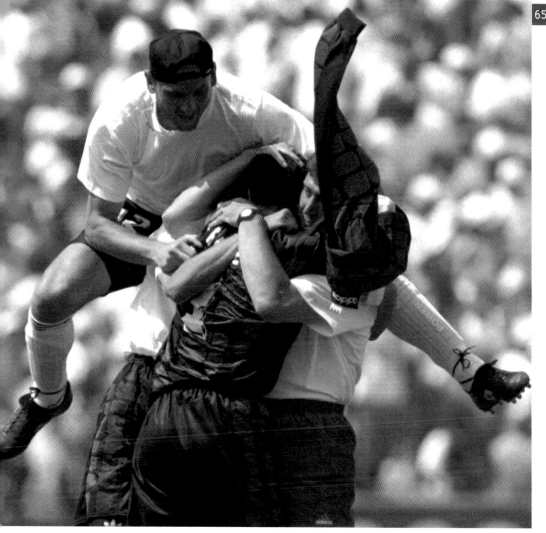

Tardelli, Marco
Juventus, Italy

THE WORLD CUP FINAL, 1982. Italy are defending a 1-0 lead in the Bernabeu against West Germany. With a little over 20 minutes left, the ball falls to an Italian midfielder on the left edge of the penalty area. After a moment's adjustment, he slams a shot into the opposite corner of the net to give his team an unassailable two-goal lead. His mad-eyed, careering celebration, fists pumping, captures his nation's explosion of joy and relief. Marco Tardelli's position in Italian football history is assured.

Tardelli was already a legend at Juventus. He had made the leap from Serie C to Serie A within three years of his debut for Pisa as a 17-year-old. The heartbeat of the midfield, he helped a fabulous Juve to five Scudetto in eight seasons from 1977. The accolade, a European Cup winners' medal in 1985, will always be tarnished by other events at Heysel. The two seasons at Inter and swansong at Swiss outfit St Gallen were but a footnote.

As a coach, Tardelli's management of the victorious Italian U-21 side at Euro 2000 remains his highest achievement. His misjudged, nine-month tenure as Inter's coach ended in 2001. For mortals, it may have proved a harder pill to swallow. Tardelli will always be remembered for something greater.

☞ He was dubbed 'Schizzo' ('spurt') for his sudden turn of pace.

👆 Although not a prolific scorer, he earned a reputation at club level for grabbing important goals. He scored only six in 81 international appearances but saved one for the World Cup final.

☞ Tardelli has the fourth-highest number of full Italian caps.

☞ As a youngster, Tardelli was nearly lost to athletics. He was a promising middle-distance runner, appearing in the finals of a national youth tournament.

VITAL STATISTICS

Place of Birth:	Capanne di Careggine, Italy
Date of Birth:	24 September 1954 **Died:** n/a
Caps:	81 (Italy) **Goals (International):** 6
Clubs:	As Player: Pisa, Como, Juventus, Inter;
	As Manager: Como, Inter, Bari, Egyptian
	national team
Appearances:	Club (League): 407
Goals:	Club (League): 45
Trophies:	SA 1977, 1978, 1981, 1982, 1984; UEFAC 1977;
	CWC 1984; ESC 1984; EC 1985; WorC 1982

LEGEND RATING	
Achievement	10.0
Skill	9.0
Teamwork	9.0
Passion	10.0
Personality	8.0
TOTAL	**46.0**

Tartan Army
Scottish Revels

IN DAYS OF YORE, the England versus Scotland match brought the curtain down on the domestic season. For Scotland fans the visit to Wembley every two years became a pilgrimage of biblical proportions; ritual bathing in the fountains of Trafalgar Square was followed by a route march to Wembley that evoked echoes of Moses and the Promised Land. Inside the ground, England would invariably play out their 'home' game to the accompaniment of 75,000 baying Caledonians intent on witnessing a re-enactment of the Battle of Bannockburn. With the demise of the Home Internationals, the Tartan Army developed a worldwide reputation, as they cheerfully followed Scotland from one World Cup disaster to another. Their seemingly routine meetings with Brazil led to a sea of white legs twinkling a samba from beneath thousands of swirling kilts. They may have drunk the place dry, but they were generally more welcome, and always better behaved than the English.

☞ Wembley 1977. The Tartan Army outraged English sensibilities by dismantling the goalposts and hacking lumps from the pitch following Scotland's 2-1 win.

☞ In the 1970s and 1980s, London Underground opted to stage a weekend strike rather than transport the Tartan Army.

🖐 In their World Cup single of 1978 Ally McLeod's Tartan Army famously claimed that they 'would really shake them up when we win the World Cup'. Scotland lost to Peru.

☞ London's last traditional visit from the Tartan Army was in 1988. The Home Internationals ended the following year, dismissed by the FA as an anachronism in a crowded season.

'Anneka Rice – a challenge – get a drink in Genoa'

or

'Italy – land of no poll tax'

Tartan Army Banners during 'dry' World Cup Finals, 1990

Taylor Report
A Legacy of Laziness

IN THE WAKE of the Hillsborough disaster, the government realised that further legislation was necessary. The aftermath of the 1971 Ibrox tragedy had brought the Safety of Sports Grounds Act, but this had failed to solve the problems of crumbling stadiums and terracing, and was anachronistic in its recommendations on crowd control. The responsibility for reform was placed in the hands of Lord Justice Taylor, a High Court judge. His first report, an interim version in August 1989, produced the Football Spectators Act and created the Football Licensing Authority (FLA), while his second in 1990 criticised many aspects of football administration and put forward 76 recommendations for improvement. The sobering conclusion of the Taylor Report was that British football could not be relied upon to put its own house in order, and that all parties – administrators, police and fans – had to share in the blame for the failings that had made British football grounds a serious threat to public safety.

A welcome side-effect of the Football Spectators Act was the scrapping of the Thatcher-inspired plans for compulsory identity cards. Perimeter fencing, a contributing factor in the Hillsborough disaster, has disappeared from British grounds but remains in Europe.

☞ March 1990. Chancellor John Major announced a 2.5 per cent reduction in the tax on football pools, releasing £100 m for ground redevelopment. The Football Trust added £40 m later in the year.

☞ Many wondered why clubs that lavished millions on transfers and wages should receive extra help from the taxpayer. Both Liverpool and Glasgow Rangers received £2 m, the maximum grant permitted to one club.

☞ Taylor's recommendations on all-seater stadiums have not been slavishly followed. All English league grounds should have converted by 1999–2000, yet Fulham were allowed to keep terraces open during their first season back in the Premiership.

The major issues addressed in the report:

• Terrace capacities. Taylor called for a 15 per cent reduction, with restrictions on self-contained pens and the opening of perimeter gates.
• A need to drastically modernise old grounds and increase safety facilities, including the replacing of terracing with seats.
• Ticket touting should be made illegal.
• A need for responsible behaviour by players and the media.
• An urgent need for consultation between clubs, officials and fans, in particular regarding hooliganism, segregation and racist chanting.

That Save, Pelé and Moore
Brazil 1 England 0, 1970

THE SCORELINE may not suggest a classic, but this was a match for the football purist. Pitting the defending champions against the team that would replace them at the tournament's end, this was a game notable as much for its defensive and goalkeeping qualities as it was for attacking flair. England appeared to have got out of jail in the first half as Gordon Banks made an incredible stop from Pelé's header, probably the best – and certainly the most replayed – save of all time. England could not repel the Brazilian attack for ever though, and on the hour they finally surrendered to the irrepressible Jairzinho, who fired home after good work from Tostão and Pelé.

The tone of the match was set by Bobby Moore's duel with Pelé, a real clash of the titans. This was Moore's finest game, his calm, interventionist style won the admiration of the Brazilian genius who made a point of exchanging shirts with the England captain after the two had embraced warmly at the final whistle. This mutual display of respect and affection, caught by camera lenses the world over, epitomised the dignity and style with which both players conducted themselves throughout their glittering careers.

- Both teams qualified for the quarter-finals, Brazil with a 100 per cent record, England with wins against Czechoslovakia and Romania.
- The match signalled the start of a great friendship between Moore and Pelé. The Brazilian paid a heartfelt tribute on Moore's death.
- Jairzinho's goal was one of seven in the tournament; he netted in all six games and finished as the top scorer.
- England nearly snatched a draw, only for Jeff Astle to miss a sitter after coming on as substitute.
- This result was no disgrace for England; Brazil scored at least three goals in every other game at the Finals.

SCORERS	Jairzinho
EVENT	World Cup Finals Group Match, Estadio Jalisco, Guadalajara, Mexico, 7 June 1970
BRAZIL	(Man: Mario Zagalo) 1. Felix 2. Carlos Alberto 3. Piazza 4. Brito 5. Everaldo 6. Clodoaldo 7. Paulo Cesar Lima 8. Jairzinho 9. Tostão (Roberto) 10. Pelé 11. Rivelino
ENGLAND	(Man: Sir Alf Ramsey) 1. Banks 2. Wright 3. Cooper 4. Mullery 5. Labone 6. Moore 7. Lee (Astle) 8. Ball 9. R Charlton (Bell) 10. Hurst 11. Peters

Theatre of Dreams
Old Trafford, Manchester

MANCHESTER UNITED'S MAGNIFICENT 'Theatre of Dreams' is currently the biggest club ground in England, having been modernised extensively in recent seasons. Its 68,000 seats are filled for every home game.

First opened in 1910, Old Trafford has enjoyed an eventful existence, not least during the Second World War. German bombing destroyed the main stand and extensively damaged other sections of the ground, forcing United to play home games at Maine Road for a couple of seasons. Old Trafford has long been a natural choice for important games needing a neutral venue. It staged three matches during the 1966 World Cup and was a key host in Euro 96, providing the semi-final arena for the Czech Republic's nail-biting penalty win. In domestic football, it was chosen as the venue for the 1915 'khaki' Cup final and replays in 1911 and 1970, in addition to countless semi-final ties.

Today, fans from around the globe make daily pilgrimages to the stadium, not least to add to United's impressive coffers in the huge superstore adjacent to the ground. The modern Old Trafford is no longer just a place to watch football.

- Despite the magnificent surroundings, sections of the crowd persist in standing, leading to periodic threats of closure by the city council.
- The most poignant monuments are the plaque and memorial clock commemorating the players, officials and journalists who died in the 1958 Munich air crash.
- Old Trafford's record crowd of 76,962 stands for the 1939 FA Cup semi-final between Wolves and Grimsby.
- The giant new North Stand is the biggest in the UK and supports the world's longest cantilevered roof.
- Old Trafford's address is now Sir Matt Busby Way. A statue to its greatest manager stands outside the ground.

VITAL STATISTICS

Location:	Manchester, England
Local Club:	Manchester United
Date Built:	1910
Current Capacity:	68,936
Max. Capacity:	76,962

They Think It's All Over
England 4 West Germany 2, 1966

'SOME PEOPLE ARE ON THE PITCH, they think it's all over … it is now. It's four'. Thus BBC commentator Kenneth Wolstenholme brought the curtain down on the 1966 World Cup. If he could claim royalties, he would now be wealthy enough to buy the FA itself. England's sixth game of the Finals brought a unique experience; for the first time in the tournament they went a goal behind, Haller taking advantage of a Ray Wilson error. But six minutes later, rising to meet a perfectly weighted free-kick from Moore, Hurst leveled with a crisp header. In the second half England appeared to have won it through Peters with 12 minutes left, only for Weber to put celebrations on ice with a last-gasp equaliser. After 10 minutes of extra-time came the flashpoint. Hurst's shot rebounded off the underside of the bar and, controversially (and probably wrongly), Azerbaijani linesman Tofik Bakhramov awarded a goal to England. Hurst completed his hat-trick in the dying moments but by then the Germans were already a beaten side. The country that invented the game could finally call itself world champions.

- Geoff Hurst remains the only scorer of a hat-trick in a World Cup final. He found the net with his head, right and left foot.
- Germany added to an unenviable record. In five successive World Cup Finals, the team scoring first had lost.
- Ramsey rallied his troops before extra-time with his most famous words: 'You've won it once, now go and win it again'. He remained impassive on the bench at the final whistle.
- Hurst's selection was vindication for Ramsey. Greaves was the popular choice but Hurst replaced him for the quarter-finals and retained his place.
- Ramsey was knighted shortly after the victory. Both Bobby Charlton and Hurst have since received the same award.

SCORERS   **England:** Hurst (3); Peters
             West Germany: Haller, Weber
EVENT   World Cup Final, Wembley, 30 July 1966

ENGLAND   (Man: Alf Ramsey)
         1. Banks 2. Cohen 3. Wilson 4. Stiles 5. J Charlton 6. Moore 7. Ball
         8. Hurst 9. R Charlton 10. Hunt 11. Peters
W. GERMANY (Man: Helmut Schoen)
         1. Tilkowski 2. Hottges 3. Schnellinger 4. Beckenbauer 5. Schulz 6. Weber
         7. Held 8. Haller 9. Seeler 10. Overath 11. Emmerich

Thijssen, Frans & Muhren, Arnold
Ipswich Town

IN 1970S BRITAIN, foreign footballers were as rare as short back and sides, so when Spurs announced the signings of the Argentine stars Osvaldo Ardiles and Ricky Villa it caused a sensation. In comparison, Frans Thijssen and Arnold Muhren slipped into Portman Road almost unnoticed. But their deft skills and vision were soon the talk of the First Division.

Cultured midfielders both, they brought the passing principles of 'Total Football' to Ipswich and, in combination with the tigerish John Wark, formed the engine of Bobby Robson's 1981 UEFA Cup winners. Muhren later moved on to Manchester United in a lucrative deal. Although he won the FA Cup in 1983, his frequent injuries meant neither he nor United prospered (some would argue that his lengthy absence in the 1983–84 season cost United the title). His signing by Ajax in 1984 proved to be Muhren's Indian summer, and resulted in his recall for Holland. Aged 37, he was a member of the Dutch team that won the European Championships in 1988. Thijssen, meanwhile, struggled to maintain his form after leaving Ipswich, becoming an itinerant and peripheral figure.

☝ Thijssen was PFA Footballer of the Year in 1981, while Muhren won Ipswich's Player of the Year award in his first season (1978–79).

☝ Both were members of the Ipswich team that won the UEFA Cup in 1981, defeating their Dutch countrymen, AZ67 Alkmaar, 5-4 in the two-legged final.

☞ 'The man with velvet feet.' John Motson waxes lyrical over Arnold Muhren.

☝ In 1988 Muhren provided the cross for the best goal ever in the European Championships – Van Basten's stunning volley in the final against Russia.

VITAL STATISTICS
FRANS THIJSSEN

Place of Birth:	Heuman, Holland		
Date of Birth:	23 January 1952	**Died:** n/a	
Caps:	14 (Holland)	**Goals (International):** 3	
Clubs:	NEC, FC Twente, Ipswich, Vancouver Whitecaps,		
	Nottingham Forest, Fortuna Sittard, FC Groningen		
Appearances:	Club (for Ipswich): 125		
Goals:	Club (for Ipswich): 10		
Trophies:	UEFAC 1981		

Achievement	6.0
Skill	8.0
Teamwork	8.0
Passion	7.0
Personality	6.0
TOTAL	**35.0**

LEGEND RATING

1981 Muhren (left) and

VITAL STATISTICS

ARNOLD MÜHREN

Place of Birth:	Volendam, Holland
Date of Birth:	2 June 1951 **Died:** n/a
Caps:	23 (Holland) **Goals (International):** 3
Clubs:	FC Twente, Ajax, Ipswich, Manchester United
Appearances:	Club (for Ipswich and Man Utd): 226
Goals:	Club (for Ipswich and Man Utd): 34
Trophies:	CWC 1987; UEFAC 1981; FAC 1983; EuroC 1988

Achievement	8.0
Skill	8.0
Teamwork	7.0
Passion	7.0
Personality	7.0
TOTAL	**37.0**

LEGEND RATING

Thirty-six – Nil
Arbroath 36 Bon Accord 0, 1885

IMAGINE, IF YOU WILL, a possible post-match interview with the Bon Accord manager: 'Aye, the lads are naturally disappointed. We always knew it would be a tough game, it's difficult to come to one of the big clubs like Arbroath and get a result. Obviously, with some of our boys being a bit sketchy on the rules, like forgetting to change ends at half-time, it made it an uphill battle. But I do feel the game turned on a couple of major decisions. One was the kick-off. Had it not happened we might well have held out for a draw. Also, the referee missed a blatant handball leading up to their 29th goal, he must have been the only person in the ground who didn't see it. If television had been invented the replay would definitely have vindicated us. Still, at least we can concentrate on the league now.' One supposes the Bon Accord keeper didn't give up his day job as a piano tuner. Scotland's biggest slaughter since Culloden is a scoreline that will probably never be topped.

- On the same day and in the same competition, Dundee Harp beat Aberdeen Rovers 35-0.
- Arbroath met their match in the fourth round, losing 5-3 at Hibernian.
- Arbroath's only other Cup exploit is a run to the semi-final in 1947.
- The score would have been even higher but for the absence of goal nets, which were not yet in common use.
- This is still a world-record victory in an official match.

EVENT   Scottish FA Cup First Round, 12 September 1885

ARBROATH   1. Milne, Jim snr 2. Collie 3. Salmond 4. Rennie 5. Milne, Jim jr 6. Bruce
7. Petrie 8. Tackett 9. Marshall 10. Crawford 11. Buick

BON ACCORD   1. Stevie Wonder 2. Long John Silver 3. Blind Pew 4. David Blunkett
5. Douglas Bader 6. Bonnie Langford 7. Basil Fotherington-Thomas
8. Thora Hird 9. Adeola Akinbiyi 10. Don Estelle 11. Toulouse Lautrec

THE HIGHLAND POST

INCREDIBLE VICTORY FOR ARBROATH

AFTER BEATING opponents Bon Accord by 36 goals to nil in the first round of the Scottish FA Cup yesterday, Arbroath's manager was said to be 'satisfied' with the way the match had gone for his team and that 'it was quite a convincing defeat'.

The Bon Accord side did not appear to find their form throughout the whole game, despite highly vocal support from their supporters, mainly family and friends of the players who all come from a small hamlet in the Grampian Mountains. Some questionable decisions were made by the referee, which worked in Arbroath's favour, giving them their 29th goal of the match.

Those Who Died Young
Footballers Cut off in Their Prime

DYING AS A RESULT of a playing injury is mercifully rare. The most famous example was Celtic goalkeeper John Thomson, who in September 1931 was Scotland's hottest prospect. Diving at the feet of Rangers' Sam English, he sustained serious head injuries and died hours later in hospital aged just 22. The funeral briefly united the sectarian divide, but English was mercilessly barracked by some Celtic fans in the following fixture. Deeply upset, he was never the same player and left Rangers the following season.

Rangers can point to a more recent tragedy. In March 1995 their former winger and legend Davie Cooper collapsed and died from a brain haemorrhage while coaching youngsters for a television programme. The 39-year-old Cooper was as fit as he had ever been and had no previous history of illness. There are other examples, but the deaths of this Glasgow pair are particularly poignant, putting football, sectarianism, rivalry and trophies in their rightful perspective.

In June 2003, the shocking death of Marc Vivien Foe was a reminder that even the fit and active can be struck down. Playing in the Confederations Cup semi-final for Cameroon against Colombia, he suffered a heart attack on the pitch and died minutes later. He was 28.

- In 1964 John White, a key member of Tottenham's double-winning side, was killed by lightning while sheltering under a tree during a round of golf.
- Laurie Cunningham and David Rocastle are the most recent English internationals to die prematurely. In 1989 Cunningham met his end behind the wheel of a car in Madrid, while Rocastle succumbed to cancer in 2001.
- Andres Escobar paid the ultimate penalty for scoring an own goal while playing for Colombia in the 1994 World Cup Finals. He upset a betting cartel and was murdered on his return.
- In 1897, Aston's Thomas Grice was fatally stabbed by his own belt buckle after what looked an innocuous tumble.

'Bill Nicholson started to talk about identifying John White's body. He broke down ... he never broke down like that.'

Dave Mackay describes the effect of John White's death.

Thrashings
Well, Des, It Was a Bit One-Sided Really

ARBROATH'S 36-0 DEFEAT of Bon Accord in 1885 is well documented as the world's biggest drubbing in a first-class game. Early fixtures were notorious for their mismatches; it would be churlish not to mention Preston's 26-0 caning of Hyde in 1887, the largest English score. In cup ties of yore, the pummelling of works' teams by well-drilled professionals was commonplace.

Despite tighter competition, mismatches still occur even at the top level (Revie's Leeds toying with Southampton in a 7-0 hammering in 1972 springs to mind). Even in the 1990s the cliché that there are 'no easy games nowadays' doesn't stand up to intense scrutiny. Manchester United versus Ipswich may have been a home banker in 1995, but 9-0 didn't result in too many claimed betting slips. But United's dominance of English football in the 1990s didn't stop them being humiliated 5-0 by Newcastle and Chelsea. Spare a thought, though, for Stanley Milton. On 6 January 1934 the Halifax goalkeeper trotted out for his debut against Stockport – and promptly let in 13 goals. Happily, he survived to be picked another day, which doesn't say much for their reserve keeper.

- American Samoa's 31-0 defeat set a new international record. FIFA weren't able to ratify the score immediately, as the scoreboard claimed 32-0.
- When Newcastle's keeper and outfield stand-in were both injured during a match at Upton Park in 1986, they turned to the vertically challenged Peter Beardsley to keep goal. West Ham won 8-0.
- Europe's record aggregate win is held by Chelsea, who once beat Jeunesse Hautcharage 21-0. The Luxembourg part-timers fielded a player with only one arm, and it wasn't the goalkeeper.
- 'We were lucky to get nil.' Oft-quoted preserve of the tight-lipped and ashen-faced manager.

'We are asking the Lord to keep the score down.'

American Samoa's coach, Tunoa Lui, prays for a miracle before a World Cup qualifier against Australia in April 2001; they lost 31-0

Too Much Bottle
Alcohol

DRINK HAS ALWAYS BEEN a strange contradiction in football. The misdemeanours of Premier League stars under the influence make for familiar tabloid revelations, yet at the same time Carling have poured millions into the FA's coffers with their sponsorship of the Premier League. At club level, the Blue Star brewery has added their familiar logo to Newcastle's black-and-white stripes in recent years. For British players, a lifestyle providing both plenty of spare time and plenty of cash has led to a thriving drinking culture. The skills of George Best and Jim Baxter can scarcely be mentioned without rueful references to the habit that so affected their lives. The great Brazilian Garrincha was to meet with an untimely end through his own alcohol addiction, while Billy Bremner's international career was curtailed following alcohol-induced incidents in a Danish nightclub. Modern casualties have included Paul Merson, and his former Arsenal team-mate Tony Adams who published an autobiography called *Addicted* in reference to his problems with the bottle. Today's use of dieticians and the cleaner habits of most continental imports have reduced the problem but, as the US government found, prohibition is completely unenforceable.

- A wilting Denis Compton was famously revived with a half-time tot of brandy during the 1950 FA Cup final. His second-half display helped Arsenal beat Liverpool 2-0.
- 1971. West Ham lost 4-0 at Blackpool in the FA Cup after several players break a club curfew and go drinking the night before. Among the players dropped for the next game is England captain Bobby Moore.
- England's footballers are snapped in the infamous 'dentist's chair' days before the start of Euro 96. The antics are repeated on the pitch, minus chair and alcohol, following Paul Gascoigne's goal in their group match against Scotland.

'I saw an advert saying "Drink Canada Dry" and thought it was an instruction.'

George Best explains his decision to cross the pond

Top Toffees
Everton's Greatest

NINE ENGLISHMEN and two Welshmen make up this blend from Everton's four great eras. All positions are contentious save two; Southall is easily the best keeper and Dixie Dean is English football's most prolific goal machine. In defence, Newton and Wilson were two of England's classiest ever full-backs, whilst the combination of Watson and Ratcliffe brought Everton a brace of titles in the 1980s. Two of the 1970 'holy trinity' are included, Ball and Kendall edging out Colin Harvey. Trevor Steven provides width, balance and sublime passing skills to right-midfield, his left-footed contemporary Sheedy is usurped by the craftsman of the 1939 Champions, Joe Mercer.

In attack, Everton enjoy an embarrassment of riches in the classic centre-forward tradition. A forward-line of Gray and Dean would make opposing defences quail. Lineker's prolific season reaped no reward and Rooney's premature departure precludes his presence.

☞ Everton's rich tradition of forwards is highlighted by the omissions from this squad – Bob Latchford, Roy Vernon and Graeme Sharp.

☞ Harry Catterick is preferred to Howard Kendall as manager. Although both won two titles, Kendall's second and third spells in charge presided over increasingly poor sides.

☞ Apart from Kendall, Colin Harvey also managed the side. His spell from 1987–90 was spent in Kendall's shadow, starting a decline from which they have never recovered.

☞ Seven of Everton's nine Championship sides are represented, the exceptions being 1891 and 1915, when competition was far weaker.

☞ Curiously, given these days of classy foreign imports, all of this squad are British except the tireless and inspirational Gravesen.

Manager: Harry Catterick

4-4-2

Neville Southall (80s/90s)

Keith Newton (60s/70s) Dave Watson (80s/90s)
Kevin Ratcliffe (C) (80s/90s) Ray Wilson (60s)

Trevor Steven (80s) Alan Ball (60s/70s) Howard Kendall (60s/70s)
Joe Mercer (30s)

Dixie Dean (30s) Andy Gray (80s)

Subs: Gordon West (G) (60s/70s) Brian Labone (D) (60s)
Thomas Gravesen (M) (2000s) Tommy Lawton (F) (30s) Joe Royle (F) (70s)

Top Toon
The Newcastle United Dream Team

A TRUE REFLECTION of Newcastle's colourful history, this squad pays respect to all the great Newcastle teams. Jimmy Lawrence, Colin Veitch and Peter McWilliam won three titles in the early part of the century, and Stan Seymour's wing-play helped Hughie Gallacher bring the bacon home in 1927. Mitchell and Milburn performed similar feats immediately after the war, while Frank Brennan and Bobby Cowell provided the solid defensive base for Milburn's heroic goal-scoring deeds. Craig and Moncur were ever-present as Newcastle struggled in the 1960s, but enjoyed better days when Malcolm Macdonald started tearing defences apart a decade later. Despite the skills of Beardsley, Gascoigne and Chris Waddle another decline followed in the 1980s and then early 1990s when, only the arrival of Kevin Keegan as manager, averted a disastrous drop into the Third Division. Keegan's unique brand of attacking football won the hearts of many neutrals as they challenged the might of Man United at the top of the Premier League. Alan Shearer is the only current player in our Dream Team. The former England captain was once overlooked by Newcastle in a trial game but, since being signed for a club record £15 m by Keegan, he has wasted little time writing himself into Geordie folklore.

☞ Three Geordie omissions: Frank Hudspeth, holder of the most outfield appearances for the club (1910–29); Joe Harvey, player and manager across five decades; and Malcolm Macdonald's striking partner, John Tudor.

🖐 Malcolm 'Supermac' Macdonald once scored all five goals in an England win over Cyprus. Sadly, he was never the same player after he left Newcastle for Arsenal.

☞ The squad has a distinctly Celtic flavour: six were capped by Scotland; Given is the current Republic of Ireland goalie; and David Craig won 25 caps for Northern Ireland.

☞ Seven Geordie boys feature in the 16. The Toon Army has always reserved its loudest applause for the local talent.

Manager: Kevin Keegan

4-2-4

Jimmy Lawrence (1900s)

David Craig (60s) Frank Brennan (40s/50s)
Bobby Moncur (C) (60s/70s) Colin Veitch (1900s)

Paul Gascoigne (80s) Peter Beardsley (90s)

Alan Shearer (90s) Jackie Milburn (40s/50s)
Malcolm Macdonald (70s) Bobby Mitchell (40s/50s)

Subs: Shay Given (G) (00s) Bobby Cowell (D) (40s/50s)
Peter McWilliam (M) (1900s) Stan Seymour (W) (20s)
Hughie Gallacher (F) (20s)

Total Football
Holland, 1970s

BUILDING ON THE SUCCESS of the great Ajax club team, Michels took a squad assembled around that side to the 1974 World Cup Finals. They had scraped through qualification, a late goal against Norway eliminating Belgium, but in Germany they were a revelation, comfortably the best team of the tournament despite their loss to the hosts in the final. All the players were comfortable on the ball, while their movement and passing were exquisite. 'Total Football' at its poetic best. Van Hanegem, stately and cultured, and the vigorous Neeskens were the team's engine room in midfield. What is often forgotten is how tough the Dutch were. If the attack wasn't firing, they were able to dig in; Krol, Rijsbergen, Haan and Neeskens were superb footballers, but they were not afraid to leave a foot in when necessary. And above all there was Cruyff. With all that talent behind him and the wiry strength of Rensenbrink next door, he was the icing on the cake, full of tricks and pace. Four years later in Argentina, without Cruyff and Van Hanegem, they were less persuasive, but still formidable opponents, and some awesome long-range shooting at altitude saw them through to a second final. Sadly, they lost again, securing their status as the greatest team never to win anything.

☞ The managers who built the two great club sides were the managers for the two World Cup campaigns (Michels from Ajax, and the Austrian, Ernst Happel, from Feyenoord).

🖑 Cruyff missed the 1978 World Cup after a dispute with Happel, followed by Van Hanegem.

☞ The 1978 campaign saw twins play in a World Cup final for the only time. Winger Rene van der Kerkhof had featured in the 1974 final as a sub, and he was joined by brother Willy in 1978.

🖐 Arie Haan's winning goal against Italy in 1978, effectively propelling Holland into the final, was from a preposterous distance, easily 40 yards.

Manager: Rinus Michels

Key Players
Wim Suurbier (D) Ruud Krol (D) Wim Rijsbergen (D)
Arie Haan (M) Wim Jansen (M) Wim Van Hanegem (M)
Johan Neeskens (M) Johnny Rep (M/F) Johan Cruyff (F)
Rob Rensenbrink (F)

Trophies
None (beaten in 1974 and 1978 World Cup Finals)

Total Let-Down
Holland 1 West Germany 2, 1974

'WE FORGOT TO SCORE the second goal.' That was Johnny Rep's take on Holland's failure to win the 1974 World Cup final, despite entering the game as clear favourites, having been overwhelmingly the best team in the tournament. It is certainly true that having taken such an early lead, Holland failed to capitalise on that advantage. They seemed content to keep the ball rather than surge forward in the way that had characterised their emergence from the group stages. Significantly, Berti Vogts, having been beaten by Cruyff for the second-minute penalty, began to gain a hold over the Dutch playmaker.

With the fluidity of the Dutch affected, the Germans began to wrestle themselves back into the match. The game turned in the 25th minute when Taylor, who deserved praise for having the guts to give the early penalty against the host nation, failed to keep his nerve and rewarded Holzenbein for an outrageous dive that wouldn't have fooled a ref in a primary school match. Holland's chance went in that moment. A typically opportunist goal from Müller put Germany 2-1 up at half-time, and the Dutch were chasing the game.

One marvellous save by Maier from Neeskens apart, West Germany were fairly comfortable in the second half, with Beckenbauer and not Cruyff emerging as the colossus.

☞ It wasn't as if Taylor wasn't warned; Holzenbein had cheated to earn a penalty in the semi-final against Poland as well, although Tomaszewski saved Hoeness' penalty on that occasion.

☞ Grabowski's introduction in the latter stages of the tournament aided Germany. His presence reduced the redoubtable Krol's ability to join the attack.

☞ Holland had struggled to qualify for the finals, pipping Belgium on goal difference. (The Belgians had cause to be miffed – they didn't concede a goal in the group and still went out!)

👆 The 4-0 demolition of Argentina in the second group stage remains the finest example of what the Dutch were all about. Their movement is bewildering to merely watch, so must have been hell to try and counter on the field.

SCORERS	**Holland:** Neeskens (pen)
	West Germany: Breitner (pen); Müller
EVENT	World Cup Final, Olympiastadion, Munich, 7 July 1974
HOLLAND	(Man: Rinus Michels)
	1. Jongbloed 2. Suurbier 3. Krol 4. Jansen 5. Rijsbergen (de Jong) 6. Haan 7. Rep 8. Neeskens 9. van Hanegem 10. Cruyff 11. Rensenbrink (van der Kerkhof)
W. GERMANY	(Man: Helmut Schoen)
	1. Maier 2. Vogts 3. Breitner 4. Bonhof 5. Schwarzenbeck 6. Beckenbauer 7. Grabowski 8. Hoeness 9. Müller 10. Overath 11. Holzenbein

Total Surrender
Argentina 3 Holland 1, 1978

AT THE END OF EXTRA-TIME, a frenzied, ticker-tape-spewing crowd erupted in an ecstasy of joy and relief. Argentina had prevailed, two strikes from Kempes and Bertoni snatching the trophy from a Dutch team cursing its luck after facing the hosts for the second successive final. It could all have been so different.

With a minute of normal time remaining, Holland were resurgent. Substitute Nanninga had wrested the initiative from Argentina seven minutes earlier, heading home for a deserved equaliser after a second half in which the Dutch had pressed consistently. Ruud Krol placed a 50-m pass into Resenbrink's stride, whose shot from a tight angle struck Fillol's far post and bounced agonisingly back into play.

For a nation desperate to exorcise the demon that had brought unthinkable defeat against Germany four years earlier, this was further proof that the Almighty's colour of choice was not orange. For Argentina, wracked by nerves since Kempes' 37th-minute opener, it provided the belief that the match was theirs for the taking.

- Holland's first-choice keeper Piet Schrijvers had been injured in the semi-final against Italy. His ageing replacement, Jan Jongbloed, was at fault for both Kempes' goals.
- Johnny Rep and Mario Kempes exchanged kisses before the final. Both had been team-mates at Valencia.
- The pre-match bonhomie ended when Argentina objected to a cast worn by Rene van der Kerkhof to protect an injured arm. The resulting row delayed the kick-off by 10 minutes.
- Typically, Holland had lost two players to disputes before the tournament began. The hammer-blow was Cruyff, who objected to Argentina's human rights record. Van Hanegem's beef was less high-minded, being a protest against the sharing of sponsorship money.
- Argentina's win will be forever tainted by bribery allegations surrounding their last group match, effectively a final eliminator. A supine Peru allowed them a 6-0 victory and a final place at the expense of rivals Brazil.

SCORERS   **Argentina:** Kempes (2); Bertoni
                     Holland: Nanninga

EVENT   World Cup Final, River Plate Stadium, Buenos Aires, 25 June 1978

ARGENTINA   (Man: Cesar Luis Menotti)
                     1. Fillol 2. Olguin 3. Galvan 4. Passarella 5. Tarantini 6. Ardiles (Larrosa) 7. Gallego
                     8. Kempes 9. Bertoni 10. Luque 11. Ortiz (Houseman)

HOLLAND   (Man: Ernst Happel)
                     1. Jongbloed 2. Poortvliet 3. Krol 4. Brandts 5. Jansen (Suurbier) 6. Neeskens 7. Haan
                     8. van der Kerkhof, W 9. van der Kerkhof, R 10. Rep (Nanninga) 11. Rensenbrink

Totti, Francesco
AS Roma, Italy

IN AN AGE when loyalty comes cheap and top players are moved around by unscrupulous agents as a matter of course, Francesco Totti is a notable exception. His loyalty to Roma: his local side and the club whom he served as a ballboy, appears unswerving. He signed as a 16-year-old in 1992 but failed to command a regular place for several seasons. Once established, his ability to unsettle defences by playing 'in the hole' between attack and midfield made him maddening to mark and a perfect foil for a more direct striker. As a result, his goals-to-game ratio is not high, but it is for his all-round contribution and ability to hold up the ball that he is most noted.

On the international stage, his talents should have shone in the 2002 World Cup Finals. Instead, the world's attention was diverted by one controversial moment in the second phase. Totti was dismissed for diving and a 10-man Italy were eliminated by a Golden Goal from South Korea.

His early exit in disgrace from Euro 2004 was an anticlimax, as his form in Serie A the previous season had raised high expectations.

- Totti made his Serie A debut in March 1993 aged only 16. His first goal came in September of the same year, three weeks before his 17th birthday.
- Omitted from the Euro 2000 semi-final versus Holland, Totti came off the bench to score a chipped penalty in the shoot-out.
- He was a member of Italy's victorious team at the 1996 U-21 European Championships.
- Totti was Man of the Match in the final of Euro 2000, despite Italy's defeat to France.
- The Roma club shop did a roaring trade selling T-shirts of Totti taunting Juventus' striker Igor Tudor after a 4-0 thrashing, incurring the wrath of Juve coach Marcello Lippi.

VITAL STATISTICS

Place of Birth:	Rome, Italy		Achievement 6.0
Date of Birth:	27 September 1976	**Died:** n/a	Skill 9.0
Caps:	42 (Italy)	**Goals (International):** 6	Teamwork 9.0
Clubs:	AS Roma		Passion 9.0
Appearances:	Club (All Matches): 297		Personality 8.0
Goals:	Club (All Matches): 103		
Trophies:	SA 2001		**TOTAL 41.0**

LEGEND RATING

Transfers
How Much? For Him?

'WHAT A WASTE OF MONEY!' This familiar chant rings out many times a season, as another striker with an inflated price-tag picks out the corner flag. These days millions of pounds routinely change hands in football's equivalent of the stock market, but it was not always thus. Alf Common's transfer fee may have been what Michael Owen now earns in the pre-match warm up, but in Edwardian England it caused a sensation. Herbert Chapman raised the stakes even further when, as Arsenal boss in 1928, his £20,000 spree (including the capture of David Jack for the world's first ever five-figure transfer) led to the Gunners being dubbed 'the Bank of England club'. But the real money was in Italy where, from around 1950 onwards, the Serie A superclubs have broken the world transfer record on an almost monthly basis; John Charles, Jimmy Greaves and Denis Law all moved to Italy for fees that were double the budget of British clubs. Yet what were once mindblowing figures are now relatively common. Looking back it is hard to believe the fuss that was made over Trevor Francis, Britain's first £1 m player. Hell, these days £1 m doesn't buy a decent reserve left-back. When Real Madrid's chairman signed the £45 m cheque for Zinedine Zidane in 2001, did the thought flicker through his mind that he was signing 45,000 Alf Commons? I doubt it.

☞ Middlesbrough signed Alf Common to save them from relegation. They are still trying to buy their way out of trouble nearly a century later.

☞ The 1960s Celtic and West Ham teams are rare examples of teams built purely with home-grown talent. A big cheque book is usually the pre-requisite of success.

☟ Best bargains? Eric Cantona and Peter Schmeichel were signed by the canny Alex Ferguson for a combined fee of less than £2 m.

☞ Inflation was rampant in 1990s Britain. The record rose from £3.5 m (Keane) to £15 m (Shearer) in six years.

'…as a matter of sport the Second Division would be more honourable than retention of place by purchase.'

Athletic News gets pious over **Middlesbrough's signing of Alf Common, the first £1,000 transfer in 1905**

Trapattoni, Giovanni

Juventus, Milan, Bayern Munich, Italy

GIOVANNI TRAPATTONI is arguably the most notable figure in post-war Italian football. No other man has been at the summit of the Italian game for so long and in so many guises.

A formidable central defender for Milan, his name became synonymous with the execution of the *catenaccio* system in the early 1960s. Ruthlessly defensive it may have been, but two European cups (1963, 1969) established Milan's reputation as one of the giants of the European club scene. His transition from Milan player to coach appeared seamless. After an unremarkable start, a move to Juventus saw the seeds bear a remarkable fruit. The Bianconeri proved unstoppable, with Zoff, Cabrini, Scirea, Rossi and co. forming the bedrock of the national side that achieved World Cup glory in 1982. At Milan, his success was built on German stars including Matthaus, Brehme and Klinsmann, so a subsequent move to Bayern Munich was unsurprising, although highly unusual for an Italian coach. Another league title followed before a return to Fiorentina. His belated elevation to national coach in 2000 has yet to bring success, and Trapattoni was criticised following Italy's second-phase exit at the 2002 World Cup. Like so many Italian managers, his fearful tactics cost him dear at Euro 2004.

- His best playing performance was his man-marking of Pelé in Italy's 3-0 victory over Brazil in the San Siro, 1963.
- Trappatoni is Serie A's most successful coach, with seven Scudetti.
- One of the oldest national coaches, Trappatoni was 63 before his elevation to the national job.

VITAL STATISTICS

Place of Birth: Cusano Milanino, Italy

Date of Birth: 17 March 1939   **Died:** n/a

Caps: 17 (Italy)   **Goals (International):** 1

Clubs: As Player: Milan; As Coach: Milan, Juventus (twice), Internazionale, Bayern Munich (twice), Cagliari, Fiorentina, Italian national team

Appearances: Club (League): 274

Goals: Club (League): 3

Trophies: As Player: EC 1963, 1969; SA 1961, 1967; CWC 1968; As Coach: SA 1977, 1978, 1981–82, 1984, 1986, 1989; EC 1985; CWC 1984; UEFAC 1977, 1991, 1993; GLT 1997

MANAGER		PLAYER	
Achievement	8	Achievement	8
Tactical Awareness	9	Skill	8
Motivation	8	Teamwork	10
Team Selection/Transfers	8	Passion	8
Personality	8	Personality	8
TOTAL	**41**	**TOTAL**	**42**

LEGEND RATING

Trautmann's Final

Manchester City 3 Birmingham City 1, 1956

ON THE FACE OF IT, this was a routine FA Cup final. The underdogs did not defy the odds, there were no comebacks, last-minute winners or 40-yard scorchers. One goalkeeper's performance, though, was unique. Bert Trautmann was already giving a fine display for Manchester City when he dived at the feet of Birmingham forward Peter Murphy and was knocked unconscious. Only partially revived, he was involved in another jarring collision five minutes later. The newsreel footage of Trautmann massaging his neck did not reveal the whole story. It wasn't until days later, after he had completed the match and picked up a winner's medal in City's 3-1 victory, that the full extent of his injury was diagnosed. Incredibly, x-rays revealed that he had suffered a broken neck and should not even have been standing up, let alone playing football. Had the modern system of three substitutes and a keeper on the bench been applied, Trautmann would almost certainly have been replaced immediately and his heroism thus diluted. In the event, his performance produced one of the FA Cup's most famous episodes in an otherwise unremarkable match.

- Trautmann was Footballer of the Year in the same season.
- Having been a German soldier and POW in the Second World War, his arrival at Maine Road brought protests and boycotts by City fans.
- Trautmann made a full recovery and was back in the team six months later.
- This match saw Trautmann overshadow Manchester City's star player, future England boss Don Revie.
- Trautmann was a converted keeper, having preferred to play centre-half in his native Bremen.

SCORERS	**Manchester City:** Hayes, Dyson, Johnstone **Birmingham City:** Kinsey
EVENT	FA Cup Final, Wembley, 5 May 1956
MAN CITY	(Man: Leslie McDowall) 1. Trautmann 2. Leivers 3. Little 4. Barnes 5. Ewing 6. Paul 7. Johnstone 8. Hayes 9. Revie 10. Dyson 11. Clarke
B'HAM CITY	(Man: Arthur Turner) 1. Merrick 2. Hall 3. Green 4. Newman 5. Smith 6. Boyd 7. Astall 8. Kinsey 9. Brown 10. Murphy 11. Govan

Treble Dutch
Ajax, 1970s

RINUS MICHELS' APPOINTMENT as coach of Ajax Amsterdam started a sequence of three successive Dutch titles, followed by a European Cup final in 1969. But even more importantly it started a culture of coaching that became 'Total Football' – the successful method of play adopted by Ajax and Holland in the 1970s. They weren't quite ready in 1969, and were easily beaten by a craftier AC Milan side, but two years later they were back and made no mistake against Panathanaikos. Michels left for Barcelona that summer, but the blueprint was in place and Ajax followed up with two more European Cups and three more titles. While Cruyff was the undoubted star and spokesman, he was not the team's only great player. A defence of Suurbier, Krol, Blankenburg and Hulshoff, with Stuy in goal didn't concede a goal in any of the European Cup finals in which they played. Haan and Rep were sound players too, both with tremendous shots from range, and Neeskens was almost the equal of the other Johan, a skilled playmaker with a steely edge.

👍 Ajax brushed aside the double winning Arsenal team on the way to winning the 1971 European Cup, beating them both home and away.

☞ Even in the 1970s, Dutch players gave better interviews in English than English players. Krol, Haan and Cruyff were all articulate and interesting.

☞ Feyenoord were not only Ajax's main domestic threat, they were also a major rival in Europe. In 1970, under another great coach, Ernst Happel, they pipped Ajax and became the first Dutch side to win the European Cup.

☞ The Ajax side was entirely Dutch. As they faded an all-German Bayern side took over, and after them English clubs dominated.

Manager: Rinus Michels

Key Players
Wim Suurbier (D) Ruud Krol (D) Johan Neeskens (M)
Arie Haan (M) Johnny Rep (F) Johan Cruyff (F)

Trophies
DLT 1970, 1972, 1973, 1977, 1979 EC 1971, 1972, 1973
ESC 1972, 1973 WCC 1972

TV & Film

Screen Soccer

FOOTBALL HAS PROVIDED a source of inspiration for dozens of filmmakers over the decades, yet for the most part they have been of a distinct 'B' movie standard. Perhaps the most famous football film is the improbable *Escape to Victory*, which tells the unlikely story of a group of prisoners of war – Bobby Moore, Pelé and Ossie Ardiles included – who plot their escape during a match against a German army team. *There's only one Jimmy Grimble*, is the latest attempt to depict the dreams and despairs of any football-mad youngster while *Gregory's Girl* cleverly used football to give an insight into the angst of adolescence. Television drama-makers have also turned to football on a regular basis, and seem particularly fascinated by the increasing presence of women in the game. In 1989 Cheri Lungi topped the ratings as *The Manageress* in charge of a struggling club, while the long-running BBC drama *Playing the Field*, based on the Doncaster Belles, charted the trials and tribulations of a women's team.

Later film offerings have included a decent stab at dramatising Nick Hornby's groundbreaking book *Fever Pitch*. In 2002, *Bend it Like Beckham* provided a novel take on an Asian girl trying to break into UK women's football. The greatest success story has to be Vinnie Jones, who has reinvented himself as a hard-man movie actor.

☞ Pelé flirted with the big screen twice in the 1980s. He first appeared in the POW drama *Escape to Victory* and again two years later in the little known *Young Giants*.

☞ *Beyond The Promised Land*, a Man Utd authorised fly-on-the-wall glimpse of Becks and the rest during the 1999–00 season, was only shown in Manchester cinemas.

☞ The boot was on the other foot when *Footballers' Wives* hit the small screen in 2002. 'They're young, they're rich, they're sexy, and they've got everything money and fame can buy,' screamed the publicity puff.

☞ *The Arsenal Stadium Mystery* is the earliest example – a 1939 black and white murder mystery set against a Highbury backdrop.

'The fans' favourite, a movie which understands like no other what makes football great.'

A *Guardian* film critic referring to the star-studded 1981 movie, *Escape to Victory*

A scene from the rightie *Escape to Victory*

Ukraine Train
Dynamo Kiev, late 1980s

IF THE DUTCH TEAM of the 1970s were the fathers of 'Total Football', the Dynamo Kiev team of the late 1980s were their second cousins once removed. Coach Lobanowski was an intelligent and imaginative man, his sullen demeanour hiding a purity of vision about what could be achieved on a football pitch.

His Kiev team came closest to achieving that vision in the 1986 European Cup Winner's Cup final against Atletico Madrid. It may have finished 3-0, but Kiev could have won by two or three times that margin and it wouldn't have flattered them. Their technique, movement and pace were outstanding and, had they not been part of the Soviet state, would surely have been celebrated more widely for their skills. Lobanowski was immediately installed as national coach. His team played outstandingly at the 1986 World Cup, and reached the final of the 1988 European Championships where, having beaten the Dutch in the group stage, they surprisingly froze against them on the big day. Kiev remain a potent side, particularly at home, but the loss of their main stars to Italian and Spanish clubs has reduced their effectiveness in European competition.

- Vassily Rats scored one of the great World Cup goals in 1986, beating French goalie Joel Bats with a strike from 40 yards.
- Belanov scored an even better one in the 4-3 defeat by Belgium in the second round, a raking shot across goal after swerving past his marker. The Soviets always looked the better side in the game, but Belgium somehow scored more goals.
- This was a team without stars, the one exception being Oleg Blokhin ('The Ukraine Train') who was the only survivor of the side that won the European Cup Winners' Cup in 1975.
- Kuznetsov signed for Rangers in 1990, but struggled with injuries inflicted by the 'hammer throwers' (Graeme Souness) in Scottish football.

Manager: Valery Lobanowski

Key Players

Sergei Baltacha (D) Vladimir Bessonov (D) Oleg Kuznetsov (D) Anatoly Demianenko (D) Vassily Rats (M) Aleksandr Zavarov (W) Sergei Aleinikov (M) Igor Belanov (F) Oleg Blokhin (F)

Ulster Untouchables
The Northern Ireland Dream Team

LIKE WALES, Northern Ireland are a nation who traditionally have been forced to rely upon spirit, passion and solid organisation rather than individual brilliance to get results and, with the exception of the last few years, they have proved better at this than the Welsh. Two memorably courageous squads made waves in the 1958 and 1982 World Cups, and those squads rightly provide the core of this side (11 of the 16).

Jennings is one of the all-time great keepers, and Gregg a more-than competent reserve. The back four were all tough, honest pros but would be dreadfully vulnerable to pace – the alternatives, like Hunter and Worthington were unfortunately from the same mould. The midfield is pretty good, the craft and industry of O'Neill and McIlroy providing a complement to Blanchflower's distribution.

Dougan provides height and power while McParland, scorer of five goals in the 1958 World Cup, gets the nod for his perseverance and pugnacity. And then there is Best. Imagine the damage he might have wreaked for his country if he had been surrounded by team-mates as talented as this.

☞ Plenty of managerial advice for Bingham; Terry Neill, Martin O'Neill and Blanchflower all cut the mustard in their club roles.

☞ Unlucky omissions? Gerry Armstrong, scorer of Northern Ireland's goal that beat hosts Spain in 1982, and his fellow forward Billy Hamilton.

☝ Omissions? Colin Clarke and Ian Dowie. Being among the top scorers does not obscure their lack of international ability.

☞ A pre-match curfew may be difficult to enforce; not too many health food and mineral-water disciples here. Be sure to get a ticket for the party if they win.

☞ There are enough jokers included without needing the slapstick of Sammy Nelson dropping his shorts.

Manager: Billy Bingham

4-3-1-2

Pat Jennings (forever!)

Pat Rice (C) (70s) Terry Neill (60s)
Chris Nicholl (70s/80s) Mal Donaghy (70s/80s)

Martin O'Neill (70s) Danny Blanchflower (50s/60s) Sammy McIlroy (70s/80s)

George Best (60s)

Peter McParland (50s) Derek Dougan (60s)

Subs: Harry Gregg (G) (50s) Allan Hunter (D) (70s) Neil Lennon (M) (90s)
Norman Whiteside (M/F) (80s) Jimmy McIlroy (W) (50s)

United Bury Their Ghosts
Manchester United 4 Benfica 1, 1968

TEN YEARS ON, this was the night that laid the ghosts of Munich to rest. At the final whistle Bobby Charlton's face, distorted with emotion, told its own story. This was a victory for the dead as well as for the living, a fitting tribute to the Busby Babes who had perished on the tarmac on that fateful night of 6 February 1958.

The pre-determined venue for the European Cup final was a huge advantage for Matt Busby's team, as half of Manchester decamped to Wembley to cheer on their heroes. They saw a cagey, goalless first half, but a rare header from Charlton appeared to have won it for United just before the hour. But Benfica pulled level through Jaime Graca after 75 minutes, and the goal galvanised the Portuguese champions. Pressing hard, Eusebio eluded Stiles in the dying minutes, only to be denied by Stepney's parry when a winner seemed certain. This incident proved to be the turning point. In extra-time United, lifted by their supporters, were irresistible. A goal of characteristic genius from George Best set them on their way, his dribble through the entire defence unleashing raptures of relief around Wembley. Kidd and Charlton twisted the knife, and Benfica were finished.

👍 Apart from Busby and Bobby Charlton, centre-half Bill Foulkes was the only other Munich survivor involved in the match.

👎 For Denis Law, it was a bittersweet night. He watched the match from a hospital bed recovering from a knee operation.

☞ Foulkes' words after the game were moving: '...for those of us who lost our friends ... our victory seemed the right tribute to their memory'.

👍 The aftermath brought several more honours. Busby was knighted, while George Best was named English and European Footballer of the Year.

☞ The 1968 team, like the Busby Babes, was largely home-grown. Only Alex Stepney and Paddy Crerand had cost a fee.

SCORERS	**United:** Charlton (2), Best, Kidd
	Benfica: Graca
EVENT	European Cup final, Wembley, 29 May 1968
MAN UTD	(Man: Matt Busby)
	1. Stepney 2. Brennan 3. Dunne 4. Crerand 5. Foulkes 6. Stiles 7. Best 8. Kidd 9. Charlton 10. Sadler 11. Aston
BENFICA	(Man: Otto Gloria)
	1. Enrique 2. Adolfo 3. Humberto 4. Jacinto 5. Cruz 6. Jaime Graca 7. Coluna 8. Jose Augusto 9. Eusebio 10. Torres 11. Simoes

Unsung Heroes

Never Mind the Badge Kissers

LOYALTY IS OFTEN cited as the quality most lacking in the modern game. Ronaldo's search for a bigger pot of gold at Real Madrid, thus ignoring Internazionale's patience with his rehabilitation, is the most glaring example.

For the less gifted, the options are more prosaic. Some players, whether out of devotion or expediency, have demonstrated season after season of unyielding service. Goalkeepers often figure in clubs' appearance records due to their ability to eke out a longer career. Pride of place must go to Steve Ogrizovic. He remained as understudy for years at Anfield watching Ray Clemence positively ooze rude health. He not only lasted another 16 years as Coventry's No. 1 but showed enough consistency to set a club record for number of appearances.

As far as clubs go, West Ham has enjoyed a greater percentage of long-servers than almost any other. Some, like Bobby Moore, enjoyed almost every decoration possible. Spare a thought for fellow defender Billy Bonds, who chalked up a Hammers' record of 663 appearances. Despite proving himself a model of consistency, his sole reward was a single England call-up. He never even got on the pitch.

☞ March 1978. Chelsea's twin stalwarts Ron Harris and Peter Bonetti each make their 700th appearance for the club on the same day.

☞ Ian Callaghan, despite 18 years of success at Anfield, waited 12 years between England caps before being recalled by Ron Greenwood in 1978.

✍ John Trollope played 770 games for Swindon over 20 years, finally hanging up his boots in 1980 – an amazing record for an outfield player.

✍ The award for Best Uncapped Player. Step forward Tony Brown of West Brom. He holds two club records, 574 appearances and 218 goals, but never got an international sniff in 17 years.

'He is part of the furniture, like a grandad. He's a miserable old git but he has such presence'

Veteran Portsmouth keeper Alan Knight receives a dubious tribute from team-mate Paul Hall.

Valderrama, Carlos
Colombia

A FLAMBOYANT PLAYER even by the standards of South American football, Carlos Valderrama scarcely needed a huge corkscrew hairstyle to attract attention. The Colombian midfielder's abilities were plain to see; he passed and moved with intelligence and vision, directing his team around the field with his artistic promptings. On the minus side his theatrical tendencies stretched patience during the 1990 World Cup Finals, where he was stretchered off in apparent agony only to return miraculously minutes later. Following 11 seasons with his native Santa Marta he made the move to Europe where, during four years with Montpellier and Valladolid of Spain, he largely flattered to deceive and picked up just a single Spanish Cup winner's medal.

Like many great players Valderrama usually reserved his best for the big occasion, his greatest game being the pivotal performance in a sensational 5-0 demolition of Argentina still fondly remembered by Colombian supporters. Much like his national side, however, Valderrama always promised more than he actually delivered.

- In 1997, Valderrama became the first Colombian to be capped 100 times.
- He was South American Footballer of the Year in 1987 and 1993.
- Most critics believe Valderrama couldn't adjust to the pace of European football. Colombia, too, were often undone by technically inferior, but quicker and stronger sides.
- Unlike his compatriot Andres Escobar, he wasn't shot as a result of his team's shortcomings in the 1994 World Cup Finals.
- The hair really was a thing to behold, deserving of the captaincy of our Hairstyles XI (see Fashion Victims, Part 1).

VITAL STATISTICS

Place of Birth:	Santa Marta, Columbia		
Date of Birth:	2 September 1961	**Died:** n/a	
Caps:	111 (Columbia)	**Goals (International):** 11	
Clubs:	Santa Marta, Millonarios, Montpellier, Valladolid, Medellin, Atletico Junior Barranquilla, Nacional, Tampa Bay Mutiny, Miami Fusion, Colorado Rapids		

LEGEND RATING	
Achievement	5.0
Skill	9.0
Teamwork	6.0
Passion	8.0
Personality	8.0
TOTAL	**36.0**

Venables, Terry

Tottenham Hotspur, England

UNTIL RESCUING MIDDLESBROUGH from the clutches of Division One in 2001, Terry Venables had never taken a footballing job north of Tottenham. In a managerial career that has spanned three decades his English employers have been almost exclusively in London, serving to reinforce his reputation as the cockney geezer with more than a hint of the Essex wide-boy about him – a reputation, it has to be said, he added to by resigning as England coach to defend himself in court against accusations of financial misdoings. Fans were sorry to see him leave the England post. As 'the people's choice' to succeed Graham Taylor he was a huge success, only narrowly failing to take England to the final of Euro 96. Venables has always had a reputation as a manager with imagination and foresight; from his time at Crystal Palace to his resurrection of Barcelona, his teams have played with flair and innovative tactical formations. At the Nou Camp he led Barca to their first league title for 11 years in 1985, and was unlucky not to add the European Cup to his sideboard the following year when, famously, all five of his allotted penalty-takers missed their kicks in the shoot-out against Steaua Bucharest in the final. He was a better coach than he was a player; despite being tipped for greatness at schoolboy level his career drifted after his second and final England appearance.

- 1991. In partnership with Alan Sugar, Venables bought Spurs. Two years later, a bitter High Court battle ended with Sugar gaining sole control.
- 1995. A judge described Venables' court evidence as 'wanton' and 'not entirely credible'.
- 1997. Venables enjoyed a brief spell as Australian national coach, then bought Portsmouth for £1.
- 2002–3 proved a tough one for Venables. He started it as Leeds' potential saviour but left before its end with Leeds in trouble.

VITAL STATISTICS

Place of Birth:	London, England		
Date of Birth:	6 January 1943	**Died:**	n/a
Caps:	2 (England)	**Goals (International):**	0
Clubs:	As Player: Chelsea, Tottenham, Queens Park Rangers, Crystal Palace; As Manager: Crystal Palace, Queens Park Rangers, Barcelona, Tottenham, English national side, Portsmouth, Australian national side, Middlesbrough, Leeds United		
Trophies:	PLA 1986; FAC 1991		

Achievement	6
Tactical Awareness	9
Motivation	8
Team Selection/Transfers	9
Personality	7
TOTAL	**39**

LEGEND RATING

Vialli, Gianluca

Chelsea, Italy

A 20-YEAR CAREER at the summit of European football ought to have been sufficient, yet it is typical of Luca Vialli's motivation that, at an age when most of his peers were looking to Serie A for coaching jobs, he should be determined to accept the challenge to resurrect his managerial career in Division One with Watford.

By rights, his first experience of management should have put him off for life; thrust into the hot seat at Chelsea in 1998 following Ruud Gullit's sacking, he was to suffer the same fate within two years despite a top-three league finish and five trophies. The Chelsea supporters certainly did not consider him a failure; such was Vialli's popularity at Stamford Bridge his name was still being chanted around the ground over a year after his departure.

As a Chelsea player Vialli was underused and played only two minutes of the 1997 FA Cup final – strange for a player who had won every major honour in his native Italy, including a League and Cup double in a glorious season in 1994–95. His international career never produced the headlines of Paolo Rossi or Roberto Baggio, but he remains one of Italy's most popular players. Latterly, Vialli's attempts to buy Watford out of trouble backfired. He left the club after a little more than a season, suing them for compensation; he eventually settled for a £1.5 m payout..

- He is one of only a handful of players to have won all three European club trophies.
- He scored both goals for Sampdoria in the 1990 European Cup Winners' Cup final.
- As Ruud Gullit's first foreign signing, Vialli's arrival started a Chelsea trend for imports.
- Discarded early from international football, Vialli won the last of his 59 caps at 28.
- 'Cheer up Luca, we love you.' Dennis Wise's T-shirt slogan, inspired by Vialli's unhappiness at Chelsea's squad rotation and his frequent omission.

VITAL STATISTICS

Place of Birth:	Cremona, Italy	
Date of Birth:	9 June 1964	**Died:** n/a
Caps:	59 (Italy)	**Goals (International):** 16
Clubs:	Cremonese, Sampdoria, Juventus, Chelsea	
Appearances:	Club (League): 467	
Goals:	Club (League): 156	
Trophies:	CWC 1990, (1998); UEFAC 1993; EC 1996;	
	SA 1991, 1995; FAC 1997, (2000); LC (1998)	

LEGEND RATING	
Achievement	8.0
Skill	8.0
Teamwork	7.0
Passion	7.0
Personality	8.0
TOTAL	**38.0**

Vieira, Patrick
Arsenal, France

PATRICK VIEIRA and Emmanuel Petit were the twin midfield turbines of the Arsenal side that won the League in 1998, a season the pair rounded off by collecting World Cup Winner's medals with France. Two years later Vieira was again in the medals, picking up a winner's gong at Euro 2000 following France's victory over Italy – all in all a fairly tidy haul for the Senegalese-born midfielder.

Vieira first emerged at Cannes where he captained the side in the French First Division at the age of 18. From there he wasted little time securing a move to AC Milan but, after failing to break into the side, he was rescued from his Milanese nightmare by Arsène Wenger who paid £3.5 m to bring him to Highbury. That fee now looks like a steal. Wenger bought a player with skill and good distribution, but also immense strength.

Since arriving in England Vieira has improved with every season, and there are signs that the fuse on his temper, so often the source of his disciplinary problems, is growing longer with age. Failure in the 2002 World Cup Finals seems to have simply driven Vieira on even harder, but injury saw him miss France's Euro 2004 quarter-final against ultimate champions Greece. His intense rivalry with Roy Keane, another uncompromising figure with an equally quick temper, has been one of the Premiership's great sub-plots in recent years.

- After being dismissed in his first two games of the 2000–01 season, he had to be persuaded not to quit English football by Arsène Wenger.
- He played only two games in Milan's first team – their loss.
- He was comfortably the best player in the 2001 FA Cup final, but still ended up on the losing side, thanks to Michael Owen.
- Vieira is exceptionally tall for a midfield player, giving his side an extra threat in the air at set-pieces.
- Viera was not a first choice for France at the 1998 World Cup, having to wait until Euro 2000 before establishing himself as his country's leading central midfielder.

VITAL STATISTICS

Place of Birth:	Dakar, Senegal	
Date of Birth:	23 June 1976	**Died:** n/a
Caps:	72 (France)	**Goals (International):** 4
Clubs:	Cannes, AC Milan, Arsenal	
Appearances:	Club (League): 310	
Goals:	Club (League): 27	
Trophies:	SA 1996; WorC 1998; EuroC 2000; LT 1998, 2002, 2004; FAC 1998, 2002	

LEGEND RATING

Achievement	9.0
Skill	8.0
Teamwork	8.5
Passion	9.0
Personality	5.5
TOTAL	**40.0**

Villa, Veni, Vici
The Aston Villa Dream Team

ASTON VILLA'S LONG HISTORY dictates that their dream team draws its personnel from a group of players spanning several generations. One of the dominant sides in the early years of the Football League, Villa won the championship six times before 1910, and remained in the top division for most of the next five decades, before the rot set in the 1960s. The next Villa side to make an impact won the league in 1981, and were a team largely without international stars – which might explain why only Cowans, Gray and Gidman make this all time XI (Dennis Mortimer and Peter Withe also came close).

Goalkeeper Sam Hardy was the first great England goalkeeper, and John Devey was Villa's most glamorous player in those early years. Massie, Walker and Dixon, though unfamiliar names to modern fans, were all excellent midfielders and David Platt would have enjoyed feeding off the nod downs of aerial superpowers, Hitchens and Gray. There are no representatives from the current, rather colourless team, although Ian Taylor deserves a mention for service and consistency, and Darius Vassell has the potential to develop into a genuine claret-and-blue icon.

- Charlie Aitken made a club record 656 appearances, many of them during Villa's days in the lower divisions.
- Nigel Spink's second game for Villa was the 1982 European Cup final. He was drafted into the team just 10 minutes after kick-off, after Jimmy Rimmer ricked his neck in the warm-up.
- Gerry Hitchens ('The Blond Bomber') shocked Villa fans by leaving for Internazionale in 1961, the same summer Jimmy Greaves also departed for Milan.
- Dixon and McParland played in the 1957 FA Cup final against Man United, with McParland scoring both goals in a 2-1 win.
- Gordon Cowans, though never given a lengthy run in the England team, was the lynchpin of Villa's European Cup success.

Manager: Ron Saunders

4-4-2

Samuel Hardy (10s)

Stan Lynn (50s) Paul McGrath (90s)
Gareth Southgate (C) (90s) Charlie Aitken (70s)

John Devey (1890s) Gordon Cowans (80s)
David Platt (80s/90s) John Dixon (40s/50s)

Gerald Hitchens (50s) Andy Gray (80s)

Subs: Nigel Spink (G) (80s/90s) John Gidman (D) (80s)
Alex Massie (M) (30s) Billy Walker (M/F) (20s) Peter McParland (50s)

Vogts, Hans-Hubert (Berti)
Borussia Mönchengladbach, West Germany

BERTI VOGTS was known in Germany as Der Terrier, acknowledgement of his tenacity and fighting spirit. Picked up by Bourussia Mönchengladbach at an early age, he developed into a competitive right back, and was an automatic choice for West Germany by the time the 1970 World Cup came around. Four years later he was still around, in an even better team with Beckenbauer, Breitner, Overath and Müller, that had won the 1992 European Championship at a canter. This time, at home, West Germany prevailed, and manager Helmut Schon's masterstroke was detailing Vogts to man-mark Johan Cruyff. After a torrid first 20 minutes Vogts got hold of the Dutch master, and Germany came back from the shock of an early penalty to win 2-1. Four years later he was captain for a disappointing campaign in Argentina. Vogts stayed at Mönchengladbach all his career – they were second only to Bayern Munich in the early 1970s, and Vogts won a plethora of domestic medals, as well as the UEFA Cup.

Vogts became a manager and coached the German national team that won the European Championship in England in 1996. In early 2002 he became the first overseas coach to be put in charge of Scotland, but found it difficult making a competitive team with a squad thin on talent. He resigned acrimoniously in October, 2004.

- Cruyff was so frustrated at the close attention he received from Vogts that he was booked for complaining vociferously at half-time. Sad as it was to see a great player suppressed, the tactic won the game.
- Vogts was frustrated in his quest to win the European Cup, the one trophy that eluded him. Mönchengladbach were beaten 3-1 by Liverpool in the 1977 final.
- His last match for West Germany was in the 1978 World Cup Finals – he scored an own goal, a sad way for a great player to go.
- In 96 internationals, Vogts scored only one goal.
- Vogts suffered torrid abuse as Scotland manager. It would appear sections of the Scottish press seem oblivious to the fact that they don't have a single international class player.

VITAL STATISTICS

Place of Birth:	Büttgen, Germany
Date of Birth:	30 December 1946 **Died:** n/a
Caps:	96 (W. Germany) **Goals (International):** 1
Clubs:	VFB Büttgen, Borussia Mönchengladbach
Appearances:	Club (League): 419
Goals:	Club (League): 32
Trophies:	WorC 1974; BLG 1970, 1971, 1975, 1976, 1977; UEFAC 1975, 1979; EuroC (1996)

LEGEND RATING	
Achievement	9.5
Skill	7.0
Teamwork	8.5
Passion	7.5
Personality	6.5
TOTAL	**39.0**

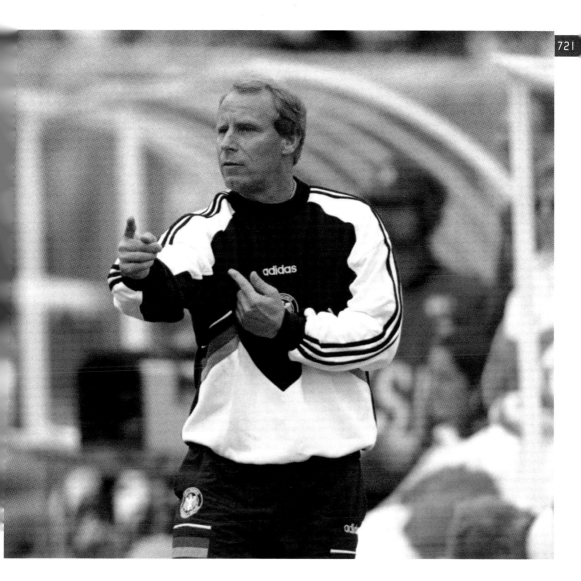

Walter, Fritz

Kaiserslautern, West Germany

THE FIRST GREAT GERMAN FOOTBALLER, Fritz Walter started his career during the war, and emerged afterwards as the biggest influence on the newly formed West German national team. A goal-scoring centre-half, Walter was a typically German player: strong and physical, he was a driving influence in the middle of the field, a genuine forerunner of Franz Beckenbauer and Lothar Matthaus. Walter was 33 when he first played at a World Cup, in Switzerland in 1954. And, as if mindful that it might be his one and only chance, he performed like a man on a mission. After destroying Austria 6-1 in the semi-final, the formidable Hungarians awaited West Germany in the final. Hungary took an early 2-0 lead but, inspired by the aggression and sheer will of Walter and the pace and finishing of Helmut Rahn, they came back to win 3-2. As it happened, 1954 was not Walter's first and last appearance at the Finals. Still going strong in 1958, he took West Germany to the semi-finals against host-nation Sweden, but picked up an injury in the game that, in addition to contributing to Germany's defeat, ended his international career.

☞ Walter's brother, Otto, also played for the West German side in 1954 – they were the first pair of brothers to play in a final.

☞ Kaiserslautern provided six players for the West German team in the 1954 final.

☞ All Fritz Walter's club football was played with Kaiserslautern, his home team. They re-named their stadium in his honour in 1985.

✎ Walter's goal-scoring rate was much higher early in his career, but he still managed two in the thrashing of Austria. Otto also scored twice.

☞ National coach Sepp Herberger tried to persuade Walter to come out of retirement for the 1962 World Cup Finals, aged 41!

VITAL STATISTICS

Place of Birth:	Kaiserslautern, Germany
Date of Birth:	31 October 1920 **Died:** 17 June 2002
Caps:	61 (W. Germany) **Goals (International):** 33
Clubs:	FC Kaiserslautern
Trophies:	WorC 1954; BLG 1951, 1953

LEGEND RATING	
Achievement	9.0
Skill	7.0
Teamwork	9.0
Passion	8.0
Personality	7.0
TOTAL	**40.0**

Watersnoodwedstrijd
France 1 Holland 2, 1953

ON THE NIGHT of 31 January 1953, the dykes of Southwest Holland collapsed. Large tracts of land were inundated; 1800 people died and 100,000 had to be evacuated. The material damage was enormous and a National Disaster Fund was founded.

Theo Timmermans, a professional footballer playing in Nîmes, France, organised a football match in support of the fund, between Dutch professionals playing abroad and the French national team. At that time Holland had no domestic professional football, and professionals playing abroad were barred from the Dutch team.

The match took place on 12 March at the Parc-des-Princes in Paris. A crowd of 39,000 people turned up, including 5000 Dutchmen. It was a momentous match for Holland: the Dutch players, who had never played together, excelled in the second half and ran out 2-1 winners against a decent French side. There was live commentary of the match, and the listeners at home learned that the most talented Dutchmen were plying their trade abroad.

The match was a breakthrough in the perception of professional football in the Netherlands. A year later the first professional club was founded, Fortuna '54, and at the end of that year paid exiles were asked to play in the Dutch team. Domestic football in Holland began to mature, and a decade later the international breakthrough followed.

☞ Kees Rijvers was coach of the Dutch team from July 1981 until November 1984.

☞ Frans de Munck, the keeper was the only 'non-French' professional. He was the unrivalled star of the match and during his whole career as a keeper he remained a household name in Holland.

👆 Another key player of this generation was the stylish centre back Cor van der Hart. He played at the highest level for 20 years in more than 1,000 matches.

👆 In French professional football Bertus de Harder was a phenomenon. He became an honorary citizen of Bordeaux.

SCORERS	**France:** Saunier
	Holland: De Harder, Appel
EVENT	Flood Disaster Game, Paris, 12 March 1953
FRANCE	(Man: Gabriel Hanot)
	1. Ruminski 2. Gianessi 3. Marche 4. Penverne 5. Jonquet 6. Gaulon 7. Kopa 8. Ujlaki 9. Saunier 10. Gardien 11. Deladerrière
HOLLAND	(Man: Edmond Delfour)
	1. De Munck 2. De Vroet 3. Van Der Hart 4. Vreeken 5. Schaap 6. Kubber 7. Van Geen 8. Timmermans 9. Appel 10. Rijvers 11. De Harder

Weah, George

AC Milan, Liberia

DISCOVERED IN 1987 by Arsène Wenger in Cameroon, where he was playing for his fifth club side, Tonerre Yaounde, Weah became the most talented and celebrated African player since Eusebio. His ceaseless charity efforts for his war-torn homeland showed a depth of personality that earned him the epithet 'light of Liberia'. His success in Europe convinced big European clubs that African players could adapt, and paved the way for a myriad of talented Africans to follow.

The North London connection continued a year later in 1988 as Weah linked up with Glenn Hoddle at Monaco. From there, in 1992, he was transferred to Paris Saint-Germain, where he collected a league championship medal before moving on to even greater glories with AC Milan in Serie A. His pace, skill and directness frightened Italian defences, and was never better demonstrated than in the stunning length-of-the-field dribble that brought him one of the greatest goals of all time in a 4-0 win over Verona at the San Siro. Some have suggested an element of tokenism in his World and European Footballer of the Year awards, but let that not obscure the fact that he leaves an important legacy, both sporting and humanitarian.

☞ Two of Weah's splendidly named African clubs include Bong Range and Invincible Eleven.

✌ Weah is three times African Footballer of the Year (1989, 1994, 1995) and World and European Footballer of the Year in 1995.

☞ Playing for Liberia guaranteed that Weah would achieve nothing at international level. Had Nigeria or Cameroon had a striker of his potency, their 1990s World Cup campaigns might have been even more interesting.

👍 A late move to England in 2000 brought an FA Cup winner's medal with Chelsea, but he was clearly on the wane.

👎 His career in England ended on a sad note when he left Man City after a public disagreement with manager Joe Royle.

VITAL STATISTICS

Place of Birth:	Monrovia, Liberia			
Date of Birth:	1 October 1966	**Died:** n/a	Achievement	7.0
Caps:	42 (Liberia)	**Goals (International):** 7	Skill	8.0
Clubs:	Tonerre Yaounde, Monaco, Paris St Germain,		Teamwork	7.0
	AC Milan, Chelsea, Manchester City, Marseille		Passion	8.0
Appearances:	Club (League): 368		Personality	8.0
Goals:	Club (League): 148			
Trophies:	FLT 1988, 1994; SA 1996 1999; FAC 2000		**TOTAL**	**38.0**

LEGEND RATING

Wembley
England

ORIGINALLY NAMED The Empire Stadium, Wembley has several nicknames including 'The Old Lady' and 'The Venue of Legends'. Built in the space of 300 days at a cost of under £750,000, it was the brainchild of architects John Simpson and Maxwell Ayrton, who worked together with the engineer Sir Owen Williams.

It opened for the 1923 Cup final between Bolton and West Ham. The first myth was duly created, as over 200,000 fans stormed the gates and were cleared with the aid of PC George Storey on his famous white horse Billy. Since then, the famous twin towers have played host to 72 FA Cup and 24 League Cup finals, as well as several European club finals. It was England's venue for Euro 96, but its greatest moments were reserved for the 1966 World Cup.

In staging the Finals, England had the advantage of playing all six games at Wembley. Charlton's goal against Mexico and Rattin's dismissal for Argentina provided the prologue and first act. The dramatic finale was reserved for the final; Hurst's hat-trick, Stiles' jig and Moore receiving the trophy are national mementos destined to be handed down through the generations.

☞ Wembley was the main venue for the 1948 Olympic Games.

✍ Amazingly for a stadium then holding 100,000, it was built in less than a year by construction experts McAlpine. Its first intended use was for the British exhibition.

☟ Despite its pageantry, Wembley was overdue a refit and closed in 2000. Its last game was very disappointing, as England squelched to a 1-0 defeat against Germany in a World Cup qualifier. It was also the last England game with Kevin Keegan as coach.

☞ After years of prevarication, a new Wembley, complete with an arch spanning the entire stadium and dominating the North-West London skyline, is slowly rising from the rubble.

VITAL STATISTICS

Location:	London, England
Local Club:	None
Date Built:	1923
Current Capacity	
(before closure):	80,000
Max. Capacity:	126,947

Wembley Wizards
Scotland, 1928

THIS WAS A TEAM celebrated not for its domination of an era, but for one game. And if, as the chant goes, you know your history, it was the sweetest game ever for all Scotland fans. The England versus Scotland clash at Wembley in 1928 ought not to have held any terrors for the home side; in the corresponding fixture the previous season, England had triumphed 2-1 at Hampden Park. Nothing could have prepared them for what was to come. Some of Scotland's best players, like so many after them, were plying their trade in England so, in theory at least, the two teams should have known each other's games well. Indeed, many of them were club team-mates. Scotland's half-back and captain Jimmy McMullan was the passing playmaker of Manchester City, and was to emerge as the man of the match. With targets as mobile as Alex James (Preston, later Arsenal), Alex Jackson (Huddersfield) and Hughie Gallacher (Newcastle) he was not short of players to hit. With England frozen like startled rabbits in the headlights of a juggernaut, Jackson helped himself to a hat-trick, leaving James and Gibson to notch the other two in a thumping 5-1 victory. For Scottish fans, that 1928 win was a symbolic act of defiance, a footballing equivalent of Bannockburn – which is why they still sing about it today.

☞ In the context of the Home Internationals, Scotland's victory was meaningless. Both teams were playing merely to avoid the ignominious wooden spoon.

☞ England blamed the heavy pitch for the result, claiming it gave the smaller, nippier Scots an advantage.

☜ Not only was it a thrashing, it was England's first defeat at Wembley.

☞ Gallacher and James commanded huge transfer fees. Gallacher was sold to Chelsea in 1930 for £10,000, while James cost over £8,500, when Herbert Chapman took him to Arsenal in 1929.

☞ England's team contained no lack of firepower; Dixie Dean scored a record 60 goals in the same season. He scarcely got a kick.

Manager: None
(team was picked by committee)

Key Players
McMullan (M) Alex James (M) Gallacher (F) Jackson (F)

Trophies
None (but this Scottish side became famous for inflicting such a heavy defeat on the Auld Enemy on their own turf)

Wenger, Arsène
Monaco, Arsenal

WHEN BRUCE RIOCH FAILED to work out at Arsenal, everyone was looking around for the big-name British manager who would take his place. After all the trophies under George Graham, there was a high level of expectation at Highbury. It came as something of a shock when they appointed Arsène Wenger, who was then working as a coach in the J-League in Japan.

His first season in full charge as a manager, at Nancy, was inauspicious – they were relegated. A move to Monaco in 1987 allowed Wenger to show his worth. A team containing Glenn Hoddle, who was to recommend him to Arsenal, won the French league a year later.

In his time at Arsenal he has introduced a new methodology and turned them from "boring, boring Arsenal" into an exciting, creative attacking team. On the downside, the team have been beset by disciplinary problems; a disgraceful exhibition in a match against Manchester United saw them lucky to avoid even more serious censure from the authorities.

☞ Strasbourg won the league title when Wenger was a player there, but he only appeared three times in that season.

👆 Wenger took Nagoya Grampus 8 from third-bottom to runners-up in the J-League in his first season.

👎 He was charged with serious disrepute after an altercation with the fourth official in the opening game of the 2000–01 season. A 12-match touchline ban was later overturned.

👆 A few flaky imports in the early years have given way to some inspired scouting. Unknowns (to British audiences) like Fabregas, Clichy, Reyes and Van Persie come straight into the side and perform at a high level.

👎 December 2004: fined £15,000 after accusing van Nistelrooy of cheating in Arsenal's traditionally ill-tempered visit to Old Trafford.

VITAL STATISTICS

Place of Birth: Strasbourg, France

Date of Birth: 1 January 1950   **Died:** n/a

Caps: 0 (France)   **Goals (International):** 0

Clubs: As Player: Strasbourg; As Manager: Nancy, Monaco, Nagoya Grampus Eight, Arsenal

Trophies: FLT 1998; LT 1998, 2002, 2004; FAC 1998, 2002, 2003

Achievement	9.0	
Tactical Awareness	8.5	
Motivation	8.0	LEGEND RATING
Team Selection/Transfers	8.0	
Personality	7.0	

TOTAL 40.5

White Horse Wembley
Bolton Wanderers 2 West Ham United 0, 1923

THE NEWLY COMPLETED Empire Stadium at Wembley had been chosen as the venue for the Cup final. Amazingly, it was not an all-ticket event, a fact which resulted in mayhem.

A realistic estimate is that 250,000 people turned up to a stadium built to hold 100,000. Most of them were allowed in, with a result that at the scheduled kick-off time of 3 p.m., thousands of fans covered the pitch.

The day was saved by one PC Storey. Mounted on his horse Billy, he helped push back the throng to just beyond the touchlines with such success that the game started only 44 minutes late. Legend has it (falsely) that he managed this feat single-handed when in fact, Billy's distinctive white appearance was the only one visible from a distance.

After such a delay, and with the crowd encroaching to within inches of the pitch, the game was not a classic. David Jack gave Bolton an advantage after two minutes that they seldom looked like losing. J.R. Smith's goal after 53 minutes would have grabbed the headlines in any other year. They had already been written by a single white horse.

☞ The FA was worried about the appeal of the new stadium and had advertised widely for fans to attend. They had to refund 10 per cent of the gate to spectators with pre-paid tickets who were unable to get to their seats.

☞ PC Storey was not scheduled to be at Wembley that afternoon. He answered an emergency call in Central London to report to the ground once the crowds got out of hand.

☞ The FA could not abandon the game: King George V was there.

☞ Bolton's first goal was aided by West Ham defender Jack Tressdern, who was caught up in the crowd after taking a throw-in, allowing David Jack a free passage. Jack's shot knocked out a spectator pressed against the net.

SCORERS	Jack, JR Smith
EVENT	FA Cup Final, Wembley, 28 April 1923
BOLTON	(Man: Charles Foweraker)
	1. Pym 2. Haworth 3. Finney 4. Nuttall 5. Seddon 6. Jennings 7. Butler 8. Jack 9. JR Smith 10. Joe Smith 11. Vizard
WEST HAM	(Man: Syd King)
	1. Hufton 2. Henderson 3. Young 4. Bishop 5. Kay 6. Tressdern 7. Richards 8. Brown 9. Watson 10. Moore 11. Ruffell

White Supremacy
Real Madrid, 1954–66

IT CAN'T HAVE BEEN much fun coaching Real Madrid in the 1970s or 1980s. How on earth do you satisfy the supporters of a club who have won the European Cup five times on the run, and have grown used to winning the league almost every year? The answer is you can't – which might explain why Real went 32 years before reclaiming their crown as champions of Europe.

Unlike the FA, the Spanish football authorities relished the opportunity the European competition presented, and this enthusiasm helped Real in those early tournaments. It also gave exposure to talented players from less prestigious clubs; even before playing Reims in the 1956 final, Real had decided to buy their playmaker, Raymond Kopa.

After that first flush of victories in Europe, Real found it harder going. Benfica and the two Milan teams emerged as threats to their supremacy (as Real struggled to replace Di Stefano and Puskas, these three won the next five tournaments). Although they never could replace those great players, Real did manage a swansong, winning the European Cup in 1966.

☞ Real knocked the young Busby Babes out of the European Cup in the 1957 semi-finals. Were it not for the air crash, they may have met again in the 1958 final, but AC Milan easily beat the makeshift United team in the semis.

✍ Miguel Munoz was a half-back in the 1956 and 1957 European Cup final teams. Three years later he coached Real to their most famous victory over Eintracht Frankfurt. He remained as manager for 14 years. (The longest run since has been three!)

✍ Amancio Amaro won nine league titles with Real Madrid, and scored their first goal in the 1966 European Cup final against Partizan Belgrade.

Managers: Pepe Villalonga
(1955–57), Luis Carniglia (1957–59) and
Miguel Munoz (1960–74)

Key Players
Alonso (G) Zarraga (D) Alfredo Di Stefano (M)
Francisco Gento (W) Jose Santamaria (D) Ferenc Puskas (F)
Raymond Kopa (M) Ignacio Zoco (M) Hector Rial (F)
Amancio Amaro (F)

Wild West
Pro Soccer in the USA

FOOTBALL HAS BEEN PLAYED in the States since the original settlers arrived from Britain in the 1600s. Historically however, the game has struggled to compete with the traditional stateside passions of American football and baseball. Although millions of youngsters now play the game, professional 'soccer' has consistently failed to make an impact. The first national league in the States was actually formed in 1895, but it was not until the mid-1970s that football began to capture the hearts and minds of the wider public. The arrival of the great Pelé at the New York Cosmos in 1975 was the catalyst for a golden era, and other soccer greats such as Franz Beckenbauer, George Best, Rodney Marsh and Zico also made their way out to the North American Soccer League before it folded in 1984. A decade of decline followed until America was chosen to host the 1994 World Cup. This sparked new interest and Major League Soccer was launched two years later. It attracted the major TV companies and sponsorship, and continues to thrive today.

☞ The Oneida Football Club was formed in 1862 in Boston and is widely regarded as the first team to be formally established in the States. It was made up of youngsters from public schools in the Boston area.

☞ The American Football Association was founded in 1895, only the fourth national association to be formed worldwide. It helped establish the first national competition – the American Cup.

☞ The United States' 1-0 victory over England in the 1950 World Cup is regarded as one of the biggest international upsets in history. England were one of the best sides in the world at the time.

'If the American League of Association Football of 1895 had been a success the sports landscape in America might be much different today.'

US sports historian Steve Holroyd

Wilkes, Faas
Inter, Valencia, Holland

WHEN ENGLAND PLAYED Holland in 1946, and won 8-2, the English press highlighted the abilities of one of the Dutch inside forwards, despite the heavy defeat. Charlton and Arsenal susbsequently tried to lure the talented Faas Wilkes to England, but he opted instead for Inter Milan. Wilkes' move sparked off a drain of Holland's major footballing talents to other countries.

A short spell in Torino was followed by a highly successful stint in Valencia. The Italians and Spanish loved his quick feet and thrilling dribbling skills – he was dubbed 'The Dutch Windmill' by the Italians, after his habit of running with his arms flailing around him.

Wilkes was limited to 38 caps for his country, almost a third of them against neighbours Belgium. The war, and a ban on foreign professionals appearing for Holland, (from 1949–55) prevented him attaining the international status his skills probably merited. Whatever the quality of the opposition, 35 goals in 38 games is no mean return.

Little known outside his own country, Faas Wilkes was the first great Dutch footballer, and the inspiration and prototype for all those household names to come.

☞ In 1952, Wilkes was in the Inter side that played Napoli in a fictional match for a comic movie about a betting scam.

☝ Wilkes was deprived of a Spanish Cup Winners' medal in 1954 when Franco barred all foreigners from playing in 'his' Copa de Generalissimo.

☝ In 1954 Faas Wilkes was Spanish Footballer of the Year, ahead of Di Stefano and Kubala.

☝ In 1954 Wilkes scored three times in one game within five minutes, in the Valencia v Barcelona match. It was his 31st birthday and the Barcelona keeper was the famous Ramallets.

VITAL STATISTICS

Place of Birth:	Rotterdam, Holland	
Date of Birth:	13 October 1923	**Died:** n/a
Caps:	38 (Holland)	**Goals (International):** 35
Clubs:	Xerxes, Internazionale, Torino, Valencia, VVV, Levante, Fortuna '54	
Appearances:	Club (All matches for Inter): 95	
Goals:	Club (All matches for Inter): 47	
Trophies:	None	

Achievement	5.0
Skill	8.0
Teamwork	7.0
Passion	8.0
Personality	8.0
TOTAL	**36.0**

LEGEND RATING

Wingless Wonders
England 1966

IT IS A LINE-UP that England fans can recite like a mantra. And yet it is a team almost as notable for the players it does not include as those that it does. The full-backs were good, honest professionals – but functional. Jimmy Armfield was a classier right-back than George Cohen, whilst Ray Wilson can count himself lucky that Terry Cooper did not arrive on the other flank until three years later. Bobby Moore and Gordon Banks provided the defensive class, natural choices in any England team. And though the midfield was solid, the emergence of Alan Mullery and Colin Bell for the next World Cup certainly hadn't weakened it (indeed, some would argue it was improved by their inclusion). The forwards present a knotty problem. Geoff Hurst vindicated his late selection, his four goals in the last three games saw off Argentina in the quarter-finals and West Germany in the final, but the player he replaced, Jimmy Greaves, was an even more prolific scorer (his 44 goals in 57 games is England's most impressive modern ratio by a distance). Roger Hunt may be the lucky man here. Whatever the argument, and many feel the 1970 side was even better, no one can deny this XI their place in England's hall of fame as the nation's only World Cup winners.

☞ This side was dubbed the 'wingless wonders' due to Alf Ramsey's reluctance to use wide players.

✎ From 1958 to 1970, only England broke Brazil's dominance of the World Cup.

☞ Cohen and Wilson were capped for a further two years. The young Alan Ball was a regular until 1975.

✎ After winning the Jules Rimet trophy, England remained undefeated for nearly a year, until Scotland beat them 3-2 at Wembley.

Manager: Alf Ramsey

Key Players
Gordon Banks(G) George Cohen (D) Ray Wilson (D)
Nobby Stiles (M) Jack Charlton (D) Bobby Moore (D)
Alan Ball (M) Geoff Hurst (F) Roger Hunt (F)
Bobby Charlton (M) Martin Peters (M)

Trophies
WorC 1966

Alf Ramsey and Bobby Moore flank the Jules Rimet trophy

Women's World Cup
New World Order

THE BRAINCHILD of former FIFA President Joao Havelange, the official Women's World Cup did not come into existence until 1991. The first tournament was staged in China and was dominated by America. They scored 20 goals in six games with striker Michelle Akers grabbing 10 on her own, including five in one game against Chinese Taipei. However, the Americans were made to fight all the way in the final by Norway, whom they eventually defeated 2-1. The second tournament was held in Sweden, and Norway gained sweet revenge by knocking the USA out at the semi-final stage. Norway then went on to lift the title courtesy of a 2-0 victory over Germany.

The US staged the finals in 1999 and the host team returned to the top of the women's game after winning a dramatic penalty shoot-out against China after the final finished goalless. They could not retain their form in 2003, losing in the semis. Sweden were beaten in the final by a flawless Germany..

- More than 63,000 fans watched the USA beat Norway in the first official Women's World Cup final in 1991.
- Brandi Chastain stripped off her top after scoring the decisive penalty for the US in the 1999 World Cup final. She later claimed it was 'momentary insanity'. The incident was given disproportionate and unedifying coverage.
- The US trio of strikers Michelle Akers, Carin Jennings and April Heinrichs scored 20 goals in six games to reach the first title.
- 90,185 fans watched the 1999 Women's World Cup final in Pasadena and millions more tuned in to it on television.
- The introduction of professionalism at Fulham could herald a new era for English women's football.
- The 2003 finals were due to be hosted by China, but FIFA made an eleventh-hour decision to hold them in the States because of the SARS epidemic.

'In some ways it's the biggest sporting event of the last decade. It's new and exciting for the United States. It will have a very far-reaching impact, not only for the United States, but for the world.'

President Bill Clinton after the USA's Women's World Cup victory over China in 1999

Pasadena, 1999. The USA raises its second World C

Wright, Billy
Wolverhampton Wanderers, England

WHEN BILLY WRIGHT passed Bob Crompton's record number of England caps in May 1952 it was his 42nd appearance. That he went on to more than double that record is a testimony to his talent, consistency and downright resilience. Wright was unlucky to play in an era when insularity reigned in British football, so was never able to develop his game properly against the more creative European sides. In 1953 he bore the brunt of criticism after England had been led a merry dance by the Hungarians at Wembley, having taken flak after the humiliating defeat to the USA in the 1950 World Cup. Abysmal tactics and selection meant Wright never made an impact on a major tournament – that was left to his natural successor, Bobby Moore.

His experiences at club level were not dissimilar. Despite Wolves' dominance of the domestic game in the 1950s, their performances in the European Cup were disappointing – a narrow defeat to Schalke, and a hammering by Barcelona. Old-fashioned he might have been, but Wright was a player of enormous integrity, an honest pro who never gave less than his lung-busting best whether playing at half-back or, as he did later in his career, in the centre of defence. Disciplined, determined and fearless he was also the perfect captain.

- In 1959 Wright made his 100th appearance for England, fittingly against Scotland. England won 1-0.
- Wright missed only three games in reaching his century. Eighty-five of his 100 appearances were as captain.
- Wright's last match for England was against the USA; an 8-1 win was partial revenge for the embarrassment in 1950.
- Wright had four years as Arsenal manager in the early 1960s, but achieved nothing and was lost to the game soon after.
- Wright was PFA Player of the Year in 1952, and was awarded a CBE on his retirement. A monument was constructed two years after his death, and now stands outside Molineux.

VITAL STATISTICS

Place of Birth:	Ironbridge, England	
Date of Birth:	6 February 1924	**Died:** 3 September 1994
Caps:	105 (England)	**Goals (International):** 3
Clubs:	Wolverhampton Wanderers	
Appearances:	Club (League): 490	
Goals:	Club (League): 13	
Trophies:	FAC 1951; LT 1954, 1958, 1959	

LEGEND RATING	
Achievement	8.0
Skill	8.0
Teamwork	9.0
Passion	10.0
Personality	6.0
TOTAL	**41.0**

Yashin, Lev
USSR

AS RUSSIA'S MOST FAMOUS and charismatic player, Lev Yashin's presence dominated Soviet football for two decades, while appearances in three World Cups brought his talents to a wider audience. Yashin made his name with Moscow Dynamo; five League titles for the club were due in no small part to his ability between the sticks.

Emerging in the European Championships in 1960, Yashin rapidly established himself as the world's top goalkeeper, a position only Gordon Banks would later challenge him for. Known as 'The Octopus' (to strikers it sometimes seemed as if he had eight arms) Yashin revolutionised the image of goalkeepers, transforming them from anonymous men in polo necks to swashbuckling match-winners. His swansong was the 1966 World Cup Finals, which found him in peak form. The tournament won him so many admirers that, later, in 1971, his testimonial was attended by Pelé, Eusebio, Bobby Charlton and Franz Beckenbauer.

Yashin's promotion to team manager of the Soviet Union was immediate upon his retirement, but with a poor squad he could never scale the heights he reached as a player.

- He was, and still is, the only goalkeeper to have ever been voted European Footballer of the Year, in 1963.
- The Soviet Union won the inaugural European Championships in 1960.
- Yashin always wore a trademark black jersey.
- Yashin skippered the Soviet Union to the semi-finals of the 1966 World Cup, where they lost 2-0 to Germany.
- One of the great shot-stoppers, Yashin saved over 100 penalties.

VITAL STATISTICS

Place of Birth:	Moscow, Russia	
Date of Birth:	22 October 1929	**Died:** 20 March 1990
Caps:	78 (USSR)	**Goals (International):** 0
Clubs:	Moscow Dynamo	
Appearances:	Club (League): 326	
Goals:	Club (League): 0	
Trophies:	EuroC 1960; SLT 1954, 1955, 1957, 1959, 1963	

LEGEND RATING	
Achievement	6.0
Skill	10.0
Teamwork	8.0
Passion	10.0
Personality	8.0
TOTAL	**42.0**

You English $&@#

Keane's Outburst

EACH SUCCESSIVE WORLD CUP is approached in an ever-increasing frenzy of media coverage. Amidst the injury bulletins and who's in/who's out speculation there is usually a juicy tale to enliven the tabloids. 2002 saw a tale to match the Bobby Moore 'shoplifting' episode and Johan Cruyff's 1978 no-show.

The Irish training facilities were crude, unworthy of a side that had exceeded expectations by even qualifying for the tournament. Roy Keane had every right to express his disappointment at this shabby treatment, and the Irish FA were deserving of scorn for their parsimony at such a high-profile event.

Mick McCarthy was in a difficult position; he probably didn't entirely disagree with Keane, but couldn't back him publicly against his employers. His already uneasy relationship with Keane was compromised, and being something of a straight-backed disciplinarian, he demanded that Keane step in line. At this point compromise was required, but that is not Keane's way. At a public team meeting he launched a fusillade of personal abuse at McCarthy that took all sense of proportion out of the matter. McCarthy, rightly on this occasion, dug his heels in even further and Keane was sent home.

☞ The saga lingered on for a week as rumours of Keane's return to the Far East abounded. But rumours they proved to be; there was no prodigal return for Keane.

☞ Keane's biographer Eamonn Dunphy, the opinionated Irish journalist, defended his charge vociferously. His credibility was shot away when he subsequently tried to vilify the Irish tactics after their splendid performance against Cameroon.

✎ Keane has a history of verbal fireworks; previous tirades include pillorying the 'prawn sandwich brigade' in the United corporate boxes, and castigating his United colleagues for lack of desire after exit from the 2001 Champions League.

'What do you think it's been like for me?'

McCarthy upbraids pressman for inane questioning

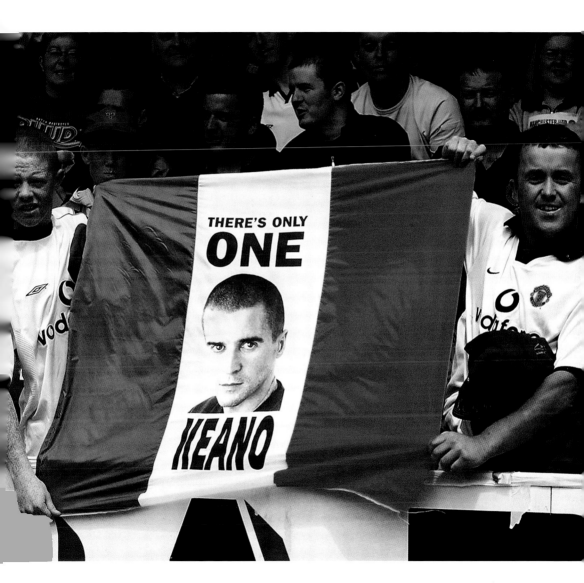

Zagallo, Mario
Brazil

WHEN BRAZIL WON the 1958 World Cup in Sweden, Mario Zagallo was an ever-present on the left wing. Similarly, in Chile in 1962, Zagallo played in every game in the tournament, scoring Brazil's opening goal against Mexico. By the time Brazil won the tournament again in 1970, Zagallo had been installed as coach.

It was another 24 years before Brazil reached the final again, winning on penalties in 1994, with Zagallo as assistant coach. In 1998, when they experienced the pain of losing a final for the first time (their 1950 loss was in a decisive group match, not a final), their coach was? Yup, you've guessed it, Mario Zagallo.

As a player Zagallo was an underrated contributor to the team. His stamina and industry allowed him to be the most effective defender of the Brazilian forwards, making him a perfect foil for the strolling Didi. As a coach he was a calming influence, realising that the key to the job was getting all his great players into a relaxed and confident frame of mind before letting them loose on the opposition. In both roles he has always been full of enthusiasm and vigour.

☞ In 1970 Zagallo took over as coach after Brazil had already qualified. Joao Saldanho, his predecessor, was deemed too unstable after he waved a revolver at one of his critics.

🖑 Zagallo has had three spells as coach of Brazilian giants Flamengo, accepting the third job offer from the club in October 2000, at the age of 68.

🖑 Zagallo scored Brazil's fourth goal in the 1958 World Cup final, using his pace and forcing the ball in at the near post.

🖑 Between 1958 and 1962, Zagallo lost his place to livewire Pepe.

VITAL STATISTICS

Place of Birth:	Maceio, Brazil					
Date of Birth:	9 August 1931	MANAGER		PLAYER		
Died:	n/a	Achievement	9	Achievement	9	
Caps:	37 (Brazil)	Tactical Awareness	8	Skill	8	
Goals (International): 4		Motivation	8	Teamwork	8	
Clubs:	Flamengo, Botafogo	Team Selection/Transfers	7	Passion	6	
Trophies:	BLT 1953, 1954, 1961, 1962;	Personality	8	Personality	7	
	WorC 1958, 1962, (1970 as coach,					
	1994 as technical advisor)	**TOTAL**	**40**	**TOTAL**	**38**	

LEGEND RATING

Zico, (Artur Antunes Coimbra)
Flamengo, Brazil

AT THE 1982 WORLD CUP, inspired by Socrates, Falcão, Cerezo and Zico, Brazil played football of an attacking brilliance not seen since 1970. It was a breath of fresh air after their dour tactics in 1978, and it allowed Zico, a huge disappointment in that earlier tournament, to show his true colours. His wiry strength and fierce shooting added firepower to the intricate movements of the men in gold – which was just as well because their other main striker, Serginho, was a donkey. Brazil's second-phase games were both classics; a 3-1 win over Argentina, featuring three brilliant goals, and an undulating 3-2 defeat by a Paolo Rossi-inspired Italy. Sadly, the 1986 tournament saw Zico back to the fitful and fretful shadow of eight years earlier. Zico's club football was principally with Flamengo, for whom he once starred in a win over a top-notch Liverpool team in the World Club Championship. A £2.5 m move to Udinese proved a bit of a waste of money for the Italians. Indeed, save for that one tournament in 1982, Zico would have been in danger of being remembered as one of the world's great unfulfilled talents.

- Sadly, Zico's last match for Brazil saw them crash out of the 1986 World Cup in a penalty shoot-out to France. After coming on as a sub, Zico had missed a penalty during the match, but had the balls to step up and score in the shoot-out.
- Zico scored a stunning hat-trick against Bolivia to clinch Brazil's place in the 1982 World Cup Finals.
- Zico scored with a trademark free-kick on his debut for Brazil in 1975.
- Kashima Antlers persuaded Zico to come to Japan to help launch the J-League.
- Zico was later appointed Sports Minister in Brazil, and was assistant coach under Zagallo at the 1998 World Cup.

VITAL STATISTICS

Place of Birth:	Rio de Janeiro, Brazil	Achievement	8.0
Date of Birth:	3 March 1953 **Died:** n/a	Skill	9.0
Caps:	71 (Brazil) **Goals (International):** 48	Teamwork	7.0
Clubs:	Flamengo, Udinese, Kashima Antlers	Passion	7.0
Appearances:	Club (All matches for Flamengo): 902	Personality	8.0
Goals:	Club (All matches for Flamengo): 727		
Trophies:	WCC 1981	**TOTAL 39.0**	

LEGEND RATING

Zidane, Zinedine
Juventus, Real Madrid, France

MARSEILLES' MOST FAMOUS footballing son has seen his career soar to unimaginable heights from inauspicious beginnings at Cannes. A three-season period from 1998 brought him winner's medals in World and European finals for France, and a world-record £45 m move from Juventus to Real Madrid, after his goals helped the Turin club to two Serie A titles. Madrid assembled their team around the Frenchman, playing some breathtaking football; a Zidane special to win the 2002 Champions League was just one highlight.

His crowning moment must remain his two goals in Paris against Brazil to bring France their first World Cup. Zidane's two-footed skills and movement bemused Brazil throughout the game, as they had bemused defenders all through the tournament. The dose was repeated two years later at Euro 2000, and Zidane was a superstar.

A slightly stooping, balding figure, he lacks the charismatic looks of Batistuta or the natural athleticism of Figo, but remains an inspiration for late developers everywhere. His professional debut was in 1986 and he remained in relative obscurity with Cannes and Bordeaux before Juventus signed him 10 years later; unthinkable humility for the most influential player of the last four years.

☞ Amazingly, Zidane's first goal did not arrive until five years after his debut for Cannes.

☝ Not always the hero, his five years at Juventus brought six red cards.

✍ He was voted World Footballer of the Year in 1998 and 2000 and European Footballer of the Year in 1998.

☝ He received the Legion d'Honneur from the French President Jacques Chirac in 1998.

☝ A poor Euro 2004 was a disappointing way to end his international career, and he seems to be struggling for motivation at Real.

VITAL STATISTICS

Place of Birth:	Marseille, France		
Date of Birth:	23 June 1972	**Died:** n/a	
Caps:	92 (France)	**Goals (International):** 26	
Clubs:	Cannes, Bordeaux, Juventus, Real Madrid		
Appearances:	Club (League): 455		
Goals:	Club (League): 80		
Trophies:	SA 1997, 1998; WorC 1998; EuroC 2000;		
	EC 2002		

	LEGEND RATING
Achievement	10.0
Skill	9.0
Teamwork	7.5
Passion	8.5
Personality	7.0
TOTAL	**42.0**

Zoff, Dino
Juventus, Italy

IN A PLAYING CAREER that lasted 20 years, Dino Zoff performed with a consistency and casual excellence that earned him a reputation, alongside Banks and Yashin, as one of the best goalkeepers Europe has ever produced. Success took its time to discover Zoff. He did not make his debut for Italy until he was 26, but quickly found his feet and was soon picking up top honours. His first triumph was at the European Championships of 1968, when Italy claimed the trophy on home soil, but his most notable achievement was to captain his country to 1982 World Cup glory in Spain at the age of 40.

It was similarly late in his career that Zoff began to pick up club trinkets, but once he got a taste for victory there was no stopping him; following his move to Juventus in 1972 he collected eight major trophies, including six Serie A titles. His retirement saw him remain with Juventus, where he became team coach in 1988, winning the UEFA Cup in 1990, but in 1992 he left to fill the vacant manager's position at Lazio.

- ✍ Zoff set an international world record in 1974 by not conceding a goal for 1,143 minutes, a sequence broken in unlikely fashion by Haiti.
- ☞ Zoff carried on playing just long enough to feature in the great Juventus side of the early 1980s – with Platini, Boniek, Tardelli and Rossi.
- ☞ His 112 Italian appearances was a national record at the time, but has since been overhauled by Paolo Maldini.
- ✍ Zoff preserved Italy's 3-2 lead over Brazil in the classic 1982 World Cup encounter with a formidable save from Oscar's header in the dying minutes.

VITAL STATISTICS

Place of Birth: Mariano del Friuli, Italy
Date of Birth: 28 February 1942   **Died:** n/a
Caps: 112 (Italy)   **Goals (International):** 0
Clubs: Udinese, Mantova, Napoli, Juventus
Appearances: Club (for Juventus): 330
Goals: Club (for Juventus): 0
Trophies: EuroC 1968; WorC 1982; SA 1973, 1975, 1977, 1978, 1981, 1982; UEFAC 1977, (1990)

LEGEND RATING	
Achievement	9.0
Skill	9.0
Teamwork	8.0
Passion	8.0
Personality	7.0
TOTAL	**41.0**

Zola, Gianfranco
Chelsea, Italy

HE MAY BE SARDINIA'S most celebrated footballer since Luigi Riva but, after thrilling crowds at Stamford Bridge during the closing seasons of his career, Gianfranco Zola is now regarded as an adopted Londoner. Too small to be a target man and never a prolific goal scorer, Zola's mercurial ball skills have created countless goals for grateful team-mates and made many accomplished defenders look like hapless novices. His trademark free-kicks rely on guile and spin rather than outright power, but he still boasts a strike rate better than some penalty-takers. None was more memorable than his opener for Chelsea on their most famous European night, a 3-1 victory over Barcelona in a Champions League quarter-final in 2001. Zola repeatedly cut an international defence to ribbons that night.

Ironically, given his dead-ball prowess, it is a missed penalty for which Italian audiences will best remember him; his uncharacteristic failure against Germany in Euro 96 resulted in the *Azzuri's* elimination from the tournament. Never a Championship winner in Italy or England, and never a huge international success, Zola will nonetheless be remembered as one of the most abundantly gifted players of his generation.

- 1996. Zola became a *bête noire* for England fans after scoring the only goal in a World Cup qualifier at Wembley.
- 1997. Named Footballer of the Year, despite joining Chelsea in mid-season.
- 2000. Voted Chelsea's greatest-ever player.
- 2001. 'There's only one Mrs Zola.' Song sung by Chelsea fans after Zola's wife was reported to have persuaded him to remain at the club for another season.
- 2002. Scored an audacious mid-air back-heeled volley versus Norwich in an FA Cup replay, probably his best-ever strike for Chelsea.
- Summer 2003. Transferred to Cagliari in his native Sardinia.

VITAL STATISTICS

Place of Birth:	Sardinia, Italy	
Date of Birth:	5 July 1966	**Died:** n/a
Caps:	35 (Italy)	**Goals (International):** 7
Clubs:	Nuorese, Torres, Napoli, Parma, Chelsea	
Appearances:	Club (League): 468	
Goals:	Club (League): 150	
Trophies:	SA 1990; UEFAC 1995; FAC 1997; CWC 1998; LC 2000	

LEGEND RATING

Achievement	6.0
Skill	9.0
Teamwork	9.0
Passion	8.0
Personality	7.0
TOTAL	**39.0**

Zubizarreta, Andoni

Barcelona, Spain

SPAIN'S MOST CAPPED PLAYER was one of Europe's most consistent goalkeepers of the last 20 years. Unfussy and dependable, Zubizarreta was a fixture in the Spanish side much in the way Zoff and Shilton had been for England a few years earlier. He played his entire career in his homeland, where he won incalculable respect, and a few trophies to boot. His talent was spotted early by Athletic Bilbao who recognised his potential while 'Zubi' was still at his first club, Alaves. But after four seasons at Bilbao, during which time he won two La Liga titles, Barcelona whisked him off to the Nou Camp for £1.2 m.

The European Cup provided Zubizarreta with both his greatest triumph and disaster. In 1992 his clean sheet made a single goal against Sampdoria sufficient for Barca to win their first European Cup, but that was all forgotten two years later when the final of the same competition produced a 4-0 thrashing by Milan. Football's reputation for showing little sentiment to its heroes was again demonstrated after that defeat; Zubizaretta was made a scapegoat and unceremoniously offloaded to Valencia.

☞ The £1.2 m paid for Zubizarreta by Barcelona in 1986 made him the world's most expensive goalkeeper.

⛸ Zubizarreta won six La Liga titles, two with Bilbao and four with Barca.

🖑 Sadly, his final game for Spain saw him make a howler against Nigeria at France 98.

🖑 Zubizarreta is the only goalkeeper to lose a penalty shoot-out against England – in the quarter-final of Euro 96.

☞ Spain's defeat to England that day ended a 31-match unbeaten run.

VITAL STATISTICS

Place of Birth:	Vitoria, Spain		
Date of Birth:	23 October 1961	**Died:** n/a	
Caps:	126 (Spain)	**Goals (International):** 0	
Clubs:	Alaves, Atletico Bilbao, Barcelona, Valencia		
Appearances:	Club (League): 622		
Goals:	Club (League): 0		
Trophies:	EC 1992; PLA 1983, 1984, 1991, 1992, 1993, 1994; CWC 1989		

Achievement	7.0
Skill	8.0
Teamwork	7.0
Passion	8.0
Personality	6.0
TOTAL	**36.0**

LEGEND RATING

Index